WOLF GIRL AND BLACK PRINCE

1

STORY & ART BY
Ayuko Hatta

CONTENTS

VOLUME

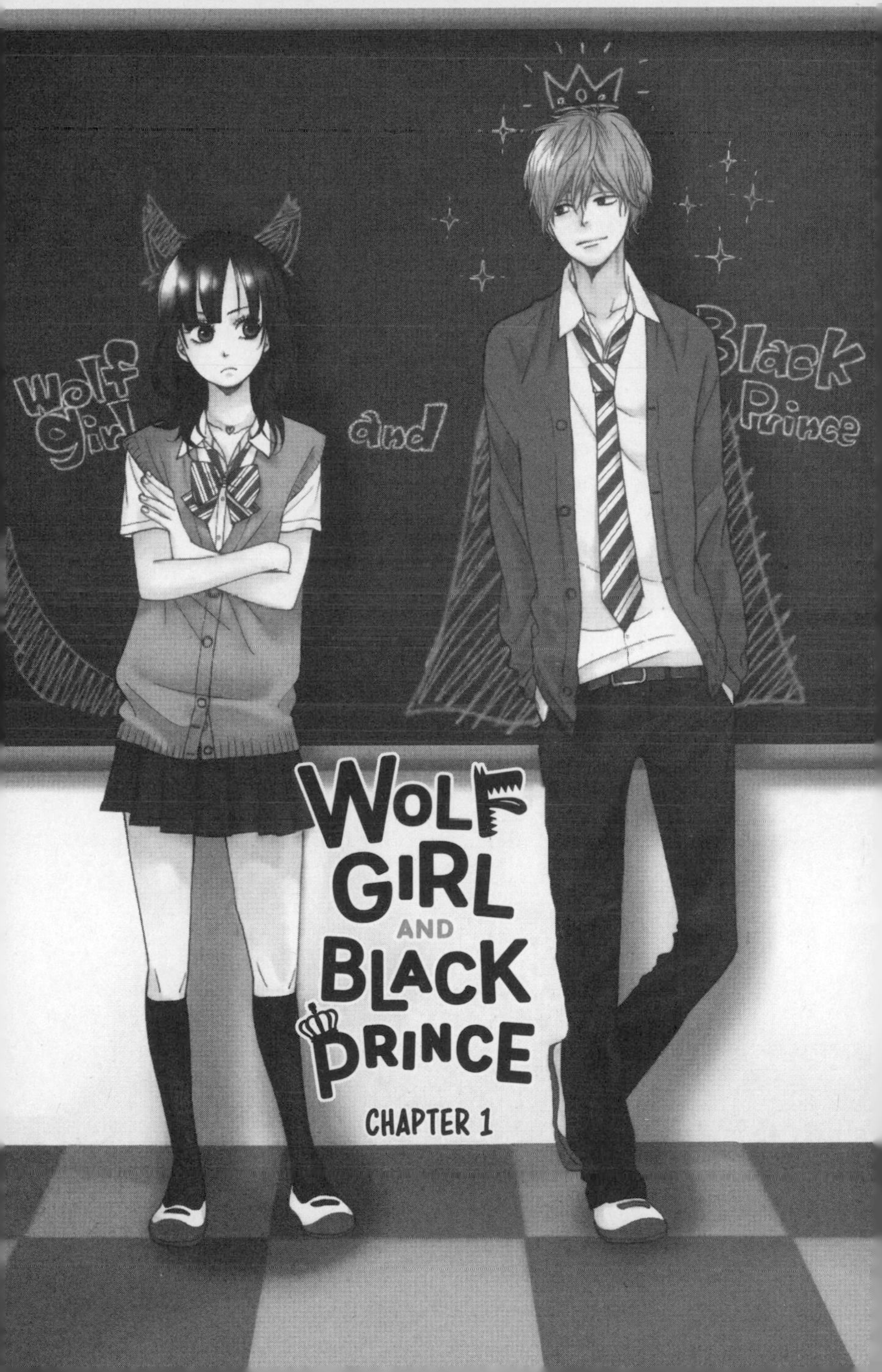
Wolf Girl and Black Prince
WOLF GIRL AND BLACK PRINCE
CHAPTER 1

Greetings to all the new faces and hello again to the old ones! I'm Hatta. Thank you for picking up volume 1 of *Wolf Girl and Black Prince*. This is my fourth published work, but the first to have a "1" next to the title! Yahoo! I'm over the moon! This wouldn't have been possible without all of you. Seriously! I can't thank you all enough! Thank you so, so much!!!

Please look forward to volume 2 as well. Actually, I guess it's a little early to ask that of you! Sorry, ever so sorry... Please just enjoy volume 1 for now.

See you again soon!

Ayuko Hatta

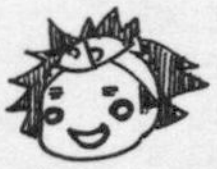

September 2011

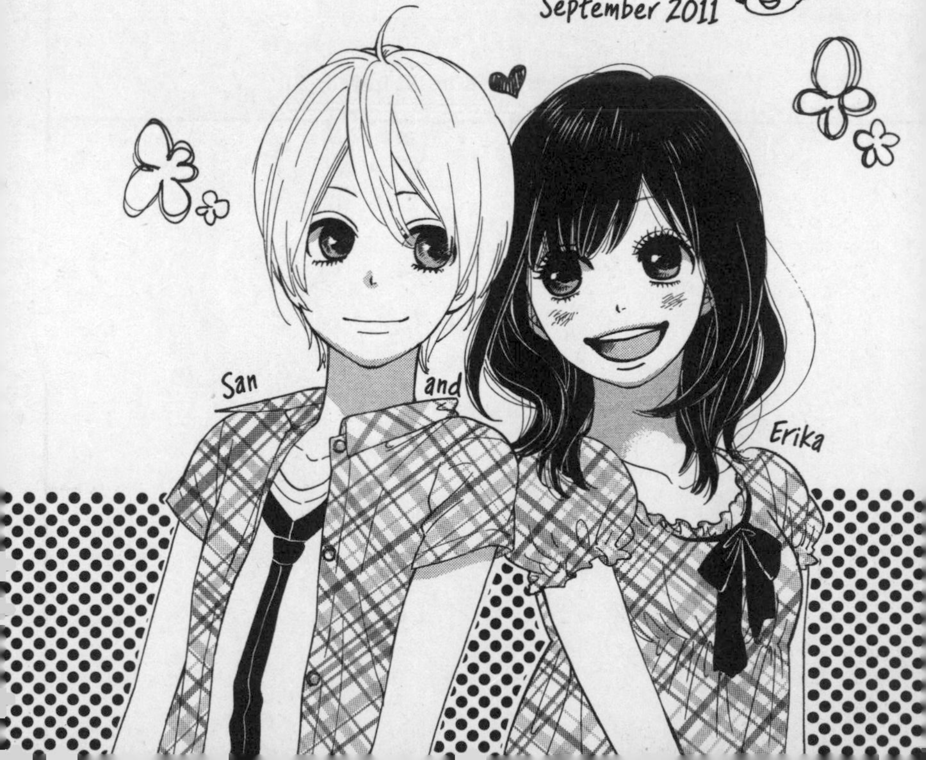
San
and
Erika

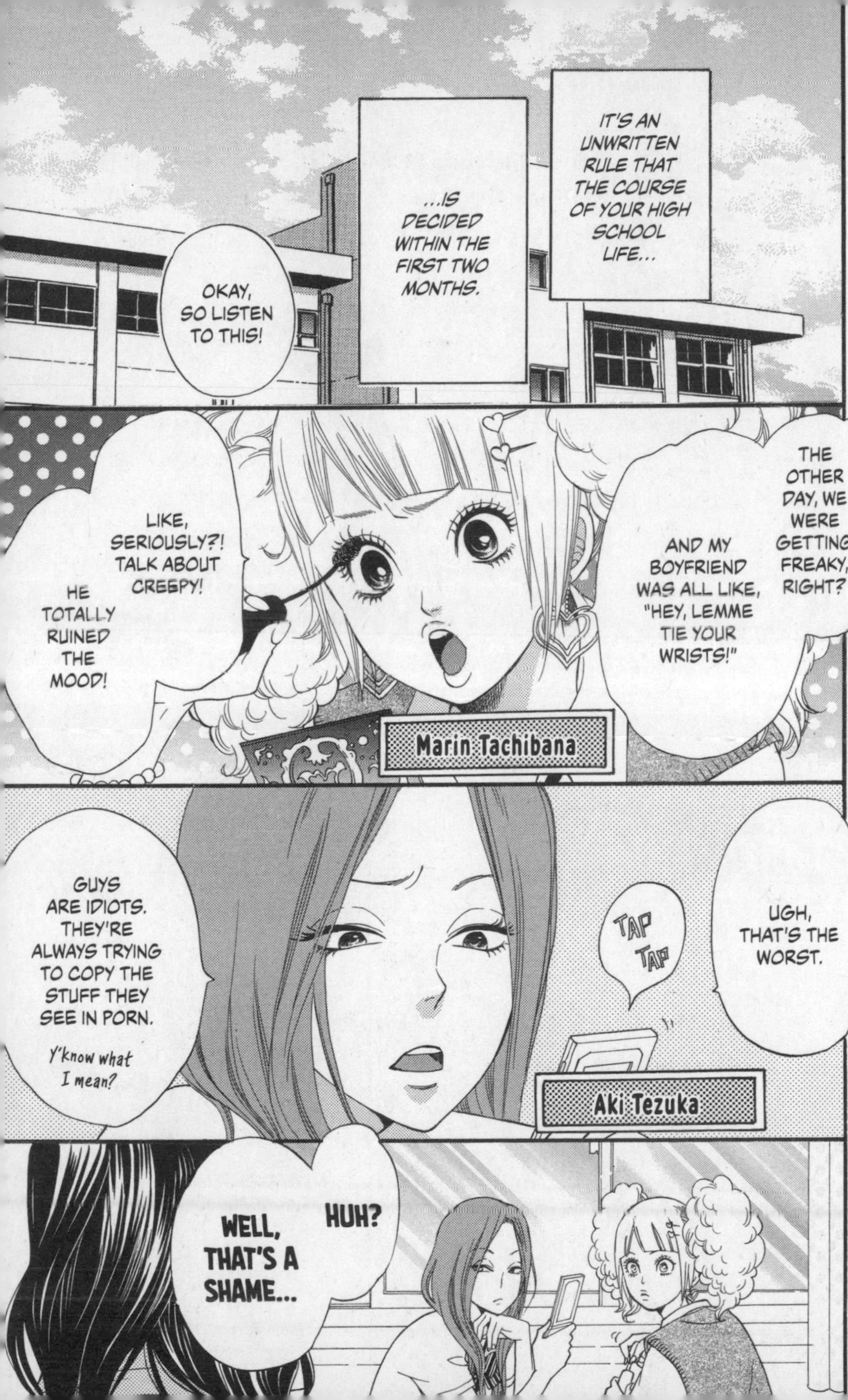
IT'S AN UNWRITTEN RULE THAT THE COURSE OF YOUR HIGH SCHOOL LIFE...
...IS DECIDED WITHIN THE FIRST TWO MONTHS.
OKAY, SO LISTEN TO THIS!
THE OTHER DAY, WE WERE GETTING FREAKY, RIGHT?
AND MY BOYFRIEND WAS ALL LIKE, "HEY, LEMME TIE YOUR WRISTS!"
Marin Tachibana
LIKE, SERIOUSLY?! TALK ABOUT CREEPY!
HE TOTALLY RUINED THE MOOD!
UGH, THAT'S THE WORST.
TAP TAP
Aki Tezuka
GUYS ARE IDIOTS. THEY'RE ALWAYS TRYING TO COPY THE STUFF THEY SEE IN PORN.
Y'know what I mean?
HUH?
WELL, THAT'S A SHAME...

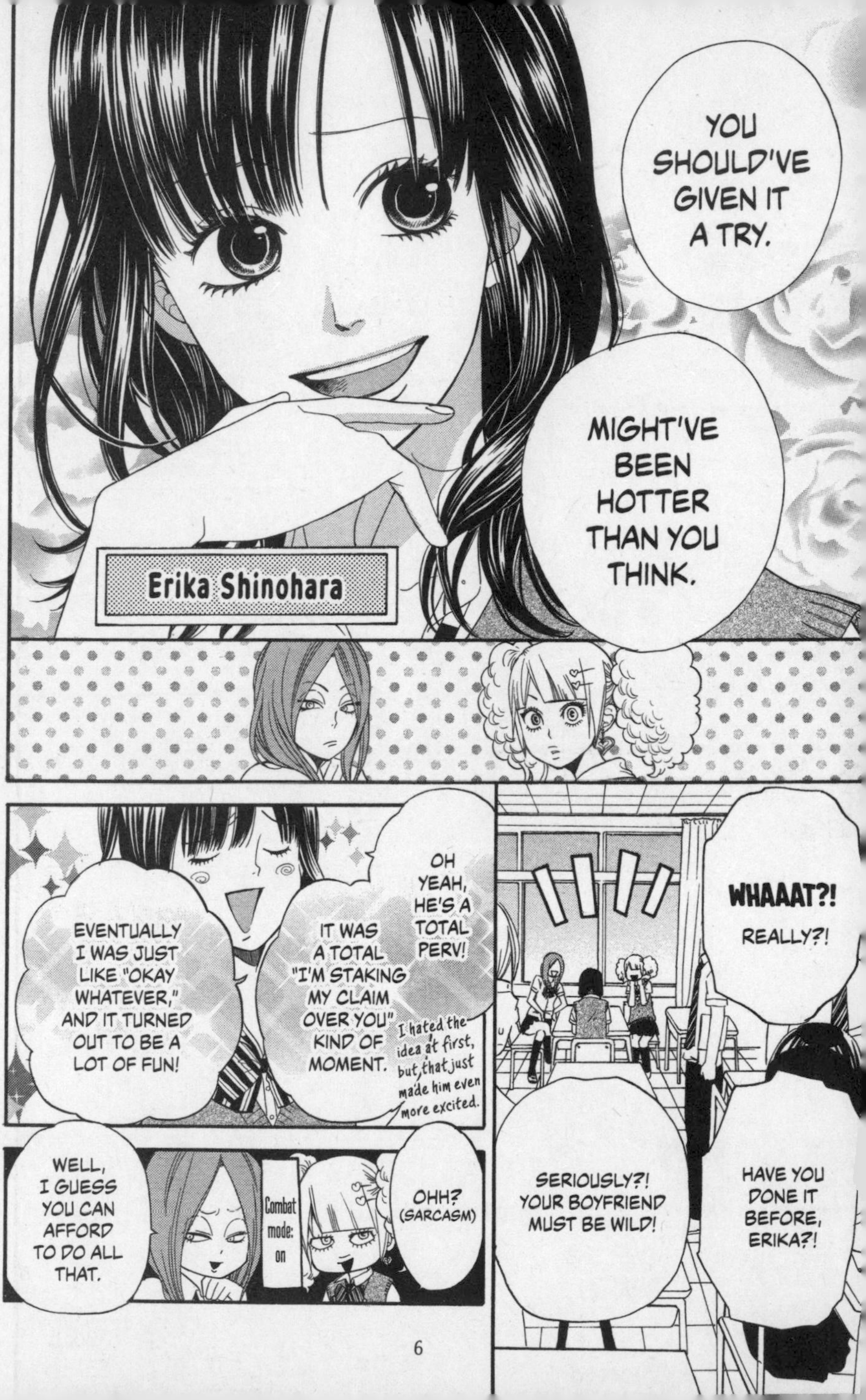
YOU SHOULD'VE GIVEN IT A TRY.
MIGHT'VE BEEN HOTTER THAN YOU THINK.
Erika Shinohara
WHAAAT?! REALLY?!
HAVE YOU DONE IT BEFORE, ERIKA?!
SERIOUSLY?! YOUR BOYFRIEND MUST BE WILD!
OH YEAH, HE'S A TOTAL PERV!
IT WAS A TOTAL "I'M STAKING MY CLAIM OVER YOU" KIND OF MOMENT.
I hated the idea at first, but that just made him even more excited.
EVENTUALLY I WAS JUST LIKE "OKAY WHATEVER," AND IT TURNED OUT TO BE A LOT OF FUN!
OHH? (SARCASM)
Combat mode: on
WELL, I GUESS YOU CAN AFFORD TO DO ALL THAT.

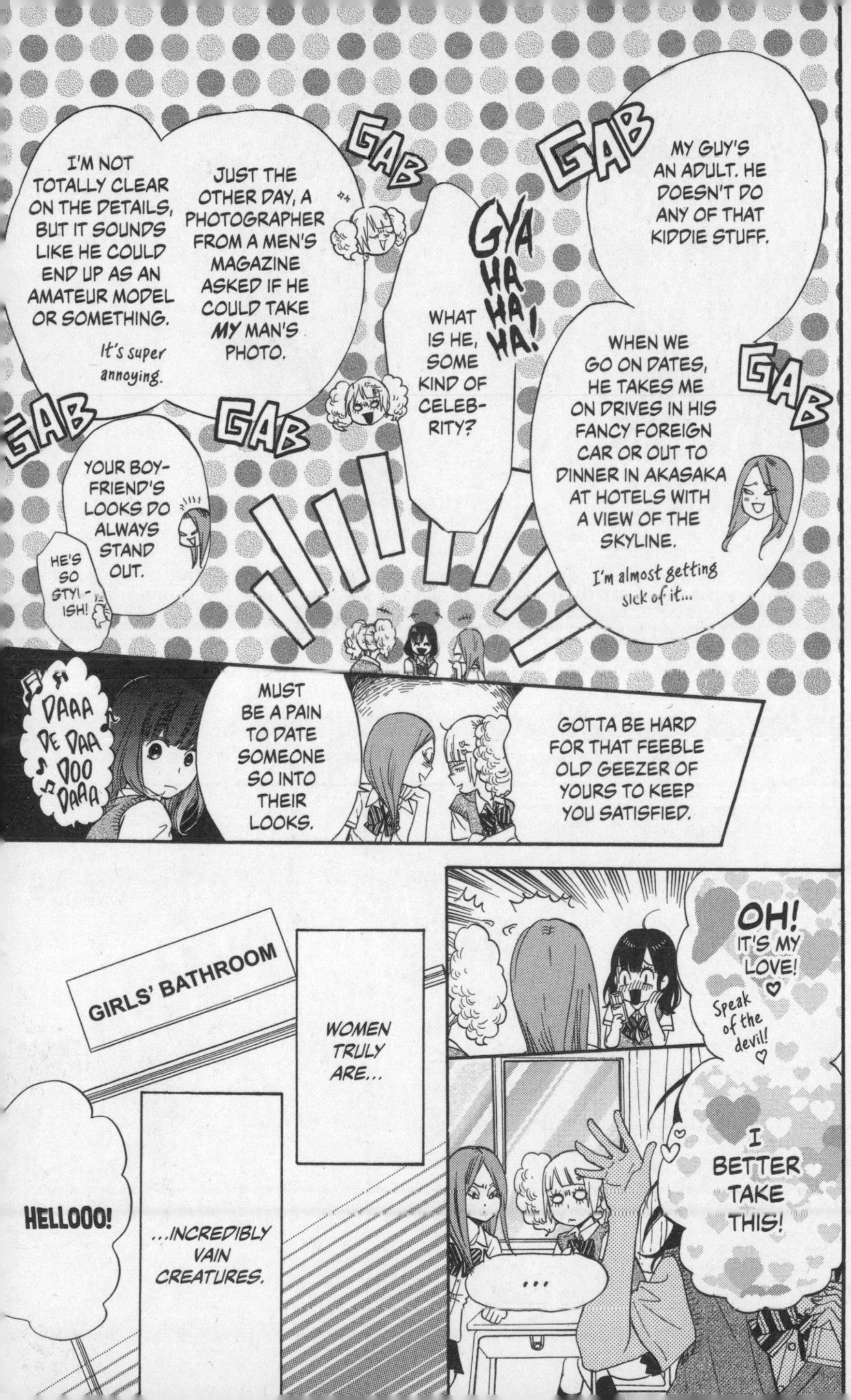
GAB
MY GUY'S AN ADULT. HE DOESN'T DO ANY OF THAT KIDDIE STUFF.
WHEN WE GO ON DATES, HE TAKES ME ON DRIVES IN HIS FANCY FOREIGN CAR OR OUT TO DINNER IN AKASAKA AT HOTELS WITH A VIEW OF THE SKYLINE.
I'm almost getting sick of it...
GAB
GYA HA HA HA HA!
WHAT IS HE, SOME KIND OF CELEB-RITY?
GAB
JUST THE OTHER DAY, A PHOTOGRAPHER FROM A MEN'S MAGAZINE ASKED IF HE COULD TAKE *MY* MAN'S PHOTO.
I'M NOT TOTALLY CLEAR ON THE DETAILS, BUT IT SOUNDS LIKE HE COULD END UP AS AN AMATEUR MODEL OR SOMETHING.
It's super annoying.
GAB
GAB
YOUR BOY-FRIEND'S LOOKS DO ALWAYS STAND OUT.
HE'S SO STYL-ISH!
GOTTA BE HARD FOR THAT FEEBLE OLD GEEZER OF YOURS TO KEEP YOU SATISFIED.
MUST BE A PAIN TO DATE SOMEONE SO INTO THEIR LOOKS.
DAAA DE DAA DOO DAAA
OH! IT'S MY LOVE!
Speak of the devil!
I BETTER TAKE THIS!
...
GIRLS' BATHROOM
WOMEN TRULY ARE...
...INCREDIBLY VAIN CREATURES.
HELLOOO!

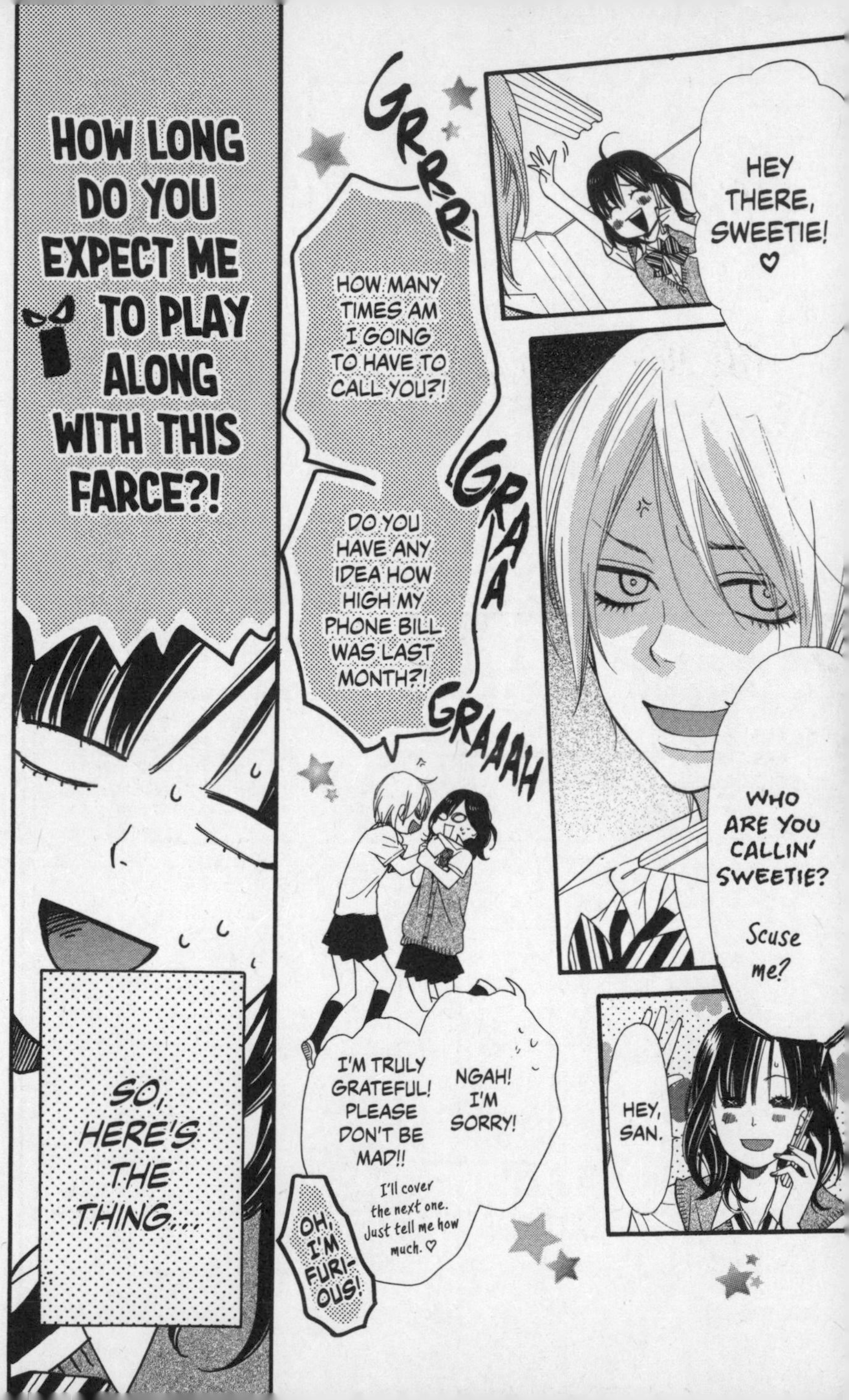
HEY THERE, SWEETIE! ♡
WHO ARE YOU CALLIN' SWEETIE?
Scuse me?
HEY, SAN.
GRRRR
HOW MANY TIMES AM I GOING TO HAVE TO CALL YOU?!
GRAAA
DO YOU HAVE ANY IDEA HOW HIGH MY PHONE BILL WAS LAST MONTH?!
GRAAAH
NGAH! I'M SORRY!
I'M TRULY GRATEFUL! PLEASE DON'T BE MAD!!
I'll cover the next one. Just tell me how much. ♡
OH, I'M FURI-OUS!
HOW LONG DO YOU EXPECT ME TO PLAY ALONG WITH THIS FARCE?!
SO, HERE'S THE THING....

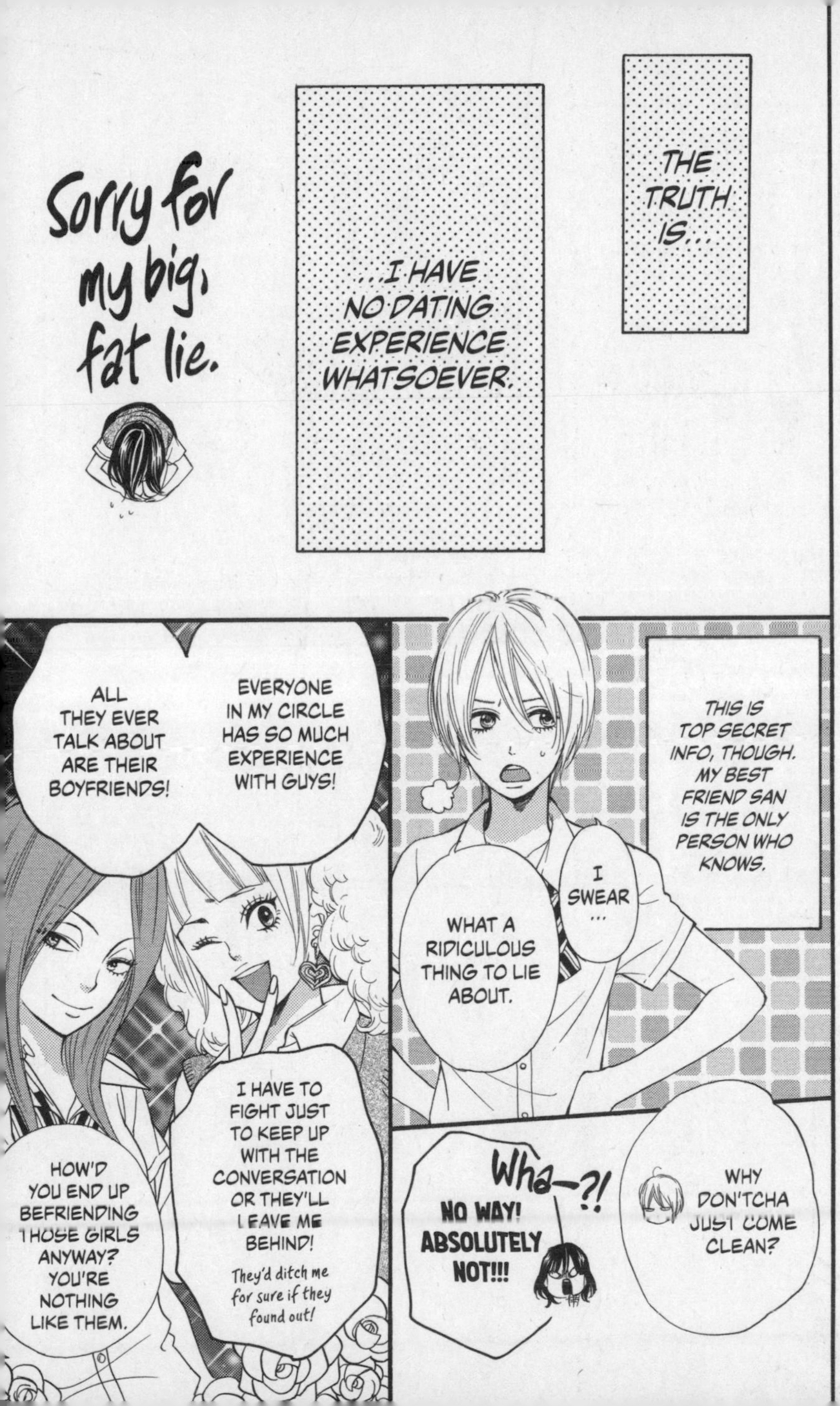
THE TRUTH IS...
...I HAVE NO DATING EXPERIENCE WHATSOEVER.
Sorry for my big, fat lie.
THIS IS TOP SECRET INFO, THOUGH. MY BEST FRIEND SAN IS THE ONLY PERSON WHO KNOWS.
I SWEAR...
WHAT A RIDICULOUS THING TO LIE ABOUT.
WHY DON'TCHA JUST COME CLEAN?
Wha-?!
NO WAY! ABSOLUTELY NOT!!!
EVERYONE IN MY CIRCLE HAS SO MUCH EXPERIENCE WITH GUYS!
ALL THEY EVER TALK ABOUT ARE THEIR BOYFRIENDS!
I HAVE TO FIGHT JUST TO KEEP UP WITH THE CONVERSATION OR THEY'LL LEAVE ME BEHIND!
They'd ditch me for sure if they found out!
HOW'D YOU END UP BEFRIENDING THOSE GIRLS ANYWAY? YOU'RE NOTHING LIKE THEM.

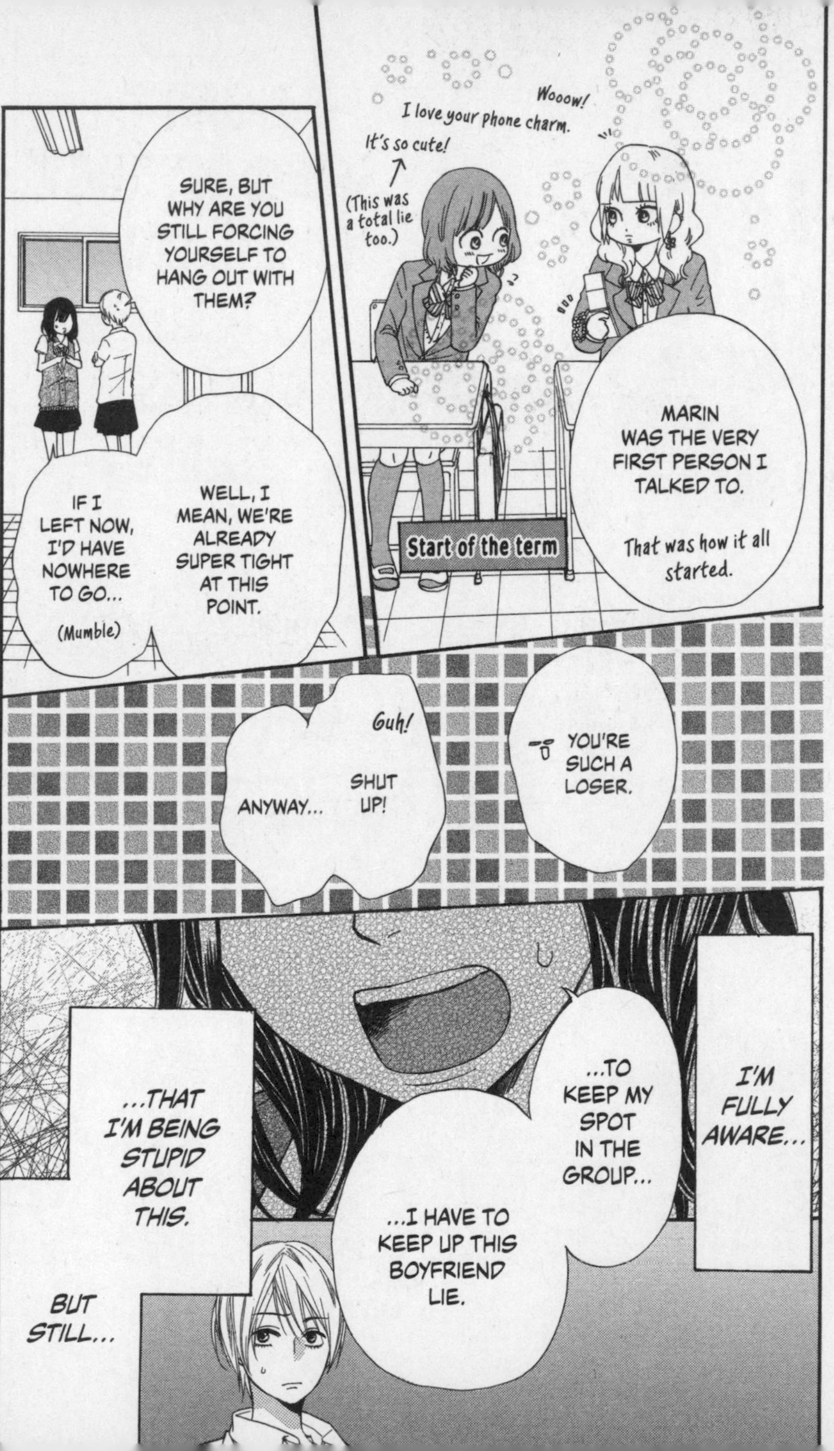
Start of the term
MARIN WAS THE VERY FIRST PERSON I TALKED TO.
That was how it all started.
Wooow!
I love your phone charm.
It's so cute!
(This was a total lie too.)
SURE, BUT WHY ARE YOU STILL FORCING YOURSELF TO HANG OUT WITH THEM?
WELL, I MEAN, WE'RE ALREADY SUPER TIGHT AT THIS POINT.
IF I LEFT NOW, I'D HAVE NOWHERE TO GO...
(Mumble)
YOU'RE SUCH A LOSER.
Guh!
SHUT UP!
ANYWAY...
I'M FULLY AWARE...
...THAT I'M BEING STUPID ABOUT THIS.
BUT STILL...
...TO KEEP MY SPOT IN THE GROUP...
...I HAVE TO KEEP UP THIS BOYFRIEND LIE.

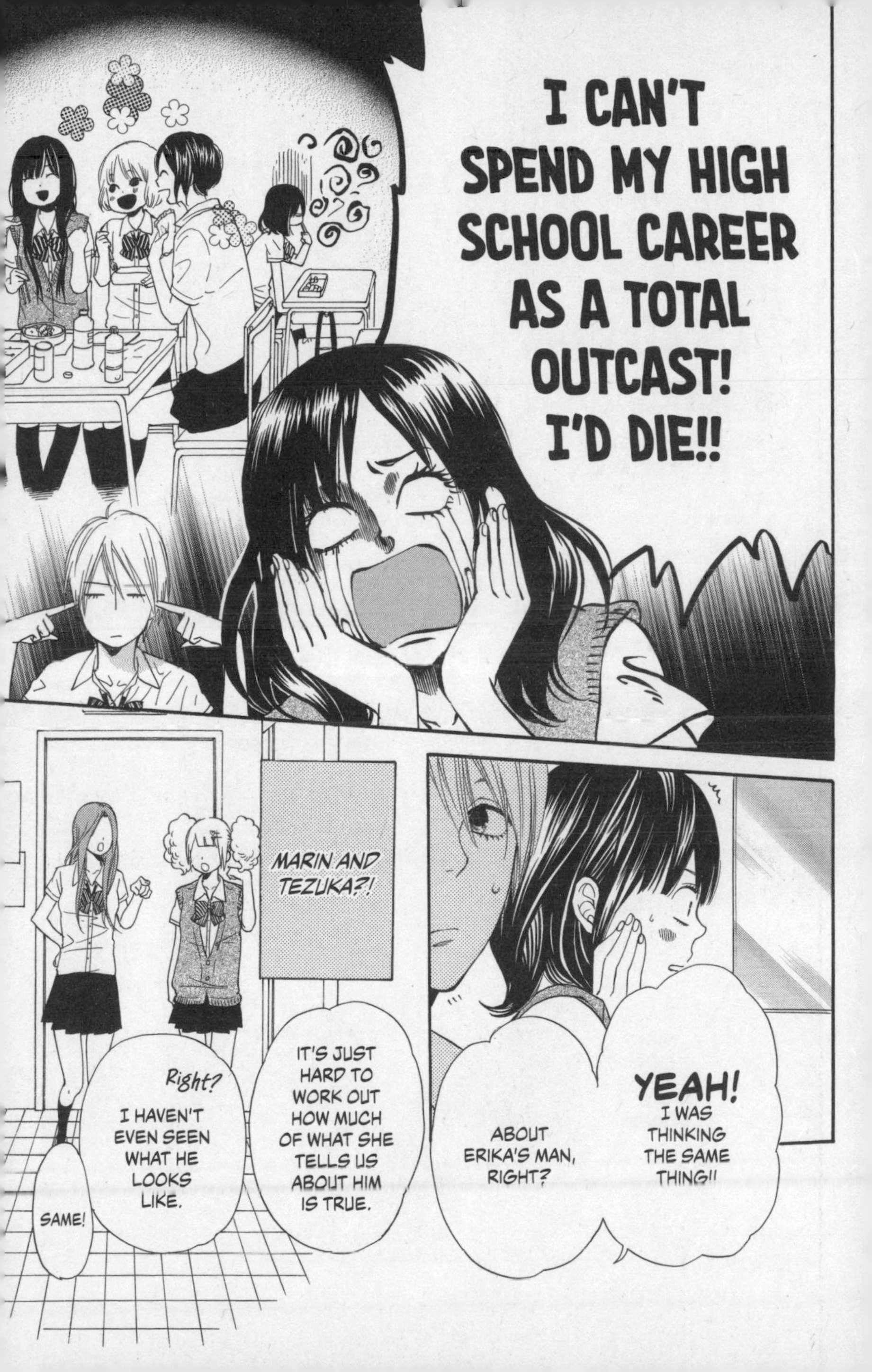
I CAN'T SPEND MY HIGH SCHOOL CAREER AS A TOTAL OUTCAST! I'D DIE!!
YEAH! I WAS THINKING THE SAME THING!!
ABOUT ERIKA'S MAN, RIGHT?
MARIN AND TEZUKA?!
IT'S JUST HARD TO WORK OUT HOW MUCH OF WHAT SHE TELLS US ABOUT HIM IS TRUE.
Right? I HAVEN'T EVEN SEEN WHAT HE LOOKS LIKE.
SAME!

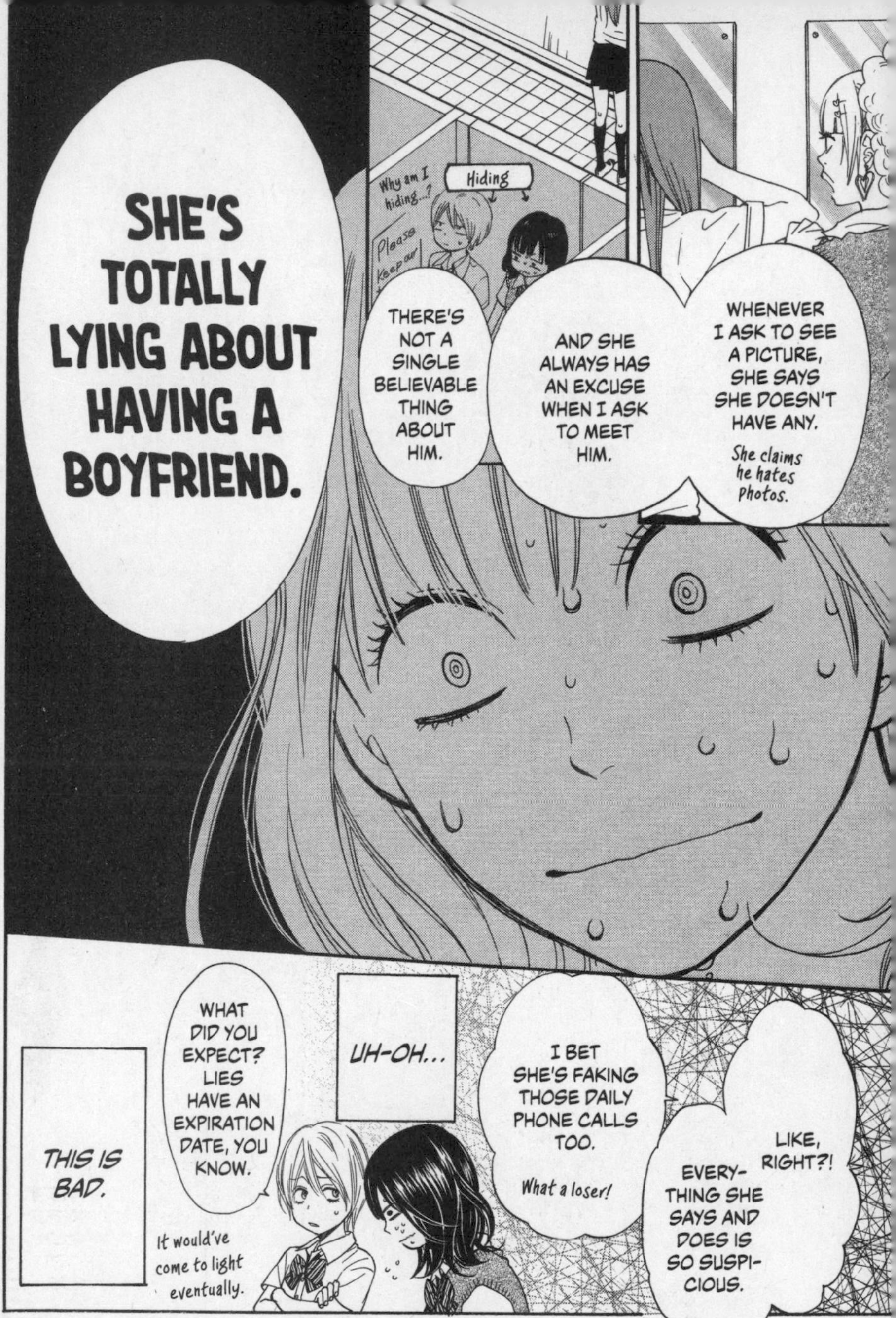
Why am I hiding...?
Hiding
WHENEVER I ASK TO SEE A PICTURE, SHE SAYS SHE DOESN'T HAVE ANY.
She claims he hates photos.
AND SHE ALWAYS HAS AN EXCUSE WHEN I ASK TO MEET HIM.
THERE'S NOT A SINGLE BELIEVABLE THING ABOUT HIM.
SHE'S TOTALLY LYING ABOUT HAVING A BOYFRIEND.
LIKE, RIGHT?!
EVERY-THING SHE SAYS AND DOES IS SO SUSPICIOUS.
I BET SHE'S FAKING THOSE DAILY PHONE CALLS TOO.
What a loser!
UH-OH...
WHAT DID YOU EXPECT? LIES HAVE AN EXPIRATION DATE, YOU KNOW.
It would've come to light eventually.
THIS IS BAD.

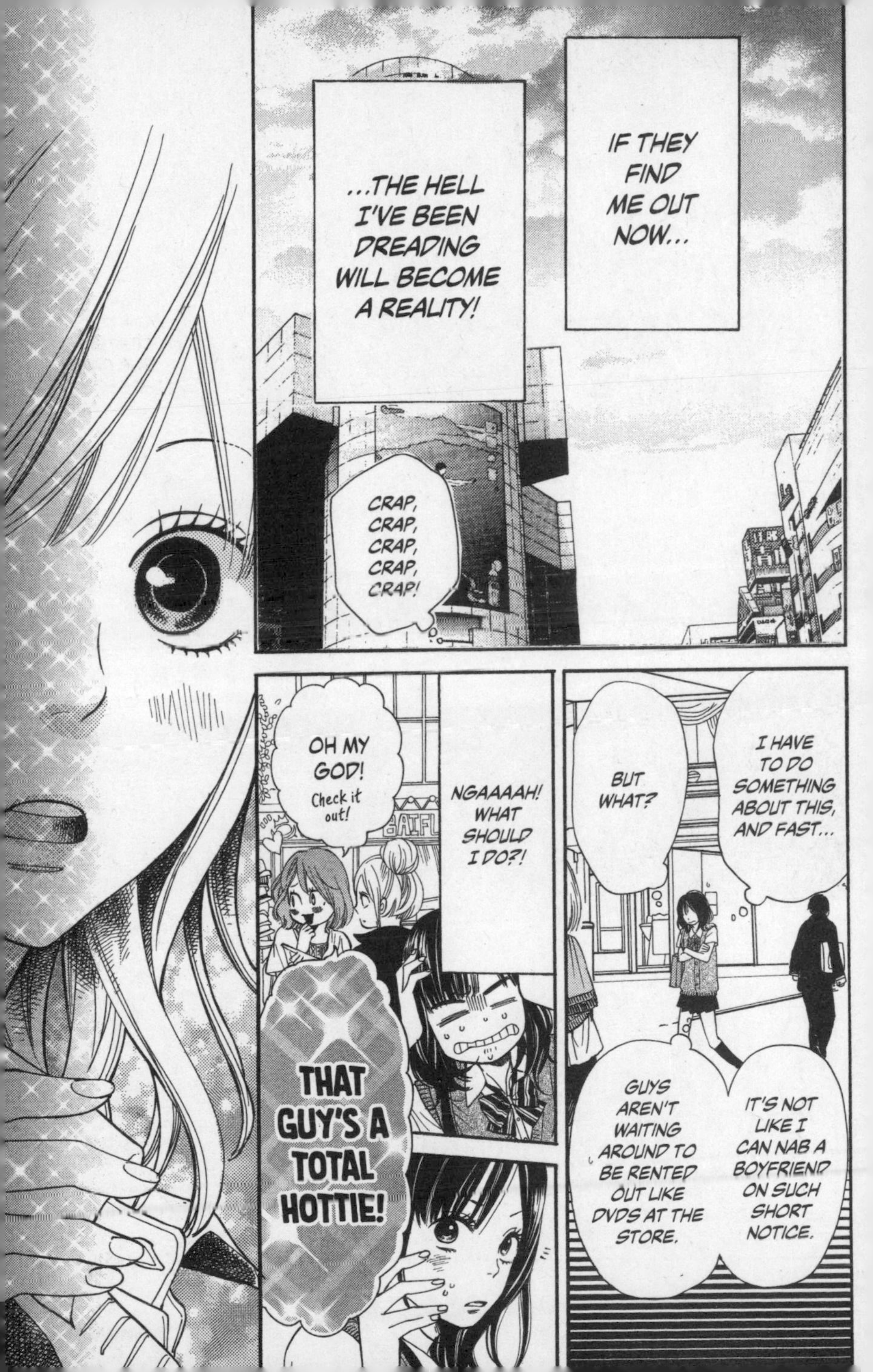
IF THEY FIND ME OUT NOW...
...THE HELL I'VE BEEN DREADING WILL BECOME A REALITY!
CRAP, CRAP, CRAP, CRAP, CRAP!
I HAVE TO DO SOMETHING ABOUT THIS, AND FAST...
BUT WHAT?
IT'S NOT LIKE I CAN NAB A BOYFRIEND ON SUCH SHORT NOTICE.
GUYS AREN'T WAITING AROUND TO BE RENTED OUT LIKE DVDS AT THE STORE.
NGAAAAH! WHAT SHOULD I DO?!
OH MY GOD! Check it out!
THAT GUY'S A TOTAL HOTTIE!

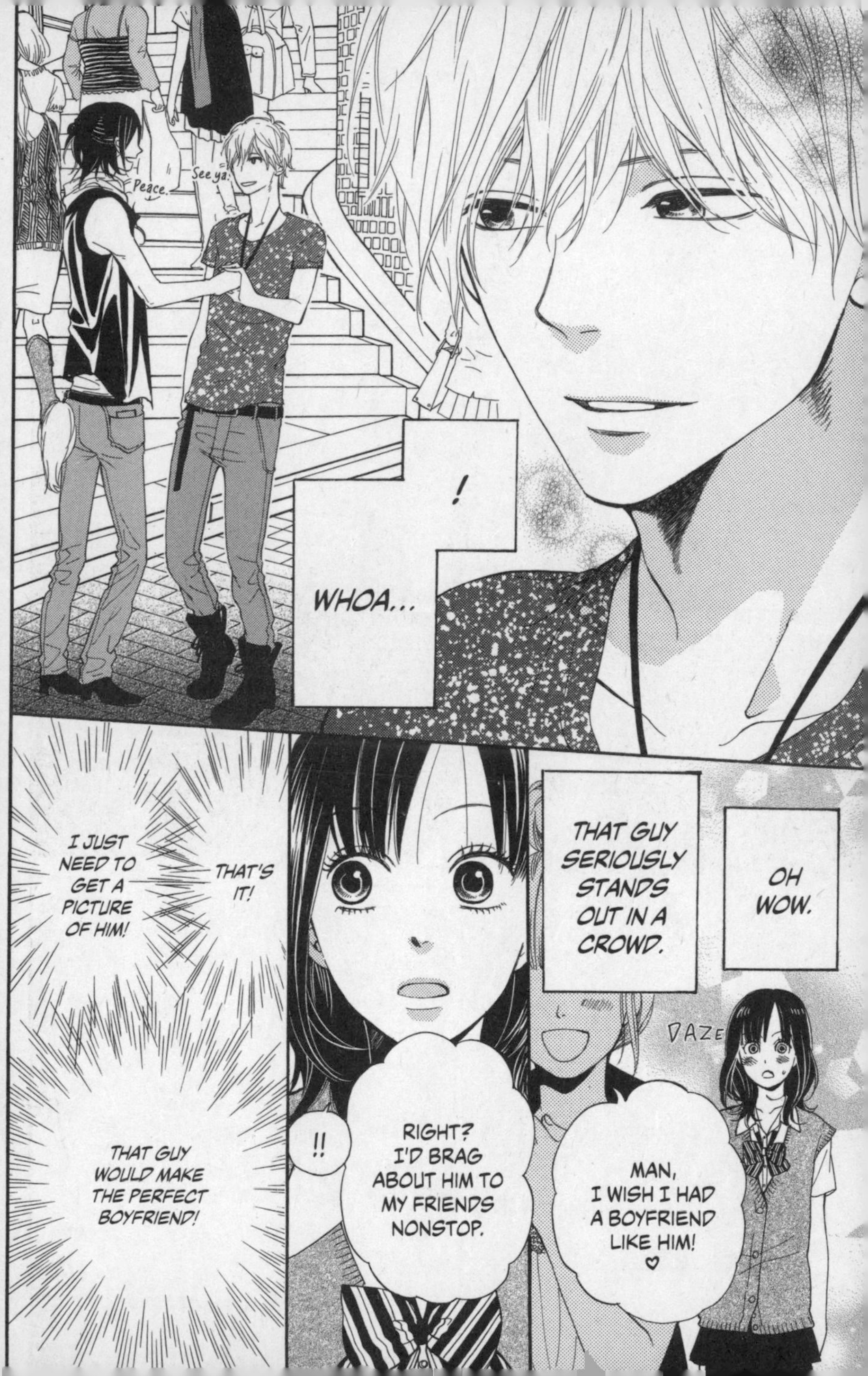
!
WHOA...
See ya.
Peace.
OH WOW.
THAT GUY SERIOUSLY STANDS OUT IN A CROWD.
DAZE
MAN, I WISH I HAD A BOYFRIEND LIKE HIM! ♡
RIGHT? I'D BRAG ABOUT HIM TO MY FRIENDS NONSTOP.
!!
THAT'S IT!
I JUST NEED TO GET A PICTURE OF HIM!
THAT GUY WOULD MAKE THE PERFECT BOYFRIEND!

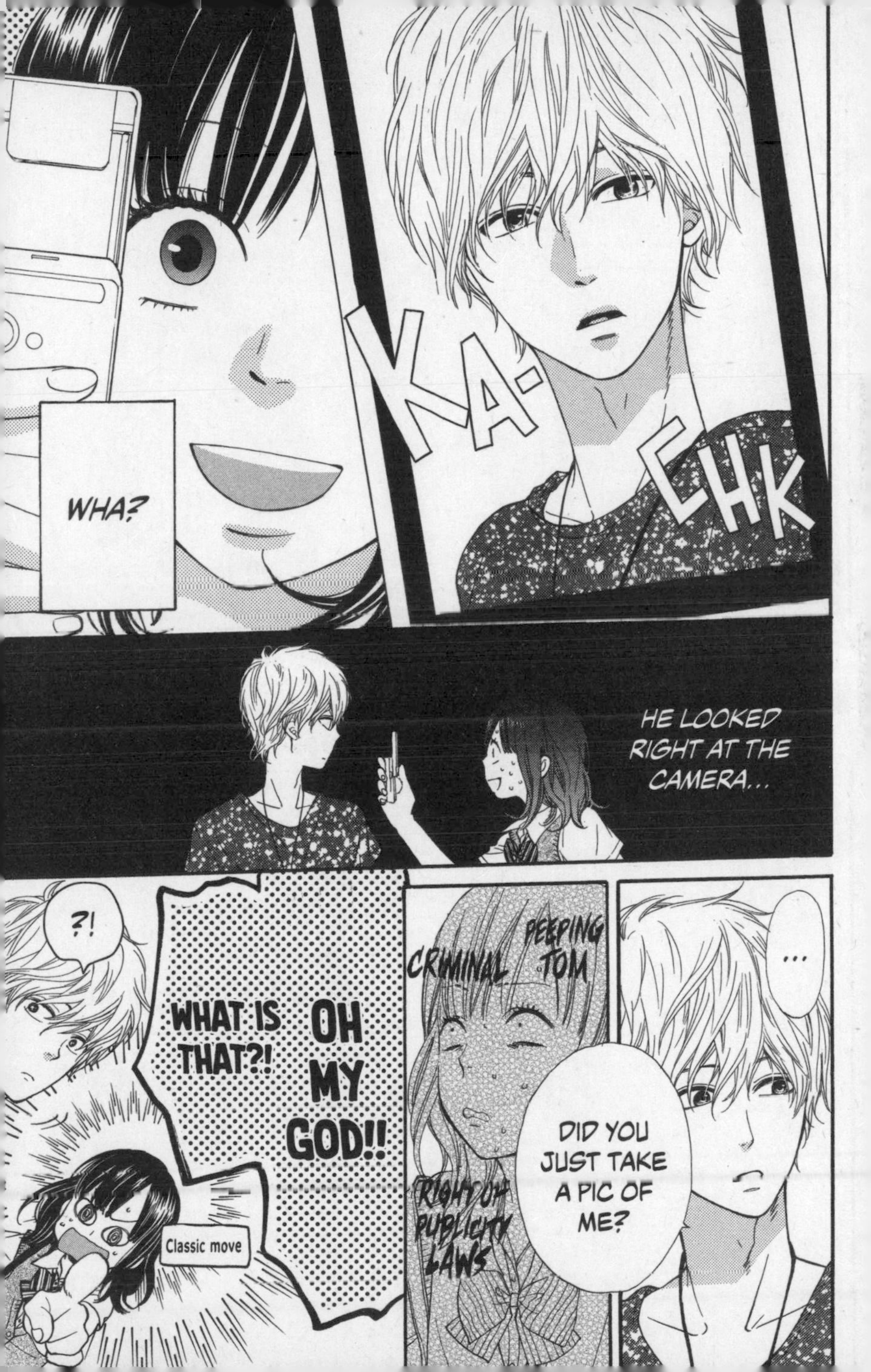
KA-CHK
WHA?
HE LOOKED RIGHT AT THE CAMERA...
...
DID YOU JUST TAKE A PIC OF ME?
PEEPING TOM
CRIMINAL
RIGHT OF PUBLICITY LAWS
?!
OH MY GOD!!
WHAT IS THAT?!
Classic move

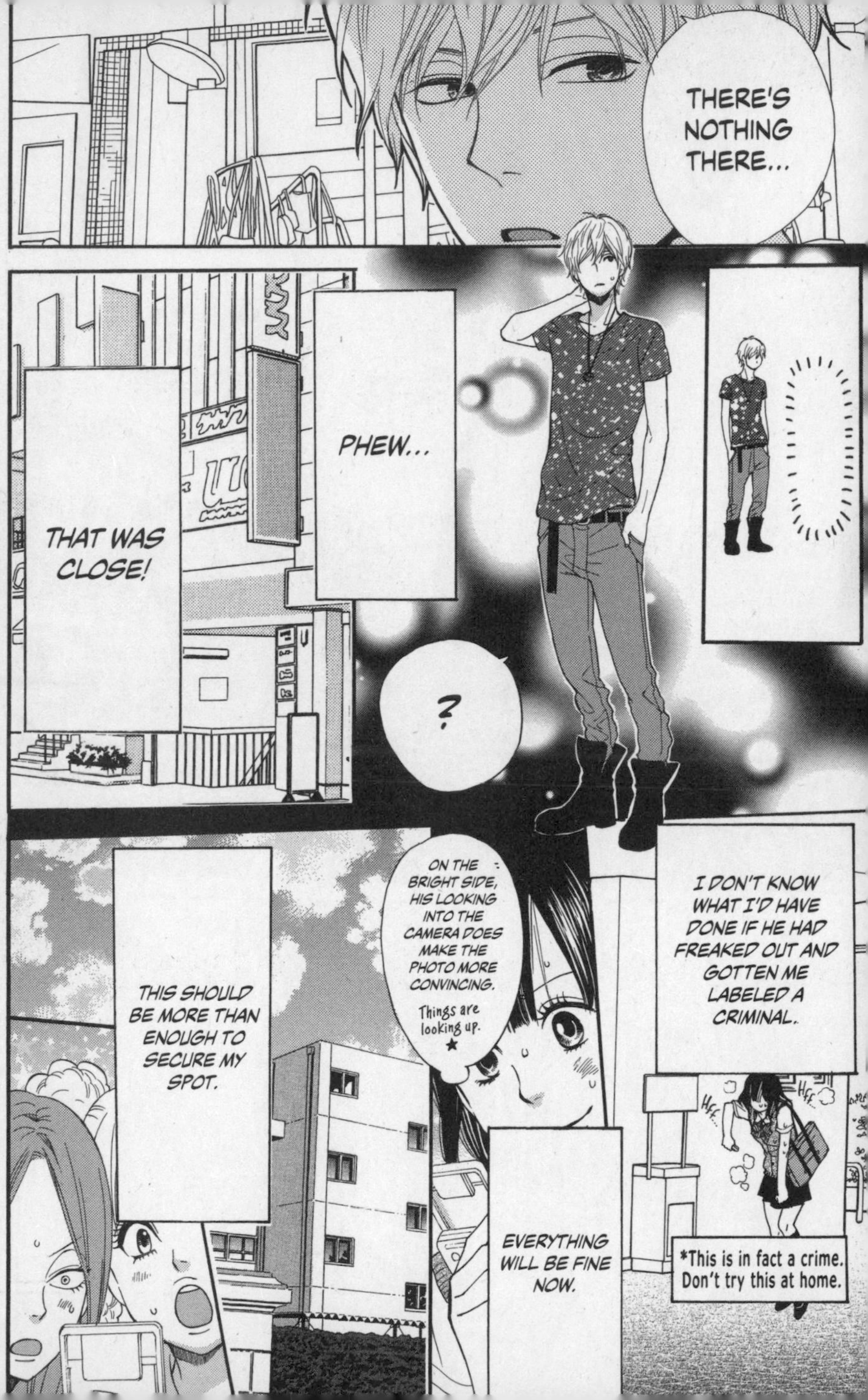
THERE'S NOTHING THERE...
?
PHEW...
THAT WAS CLOSE!
I DON'T KNOW WHAT I'D HAVE DONE IF HE HAD FREAKED OUT AND GOTTEN ME LABELED A CRIMINAL.
*This is in fact a crime. Don't try this at home.
ON THE BRIGHT SIDE, HIS LOOKING INTO THE CAMERA DOES MAKE THE PHOTO MORE CONVINCING.
Things are looking up. ★
EVERYTHING WILL BE FINE NOW.
THIS SHOULD BE MORE THAN ENOUGH TO SECURE MY SPOT.

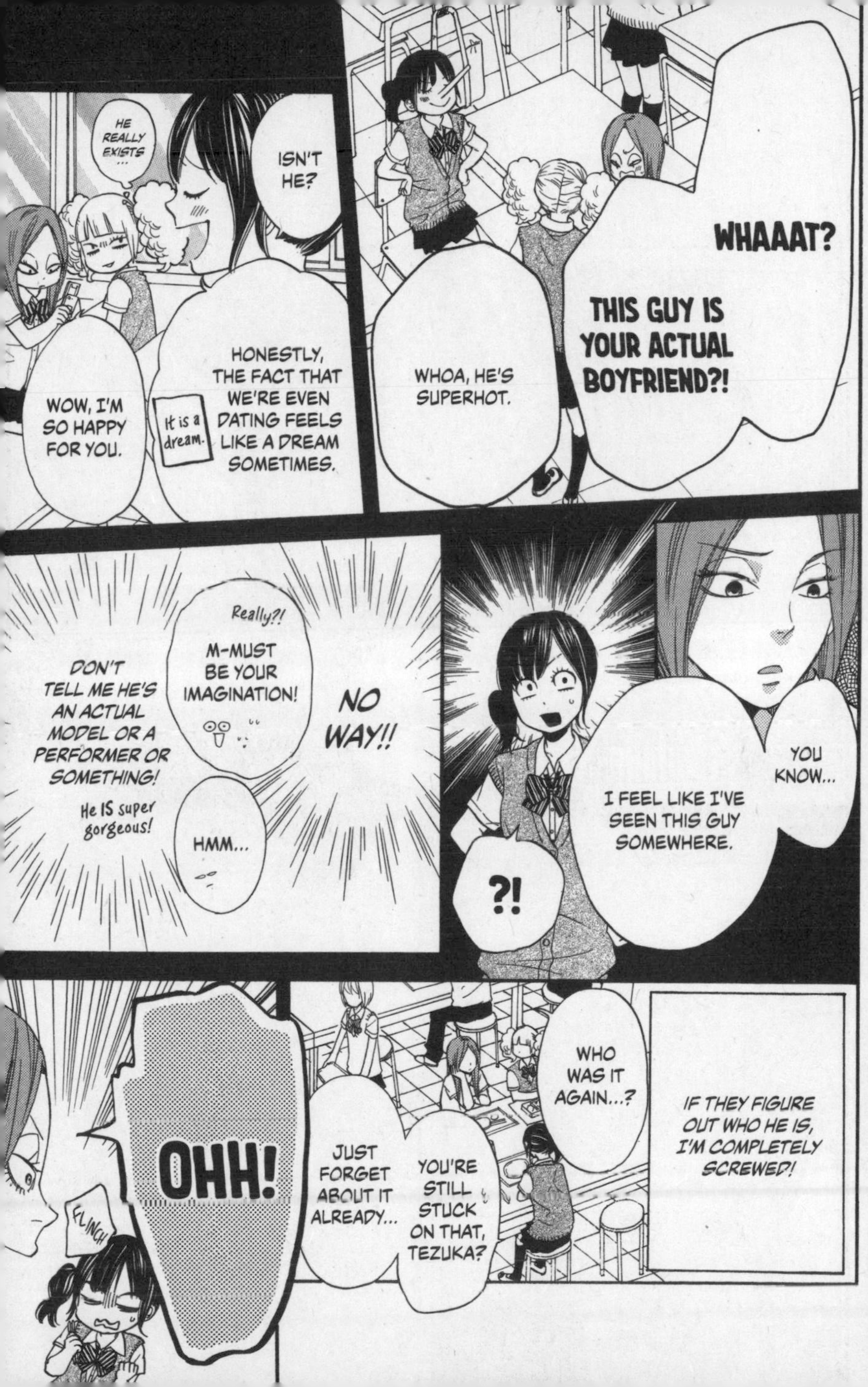
WHAAAT?
THIS GUY IS YOUR ACTUAL BOYFRIEND?!
WHOA, HE'S SUPERHOT.
ISN'T HE?
HE REALLY EXISTS...
HONESTLY, THE FACT THAT WE'RE EVEN DATING FEELS LIKE A DREAM SOMETIMES.
It is a dream.
WOW, I'M SO HAPPY FOR YOU.
YOU KNOW...
I FEEL LIKE I'VE SEEN THIS GUY SOMEWHERE.
?!
NO WAY!!
Really?!
M-MUST BE YOUR IMAGINATION!
DON'T TELL ME HE'S AN ACTUAL MODEL OR A PERFORMER OR SOMETHING!
He IS super gorgeous!
HMM...
IF THEY FIGURE OUT WHO HE IS, I'M COMPLETELY SCREWED!
WHO WAS IT AGAIN...?
YOU'RE STILL STUCK ON THAT, TEZUKA?
JUST FORGET ABOUT IT ALREADY...
OHH!
FLINCH

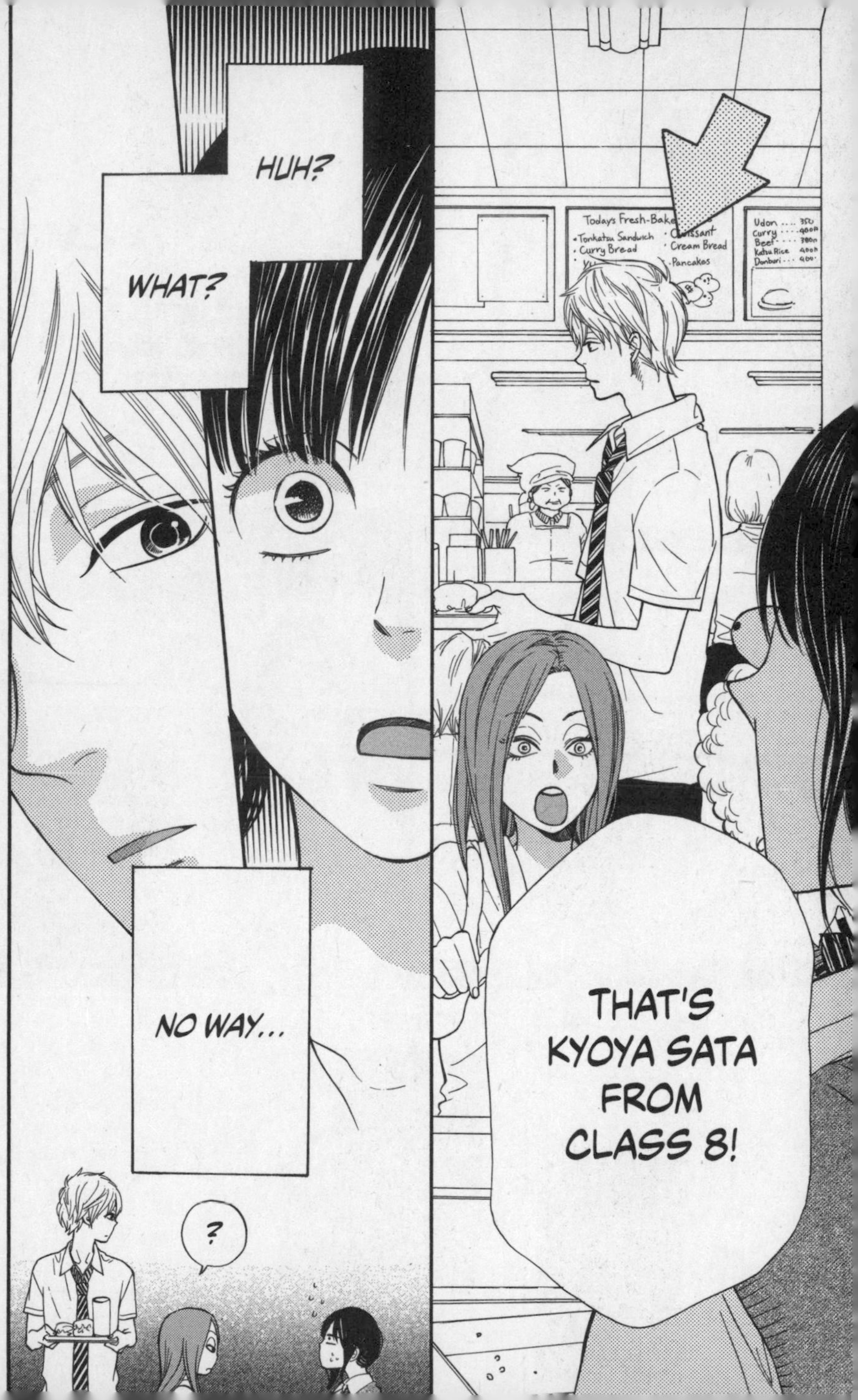
Todays Fresh-Bake
Tonkatsu Sandwich
Curry Bread
Cream Bread
Pancakes
Udon
Curry
Beef
Katsu Rice
Donburi
THAT'S KYOYA SATA FROM CLASS 8!
HUH?
WHAT?
NO WAY...
?

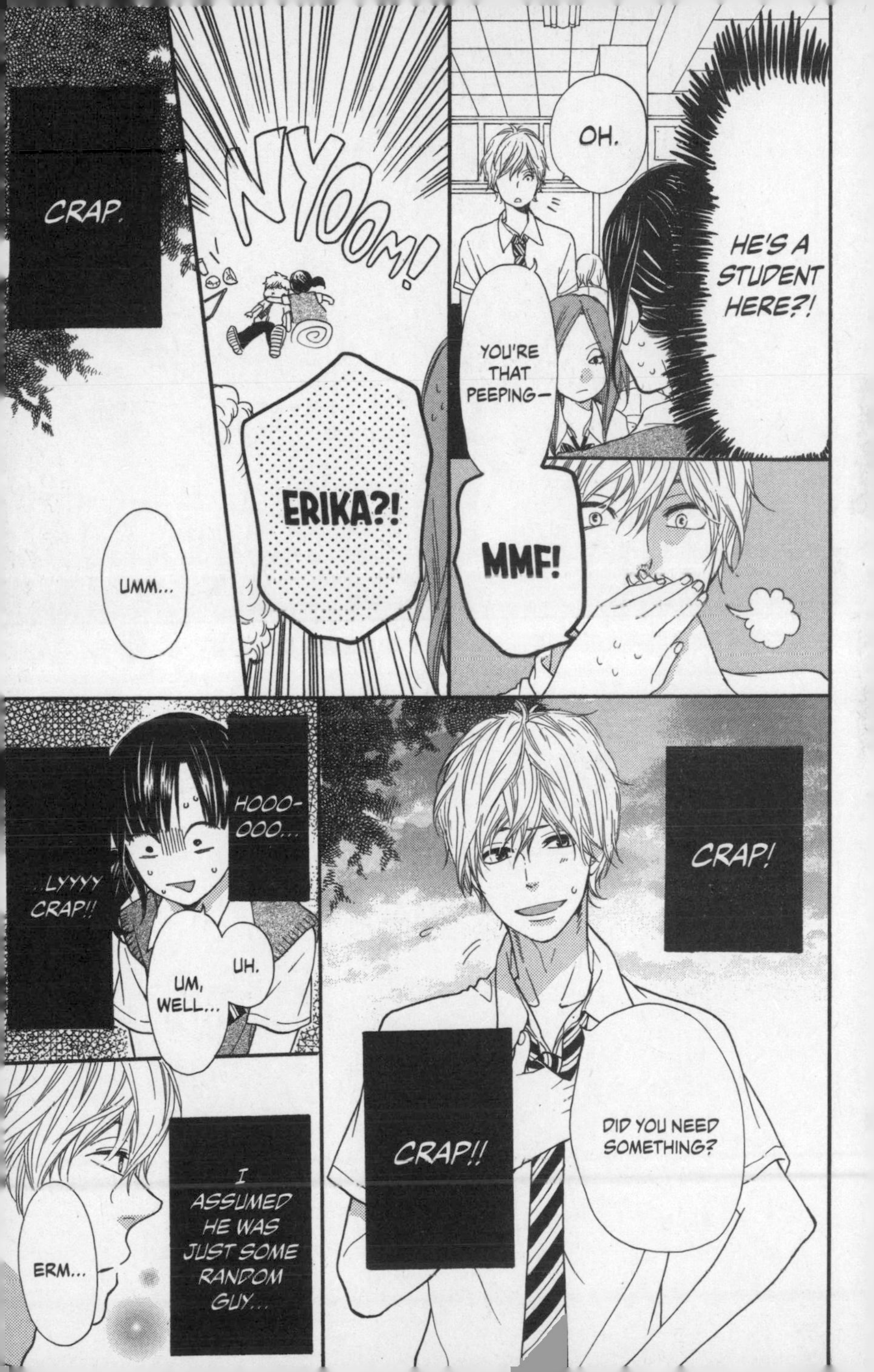
OH.
HE'S A STUDENT HERE?!
YOU'RE THAT PEEPING—
MMF!
NYOOM!
ERIKA?!
CRAP.
UMM...
CRAP!
DID YOU NEED SOMETHING?
CRAP!!
HOOO-OOO...
UH.
UM, WELL...
...LYYYY CRAP!!
I ASSUMED HE WAS JUST SOME RANDOM GUY...
ERM...

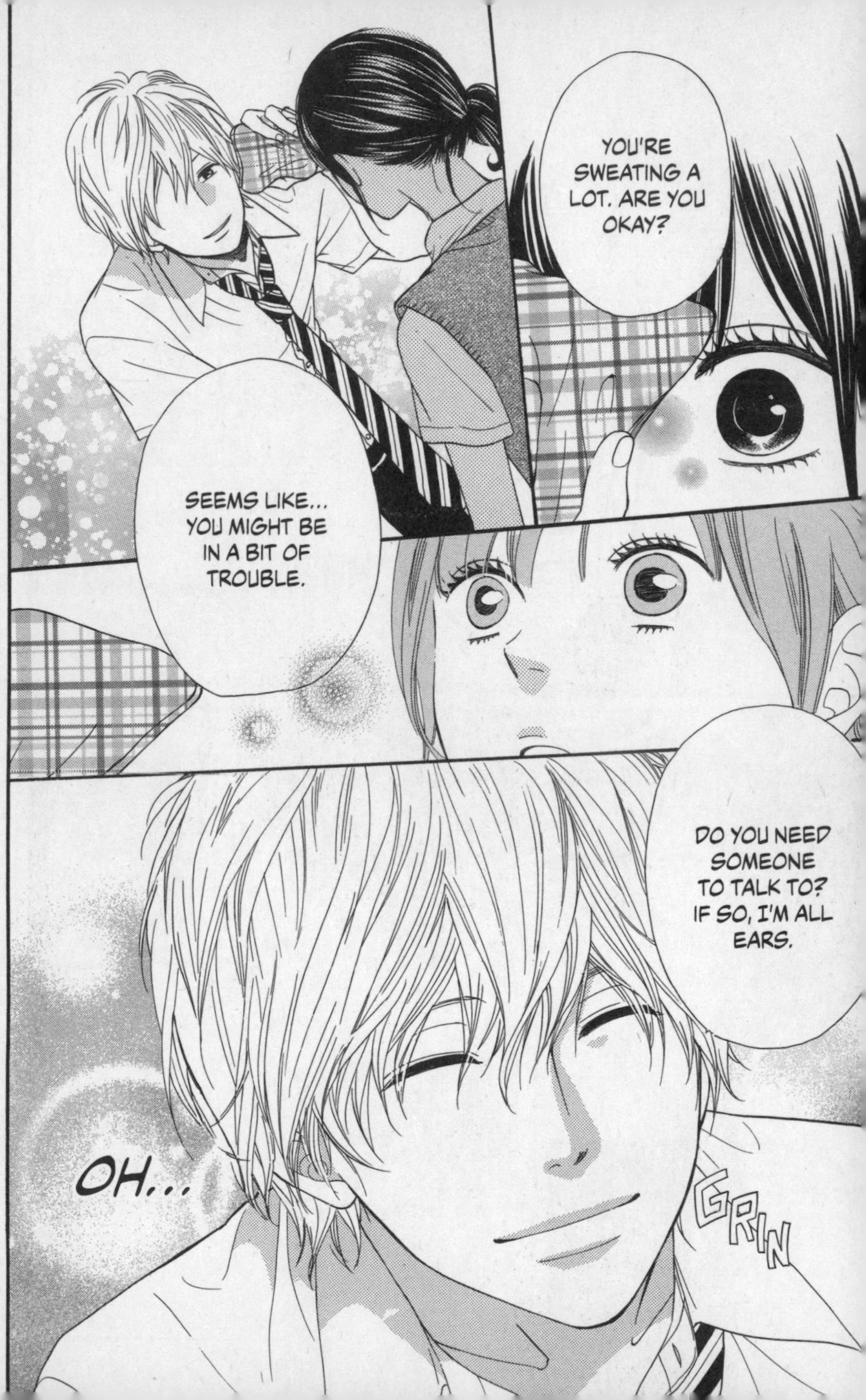
YOU'RE SWEATING A LOT. ARE YOU OKAY?
SEEMS LIKE... YOU MIGHT BE IN A BIT OF TROUBLE.
DO YOU NEED SOMEONE TO TALK TO? IF SO, I'M ALL EARS.
GRIN
OH...

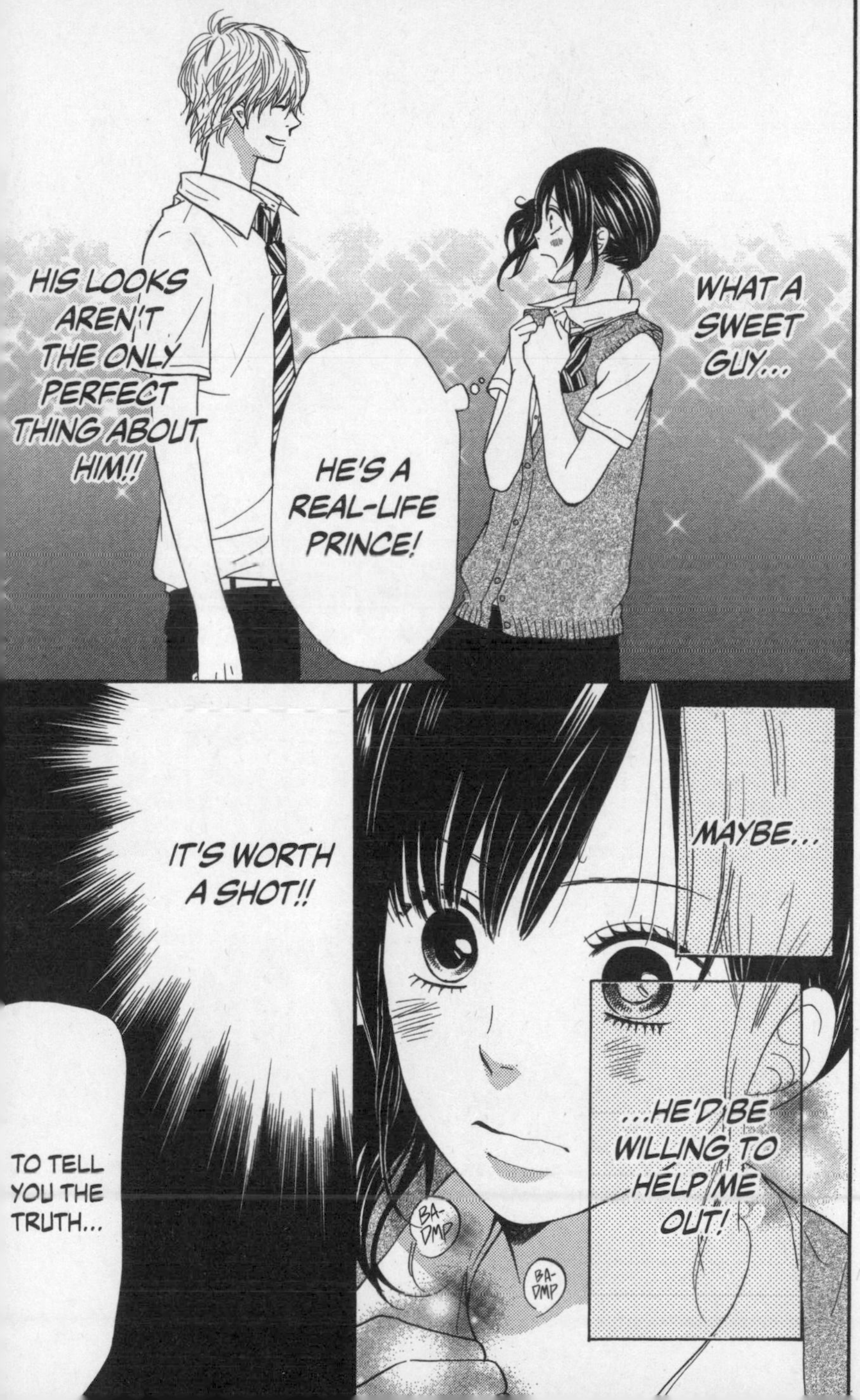
WHAT A SWEET GUY...
HIS LOOKS AREN'T THE ONLY PERFECT THING ABOUT HIM!!
HE'S A REAL-LIFE PRINCE!
MAYBE...
...HE'D BE WILLING TO HELP ME OUT!
BA-DMP
BA-DMP
IT'S WORTH A SHOT!!
TO TELL YOU THE TRUTH...

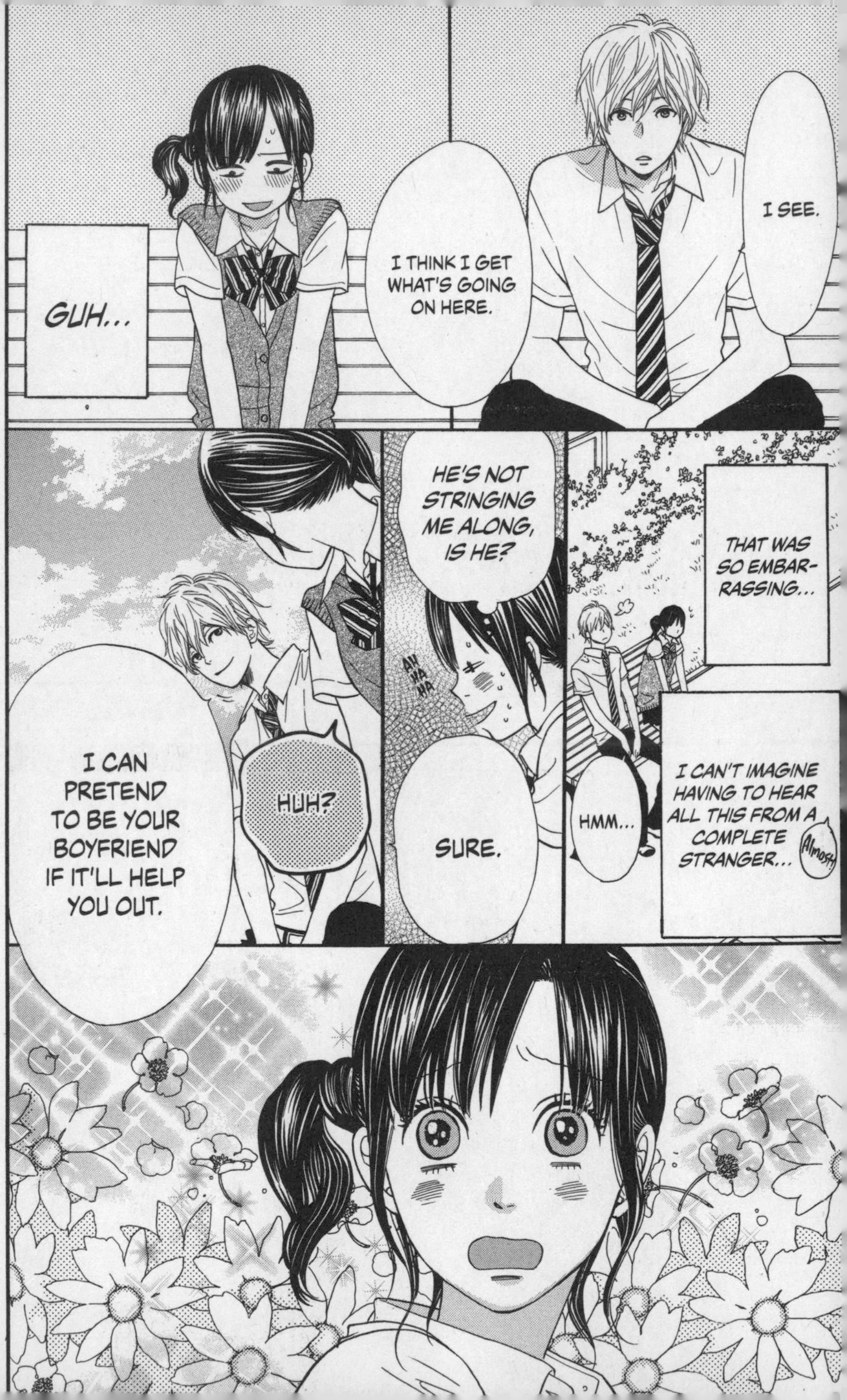
I SEE.
I THINK I GET WHAT'S GOING ON HERE.
GUH...
THAT WAS SO EMBARRASSING...
I CAN'T IMAGINE HAVING TO HEAR ALL THIS FROM A COMPLETE STRANGER...
Almost
HMM...
HE'S NOT STRINGING ME ALONG, IS HE?
AH HA HA
SURE.
HUH?
I CAN PRETEND TO BE YOUR BOYFRIEND IF IT'LL HELP YOU OUT.

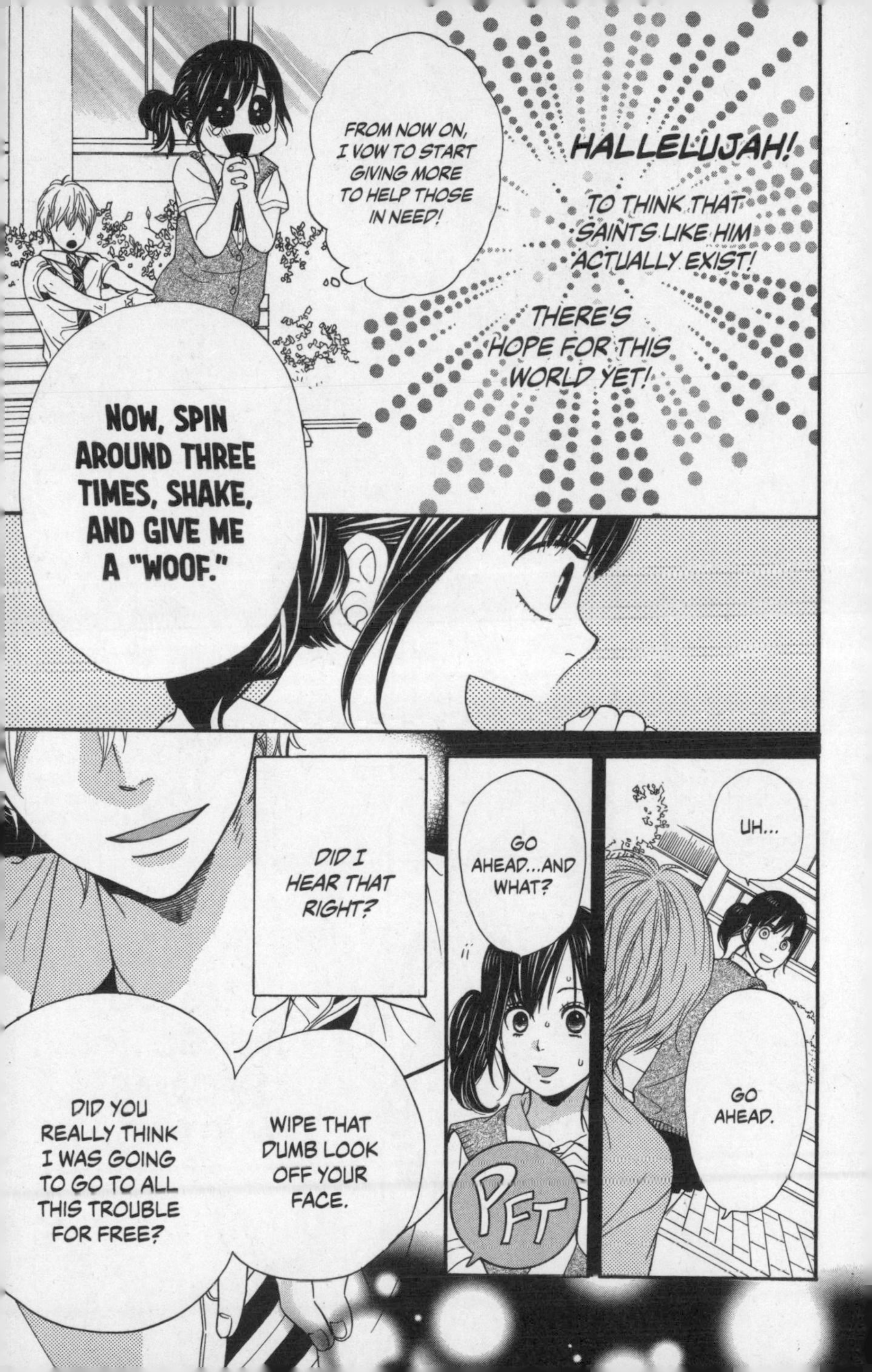
HALLELUJAH!
TO THINK THAT SAINTS LIKE HIM ACTUALLY EXIST!
THERE'S HOPE FOR THIS WORLD YET!
FROM NOW ON, I VOW TO START GIVING MORE TO HELP THOSE IN NEED!
NOW, SPIN AROUND THREE TIMES, SHAKE, AND GIVE ME A "WOOF."
UH...
GO AHEAD.
GO AHEAD...AND WHAT?
PFT
DID I HEAR THAT RIGHT?
WIPE THAT DUMB LOOK OFF YOUR FACE.
DID YOU REALLY THINK I WAS GOING TO GO TO ALL THIS TROUBLE FOR FREE?

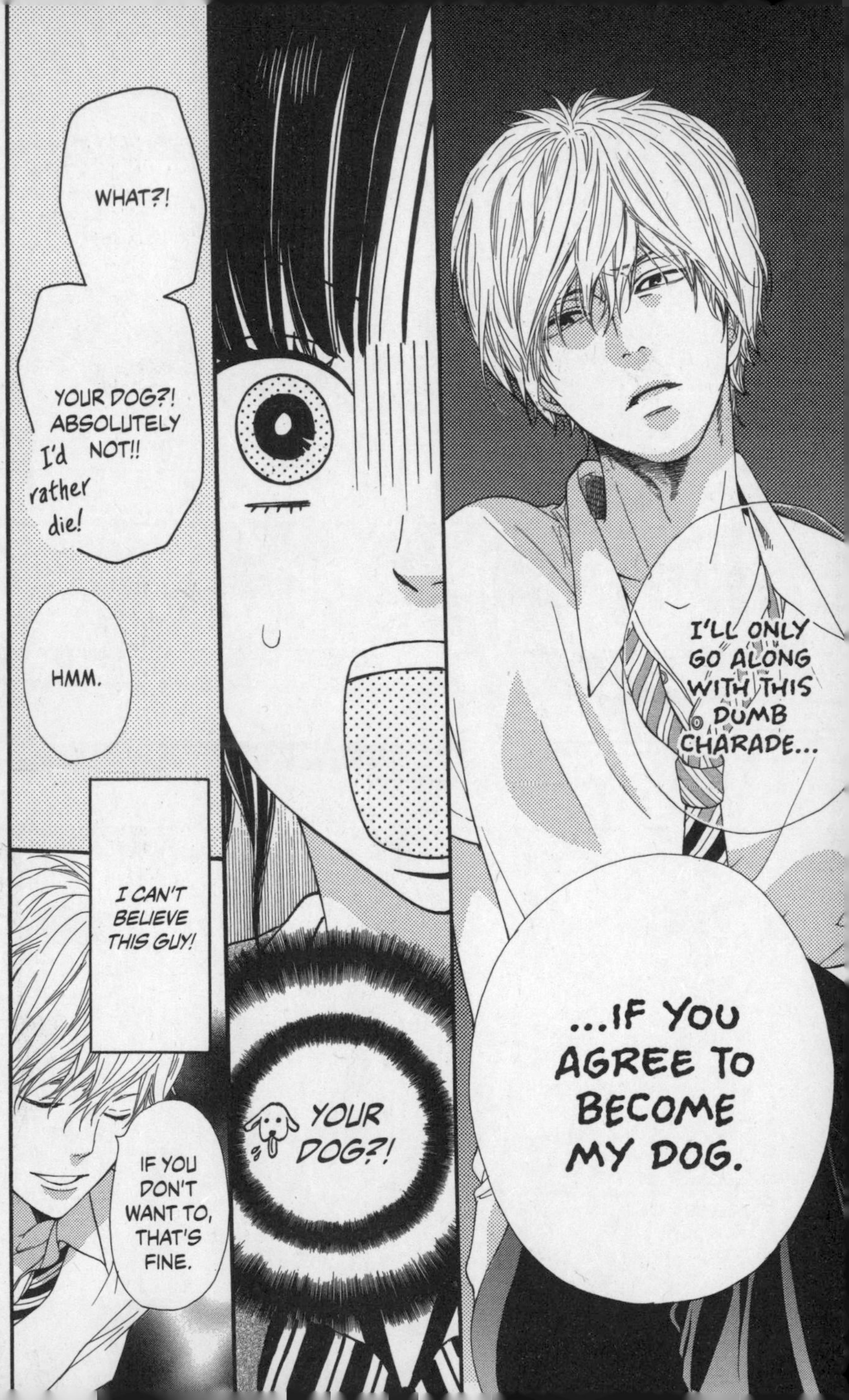
I'LL ONLY GO ALONG WITH THIS DUMB CHARADE...
...IF YOU AGREE TO BECOME MY DOG.
YOUR DOG?!
WHAT?!
YOUR DOG?! ABSOLUTELY NOT!!
I'd rather die!
HMM.
I CAN'T BELIEVE THIS GUY!
IF YOU DON'T WANT TO, THAT'S FINE.

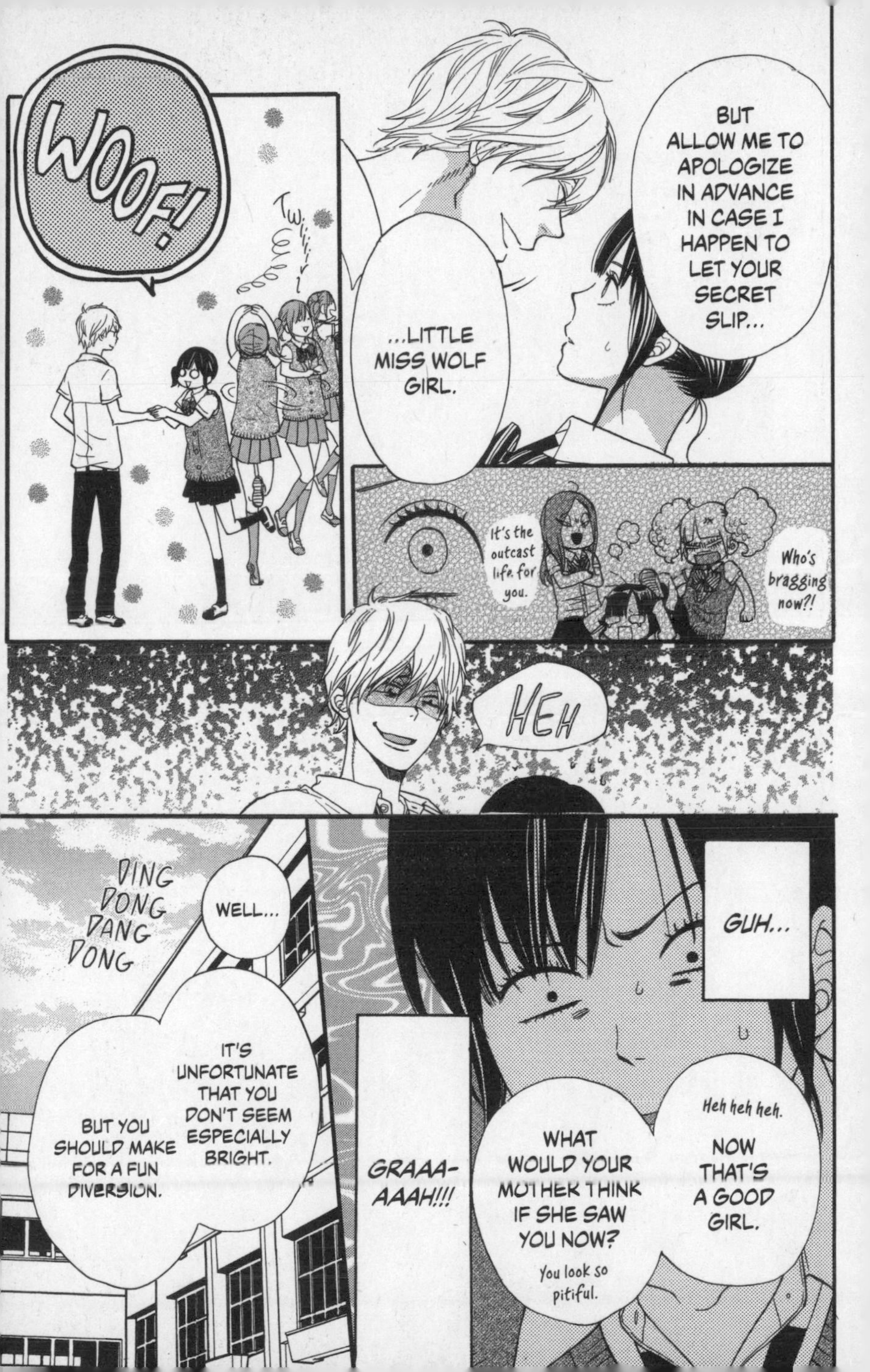
BUT ALLOW ME TO APOLOGIZE IN ADVANCE IN CASE I HAPPEN TO LET YOUR SECRET SLIP...
...LITTLE MISS WOLF GIRL.
Who's bragging now?!
It's the outcast life for you.
WOOF!
HEH
GUH...
Heh heh heh.
NOW THAT'S A GOOD GIRL.
WHAT WOULD YOUR MOTHER THINK IF SHE SAW YOU NOW?
You look so pitiful.
GRAAA-AAAH!!!
WELL...
IT'S UNFORTUNATE THAT YOU DON'T SEEM ESPECIALLY BRIGHT.
BUT YOU SHOULD MAKE FOR A FUN DIVERSION.
DING DONG DANG DONG

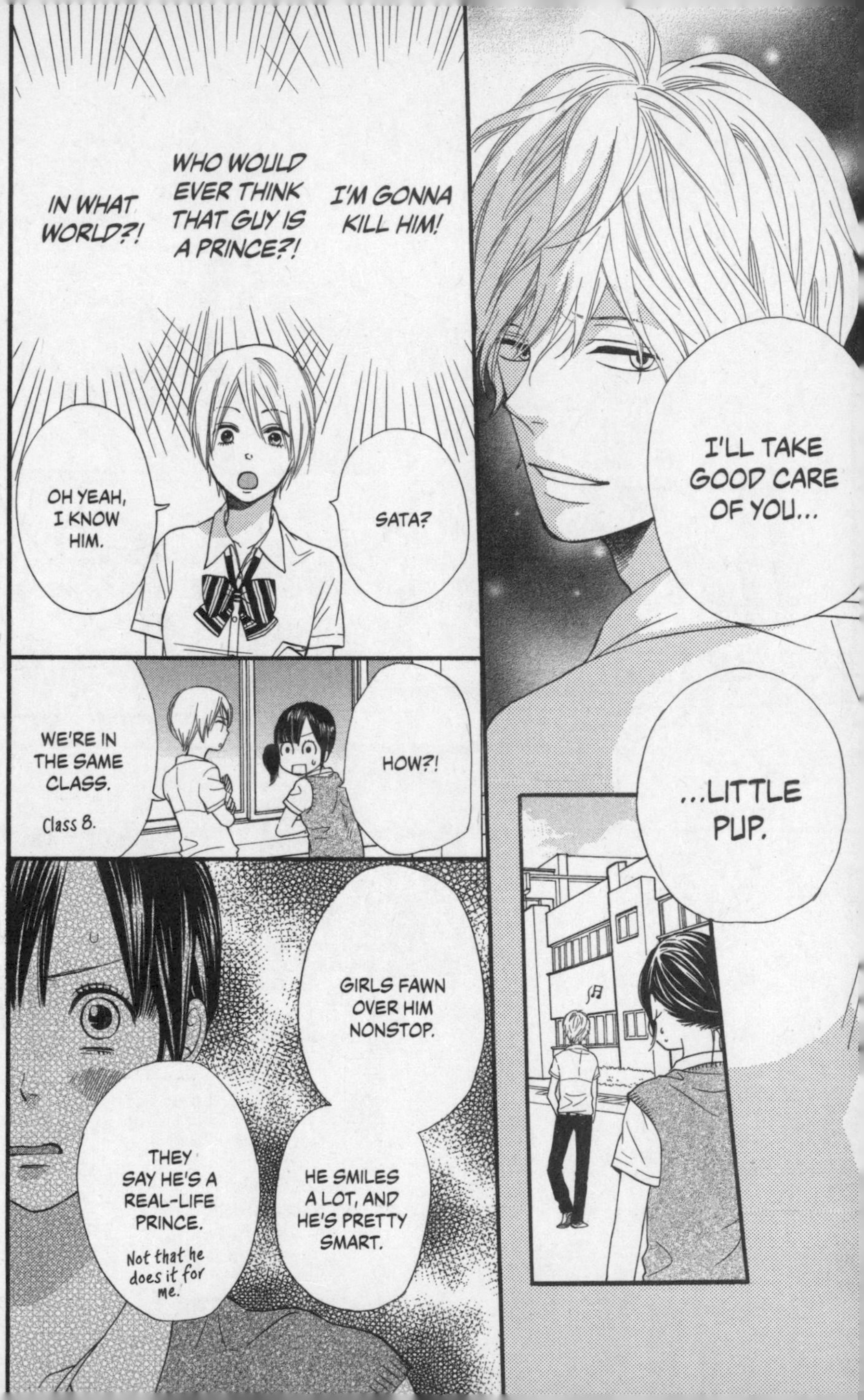
I'LL TAKE GOOD CARE OF YOU...
...LITTLE PUP.
I'M GONNA KILL HIM!
WHO WOULD EVER THINK THAT GUY IS A PRINCE?!
IN WHAT WORLD?!
SATA?
OH YEAH, I KNOW HIM.
HOW?!
WE'RE IN THE SAME CLASS.
Class 8.
GIRLS FAWN OVER HIM NONSTOP.
HE SMILES A LOT, AND HE'S PRETTY SMART.
THEY SAY HE'S A REAL-LIFE PRINCE.
Not that he does it for me.

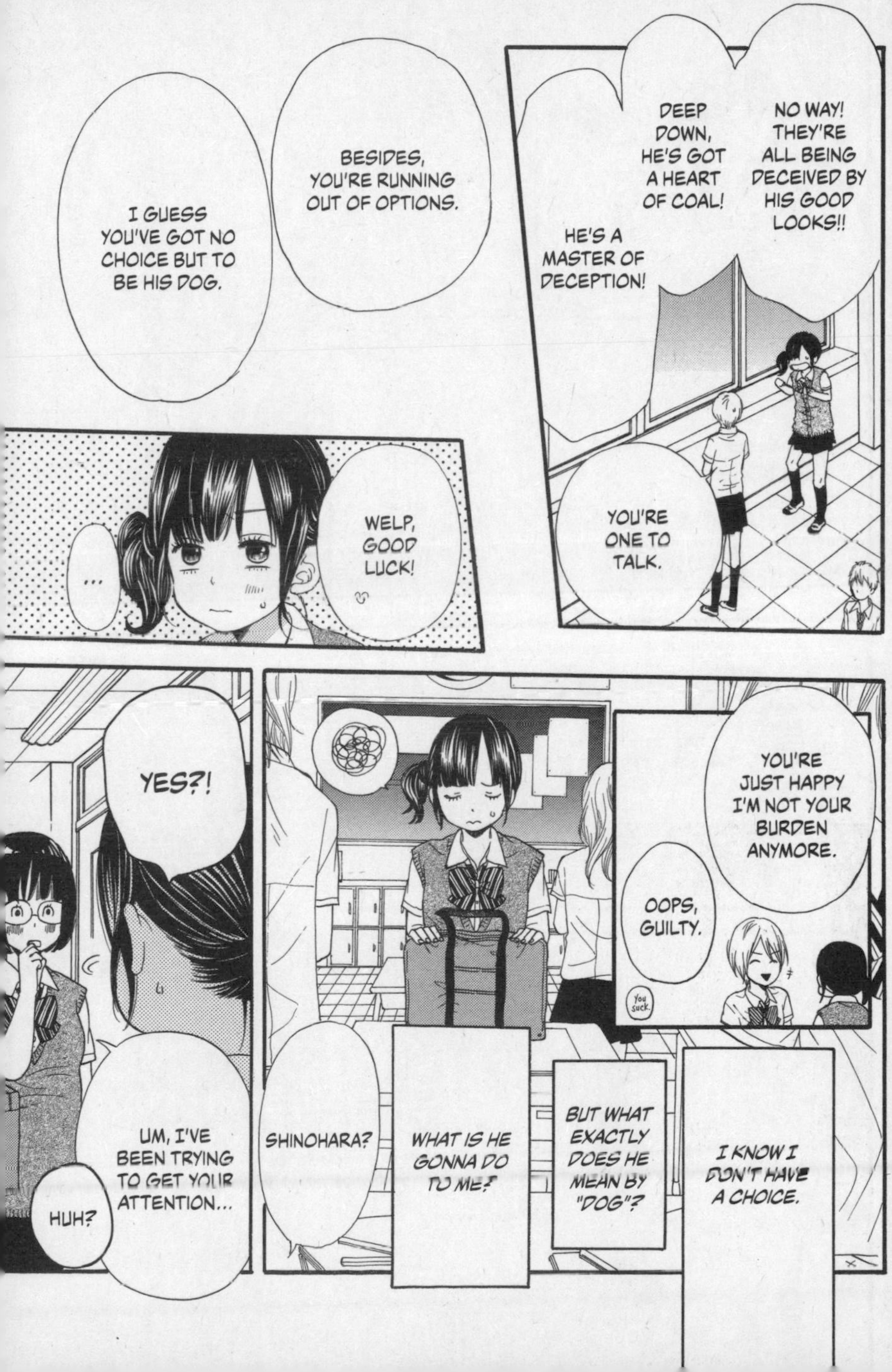
NO WAY! THEY'RE ALL BEING DECEIVED BY HIS GOOD LOOKS!!
DEEP DOWN, HE'S GOT A HEART OF COAL!
HE'S A MASTER OF DECEPTION!
YOU'RE ONE TO TALK.
BESIDES, YOU'RE RUNNING OUT OF OPTIONS.
I GUESS YOU'VE GOT NO CHOICE BUT TO BE HIS DOG.
WELP, GOOD LUCK!
...
YOU'RE JUST HAPPY I'M NOT YOUR BURDEN ANYMORE.
OOPS, GUILTY.
You suck.
I KNOW I DON'T HAVE A CHOICE.
BUT WHAT EXACTLY DOES HE MEAN BY "DOG"?
WHAT IS HE GONNA DO TO ME?
SHINOHARA?
UM, I'VE BEEN TRYING TO GET YOUR ATTENTION...
HUH?
YES?!

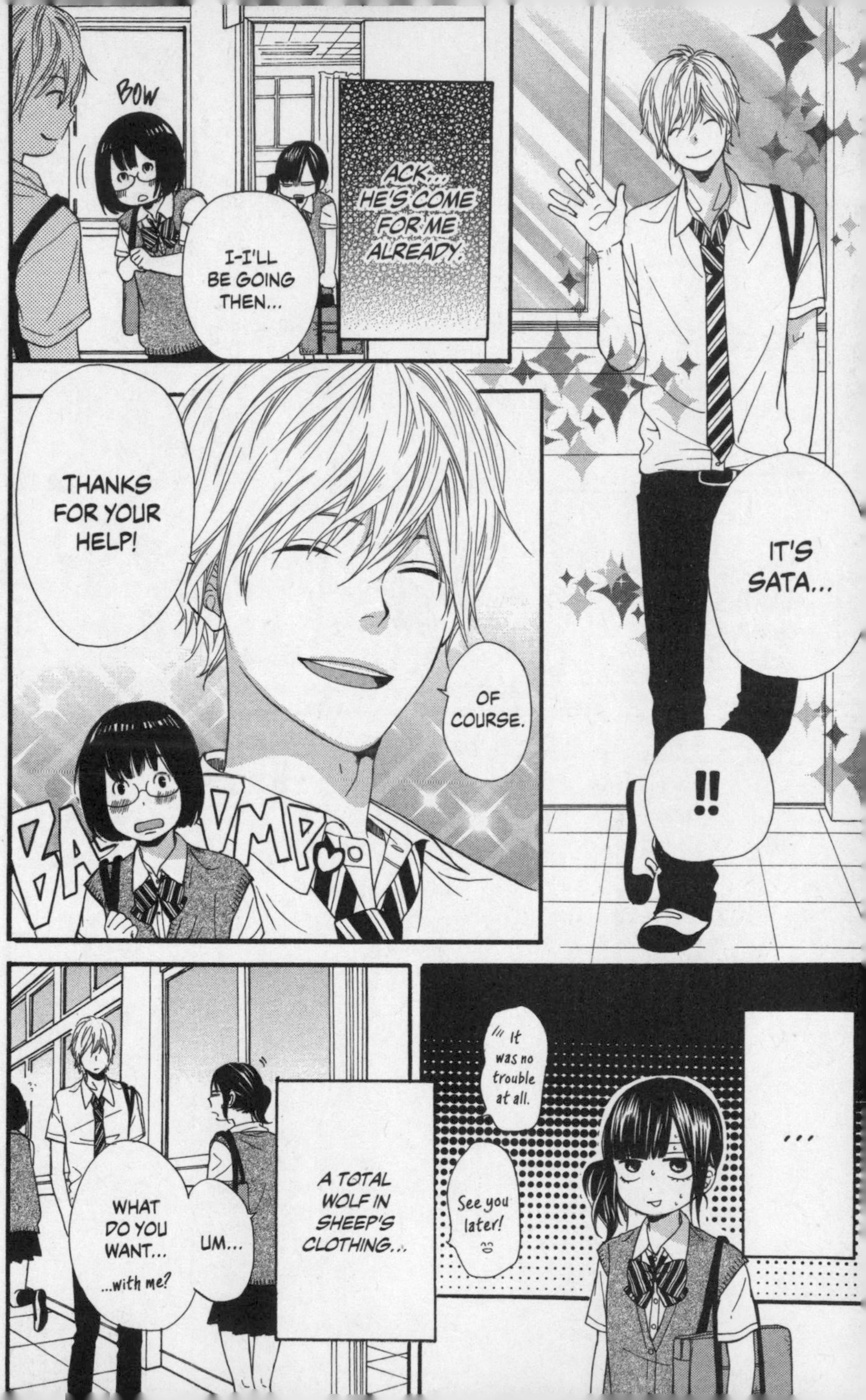

IT'S SATA...
!!
ACK... HE'S COME FOR ME ALREADY.
BOW
I-I'LL BE GOING THEN...
THANKS FOR YOUR HELP!
OF COURSE.
...
It was no trouble at all.
See you later!
A TOTAL WOLF IN SHEEP'S CLOTHING...
UM...
WHAT DO YOU WANT... ...with me?

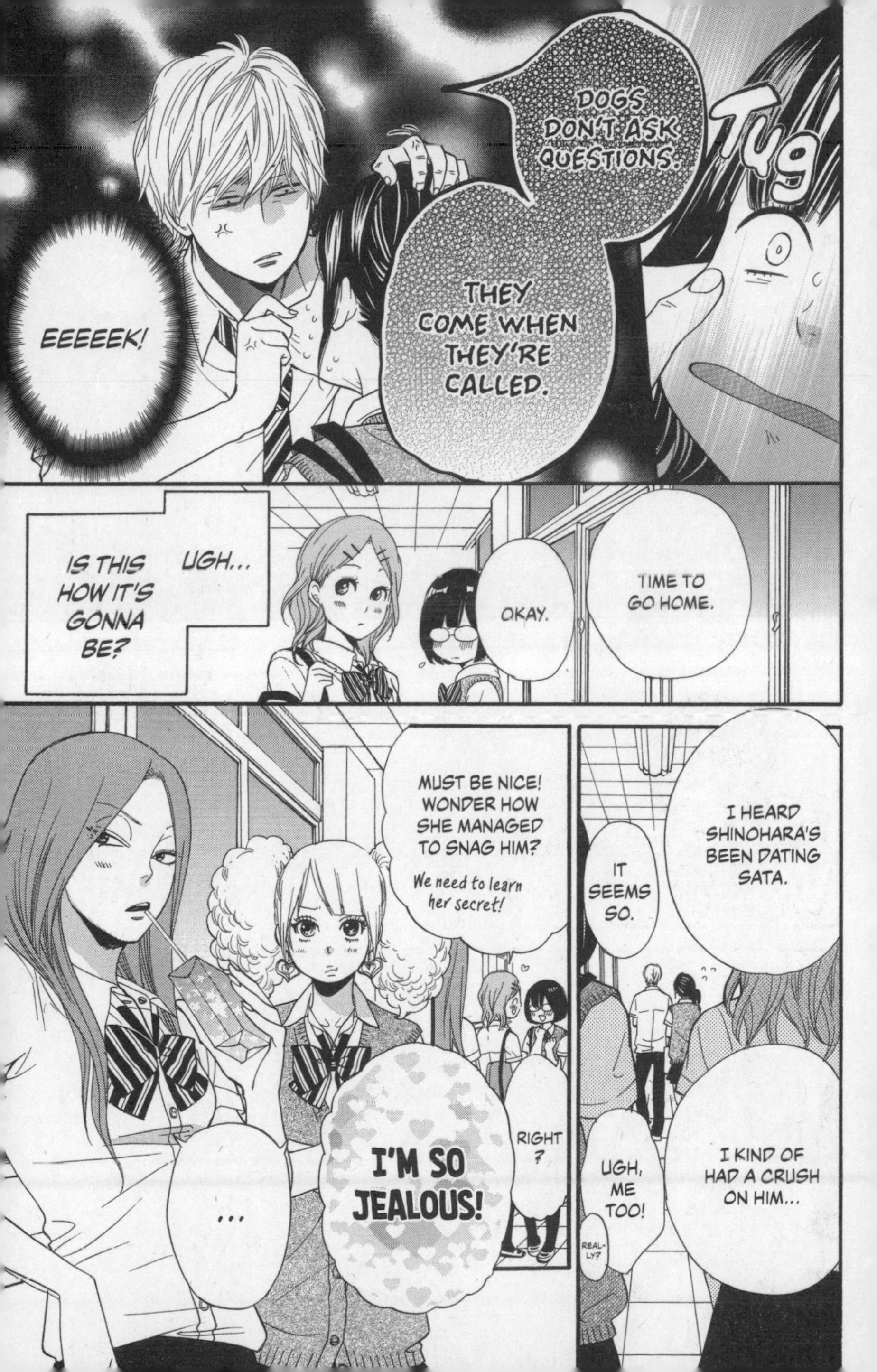
Tug
DOGS DON'T ASK QUESTIONS.
THEY COME WHEN THEY'RE CALLED.
EEEEEK!
TIME TO GO HOME.
OKAY.
UGH...
IS THIS HOW IT'S GONNA BE?
I HEARD SHINOHARA'S BEEN DATING SATA.
IT SEEMS SO.
I KIND OF HAD A CRUSH ON HIM...
UGH, ME TOO!
REAL-LY?
MUST BE NICE! WONDER HOW SHE MANAGED TO SNAG HIM?
We need to learn her secret!
RIGHT?
I'M SO JEALOUS!
...

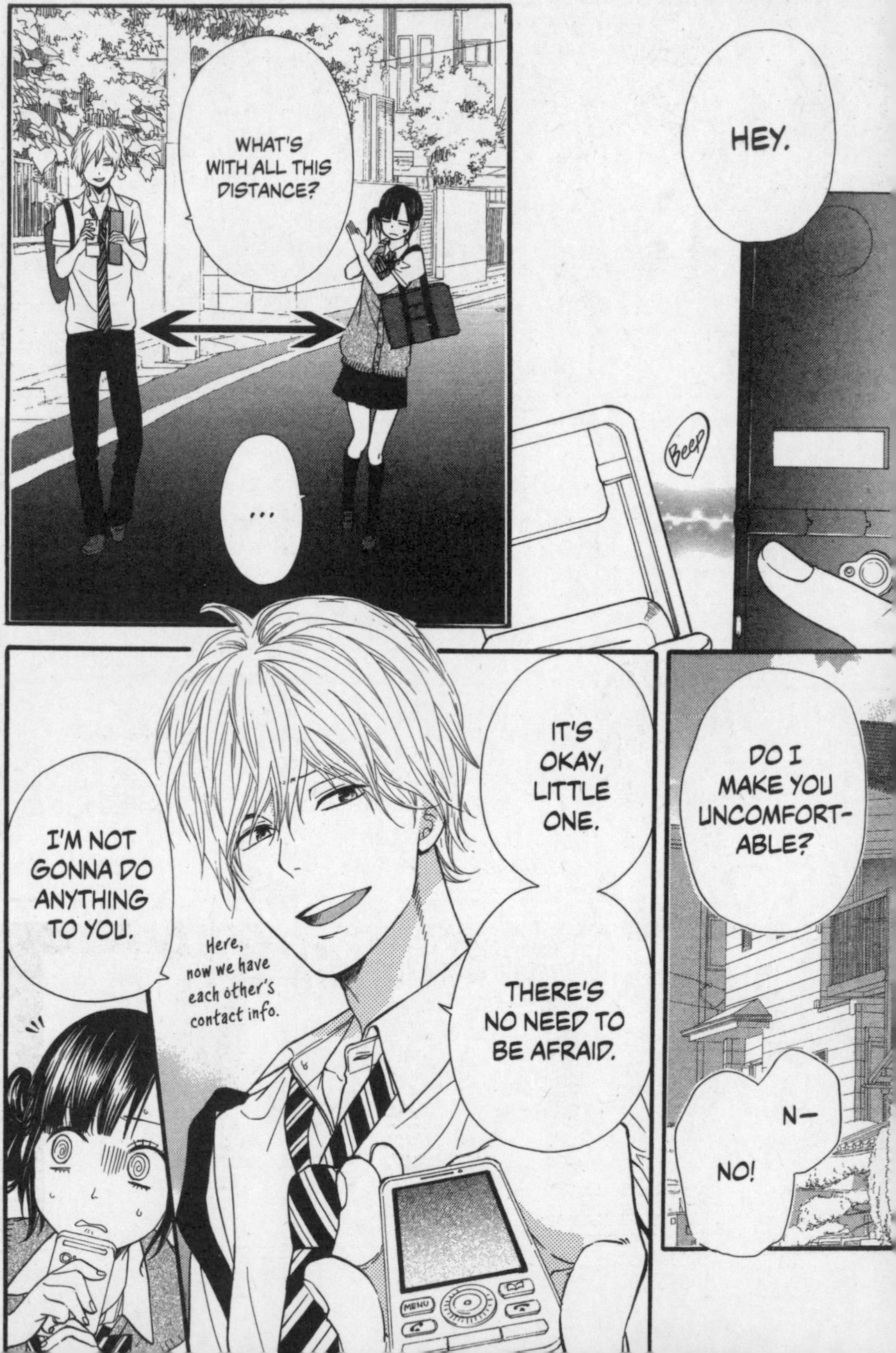
HEY.
Beep
WHAT'S WITH ALL THIS DISTANCE?
...
DO I MAKE YOU UNCOMFORT-ABLE?
N— NO!
IT'S OKAY, LITTLE ONE.
THERE'S NO NEED TO BE AFRAID.
I'M NOT GONNA DO ANYTHING TO YOU.
Here, now we have each other's contact info.

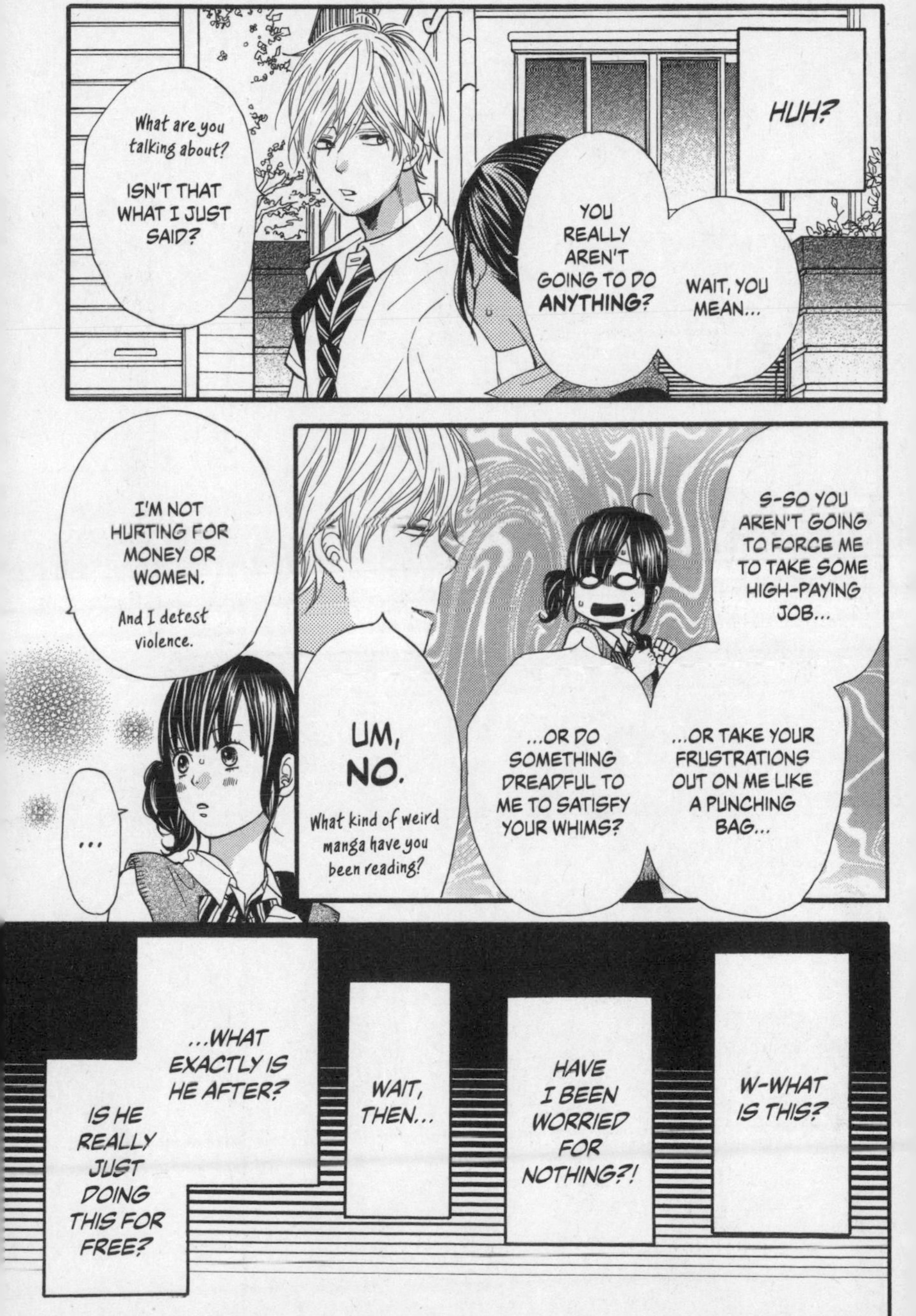
HUH?
WAIT, YOU MEAN...
YOU REALLY AREN'T GOING TO DO ANYTHING?
What are you talking about?
ISN'T THAT WHAT I JUST SAID?
S-SO YOU AREN'T GOING TO FORCE ME TO TAKE SOME HIGH-PAYING JOB...
...OR TAKE YOUR FRUSTRATIONS OUT ON ME LIKE A PUNCHING BAG...
...OR DO SOMETHING DREADFUL TO ME TO SATISFY YOUR WHIMS?
UM, NO.
What kind of weird manga have you been reading?
I'M NOT HURTING FOR MONEY OR WOMEN.
And I detest violence.
...
W-WHAT IS THIS?
HAVE I BEEN WORRIED FOR NOTHING?!
WAIT, THEN...
...WHAT EXACTLY IS HE AFTER?
IS HE REALLY JUST DOING THIS FOR FREE?

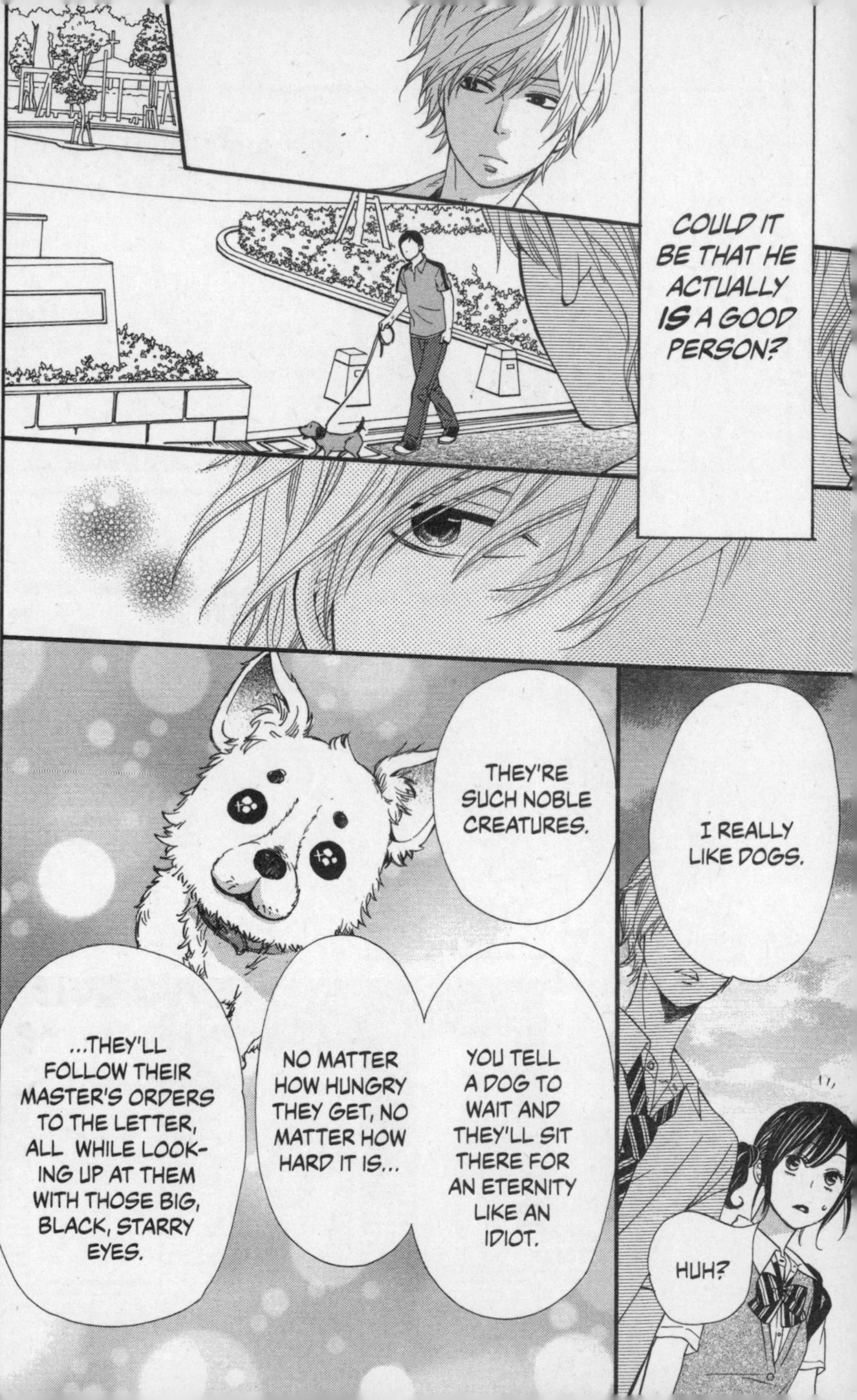
COULD IT BE THAT HE ACTUALLY IS A GOOD PERSON?
I REALLY LIKE DOGS.
HUH?
THEY'RE SUCH NOBLE CREATURES.
YOU TELL A DOG TO WAIT AND THEY'LL SIT THERE FOR AN ETERNITY LIKE AN IDIOT.
NO MATTER HOW HUNGRY THEY GET, NO MATTER HOW HARD IT IS...
...THEY'LL FOLLOW THEIR MASTER'S ORDERS TO THE LETTER, ALL WHILE LOOKING UP AT THEM WITH THOSE BIG, BLACK, STARRY EYES.

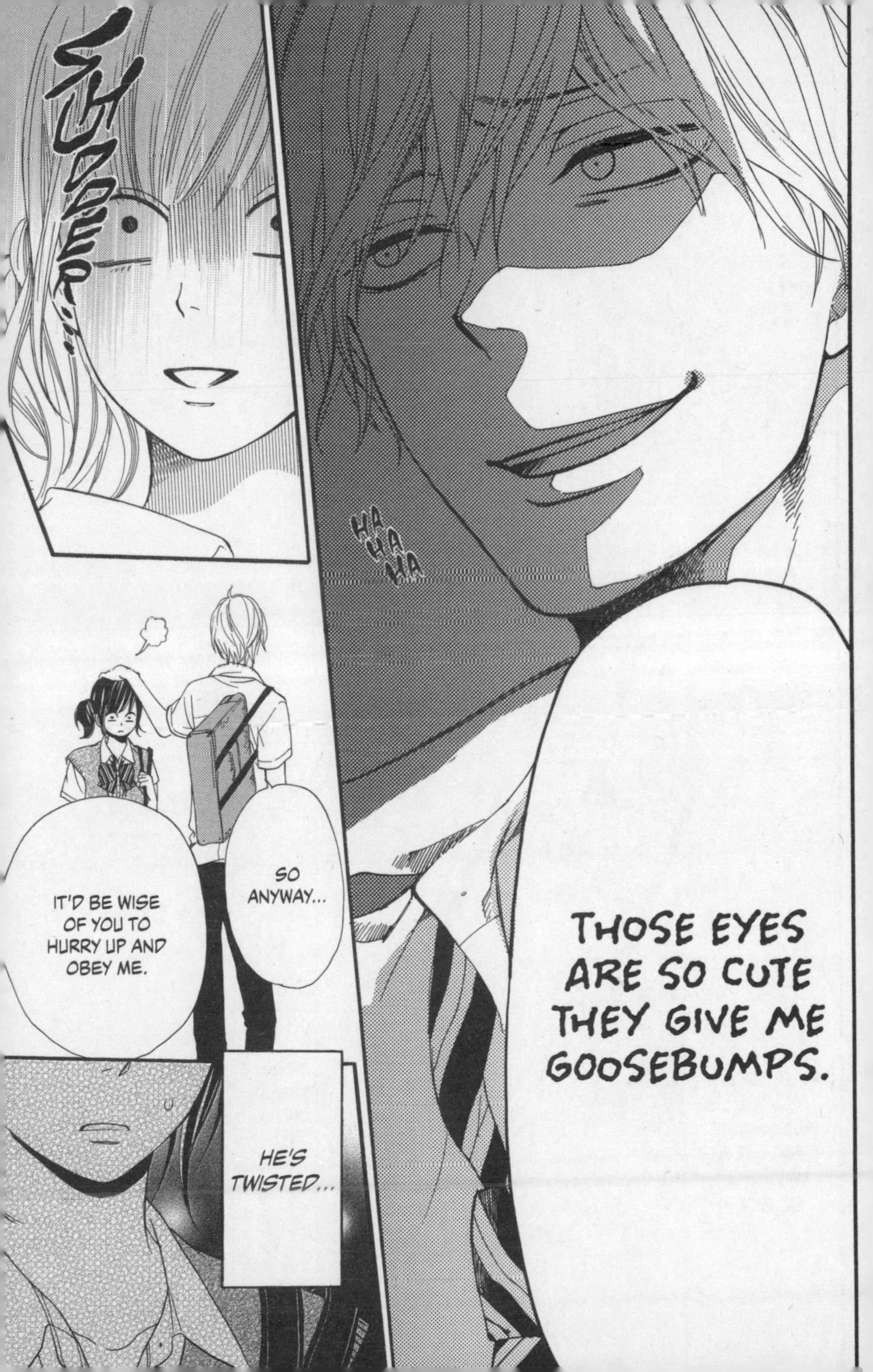
HA HA HA
THOSE EYES ARE SO CUTE THEY GIVE ME GOOSEBUMPS.
SHUDDER...
SO ANYWAY...
IT'D BE WISE OF YOU TO HURRY UP AND OBEY ME.
HE'S TWISTED...

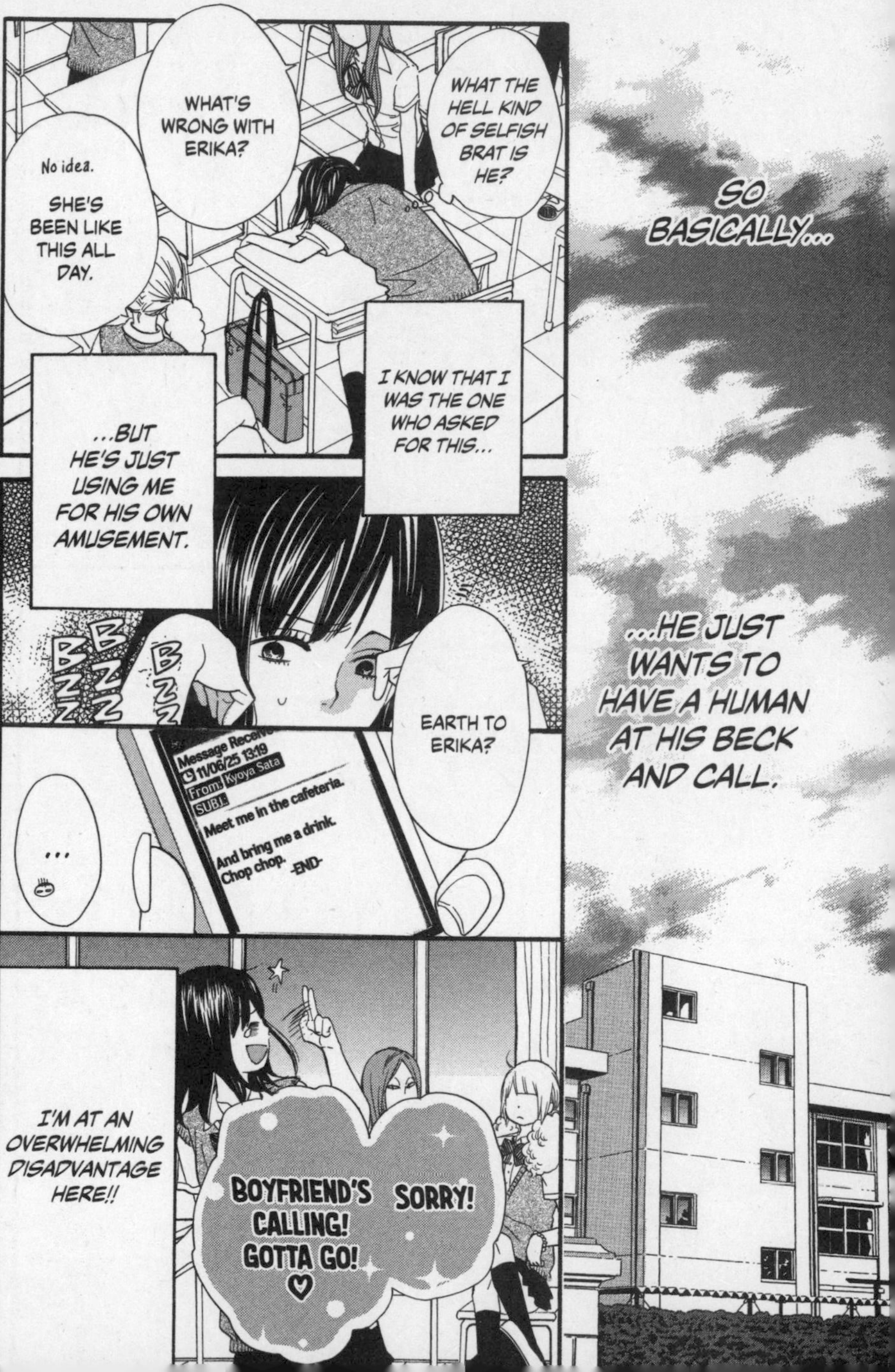
SO BASICALLY...
...HE JUST WANTS TO HAVE A HUMAN AT HIS BECK AND CALL.
WHAT THE HELL KIND OF SELFISH BRAT IS HE?
WHAT'S WRONG WITH ERIKA?
No idea.
SHE'S BEEN LIKE THIS ALL DAY.
I KNOW THAT I WAS THE ONE WHO ASKED FOR THIS...
...BUT HE'S JUST USING ME FOR HIS OWN AMUSEMENT.
BZZ BZZ
BZZ
EARTH TO ERIKA?
Message Rece
11/06/25 13:19
From: Kyoya Sata
SUBJ:
Meet me in the cafeteria.
And bring me a drink.
Chop chop.
-END-
...
SORRY!
BOYFRIEND'S CALLING! GOTTA GO! ♥
I'M AT AN OVERWHELMING DISADVANTAGE HERE!!

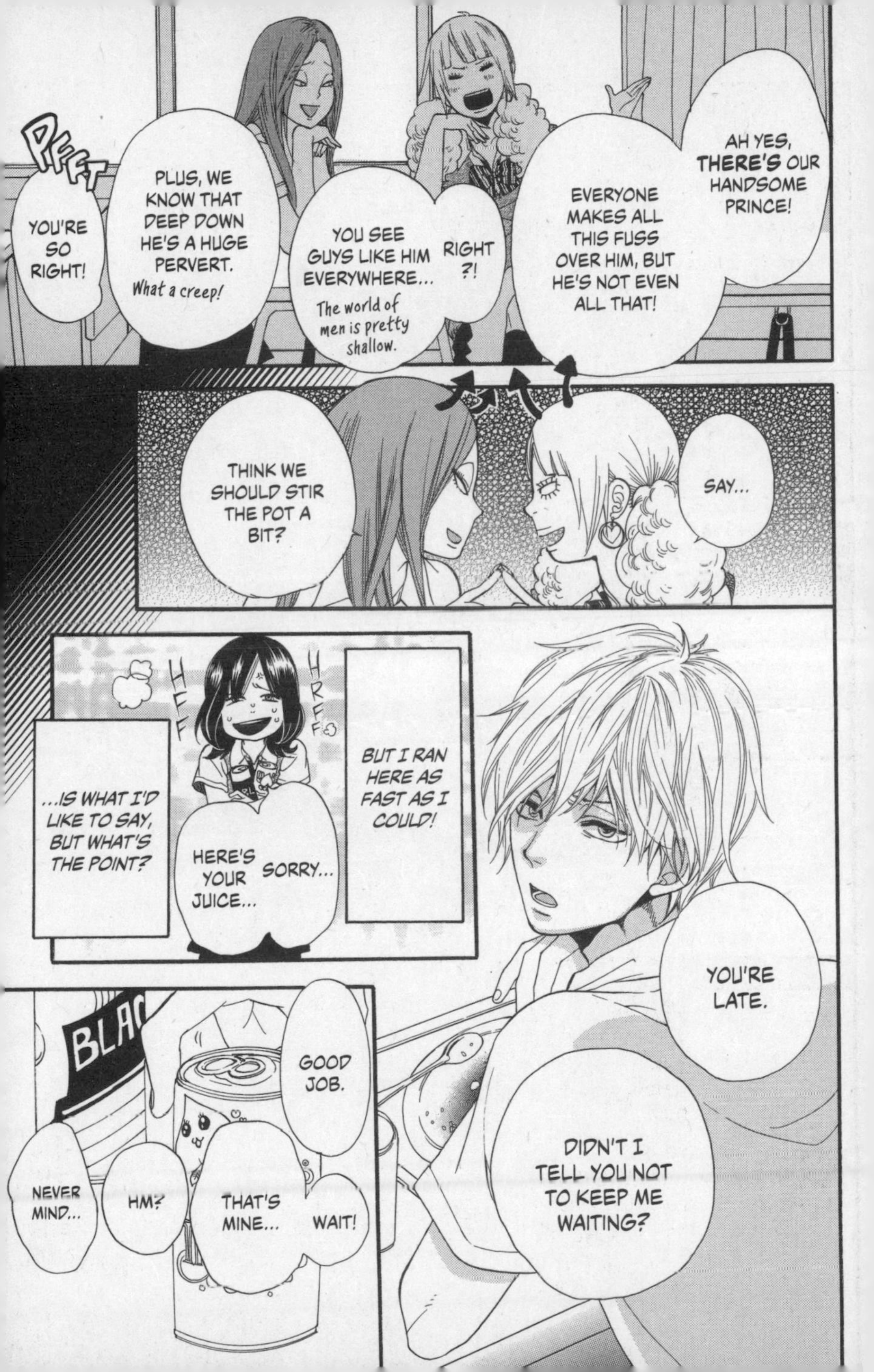
AH YES, **THERE'S** OUR HANDSOME PRINCE!
EVERYONE MAKES ALL THIS FUSS OVER HIM, BUT HE'S NOT EVEN ALL THAT!
RIGHT?!
YOU SEE GUYS LIKE HIM EVERYWHERE...
The world of men is pretty shallow.
PLUS, WE KNOW THAT DEEP DOWN HE'S A HUGE PERVERT.
What a creep!
PFFT
YOU'RE SO RIGHT!
SAY...
THINK WE SHOULD STIR THE POT A BIT?
YOU'RE LATE.
DIDN'T I TELL YOU NOT TO KEEP ME WAITING?
BUT I RAN HERE AS FAST AS I COULD!
HRFF
HFF
SORRY...
HERE'S YOUR JUICE...
...IS WHAT I'D LIKE TO SAY, BUT WHAT'S THE POINT?
GOOD JOB.
WAIT!
THAT'S MINE...
HM?
NEVER MIND...
BLAC

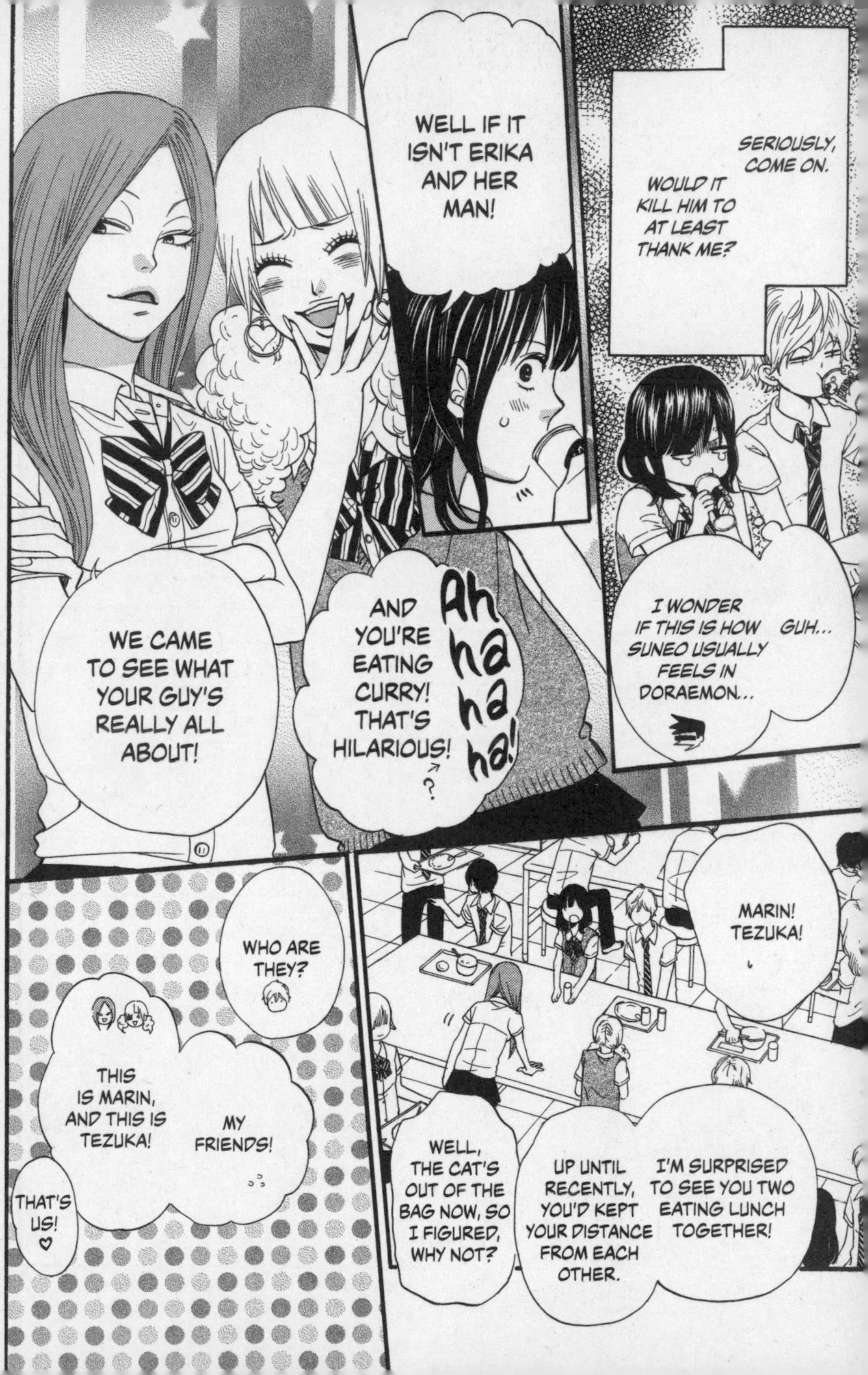
SERIOUSLY, COME ON.
WOULD IT KILL HIM TO AT LEAST THANK ME?
GUH...
I WONDER IF THIS IS HOW SUNEO USUALLY FEELS IN DORAEMON...
WELL IF IT ISN'T ERIKA AND HER MAN!
Ah ha ha ha ha!
AND YOU'RE EATING CURRY! THAT'S HILARIOUS!
?
WE CAME TO SEE WHAT YOUR GUY'S REALLY ALL ABOUT!
MARIN! TEZUKA!
I'M SURPRISED TO SEE YOU TWO EATING LUNCH TOGETHER!
UP UNTIL RECENTLY, YOU'D KEPT YOUR DISTANCE FROM EACH OTHER.
WELL, THE CAT'S OUT OF THE BAG NOW, SO I FIGURED, WHY NOT?
WHO ARE THEY?
MY FRIENDS!
THIS IS MARIN, AND THIS IS TEZUKA!
THAT'S US! ♡

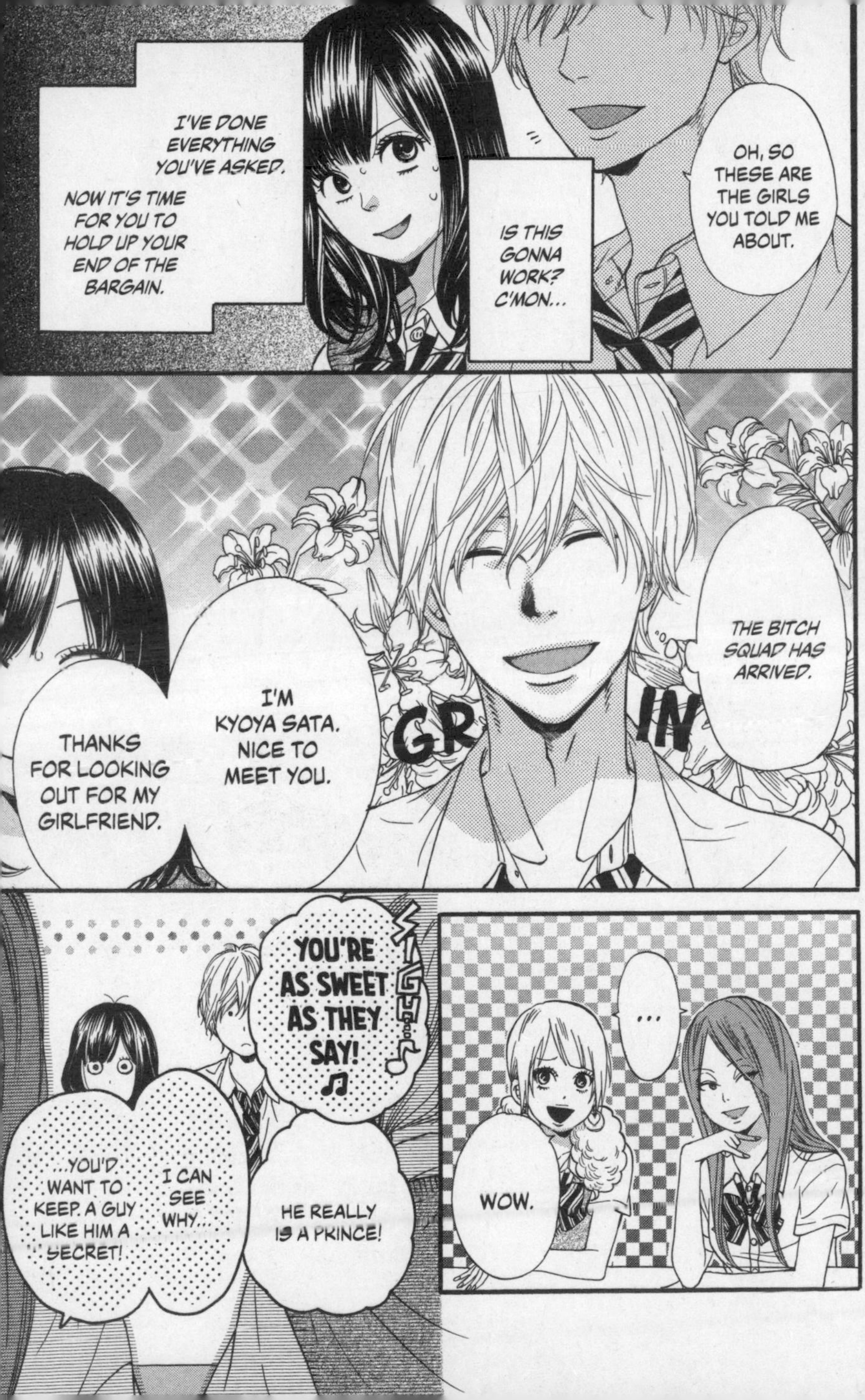
OH, SO THESE ARE THE GIRLS YOU TOLD ME ABOUT.
IS THIS GONNA WORK? C'MON...
I'VE DONE EVERYTHING YOU'VE ASKED.
NOW IT'S TIME FOR YOU TO HOLD UP YOUR END OF THE BARGAIN.
THE BITCH SQUAD HAS ARRIVED.
GRIN
I'M KYOYA SATA. NICE TO MEET YOU.
THANKS FOR LOOKING OUT FOR MY GIRLFRIEND.
...
WOW.
YOU'RE AS SWEET AS THEY SAY! ♫
HE REALLY IS A PRINCE!
I CAN SEE WHY...
...YOU'D WANT TO KEEP A GUY LIKE HIM A SECRET!

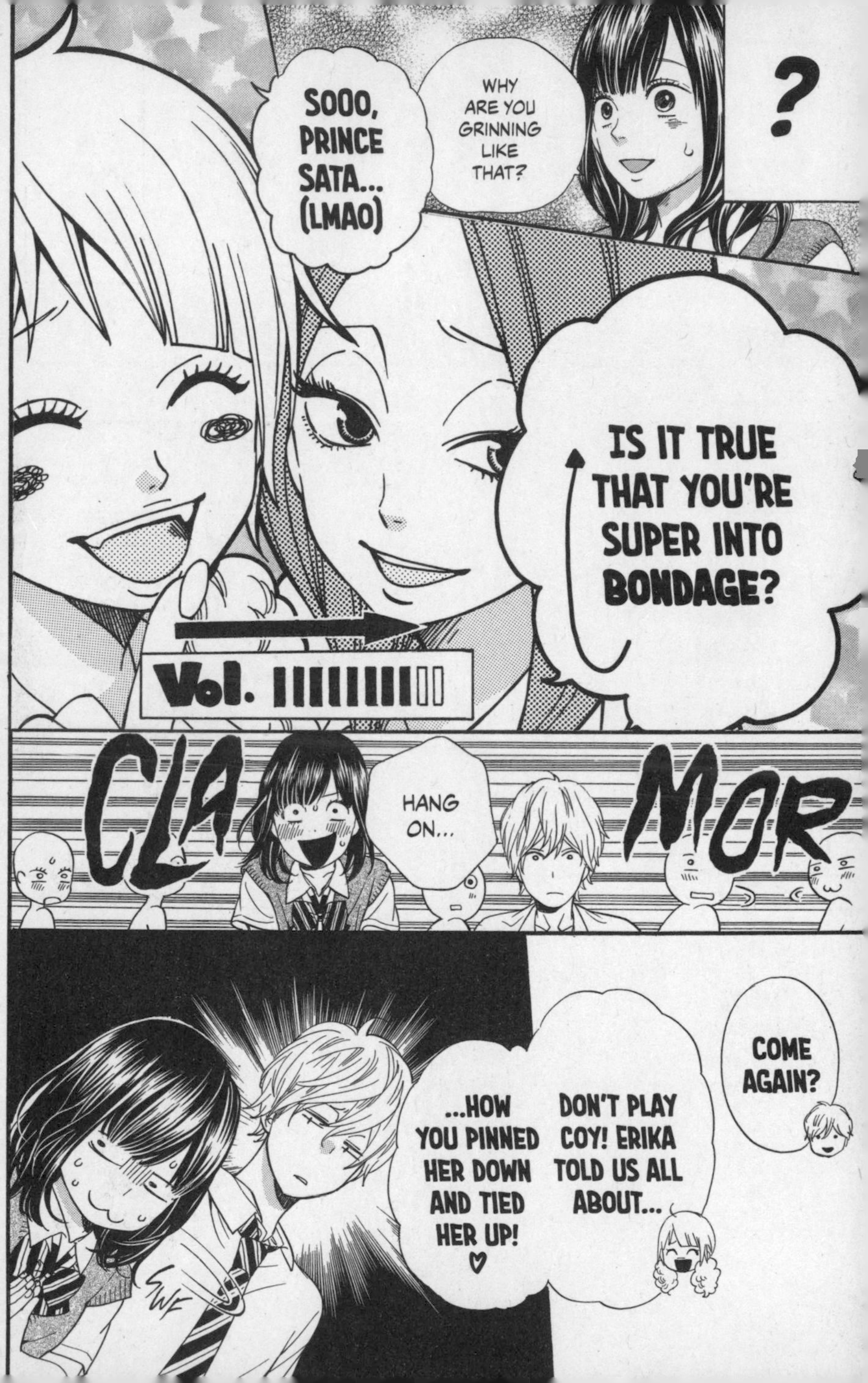
?
WHY ARE YOU GRINNING LIKE THAT?
SOOO, PRINCE SATA... (LMAO)
IS IT TRUE THAT YOU'RE SUPER INTO BONDAGE?
Vol.
CLAMOR
HANG ON...
COME AGAIN?
DON'T PLAY COY! ERIKA TOLD US ALL ABOUT...
...HOW YOU PINNED HER DOWN AND TIED HER UP! ♡

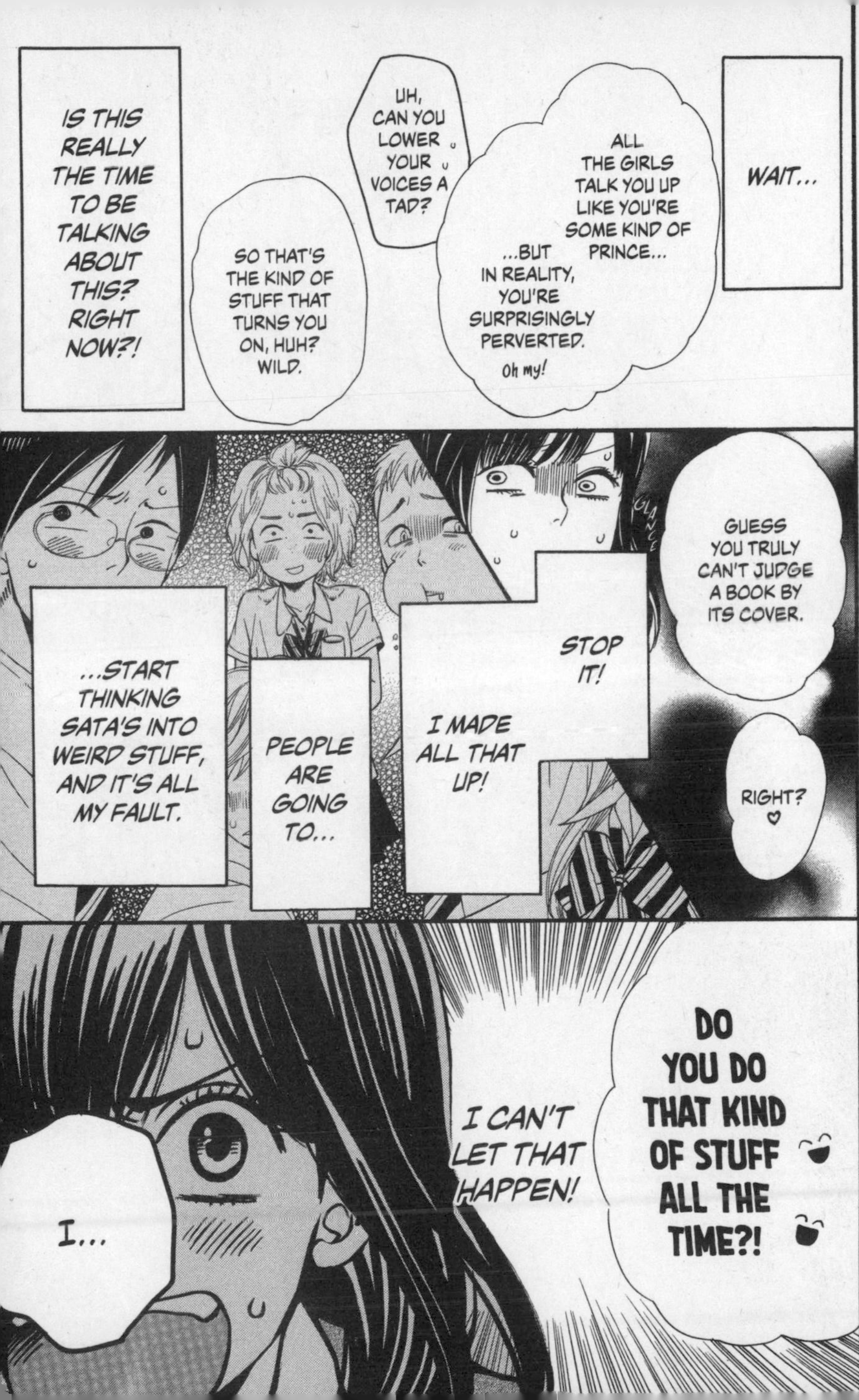
WAIT...
ALL THE GIRLS TALK YOU UP LIKE YOU'RE SOME KIND OF PRINCE...
...BUT IN REALITY, YOU'RE SURPRISINGLY PERVERTED.
Oh my!
UH, CAN YOU LOWER YOUR VOICES A TAD?
SO THAT'S THE KIND OF STUFF THAT TURNS YOU ON, HUH? WILD.
IS THIS REALLY THE TIME TO BE TALKING ABOUT THIS? RIGHT NOW?!
GUESS YOU TRULY CAN'T JUDGE A BOOK BY ITS COVER.
RIGHT? ♡
GLANCE
STOP IT!
I MADE ALL THAT UP!
PEOPLE ARE GOING TO...
...START THINKING SATA'S INTO WEIRD STUFF, AND IT'S ALL MY FAULT.
DO YOU DO THAT KIND OF STUFF ALL THE TIME?!
I CAN'T LET THAT HAPPEN!
I...

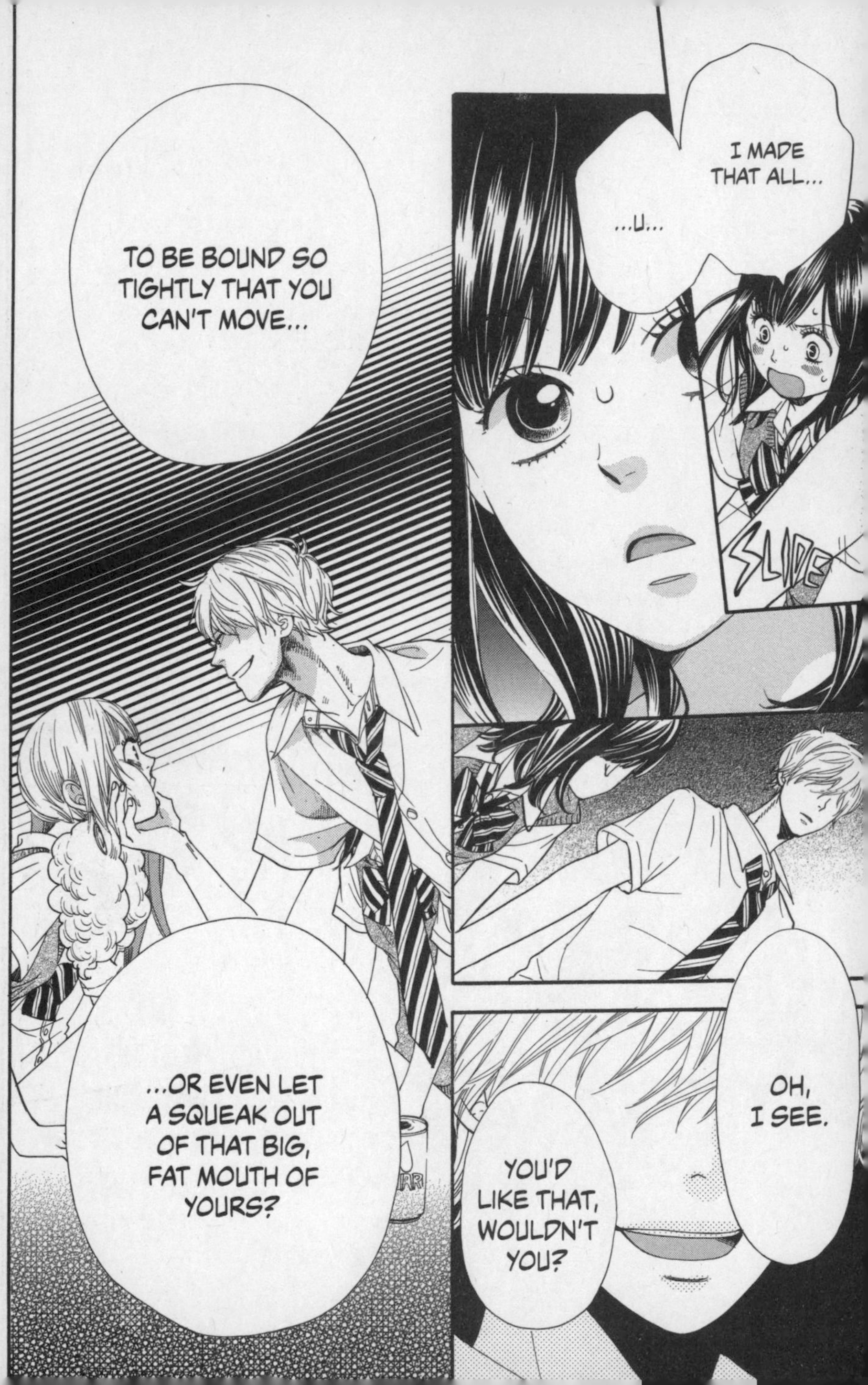
I MADE THAT ALL...
...U...
SLIDE
OH, I SEE.
YOU'D LIKE THAT, WOULDN'T YOU?
TO BE BOUND SO TIGHTLY THAT YOU CAN'T MOVE...
...OR EVEN LET A SQUEAK OUT OF THAT BIG, FAT MOUTH OF YOURS?

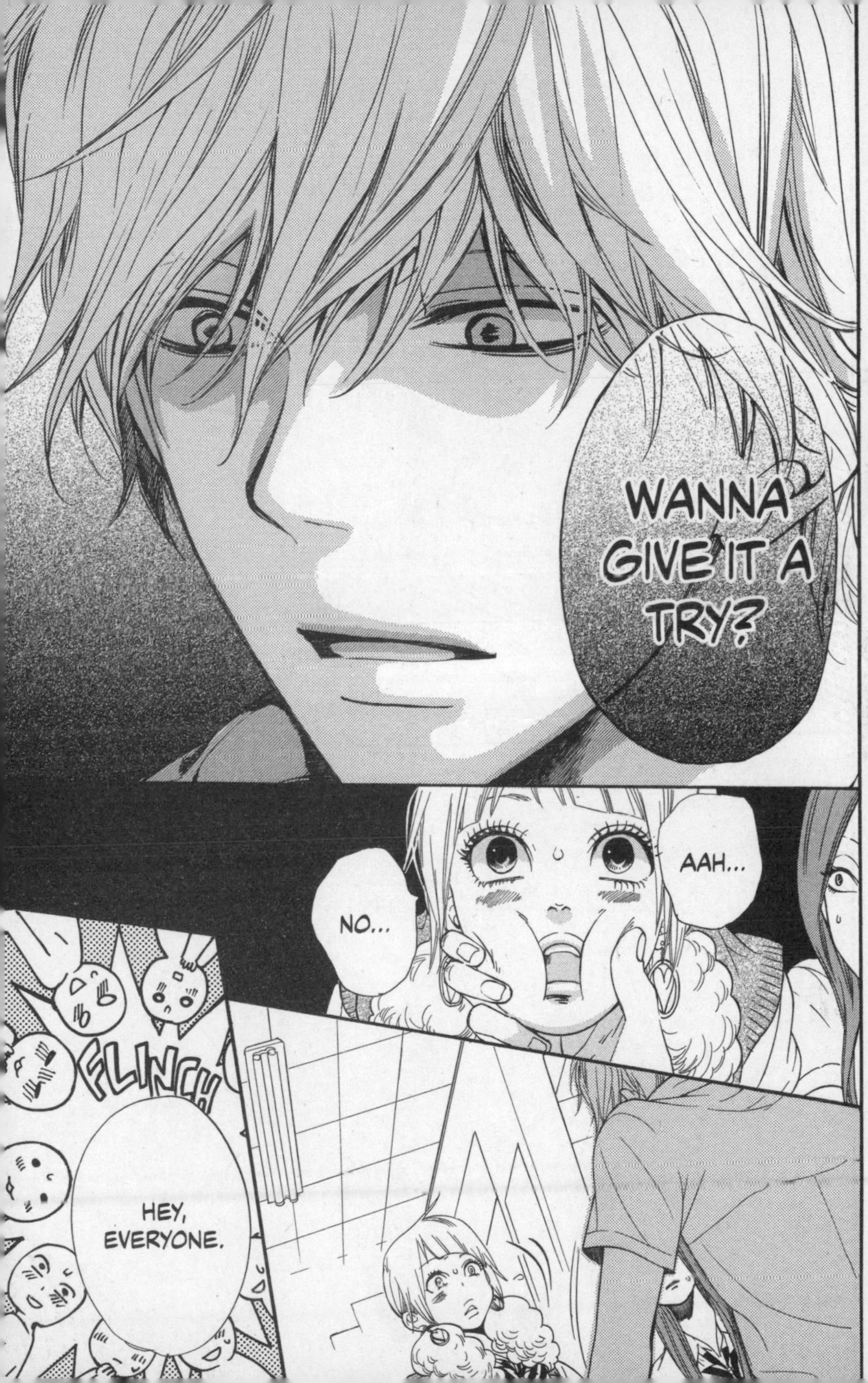
WANNA GIVE IT A TRY?
AAH...
NO...
FLINCH
HEY, EVERYONE.

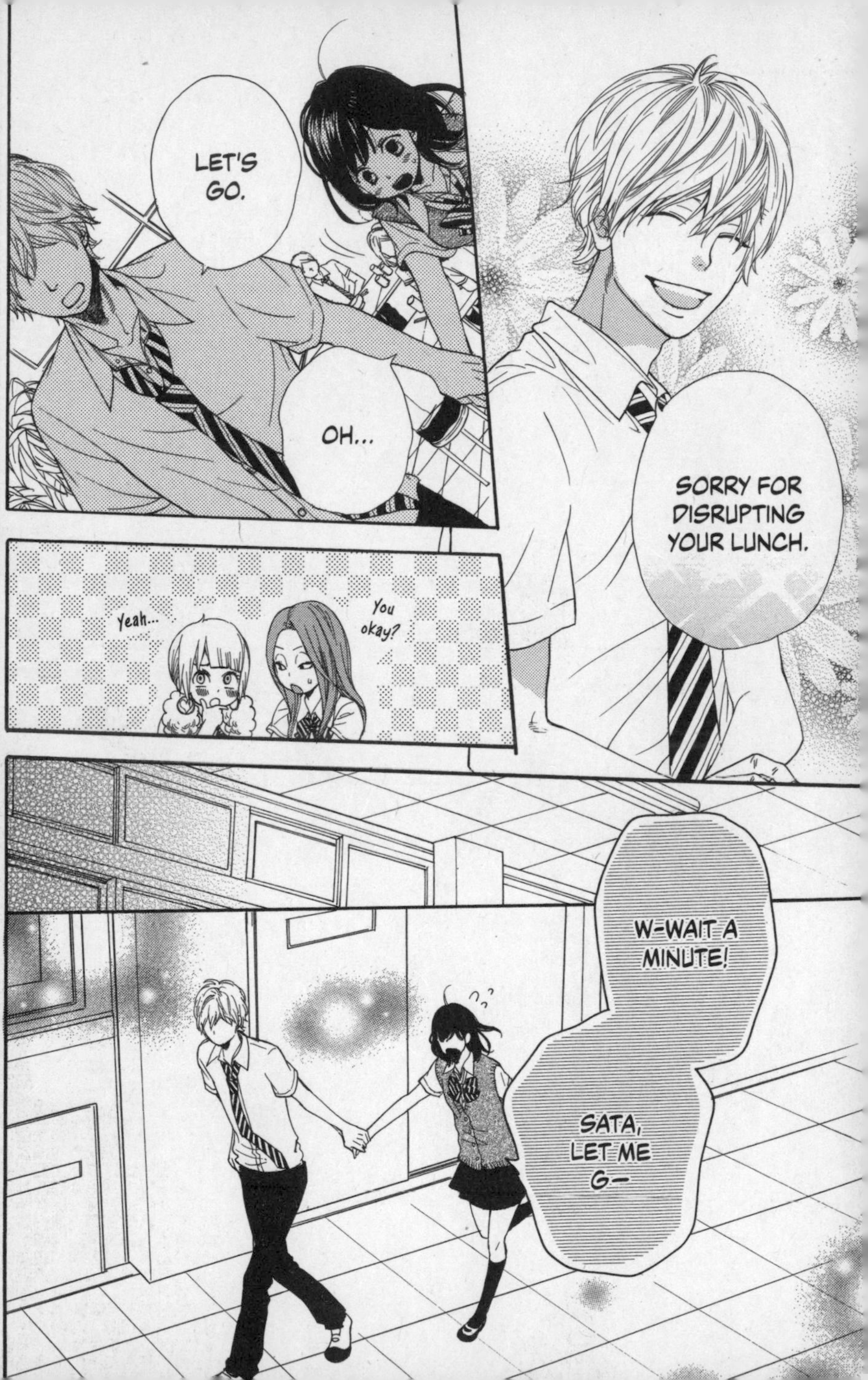
SORRY FOR DISRUPTING YOUR LUNCH.
LET'S GO.
OH...
You okay?
Yeah...
W-WAIT A MINUTE!
SATA, LET ME G—

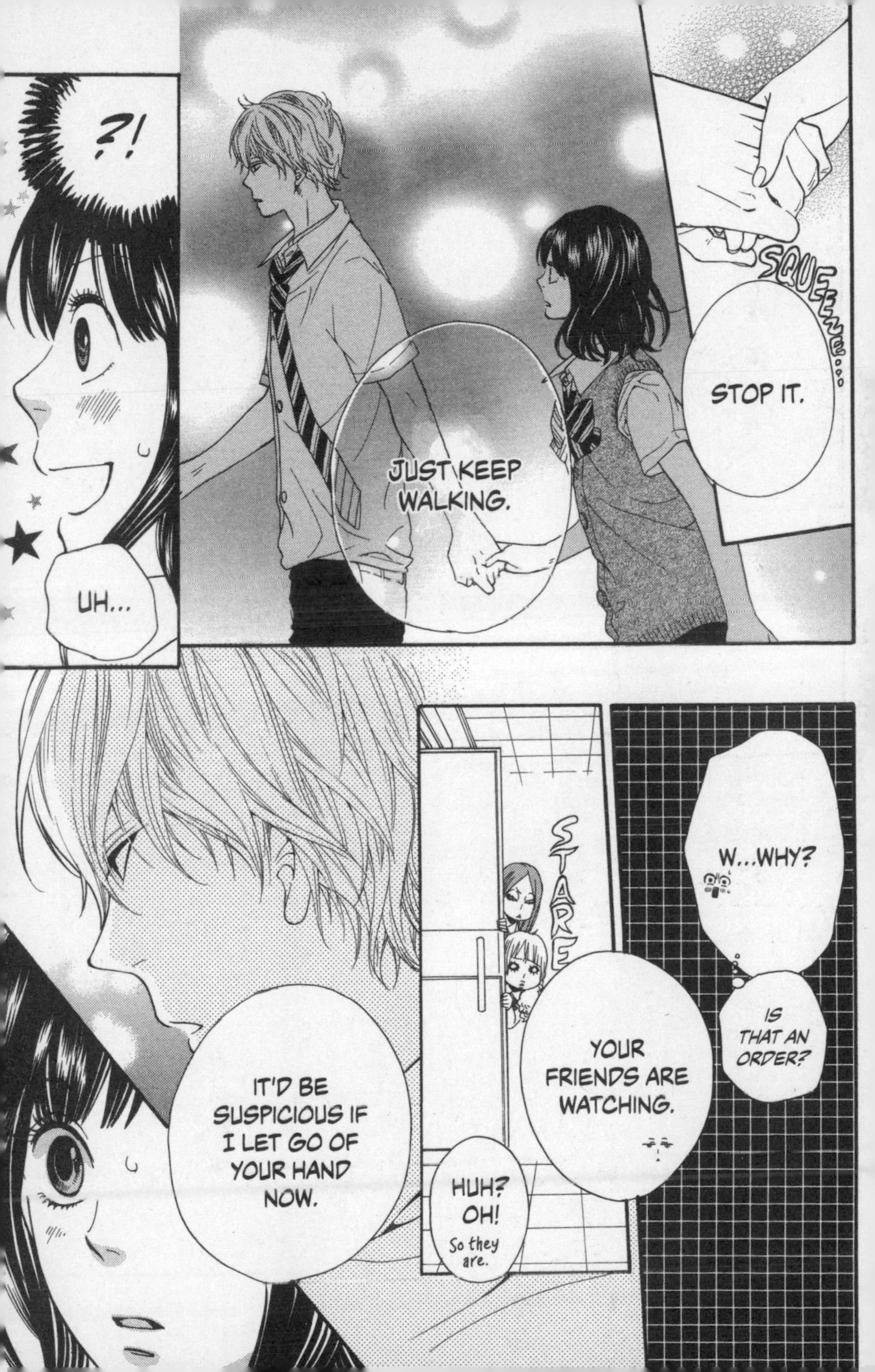
SQUEEEZE...
STOP IT.
JUST KEEP WALKING.
?!
UH...
W...WHY?
IS THAT AN ORDER?
STARE
YOUR FRIENDS ARE WATCHING.
HUH? OH!
So they are.
IT'D BE SUSPICIOUS IF I LET GO OF YOUR HAND NOW.

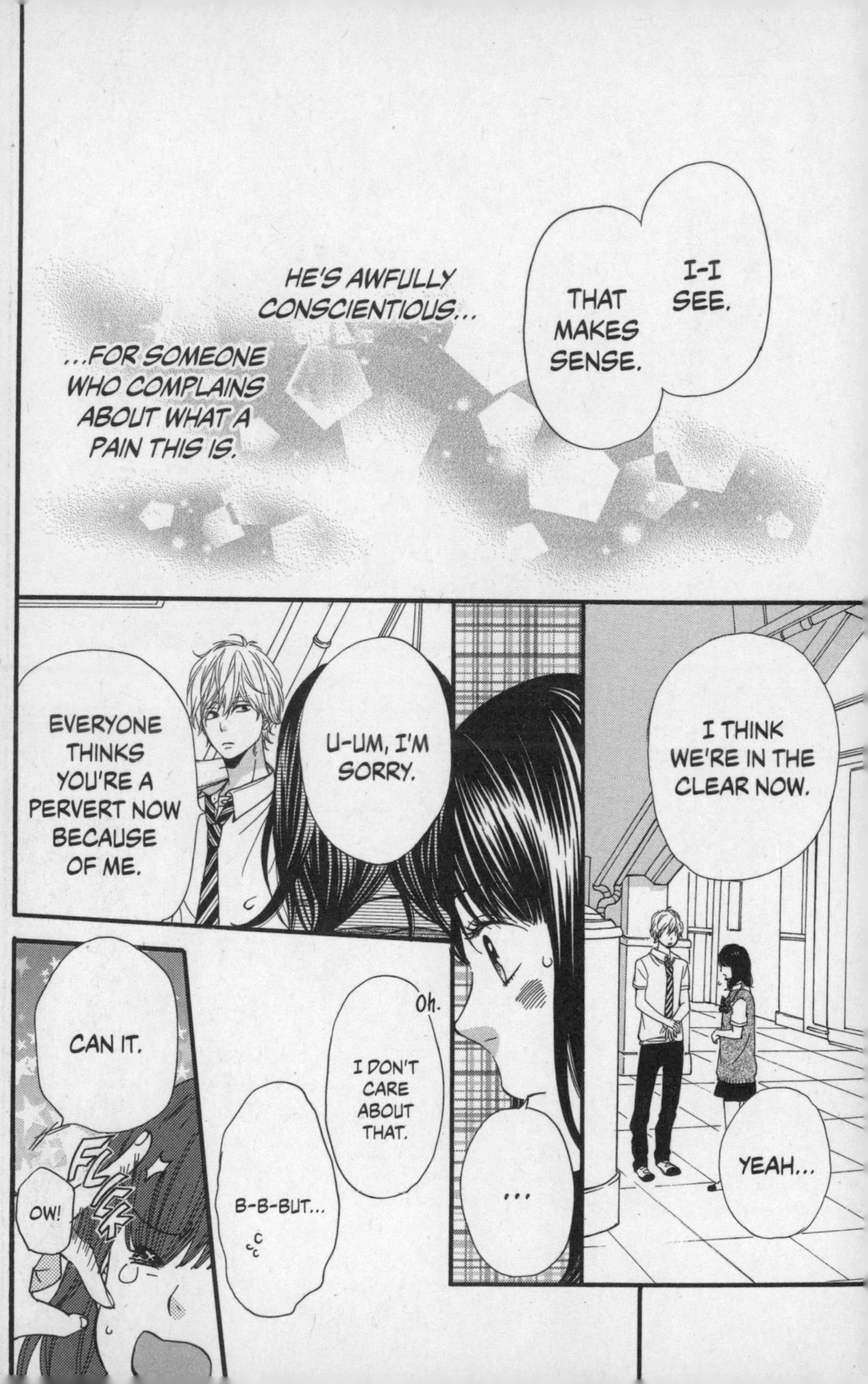

I-I SEE.
THAT MAKES SENSE.
HE'S AWFULLY CONSCIENTIOUS...
...FOR SOMEONE WHO COMPLAINS ABOUT WHAT A PAIN THIS IS.
I THINK WE'RE IN THE CLEAR NOW.
YEAH...
...
U-UM, I'M SORRY.
EVERYONE THINKS YOU'RE A PERVERT NOW BECAUSE OF ME.
Oh.
I DON'T CARE ABOUT THAT.
B-B-BUT...
CAN IT.
FLICK
OW!

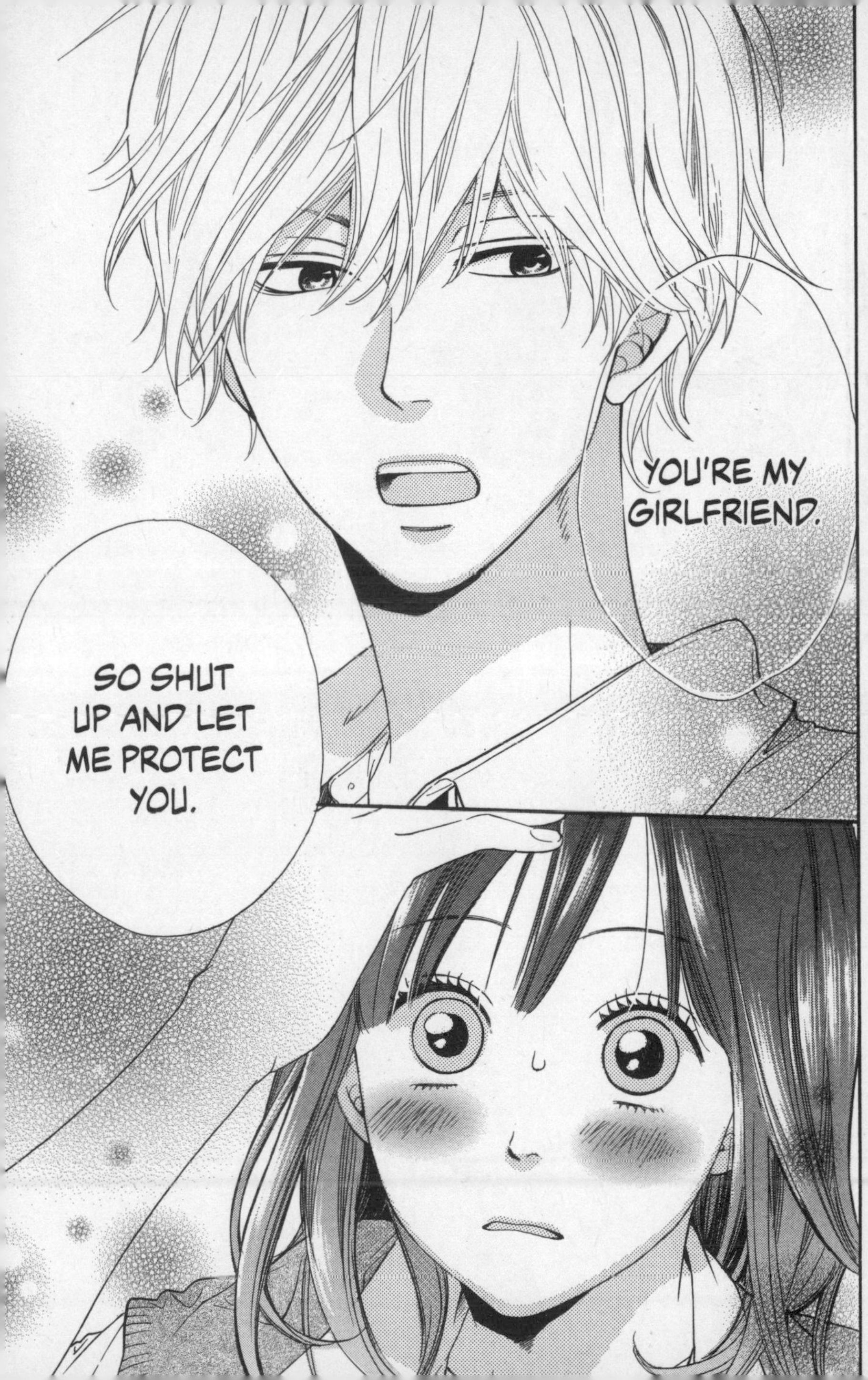
YOU'RE MY GIRLFRIEND.
SO SHUT UP AND LET ME PROTECT YOU.

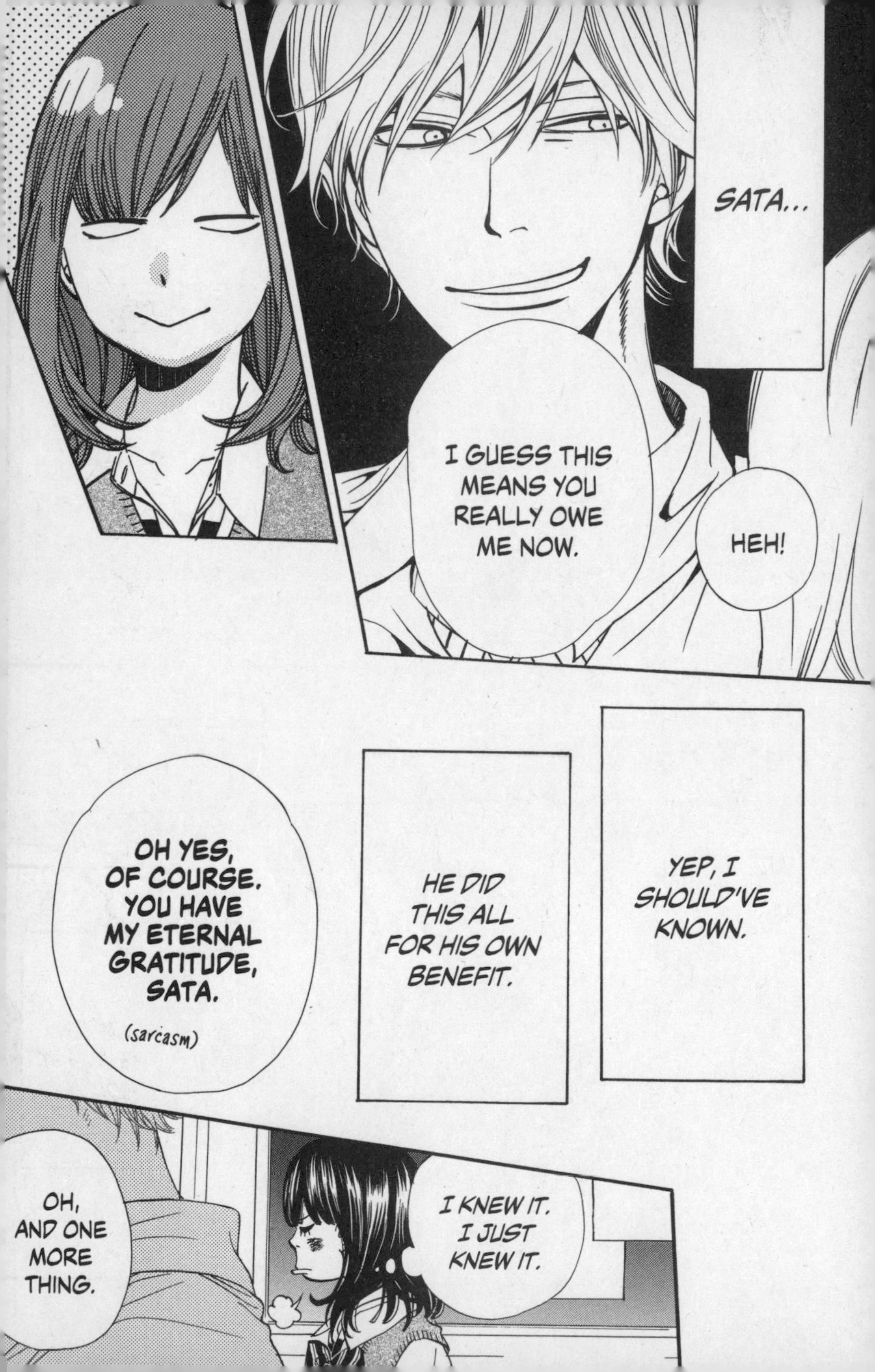
SATA...
HEH!
I GUESS THIS MEANS YOU REALLY OWE ME NOW.
YEP, I SHOULD'VE KNOWN.
HE DID THIS ALL FOR HIS OWN BENEFIT.
OH YES, OF COURSE. YOU HAVE MY ETERNAL GRATITUDE, SATA.
(sarcasm)
I KNEW IT. I JUST KNEW IT.
OH, AND ONE MORE THING.

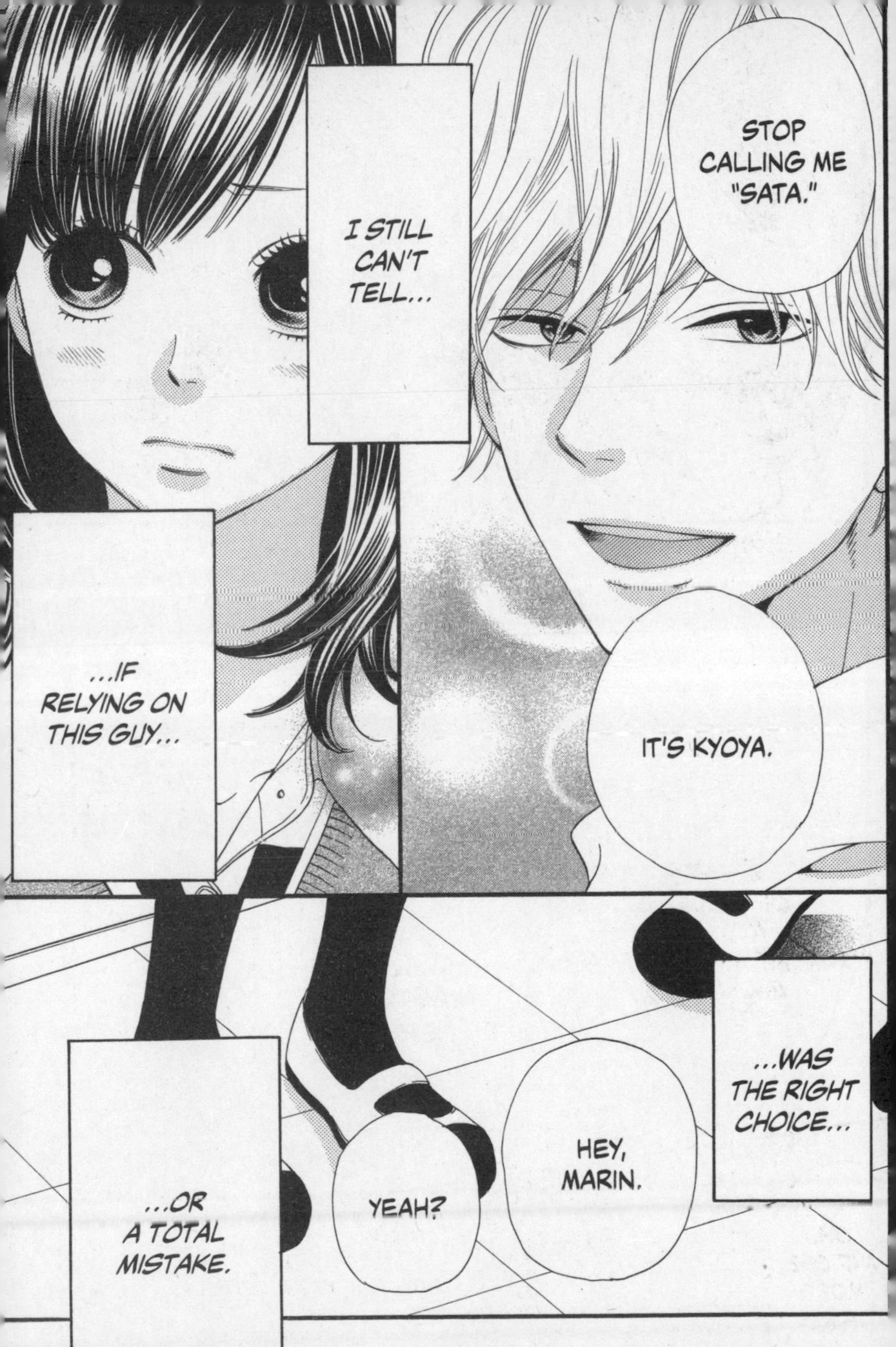
STOP CALLING ME "SATA."
IT'S KYOYA.
I STILL CAN'T TELL...
...IF RELYING ON THIS GUY...
...WAS THE RIGHT CHOICE...
HEY, MARIN.
YEAH?
...OR A TOTAL MISTAKE.

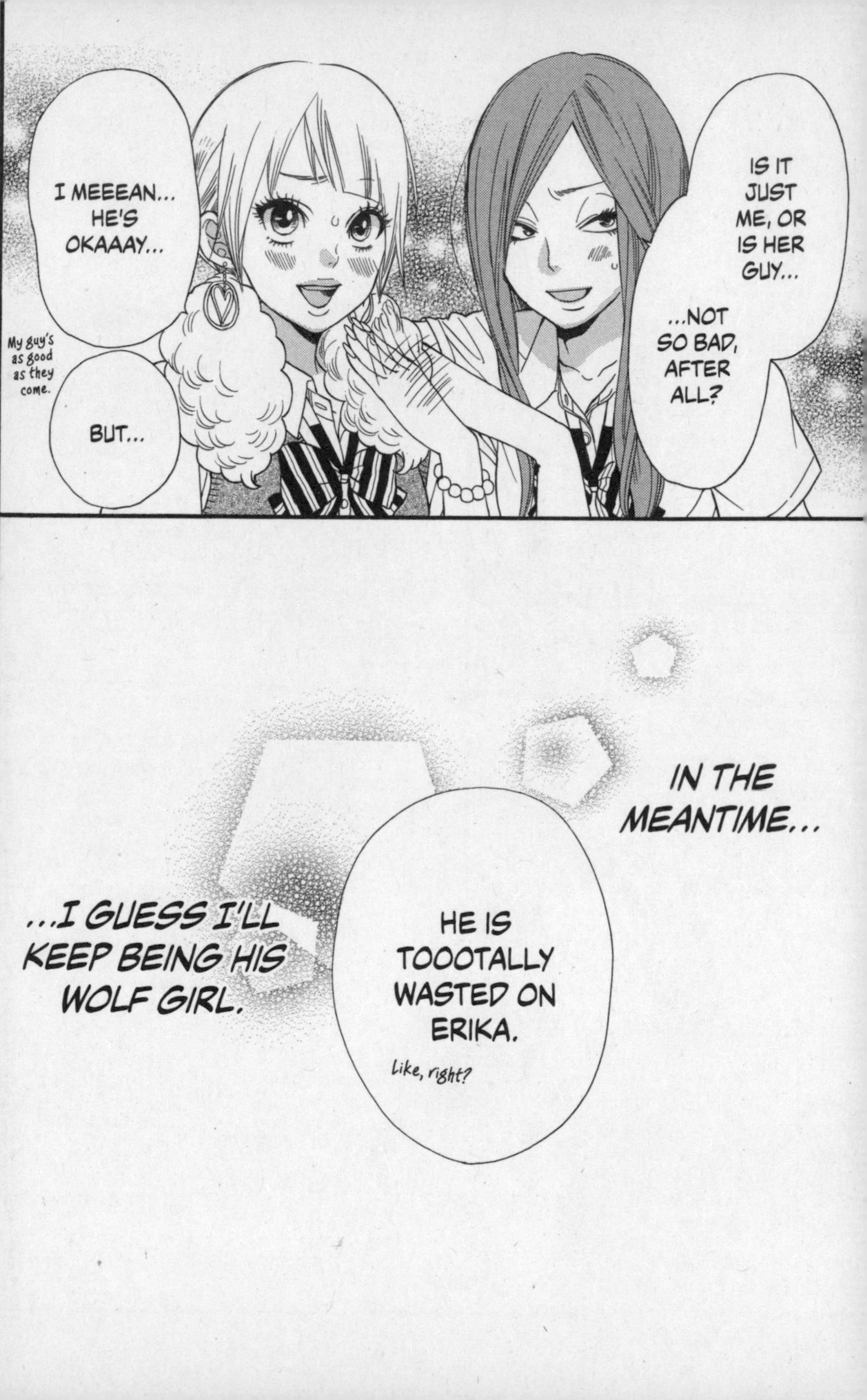
IS IT JUST ME, OR IS HER GUY...
...NOT SO BAD, AFTER ALL?
I MEEEAN... HE'S OKAAAY...
BUT...
My guy's as good as they come.
IN THE MEANTIME...
HE IS TOOOTALLY WASTED ON ERIKA.
Like, right?
...I GUESS I'LL KEEP BEING HIS WOLF GIRL.

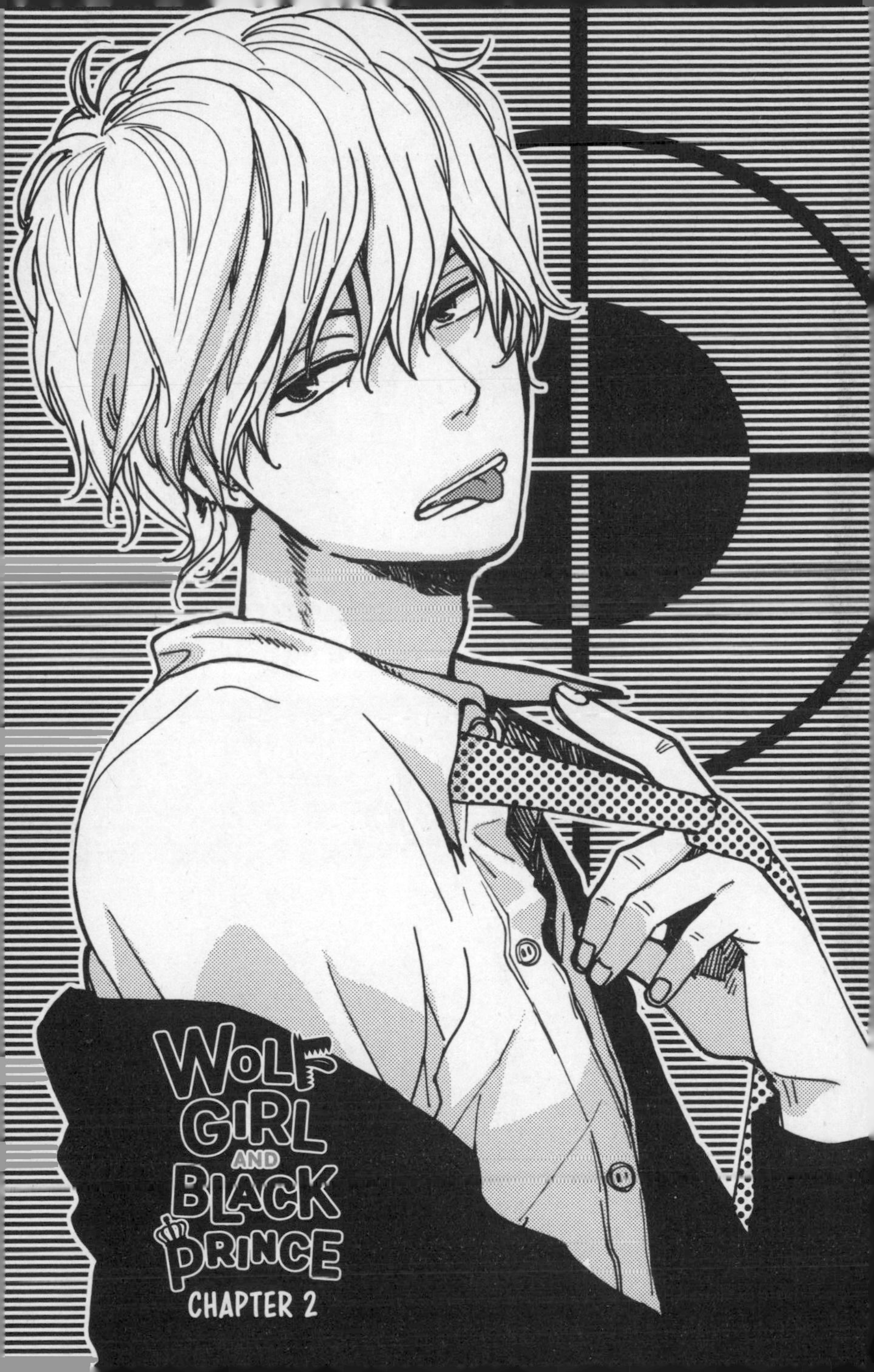
WOLF GIRL AND BLACK PRINCE
CHAPTER 2

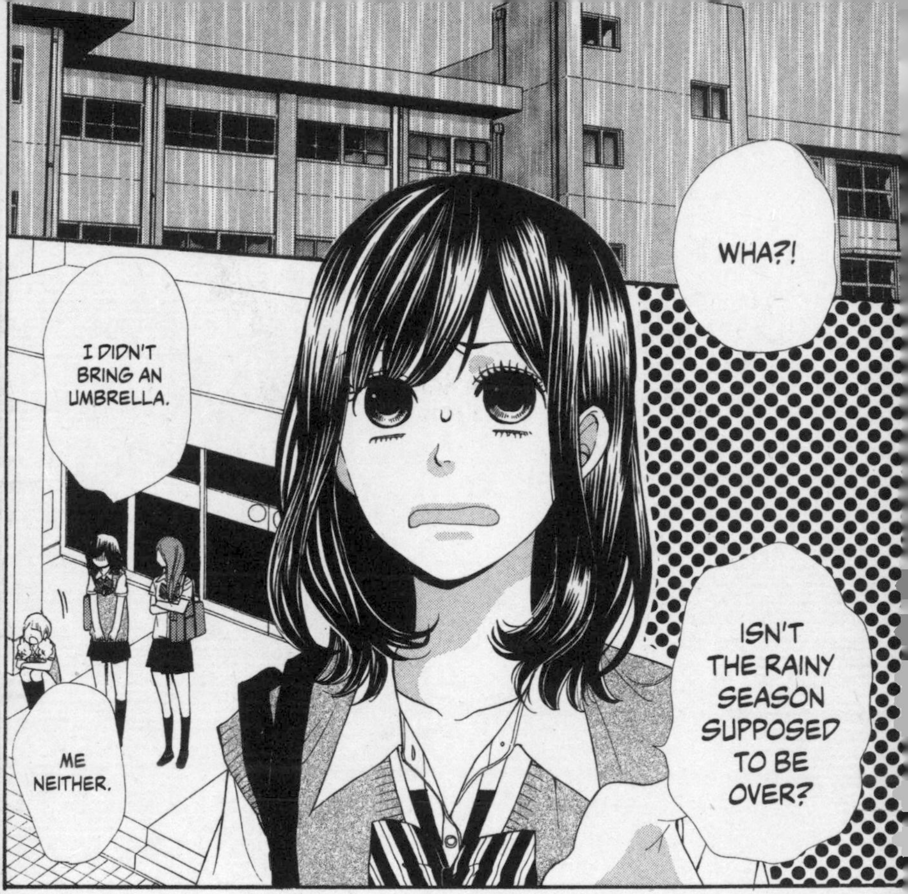
WHA?!
ISN'T THE RAINY SEASON SUPPOSED TO BE OVER?
I DIDN'T BRING AN UMBRELLA.
ME NEITHER.

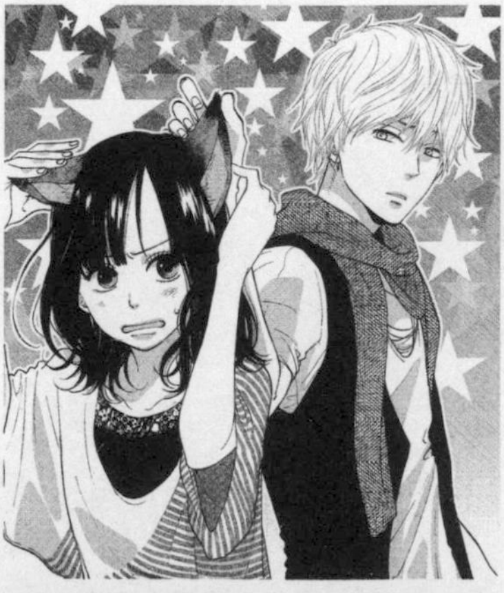

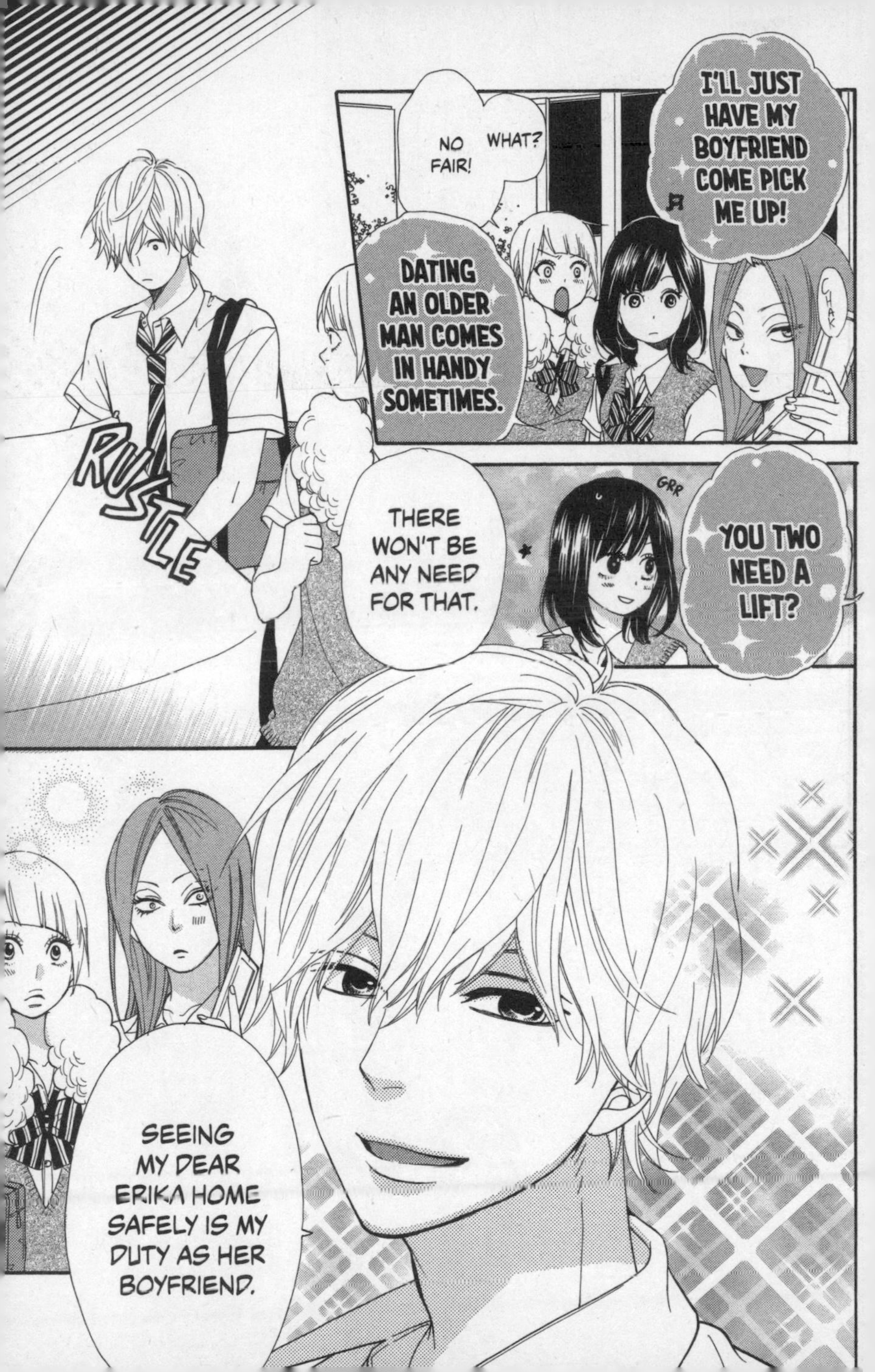

I'LL JUST HAVE MY BOYFRIEND COME PICK ME UP!
CHAK
WHAT?
NO FAIR!
DATING AN OLDER MAN COMES IN HANDY SOMETIMES.
GRR
YOU TWO NEED A LIFT?
THERE WON'T BE ANY NEED FOR THAT.
RUSTLE
SEEING MY DEAR ERIKA HOME SAFELY IS MY DUTY AS HER BOYFRIEND.

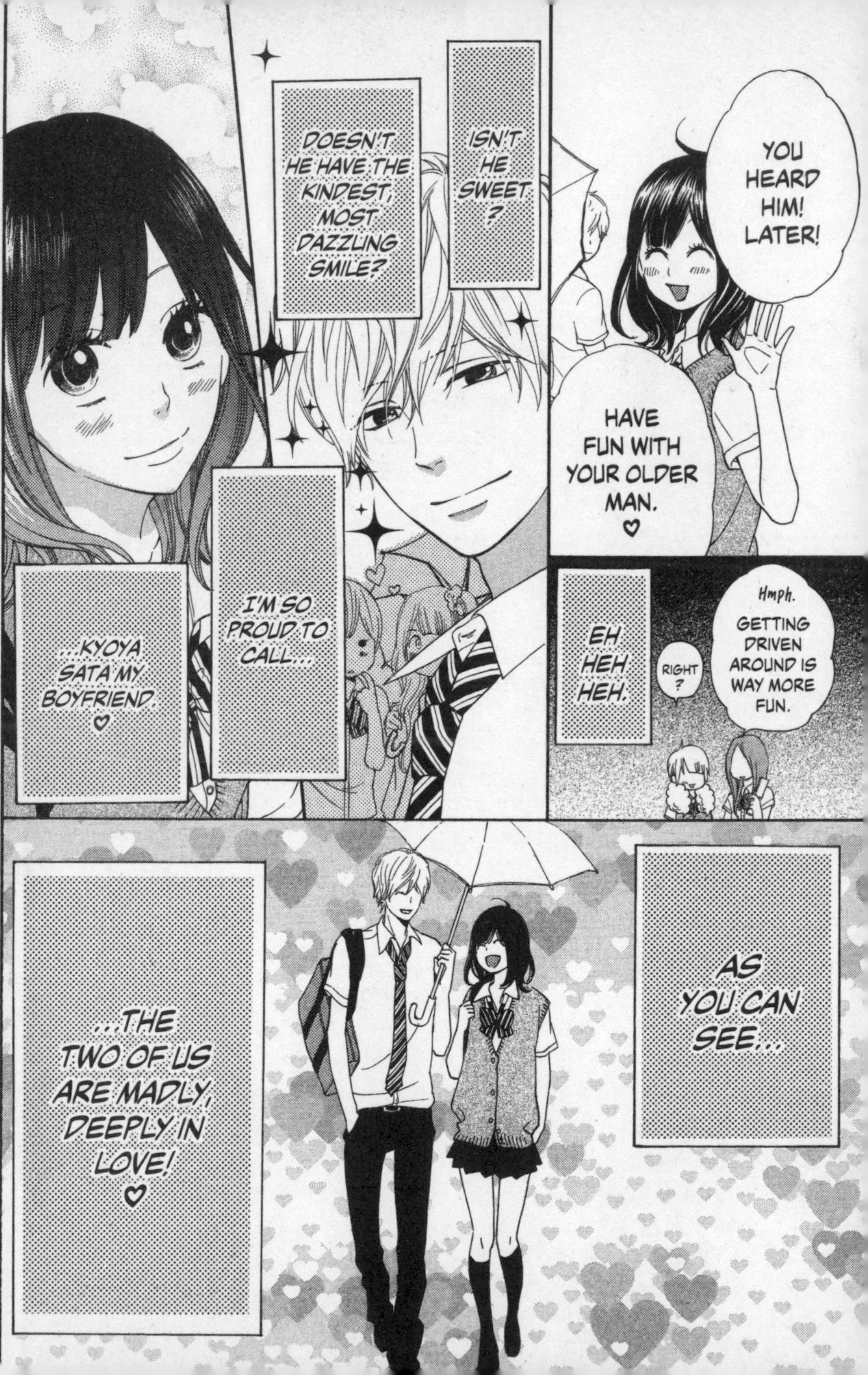
YOU HEARD HIM! LATER!
HAVE FUN WITH YOUR OLDER MAN. ♡
Hmph. GETTING DRIVEN AROUND IS WAY MORE FUN.
RIGHT?
EH HEH HEH.
ISN'T HE SWEET?
DOESN'T HE HAVE THE KINDEST, MOST DAZZLING SMILE?
I'M SO PROUD TO CALL...
...KYOYA SATA MY BOYFRIEND. ♡
AS YOU CAN SEE...
...THE TWO OF US ARE MADLY, DEEPLY IN LOVE! ♡

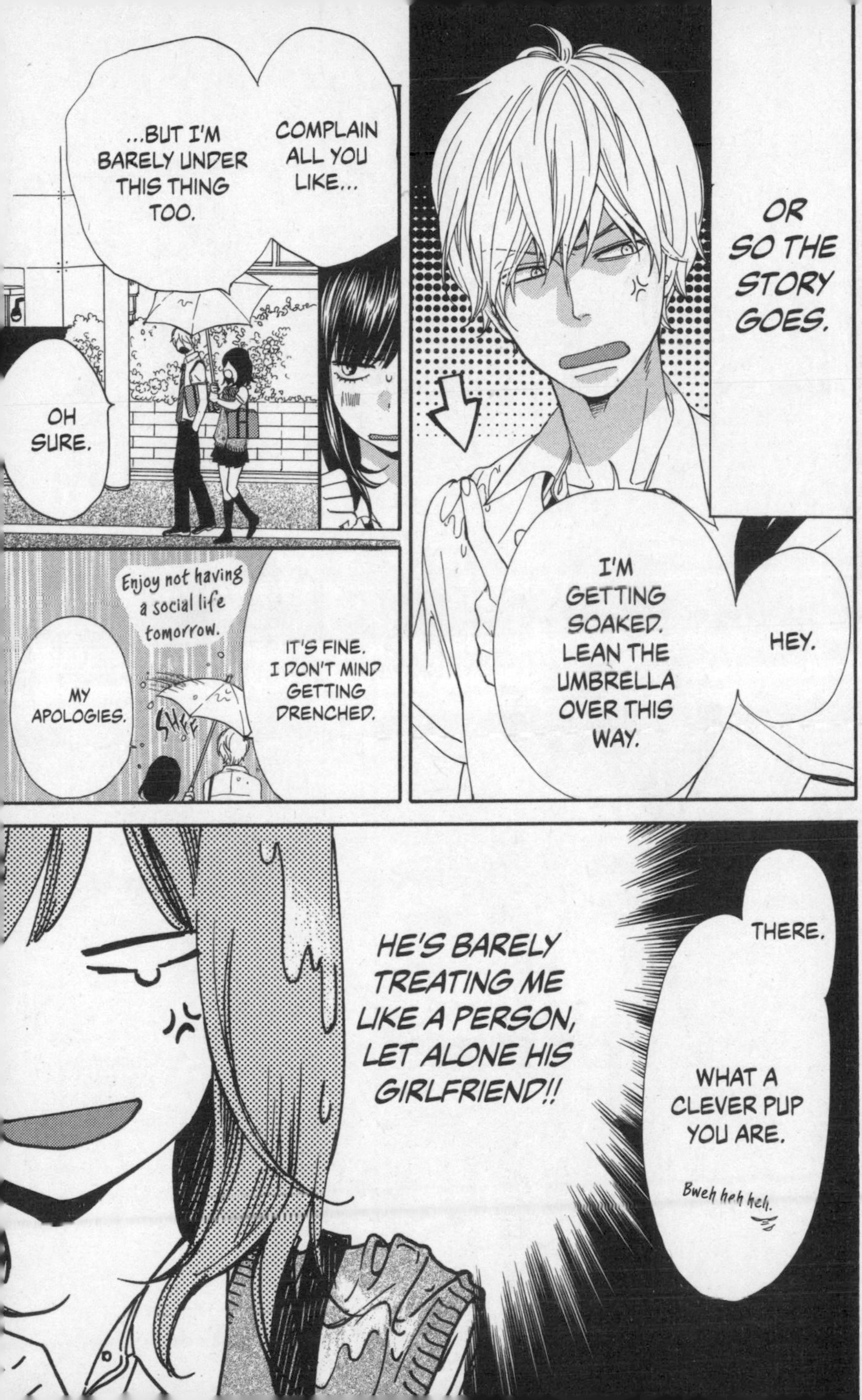
OR SO THE STORY GOES.
HEY.
I'M GETTING SOAKED. LEAN THE UMBRELLA OVER THIS WAY.
COMPLAIN ALL YOU LIKE...
...BUT I'M BARELY UNDER THIS THING TOO.
OH SURE.
IT'S FINE. I DON'T MIND GETTING DRENCHED.
Enjoy not having a social life tomorrow.
MY APOLOGIES.
THERE.
WHAT A CLEVER PUP YOU ARE.
Bweh heh heh.
HE'S BARELY TREATING ME LIKE A PERSON, LET ALONE HIS GIRLFRIEND!!

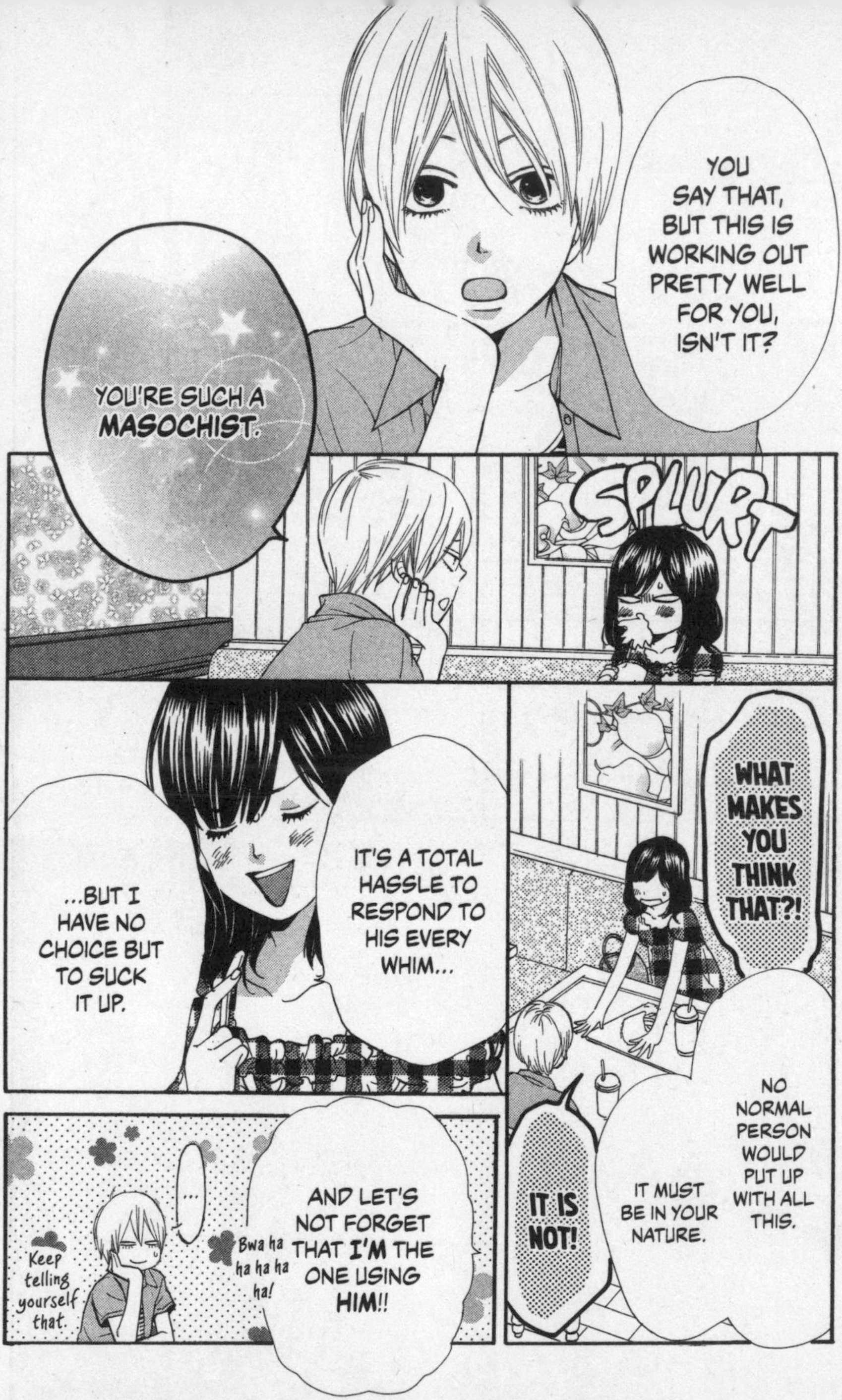
YOU SAY THAT, BUT THIS IS WORKING OUT PRETTY WELL FOR YOU, ISN'T IT?
YOU'RE SUCH A MASOCHIST.
SPLURT
WHAT MAKES YOU THINK THAT?!
NO NORMAL PERSON WOULD PUT UP WITH ALL THIS.
IT MUST BE IN YOUR NATURE.
IT IS NOT!
IT'S A TOTAL HASSLE TO RESPOND TO HIS EVERY WHIM...
...BUT I HAVE NO CHOICE BUT TO SUCK IT UP.
AND LET'S NOT FORGET THAT I'M THE ONE USING HIM!!
Bwa ha ha ha ha ha!
...
Keep telling yourself that.

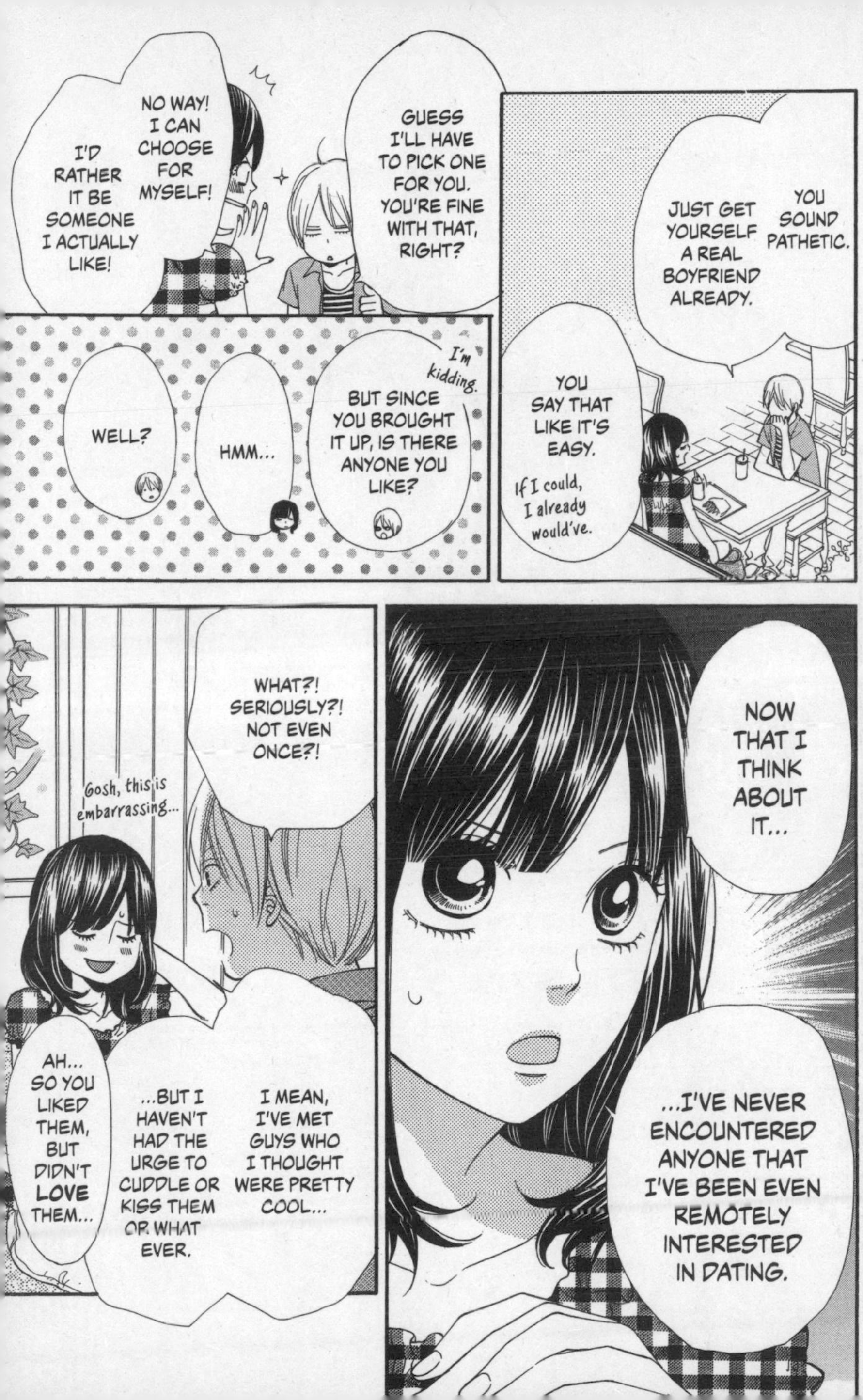
YOU SOUND PATHETIC.
JUST GET YOURSELF A REAL BOYFRIEND ALREADY.
YOU SAY THAT LIKE IT'S EASY.
If I could, I already would've.
GUESS I'LL HAVE TO PICK ONE FOR YOU. YOU'RE FINE WITH THAT, RIGHT?
NO WAY! I CAN CHOOSE FOR MYSELF!
I'D RATHER IT BE SOMEONE I ACTUALLY LIKE!
I'm kidding.
BUT SINCE YOU BROUGHT IT UP, IS THERE ANYONE YOU LIKE?
HMM...
WELL?
NOW THAT I THINK ABOUT IT...
...I'VE NEVER ENCOUNTERED ANYONE THAT I'VE BEEN EVEN REMOTELY INTERESTED IN DATING.
WHAT?! SERIOUSLY?! NOT EVEN ONCE?!
Gosh, this is embarrassing...
I MEAN, I'VE MET GUYS WHO I THOUGHT WERE PRETTY COOL...
...BUT I HAVEN'T HAD THE URGE TO CUDDLE OR KISS THEM OR WHAT EVER.
AH... SO YOU LIKED THEM, BUT DIDN'T **LOVE** THEM...

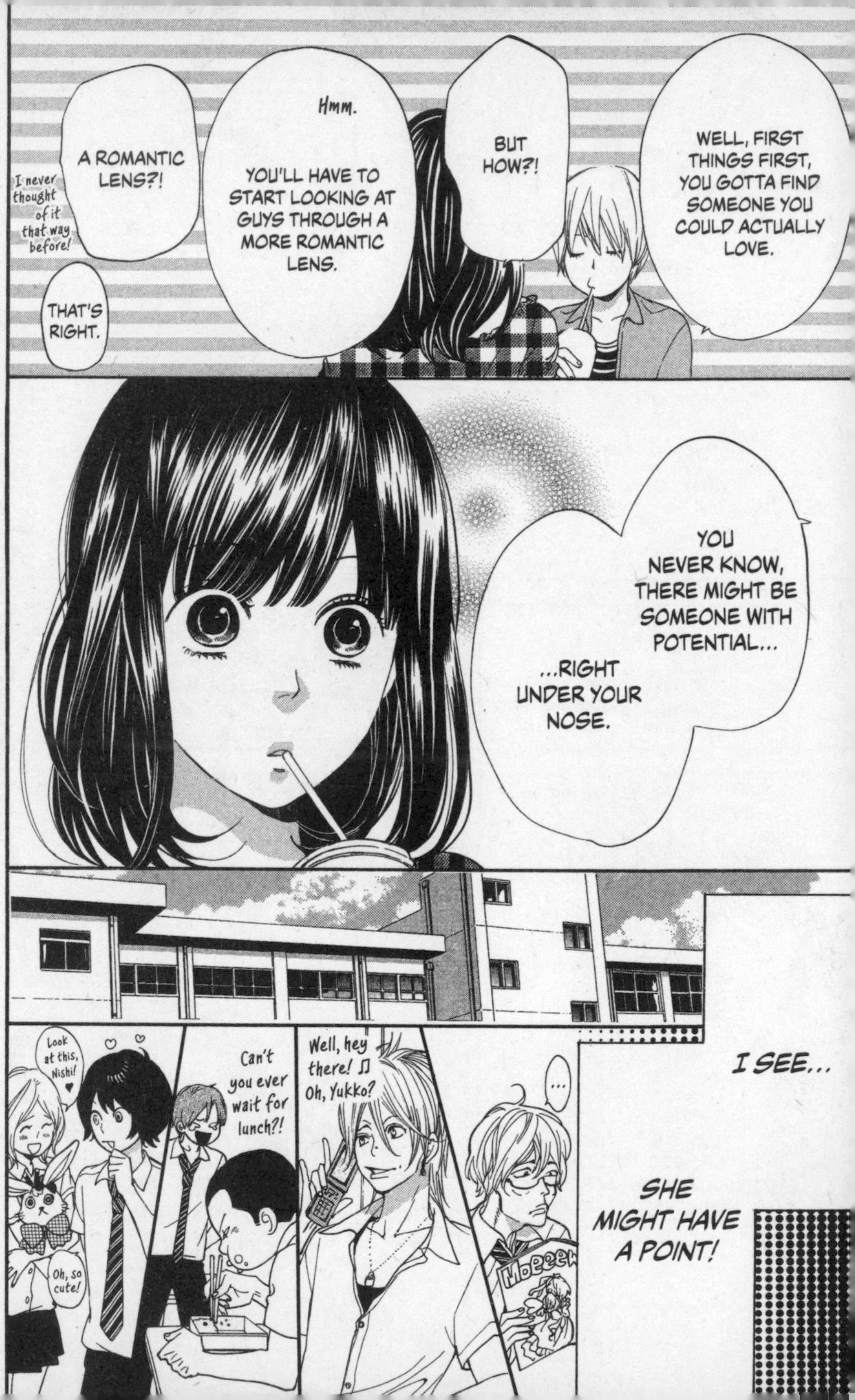
WELL, FIRST THINGS FIRST, YOU GOTTA FIND SOMEONE YOU COULD ACTUALLY LOVE.
BUT HOW?!
Hmm.
YOU'LL HAVE TO START LOOKING AT GUYS THROUGH A MORE ROMANTIC LENS.
A ROMANTIC LENS?!
I never thought of it that way before!
THAT'S RIGHT.
YOU NEVER KNOW, THERE MIGHT BE SOMEONE WITH POTENTIAL...
...RIGHT UNDER YOUR NOSE.
I SEE...
SHE MIGHT HAVE A POINT!
...
Well, hey there! ♫ Oh, Yukko?
Can't you ever wait for lunch?!
Look at this, Nishi! ♥
Oh, so cute!

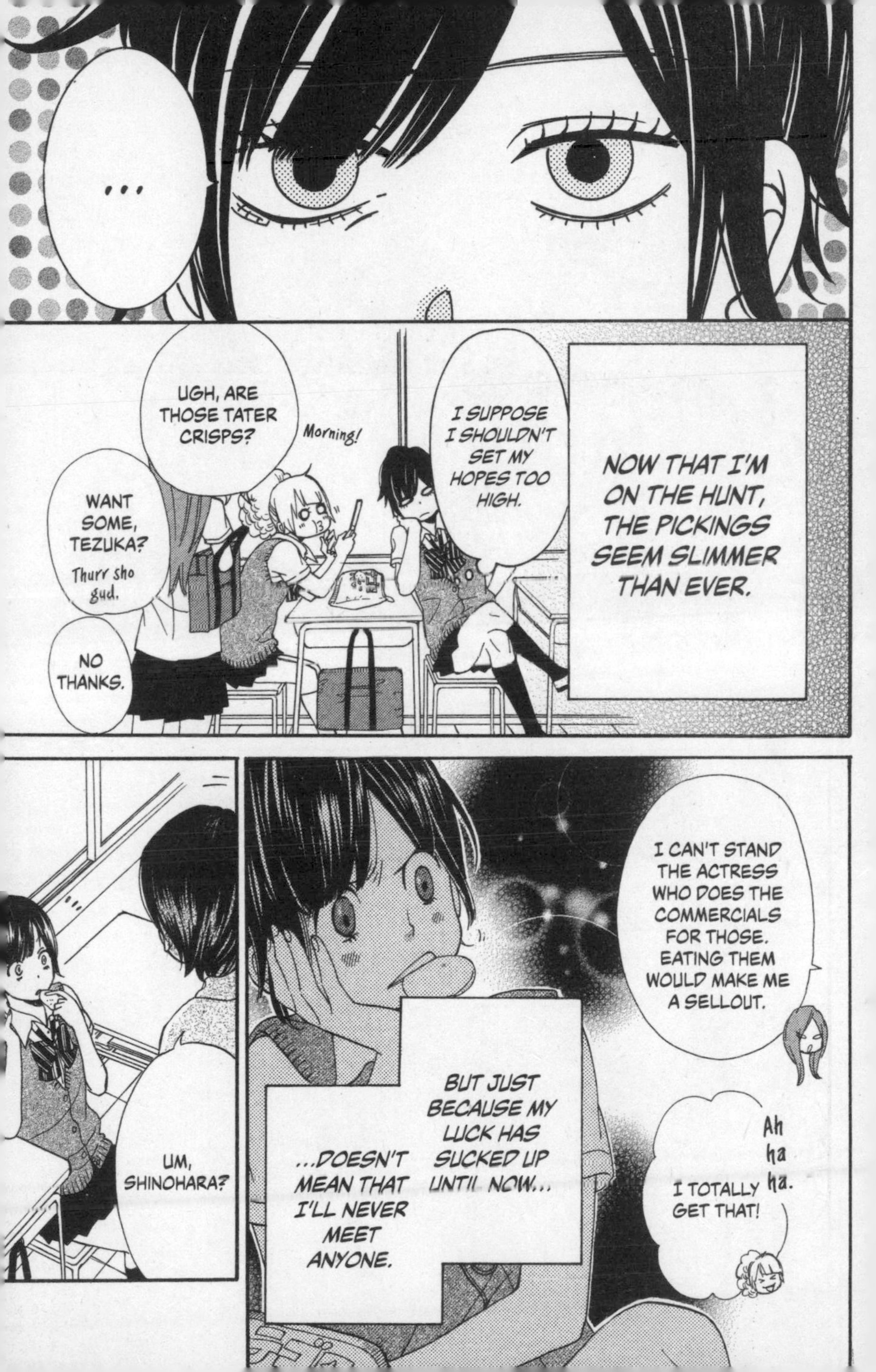
...
NOW THAT I'M ON THE HUNT, THE PICKINGS SEEM SLIMMER THAN EVER.
I SUPPOSE I SHOULDN'T SET MY HOPES TOO HIGH.
Morning!
UGH, ARE THOSE TATER CRISPS?
WANT SOME, TEZUKA? Thurr sho gud.
NO THANKS.
I CAN'T STAND THE ACTRESS WHO DOES THE COMMERCIALS FOR THOSE. EATING THEM WOULD MAKE ME A SELLOUT.
Ah ha ha.
I TOTALLY GET THAT!
BUT JUST BECAUSE MY LUCK HAS SUCKED UP UNTIL NOW...
...DOESN'T MEAN THAT I'LL NEVER MEET ANYONE.
UM, SHINOHARA?

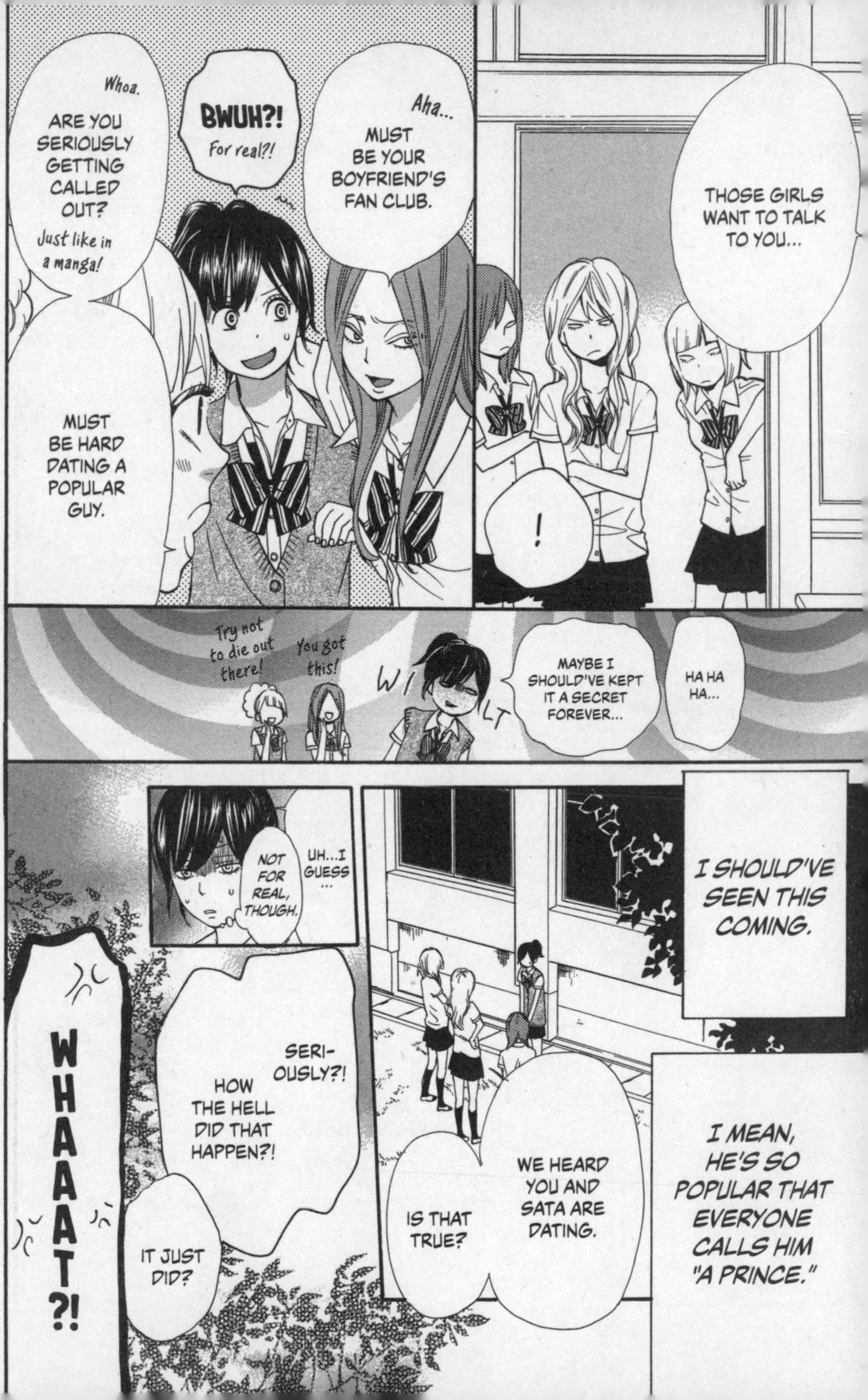
THOSE GIRLS WANT TO TALK TO YOU...
!
Aha... MUST BE YOUR BOYFRIEND'S FAN CLUB.
BWUH?! For real?!
Whoa. ARE YOU SERIOUSLY GETTING CALLED OUT? Just like in a manga!
MUST BE HARD DATING A POPULAR GUY.
HA HA HA...
MAYBE I SHOULD'VE KEPT IT A SECRET FOREVER...
WILT
You got this!
Try not to die out there!
I SHOULD'VE SEEN THIS COMING.
I MEAN, HE'S SO POPULAR THAT EVERYONE CALLS HIM "A PRINCE."
WE HEARD YOU AND SATA ARE DATING.
IS THAT TRUE?
UH...I GUESS...
NOT FOR REAL, THOUGH.
SERI-OUSLY?!
HOW THE HELL DID THAT HAPPEN?!
IT JUST DID?
WHAAAAT?!

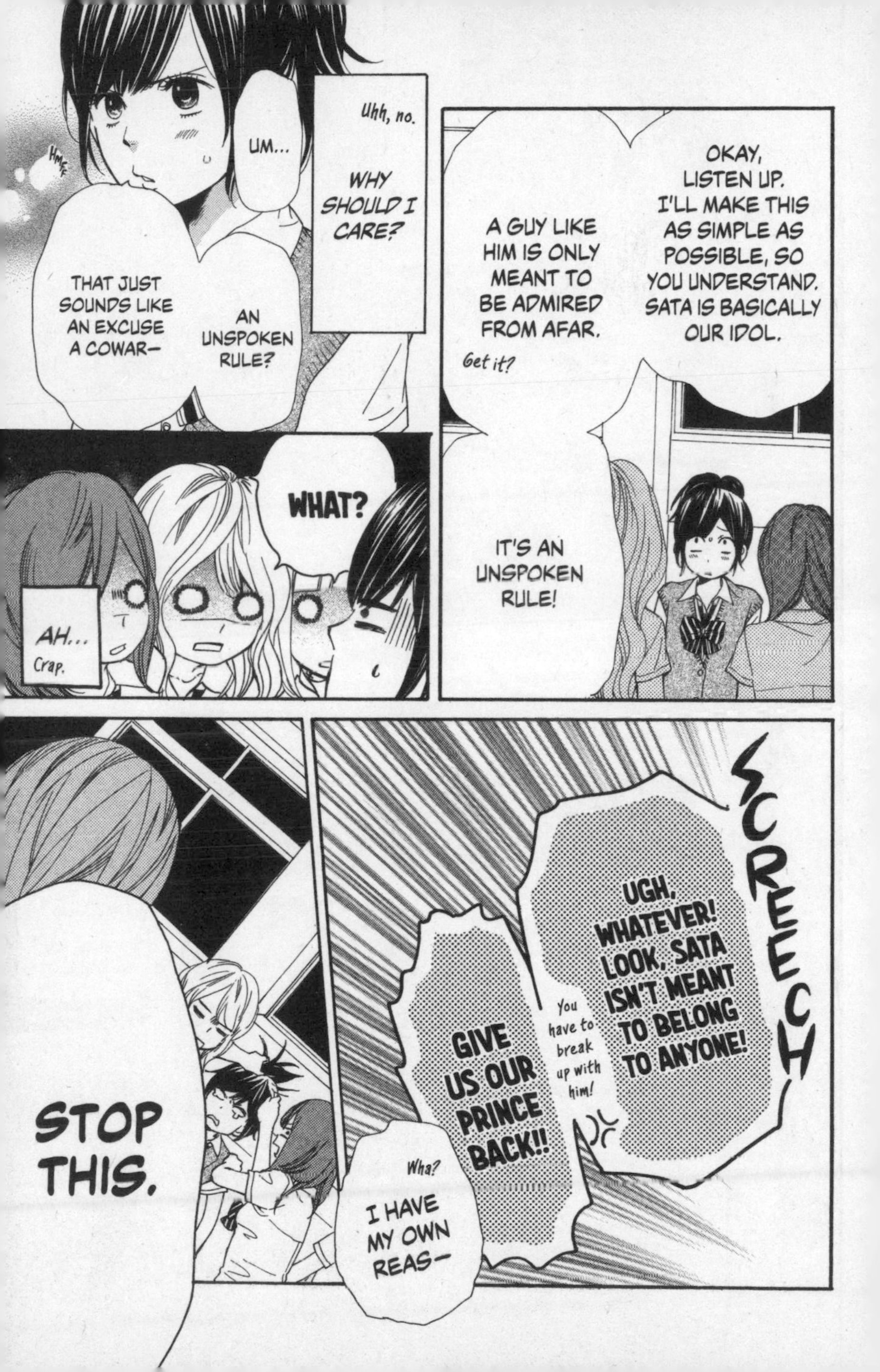

OKAY, LISTEN UP. I'LL MAKE THIS AS SIMPLE AS POSSIBLE, SO YOU UNDERSTAND. SATA IS BASICALLY OUR IDOL.
A GUY LIKE HIM IS ONLY MEANT TO BE ADMIRED FROM AFAR.
Get it?
IT'S AN UNSPOKEN RULE!
Uhh, no.
WHY SHOULD I CARE?
UM...
AN UNSPOKEN RULE?
THAT JUST SOUNDS LIKE AN EXCUSE A COWAR—
HMF
WHAT?
AH... Crap.
SCREECH
UGH, WHATEVER! LOOK, SATA ISN'T MEANT TO BELONG TO ANYONE!
You have to break up with him!
GIVE US OUR PRINCE BACK!!
Wha?
I HAVE MY OWN REAS—
STOP THIS.

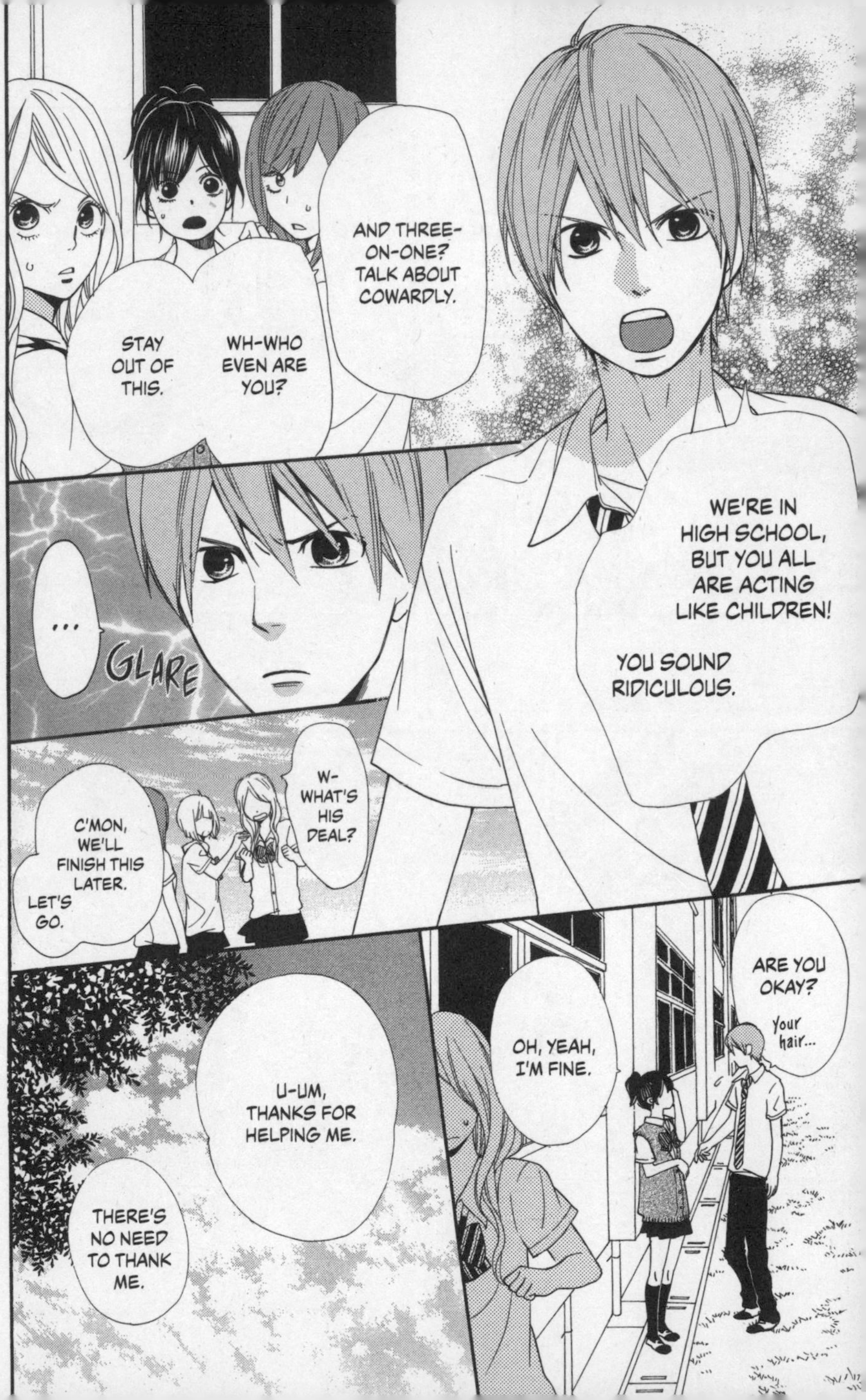
WE'RE IN HIGH SCHOOL, BUT YOU ALL ARE ACTING LIKE CHILDREN!
YOU SOUND RIDICULOUS.
AND THREE-ON-ONE? TALK ABOUT COWARDLY.
WH-WHO EVEN ARE YOU?
STAY OUT OF THIS.
GLARE
...
W-WHAT'S HIS DEAL?
C'MON, WE'LL FINISH THIS LATER.
LET'S GO.
ARE YOU OKAY?
Your hair...
OH, YEAH, I'M FINE.
U-UM, THANKS FOR HELPING ME.
THERE'S NO NEED TO THANK ME.

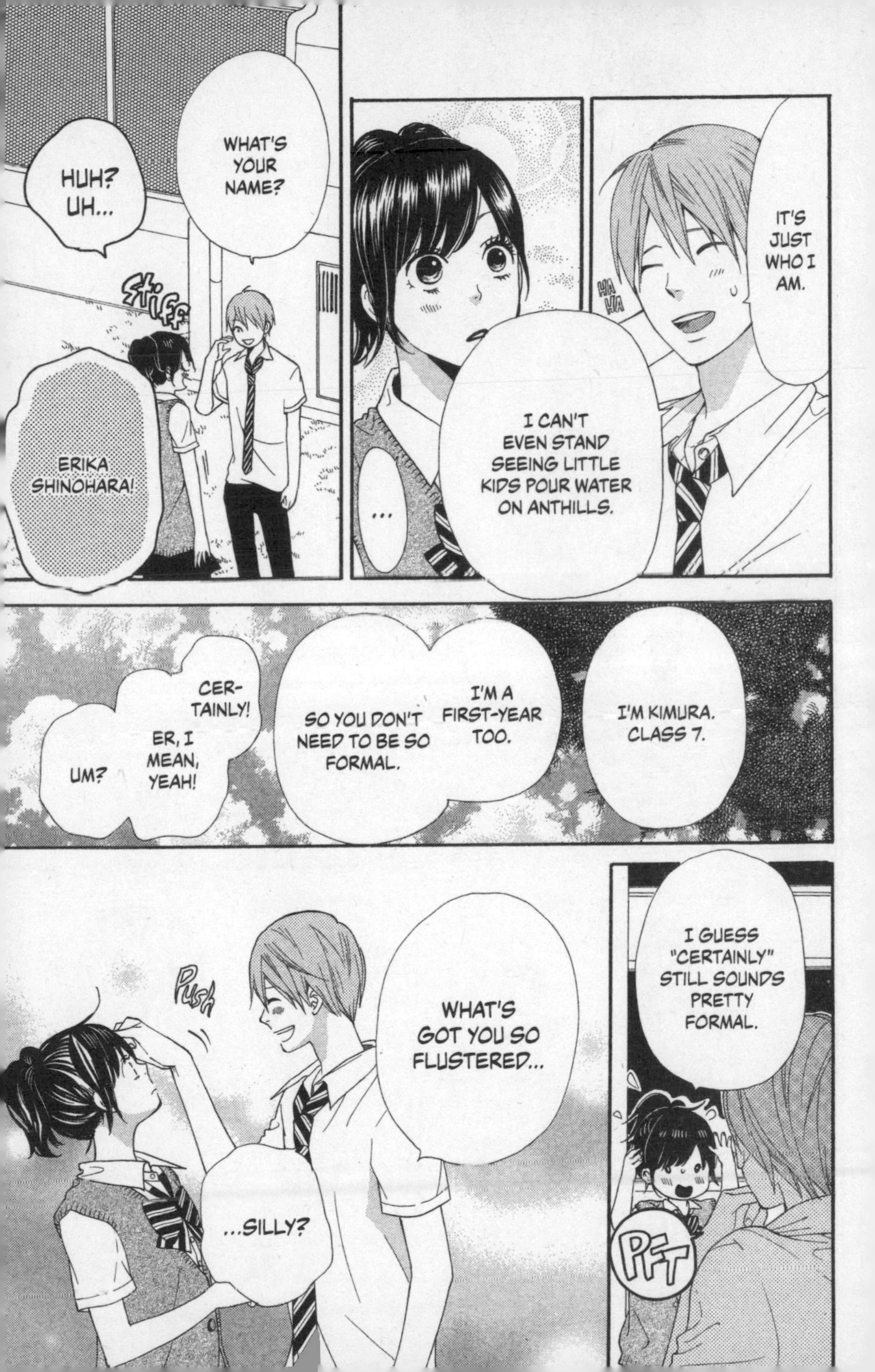
IT'S JUST WHO I AM.
HA HA
I CAN'T EVEN STAND SEEING LITTLE KIDS POUR WATER ON ANTHILLS.
...
WHAT'S YOUR NAME?
HUH? UH...
Stiff
ERIKA SHINOHARA!
I'M KIMURA. CLASS 7.
I'M A FIRST-YEAR TOO.
SO YOU DON'T NEED TO BE SO FORMAL.
CER-TAINLY!
ER, I MEAN, YEAH!
UM?
I GUESS "CERTAINLY" STILL SOUNDS PRETTY FORMAL.
PFT
WHAT'S GOT YOU SO FLUSTERED...
Push
...SILLY?

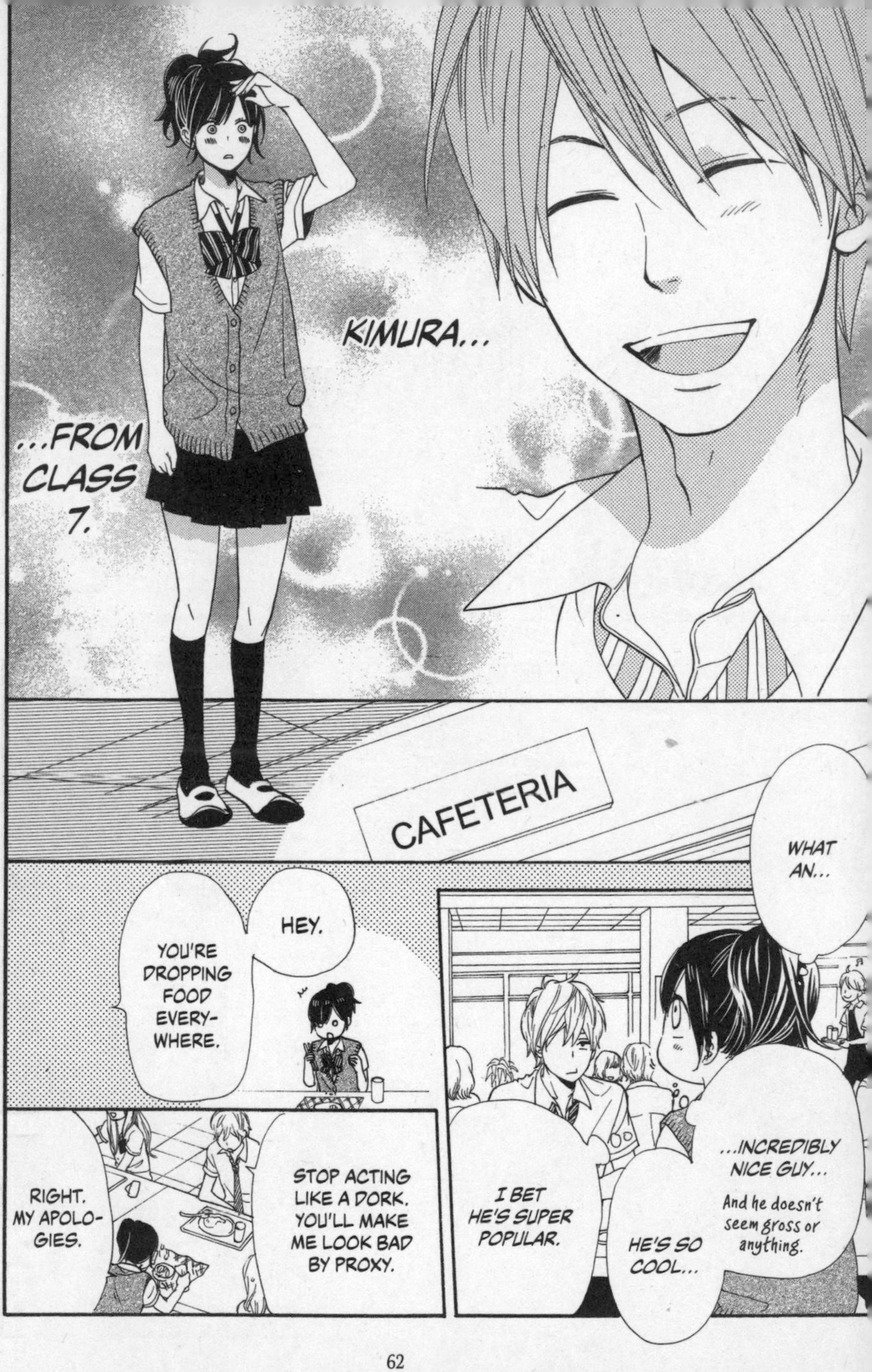
KIMURA...
...FROM CLASS 7.
CAFETERIA
WHAT AN...
...INCREDIBLY NICE GUY...
And he doesn't seem gross or anything.
HE'S SO COOL...
I BET HE'S SUPER POPULAR.
HEY.
YOU'RE DROPPING FOOD EVERY-WHERE.
STOP ACTING LIKE A DORK. YOU'LL MAKE ME LOOK BAD BY PROXY.
RIGHT. MY APOLO-GIES.

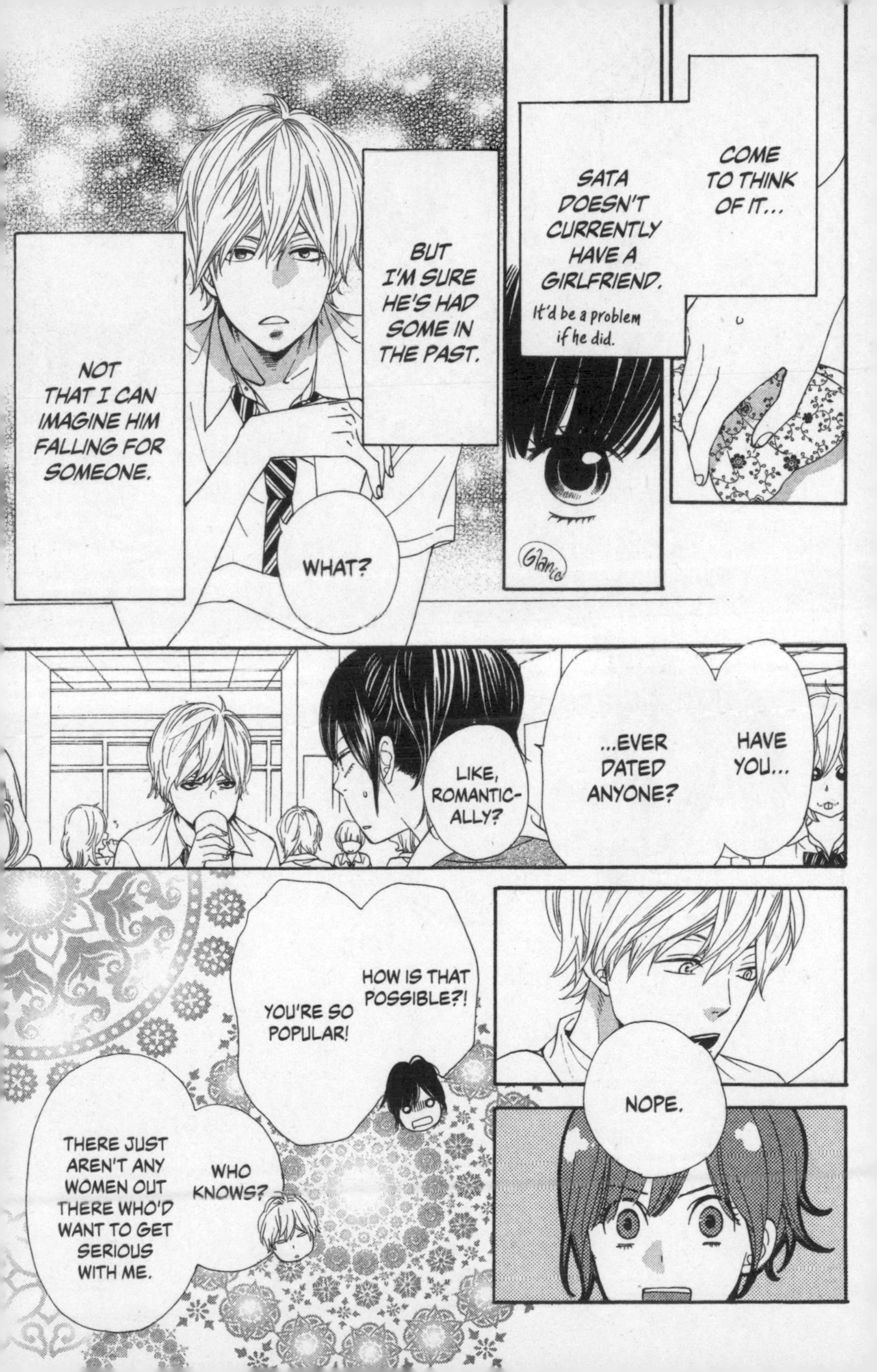
COME TO THINK OF IT...
SATA DOESN'T CURRENTLY HAVE A GIRLFRIEND.
It'd be a problem if he did.
Glance
BUT I'M SURE HE'S HAD SOME IN THE PAST.
NOT THAT I CAN IMAGINE HIM FALLING FOR SOMEONE.
WHAT?
HAVE YOU...
...EVER DATED ANYONE?
LIKE, ROMANTIC-ALLY?
NOPE.
HOW IS THAT POSSIBLE?!
YOU'RE SO POPULAR!
WHO KNOWS?
THERE JUST AREN'T ANY WOMEN OUT THERE WHO'D WANT TO GET SERIOUS WITH ME.

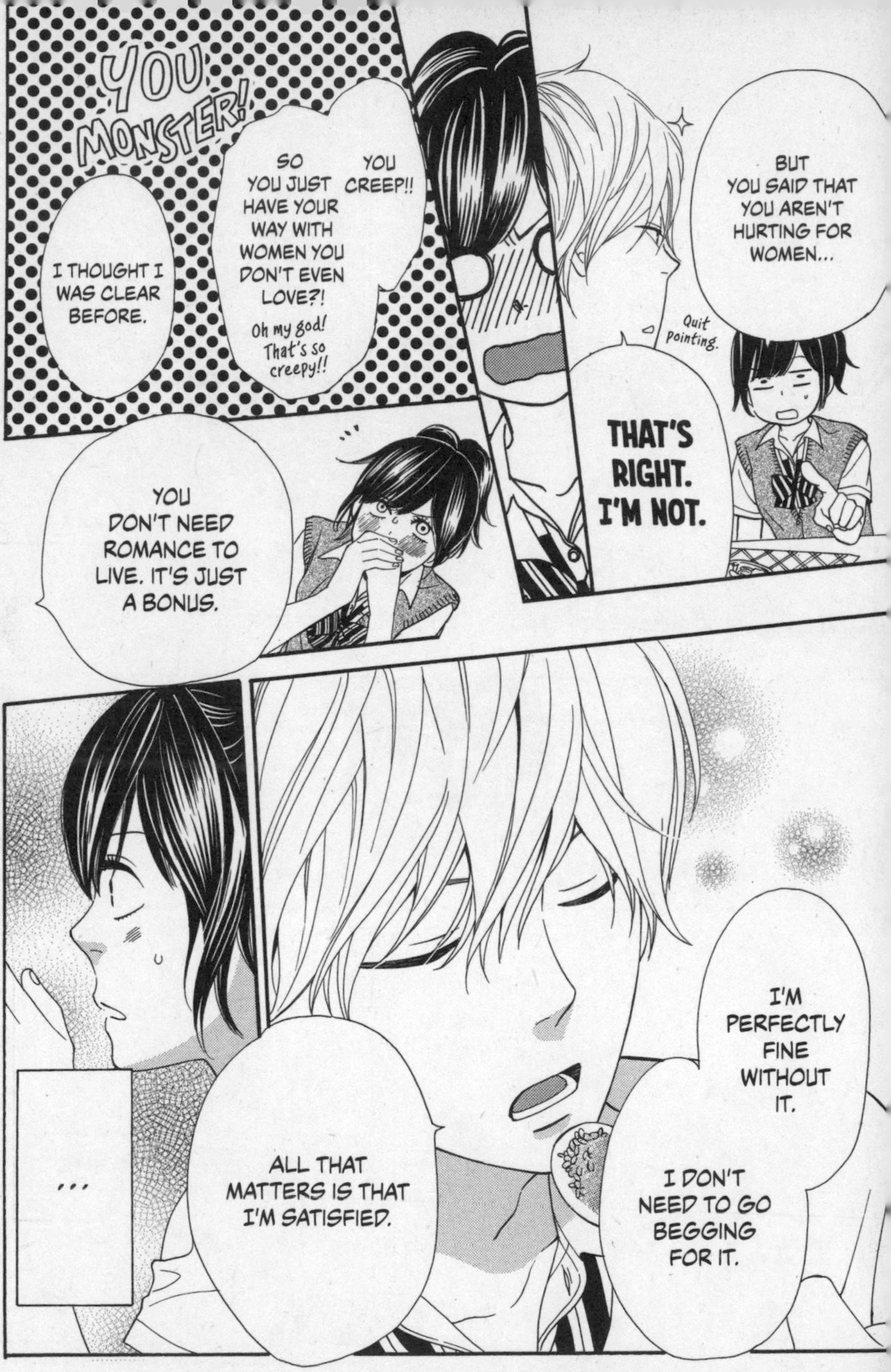
BUT YOU SAID THAT YOU AREN'T HURTING FOR WOMEN...
Quit pointing.
THAT'S RIGHT. I'M NOT.
YOU CREEP!!
SO YOU JUST HAVE YOUR WAY WITH WOMEN YOU DON'T EVEN LOVE?!
Oh my god! That's so creepy!!
YOU MONSTER!
I THOUGHT I WAS CLEAR BEFORE.
YOU DON'T NEED ROMANCE TO LIVE. IT'S JUST A BONUS.
I'M PERFECTLY FINE WITHOUT IT.
I DON'T NEED TO GO BEGGING FOR IT.
ALL THAT MATTERS IS THAT I'M SATISFIED.
...

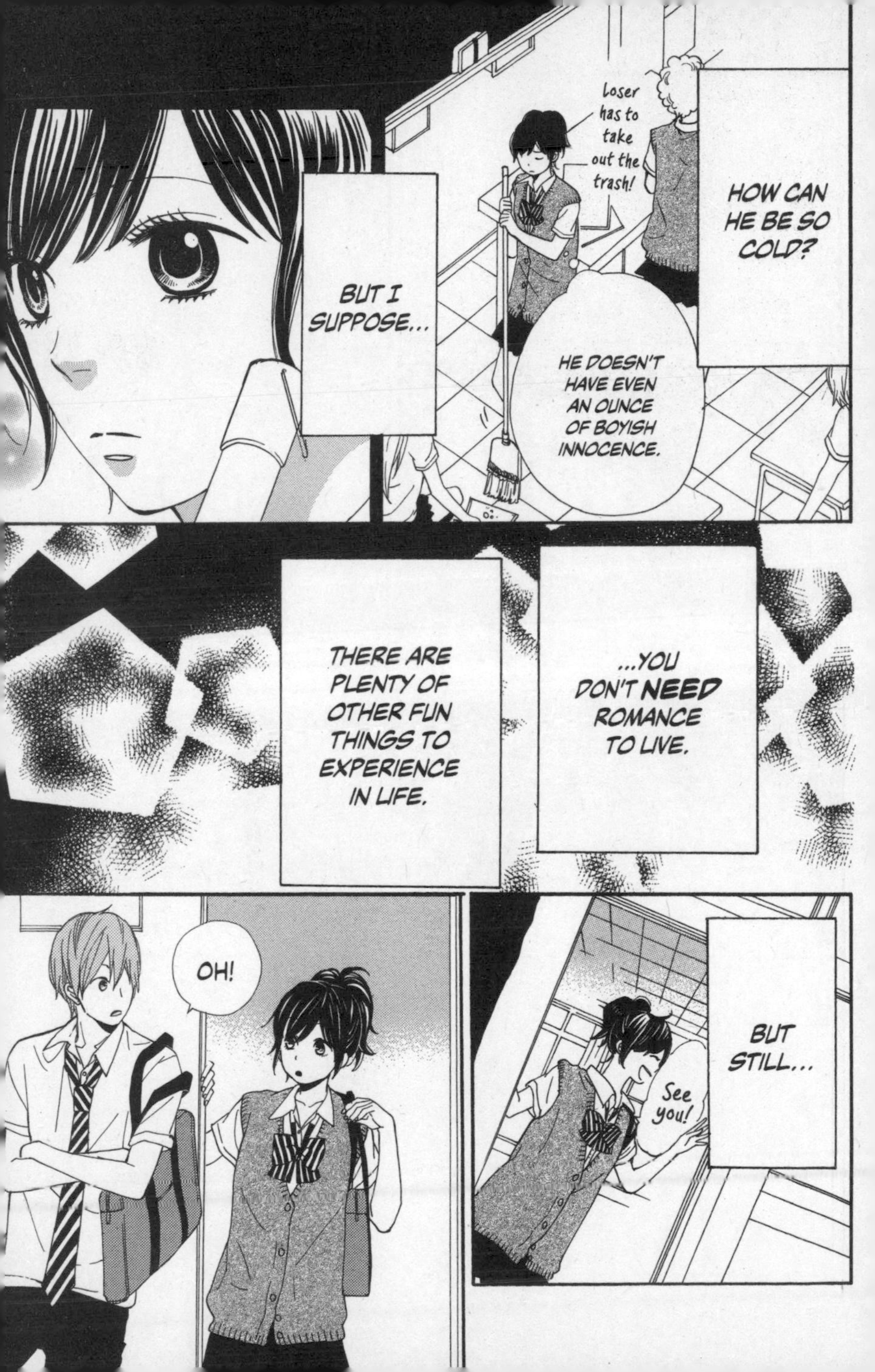
HOW CAN HE BE SO COLD?
Loser has to take out the trash!
HE DOESN'T HAVE EVEN AN OUNCE OF BOYISH INNOCENCE.
BUT I SUPPOSE...
...YOU DON'T NEED ROMANCE TO LIVE.
THERE ARE PLENTY OF OTHER FUN THINGS TO EXPERIENCE IN LIFE.
BUT STILL...
See you!
OH!

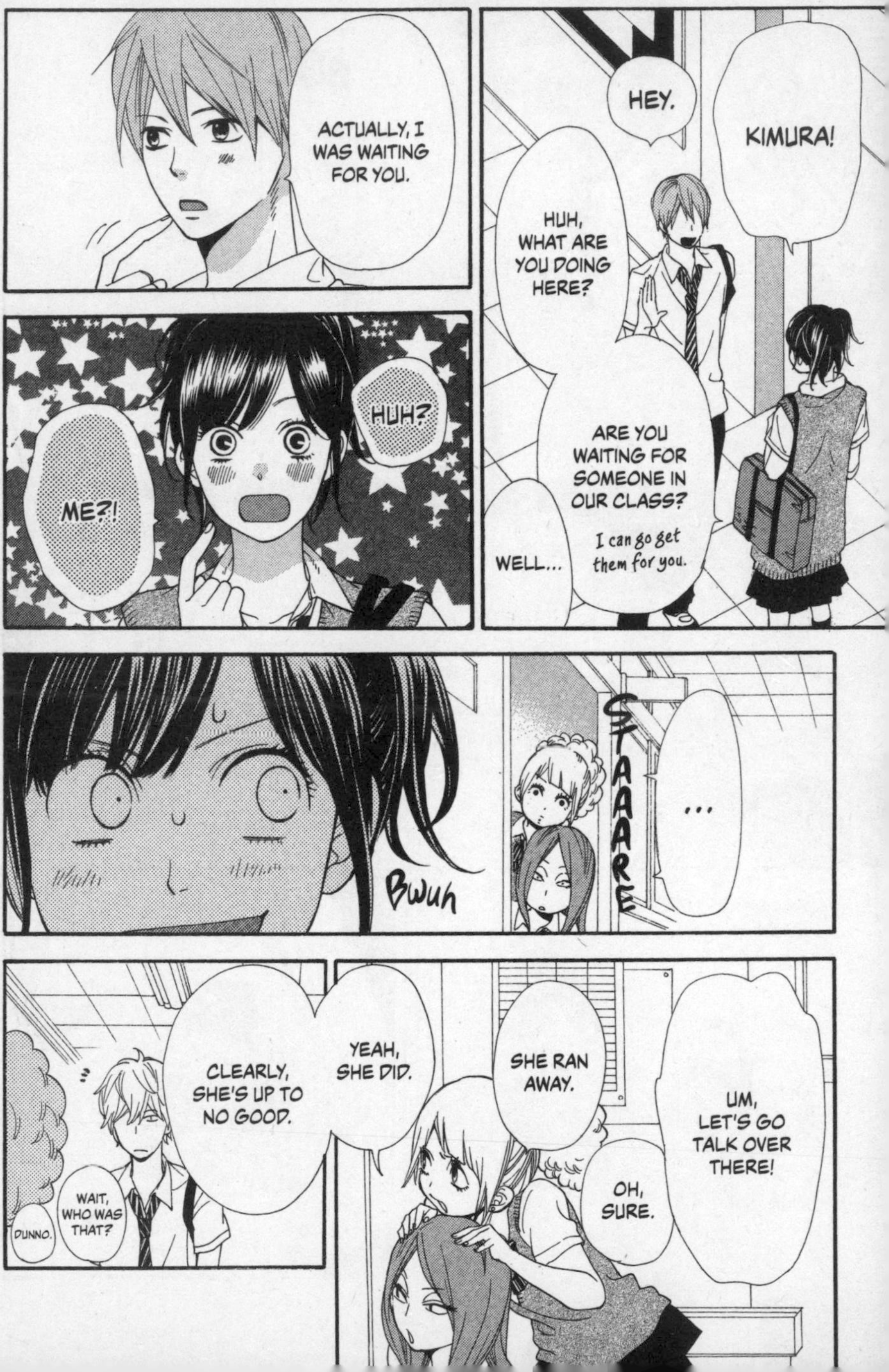
KIMURA!
HEY.
HUH, WHAT ARE YOU DOING HERE?
ARE YOU WAITING FOR SOMEONE IN OUR CLASS?
I can go get them for you.
WELL...
ACTUALLY, I WAS WAITING FOR YOU.
HUH?
ME?!
STAAAARE
...
Bwuh
UM, LET'S GO TALK OVER THERE!
OH, SURE.
SHE RAN AWAY.
YEAH, SHE DID.
CLEARLY, SHE'S UP TO NO GOOD.
WAIT, WHO WAS THAT?
DUNNO.

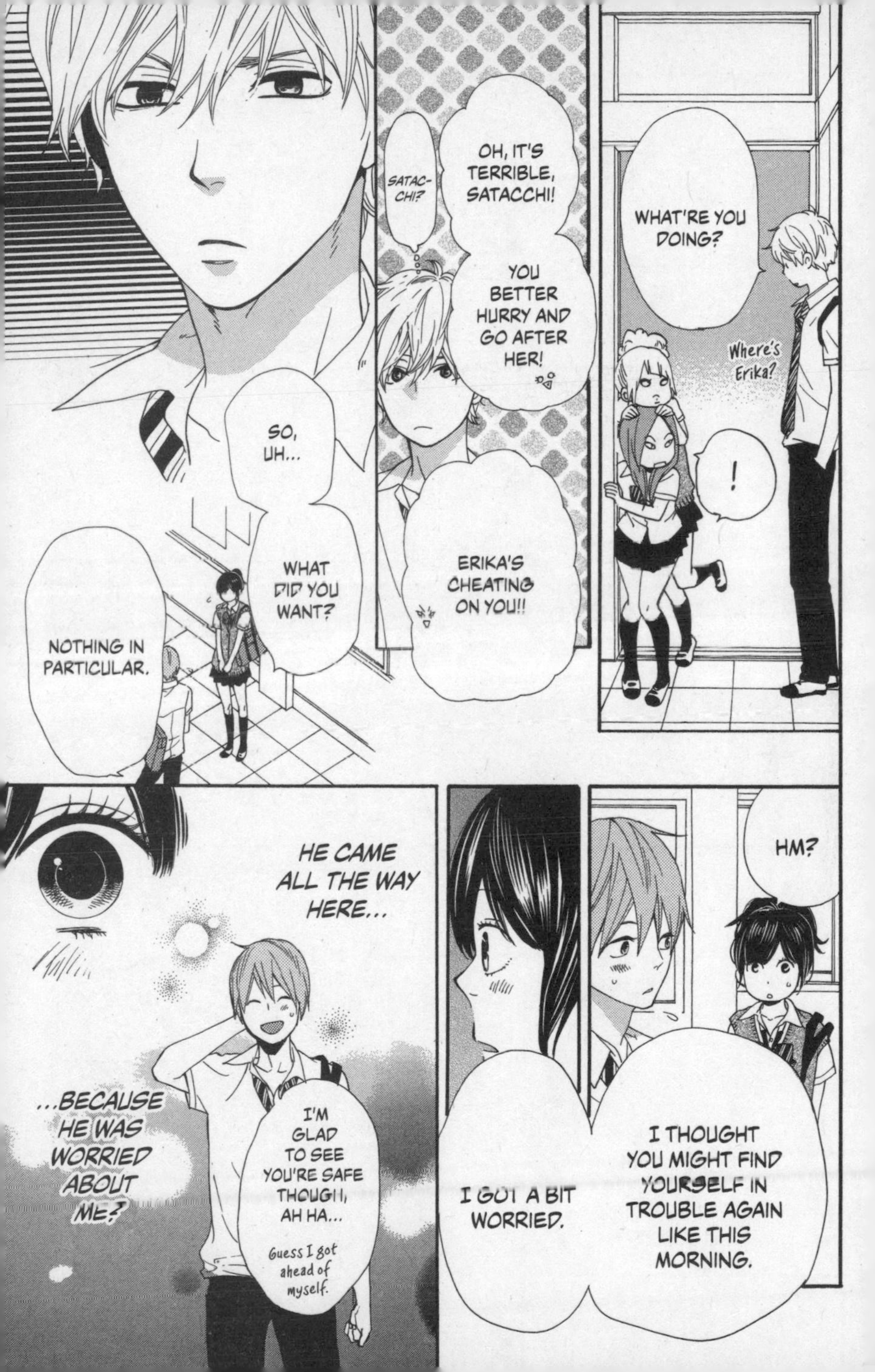

WHAT'RE YOU DOING?
Where's Erika?
!
SATAC-CHI?
OH, IT'S TERRIBLE, SATACCHI!
YOU BETTER HURRY AND GO AFTER HER!
ERIKA'S CHEATING ON YOU!!
SO, UH...
WHAT DID YOU WANT?
NOTHING IN PARTICULAR.
HM?
I THOUGHT YOU MIGHT FIND YOURSELF IN TROUBLE AGAIN LIKE THIS MORNING.
I GOT A BIT WORRIED.
HE CAME ALL THE WAY HERE...
I'M GLAD TO SEE YOU'RE SAFE THOUGH, AH HA...
Guess I got ahead of myself.
...BECAUSE HE WAS WORRIED ABOUT ME?

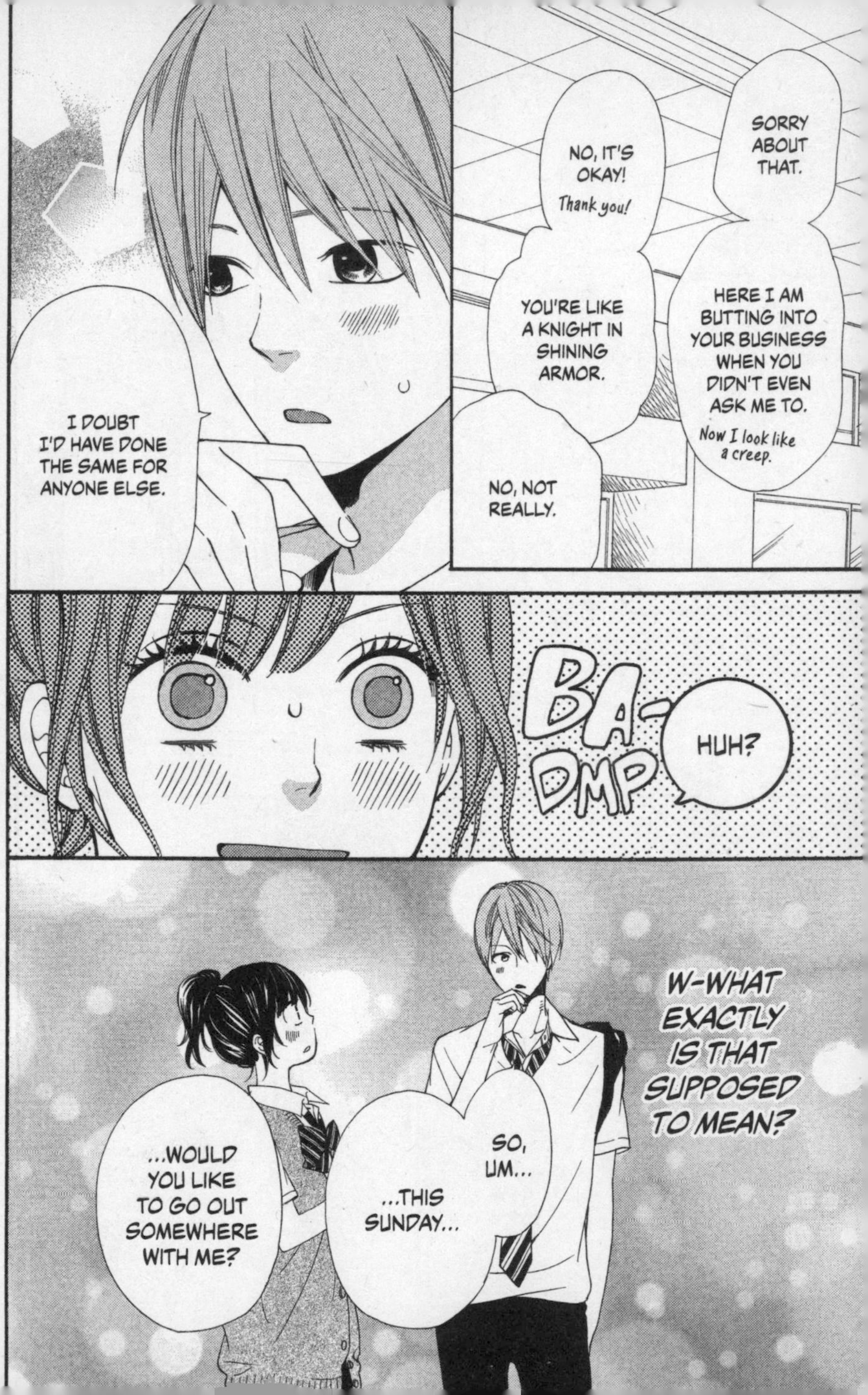
SORRY ABOUT THAT.
HERE I AM BUTTING INTO YOUR BUSINESS WHEN YOU DIDN'T EVEN ASK ME TO.
Now I look like a creep.
NO, IT'S OKAY!
Thank you!
YOU'RE LIKE A KNIGHT IN SHINING ARMOR.
NO, NOT REALLY.
I DOUBT I'D HAVE DONE THE SAME FOR ANYONE ELSE.
HUH?
BA-DMP
W-WHAT EXACTLY IS THAT SUPPOSED TO MEAN?
SO, UM...
...THIS SUNDAY...
...WOULD YOU LIKE TO GO OUT SOMEWHERE WITH ME?

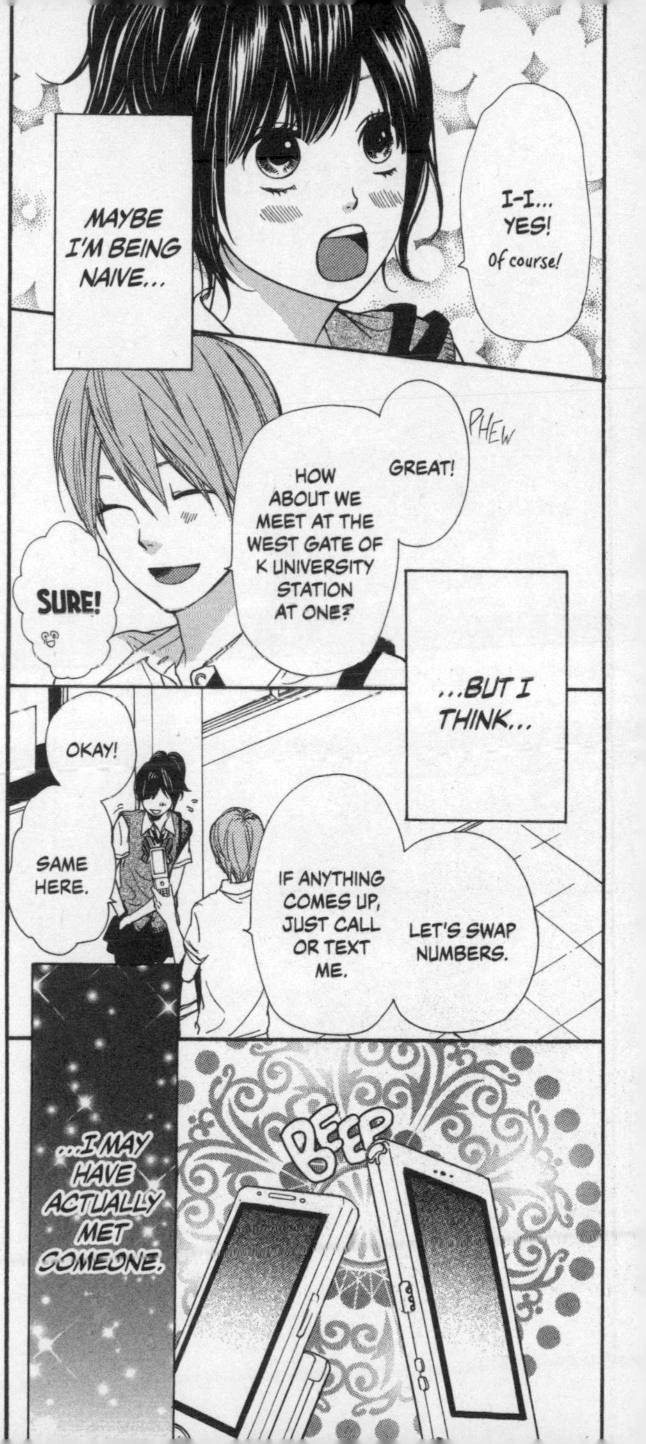
I-I... YES!
Of course!
MAYBE I'M BEING NAIVE...
PHEW
GREAT!
HOW ABOUT WE MEET AT THE WEST GATE OF K UNIVERSITY STATION AT ONE?
SURE!
...BUT I THINK...
LET'S SWAP NUMBERS.
IF ANYTHING COMES UP, JUST CALL OR TEXT ME.
OKAY!
SAME HERE.
BEEP
...I MAY HAVE ACTUALLY MET SOMEONE.

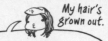

My hair's grown out.

Howdy-ho, everyone! It's September, so the temperature's finally starting to drop. It's really made the time pass easier. Not that I go out much, on account of being a bit of a homebody. Still, I'm glad to no longer have to run the AC nonstop. Think of the environment! That reminds me, the other day I went to the salon for the first time in five months. Five whole months... Even the beautician was yelling at me, like, "You should have come back sooner, Ms. Hatta!" But it's such a pain. I just don't go out that much. Plus, I actually hate going to the salon and having to talk to the staff. I always read a magazine and try to give off a "don't talk to me" vibe whenever I go. On top of that... I never know how I want my hair cut until I get there. I've been going to the same salon for five years, but that doesn't mean I'm friends with the employees. They give off too much of a normie vibe. They're all perfectly nice people though. I do love them.

It occurs to me that some of the employees might read this comic. Thanks for putting up with me.

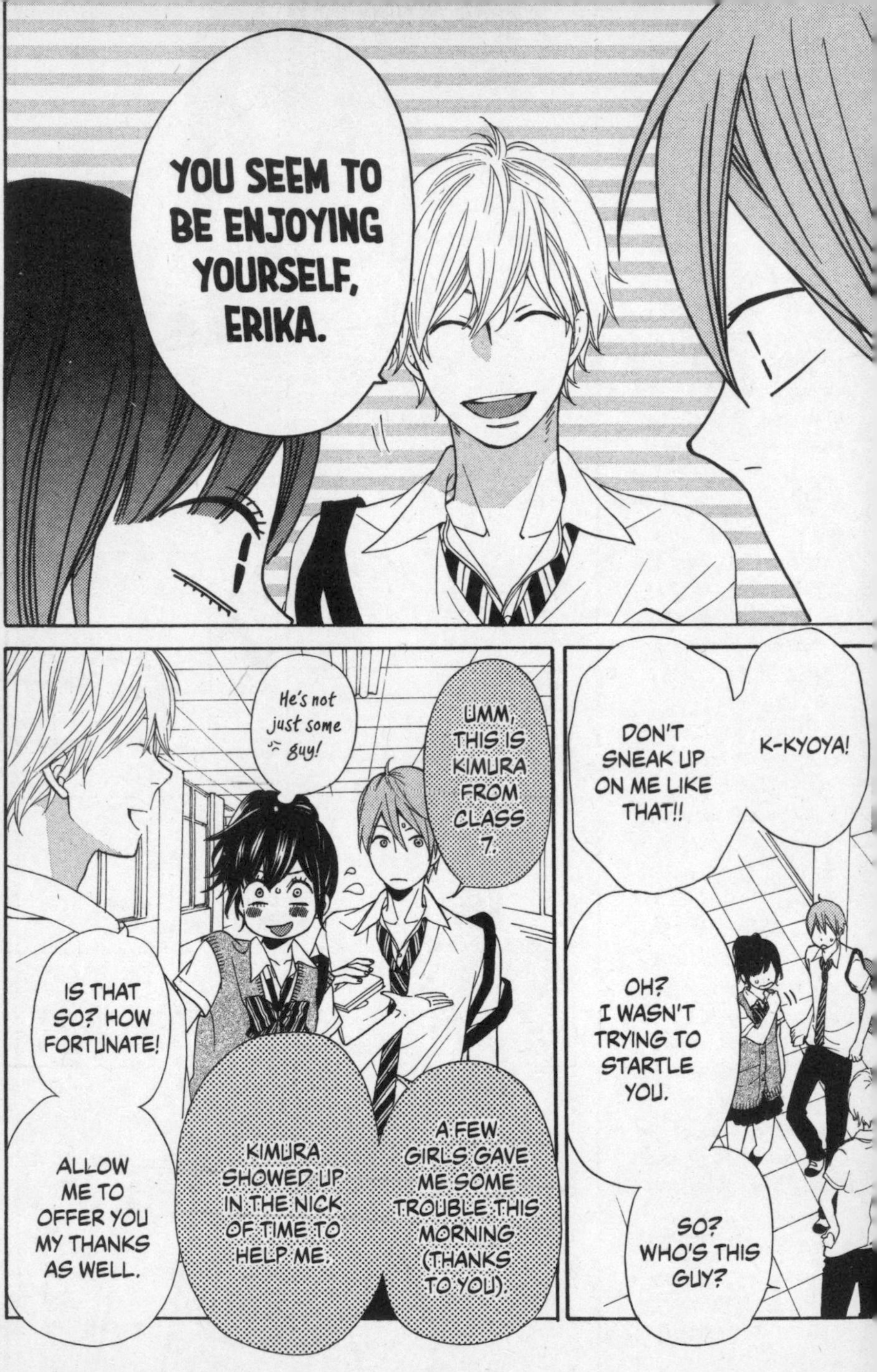
YOU SEEM TO BE ENJOYING YOURSELF, ERIKA.
K-KYOYA!
DON'T SNEAK UP ON ME LIKE THAT!!
OH? I WASN'T TRYING TO STARTLE YOU.
SO? WHO'S THIS GUY?
UMM, THIS IS KIMURA FROM CLASS 7.
He's not just some guy!
A FEW GIRLS GAVE ME SOME TROUBLE THIS MORNING (THANKS TO YOU).
KIMURA SHOWED UP IN THE NICK OF TIME TO HELP ME.
IS THAT SO? HOW FORTUNATE!
ALLOW ME TO OFFER YOU MY THANKS AS WELL.

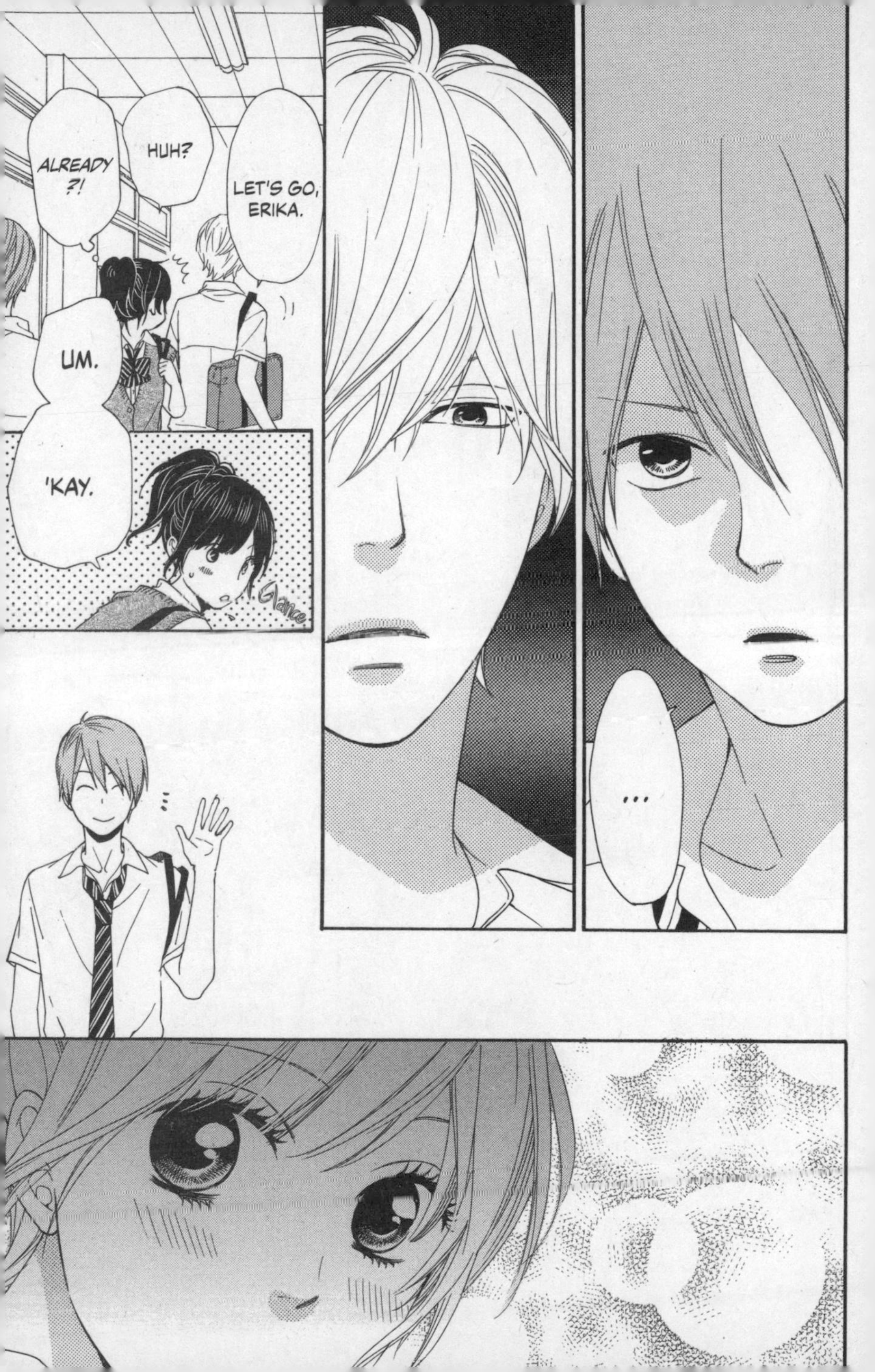
...
LET'S GO, ERIKA.
HUH?
ALREADY ?!
UM. 'KAY.
Glance

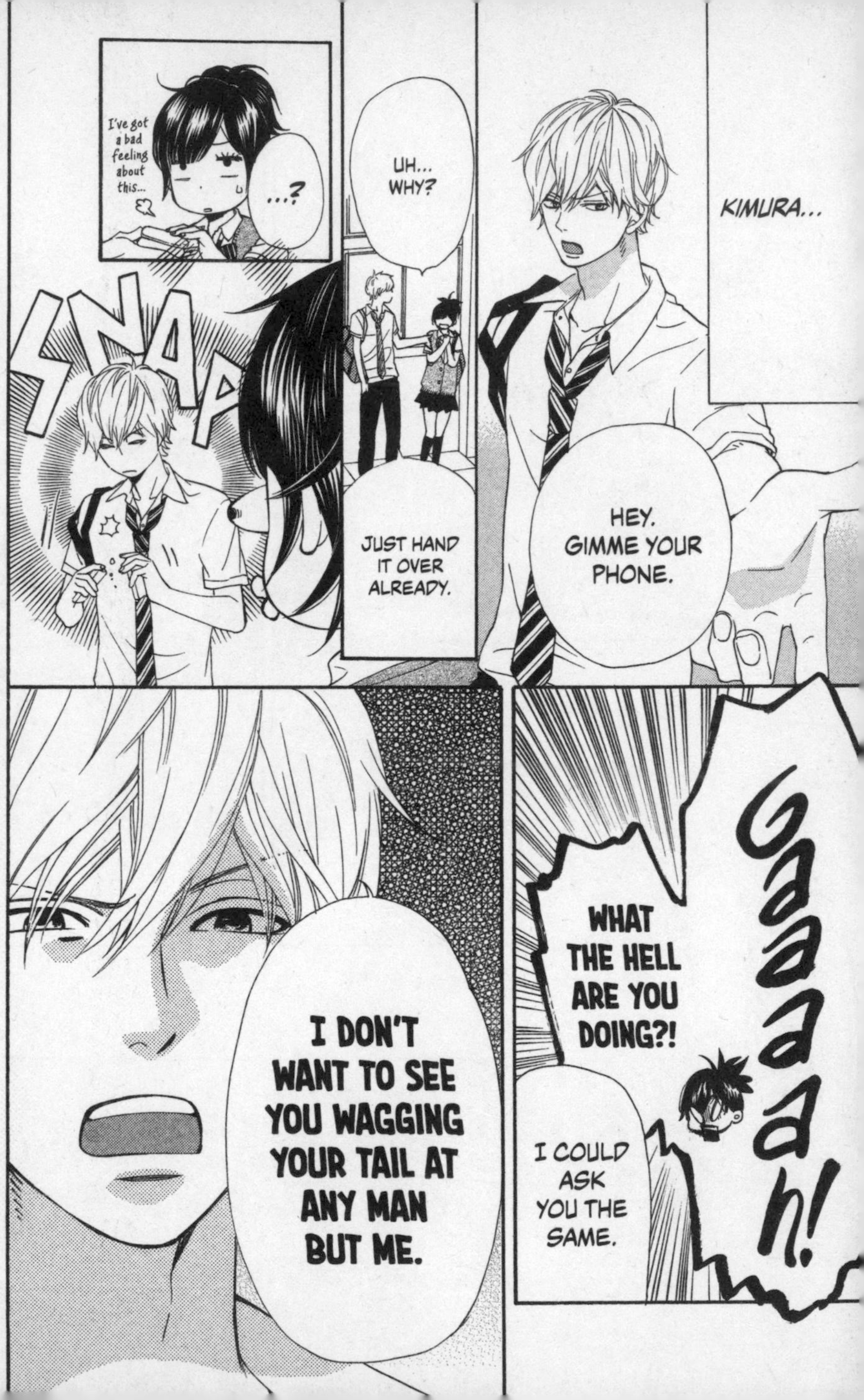
KIMURA...
HEY. GIMME YOUR PHONE.
UH... WHY?
JUST HAND IT OVER ALREADY.
...?
I've got a bad feeling about this...
SNAP
Gaaaah!
WHAT THE HELL ARE YOU DOING?!
I COULD ASK YOU THE SAME.
I DON'T WANT TO SEE YOU WAGGING YOUR TAIL AT ANY MAN BUT ME.

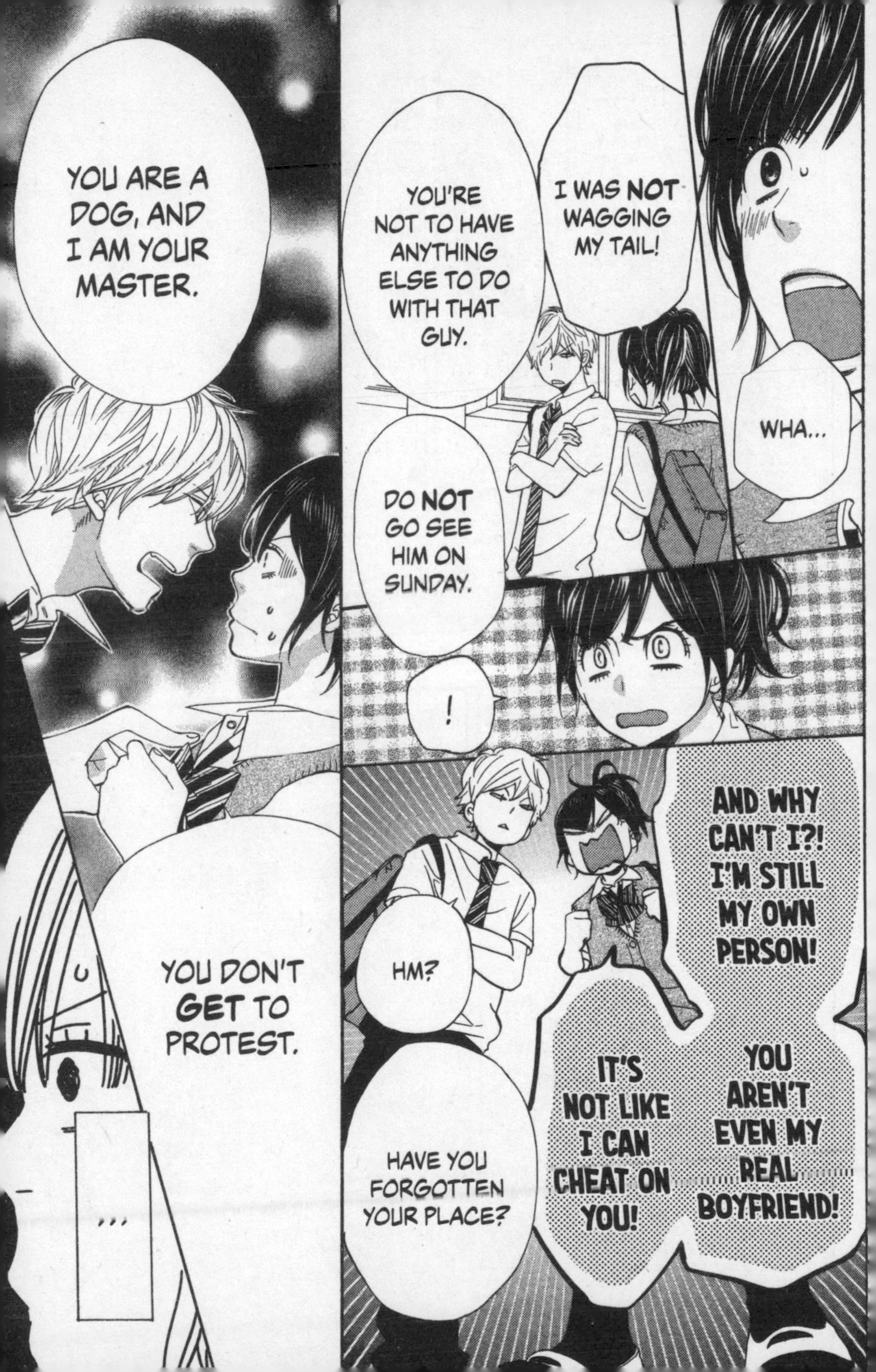
WHA...
I WAS NOT WAGGING MY TAIL!
YOU'RE NOT TO HAVE ANYTHING ELSE TO DO WITH THAT GUY.
DO NOT GO SEE HIM ON SUNDAY.
!
AND WHY CAN'T I?! I'M STILL MY OWN PERSON!
YOU AREN'T EVEN MY REAL BOYFRIEND!
IT'S NOT LIKE I CAN CHEAT ON YOU!
HM?
HAVE YOU FORGOTTEN YOUR PLACE?
YOU ARE A DOG, AND I AM YOUR MASTER.
YOU DON'T GET TO PROTEST.
...

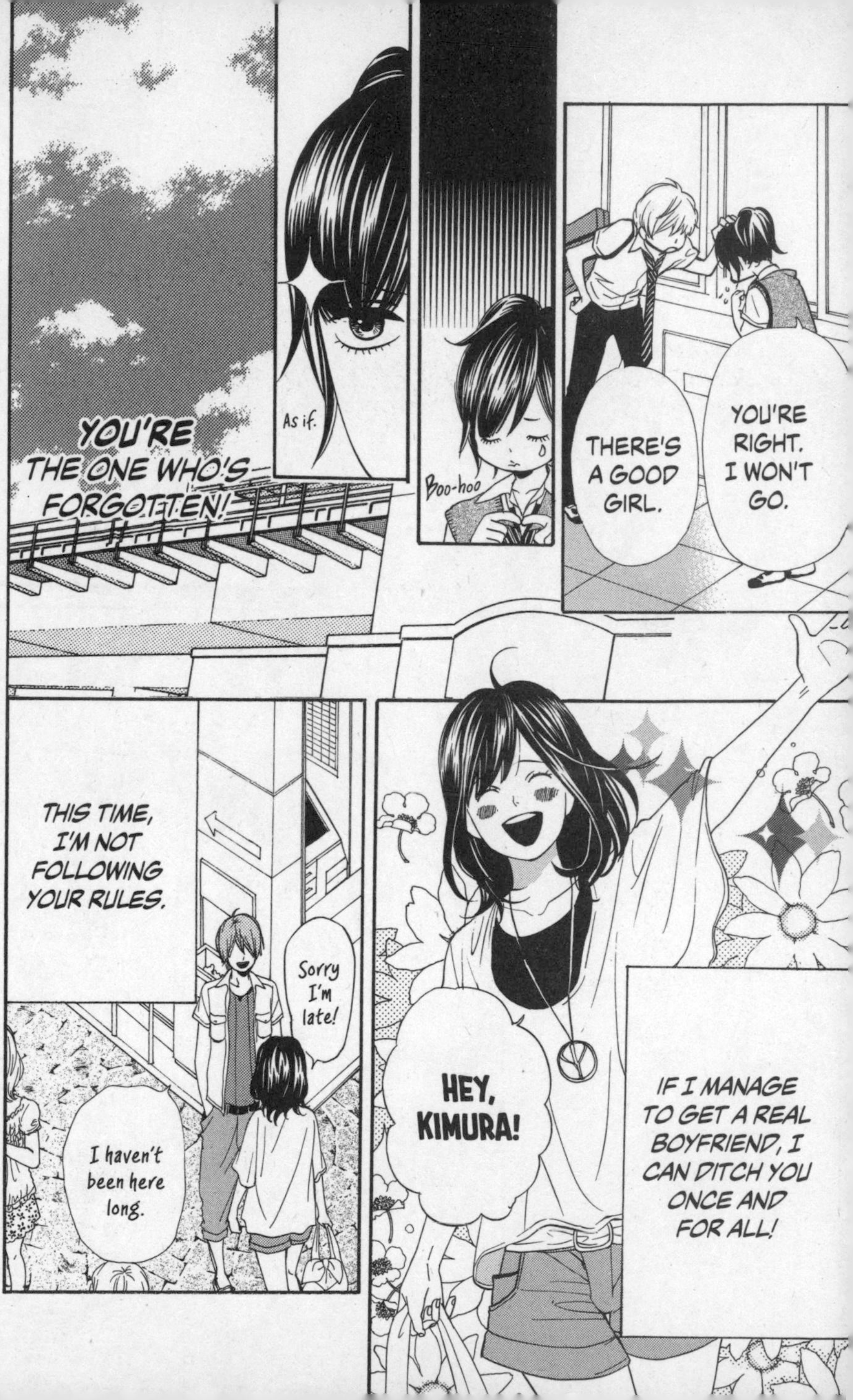
YOU'RE RIGHT. I WON'T GO.
THERE'S A GOOD GIRL.
Boo-hoo
As if.
YOU'RE THE ONE WHO'S FORGOTTEN!
IF I MANAGE TO GET A REAL BOYFRIEND, I CAN DITCH YOU ONCE AND FOR ALL!
HEY, KIMURA!
THIS TIME, I'M NOT FOLLOWING YOUR RULES.
Sorry I'm late!
I haven't been here long.

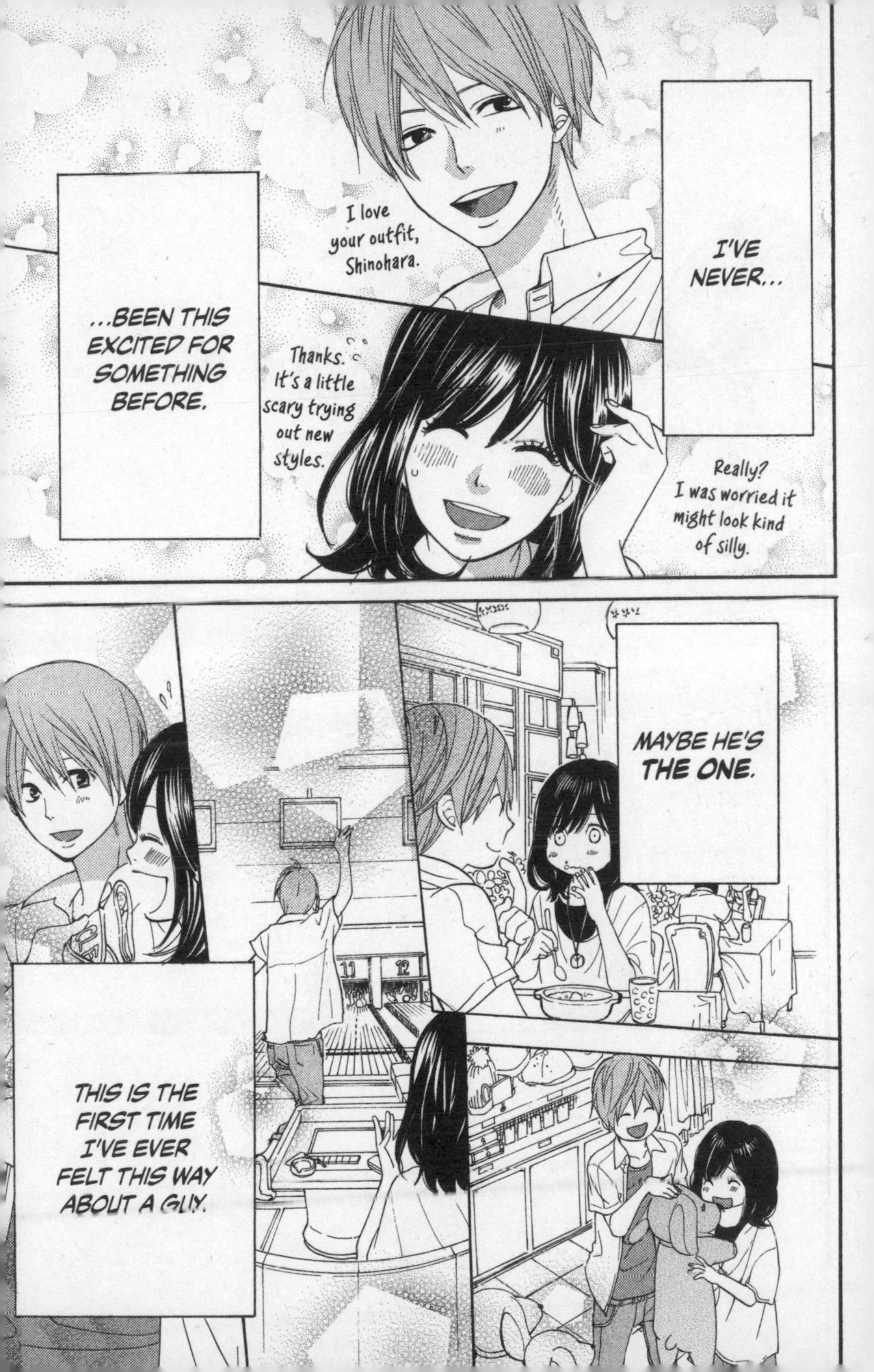
I'VE NEVER...
I love your outfit, Shinohara.
Really? I was worried it might look kind of silly.
Thanks. It's a little scary trying out new styles.
...BEEN THIS EXCITED FOR SOMETHING BEFORE.
MAYBE HE'S THE ONE.
THIS IS THE FIRST TIME I'VE EVER FELT THIS WAY ABOUT A GUY.

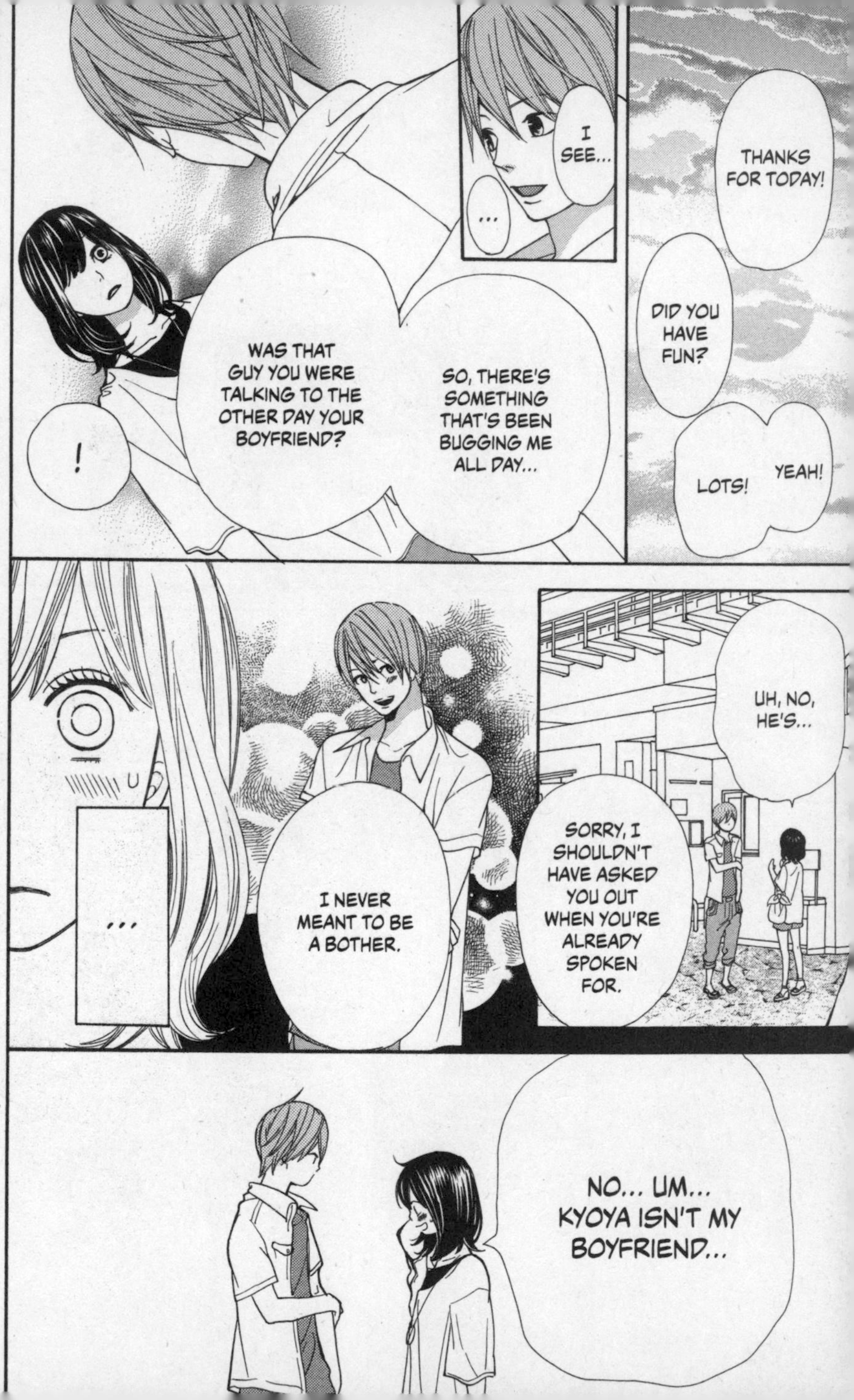
THANKS FOR TODAY!
DID YOU HAVE FUN?
YEAH!
LOTS!
I SEE...
...
SO, THERE'S SOMETHING THAT'S BEEN BUGGING ME ALL DAY...
WAS THAT GUY YOU WERE TALKING TO THE OTHER DAY YOUR BOYFRIEND?
!
UH, NO, HE'S...
SORRY, I SHOULDN'T HAVE ASKED YOU OUT WHEN YOU'RE ALREADY SPOKEN FOR.
I NEVER MEANT TO BE A BOTHER.
...
NO... UM... KYOYA ISN'T MY BOYFRIEND...

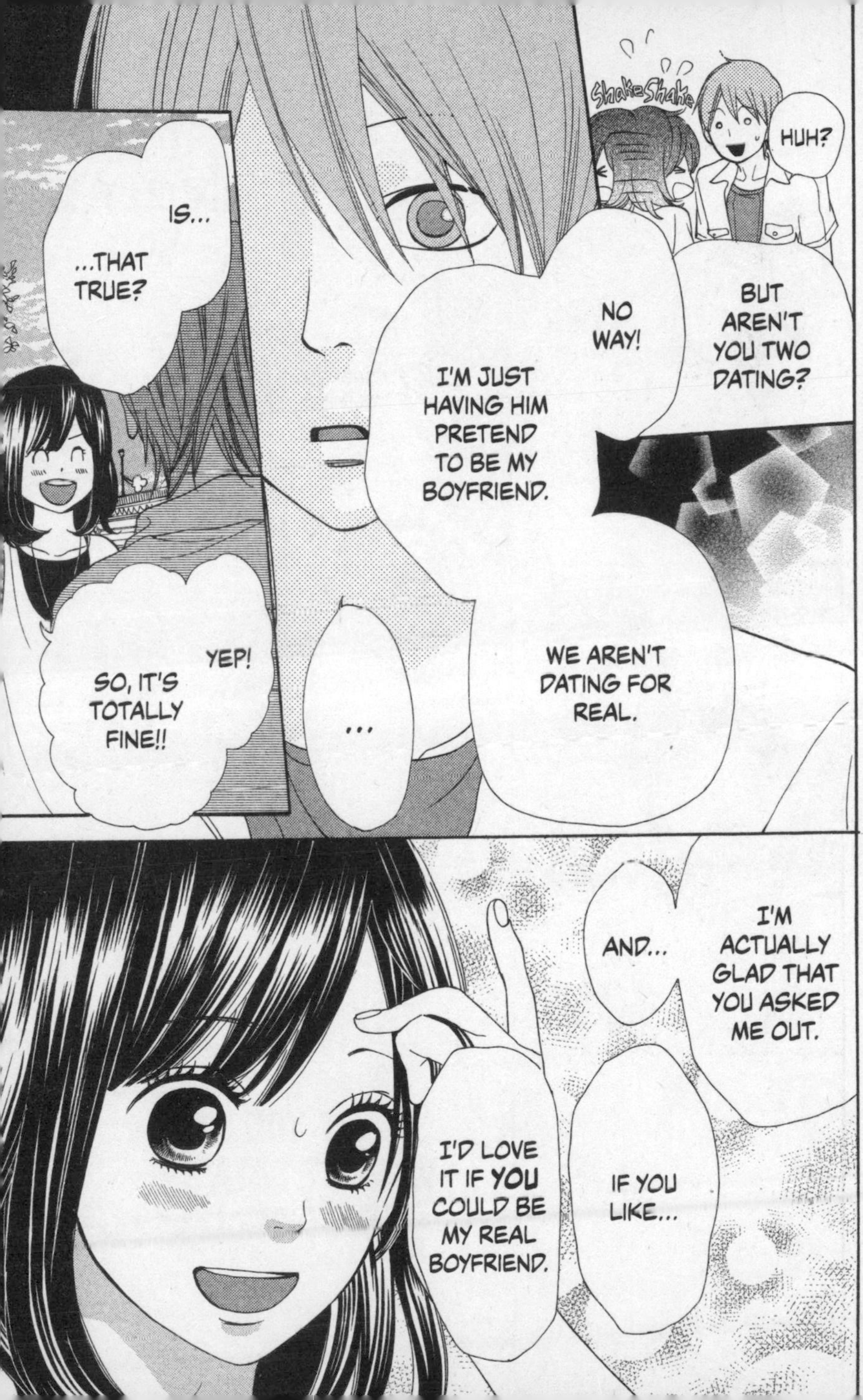
ShakeShake
HUH?
BUT AREN'T YOU TWO DATING?
NO WAY!
I'M JUST HAVING HIM PRETEND TO BE MY BOYFRIEND.
WE AREN'T DATING FOR REAL.
...
IS...
...THAT TRUE?
YEP!
SO, IT'S TOTALLY FINE!!
I'M ACTUALLY GLAD THAT YOU ASKED ME OUT.
AND...
IF YOU LIKE...
I'D LOVE IT IF **YOU** COULD BE MY REAL BOYFRIEND.

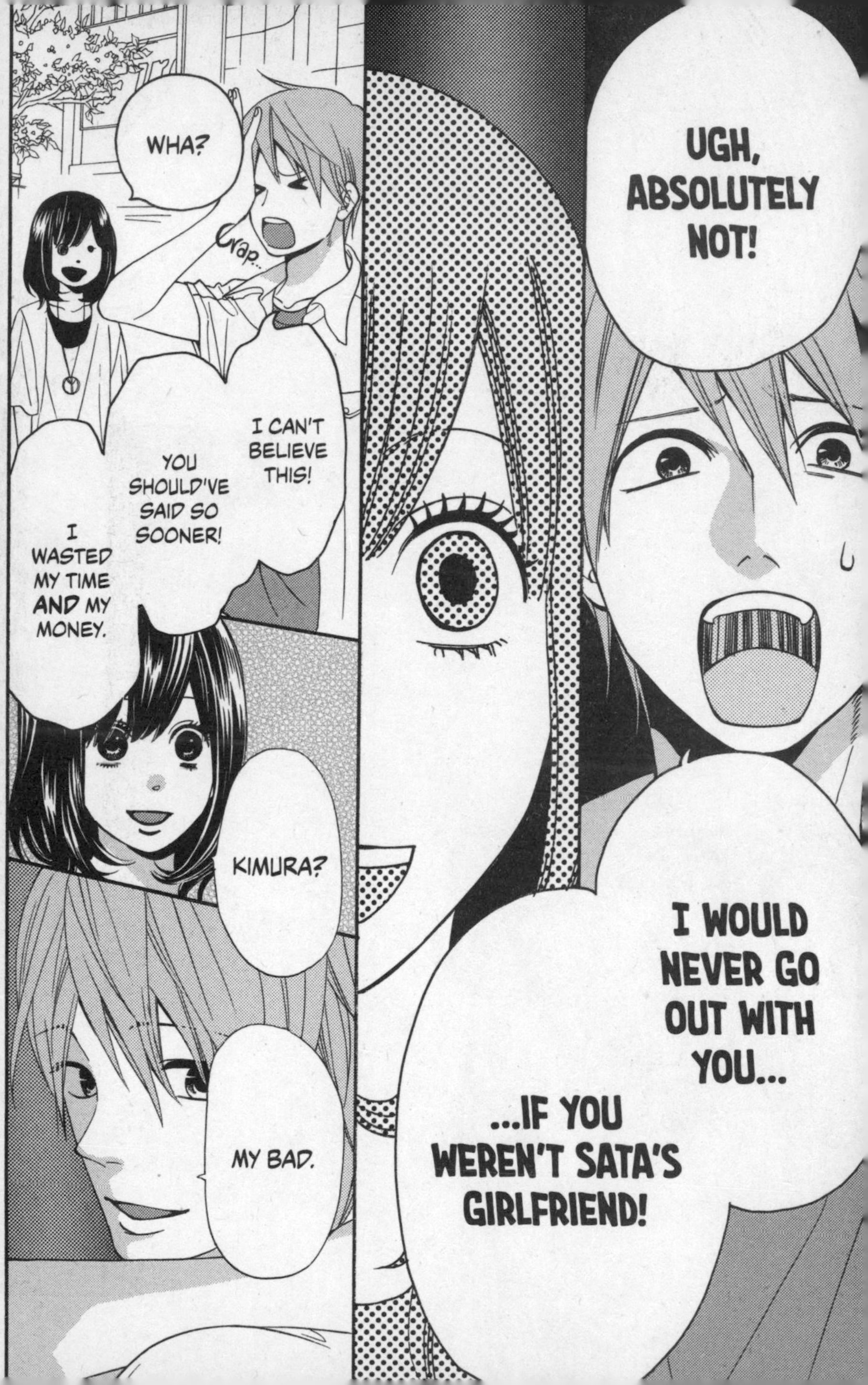
UGH, ABSOLUTELY NOT!
I WOULD NEVER GO OUT WITH YOU...
...IF YOU WEREN'T SATA'S GIRLFRIEND!
WHA?
Crap...
I CAN'T BELIEVE THIS!
YOU SHOULD'VE SAID SO SOONER!
I WASTED MY TIME AND MY MONEY.
KIMURA?
MY BAD.

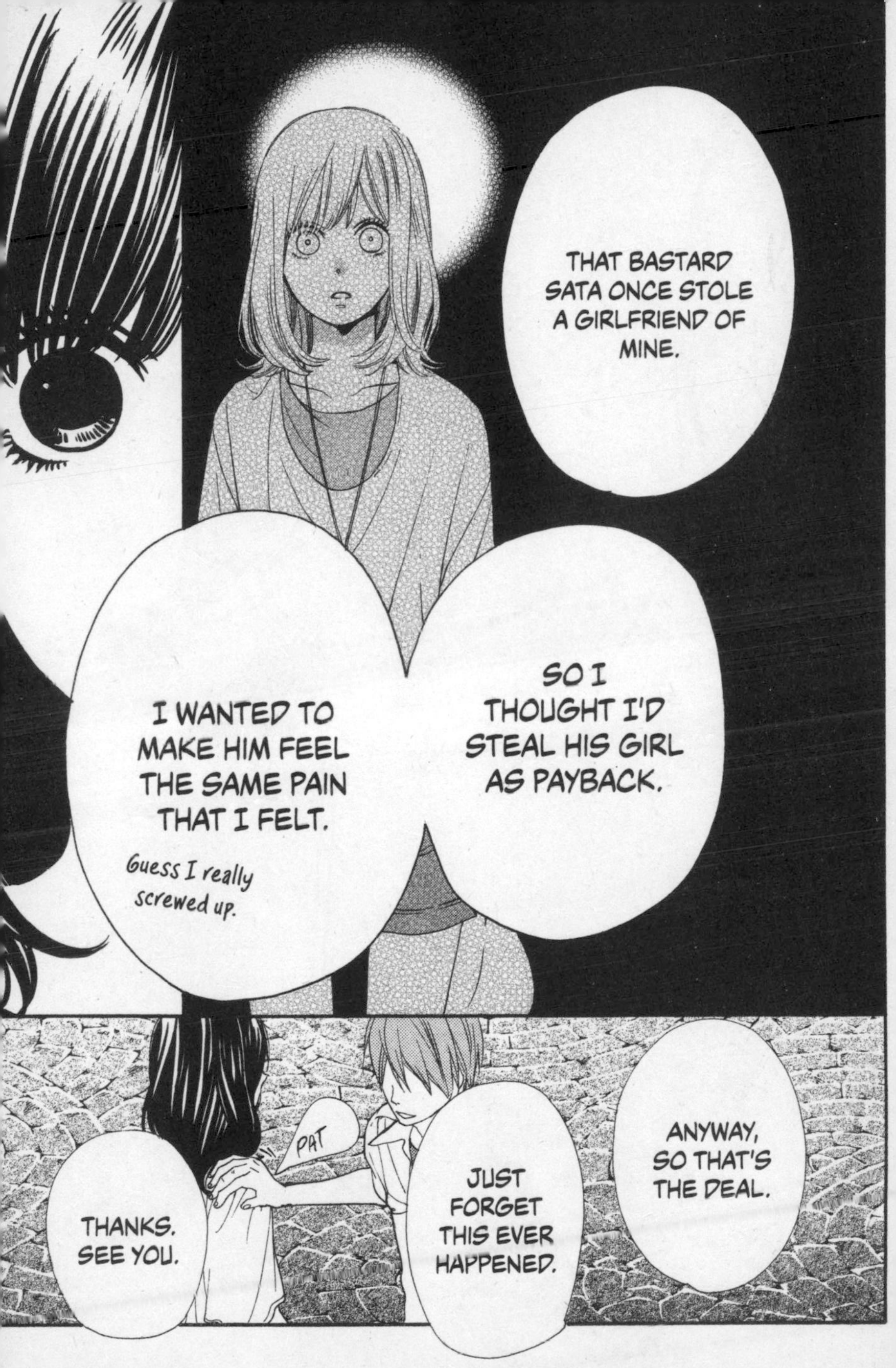
THAT BASTARD SATA ONCE STOLE A GIRLFRIEND OF MINE.
SO I THOUGHT I'D STEAL HIS GIRL AS PAYBACK.
I WANTED TO MAKE HIM FEEL THE SAME PAIN THAT I FELT.
Guess I really screwed up.
ANYWAY, SO THAT'S THE DEAL.
JUST FORGET THIS EVER HAPPENED.
PAT
THANKS. SEE YOU.

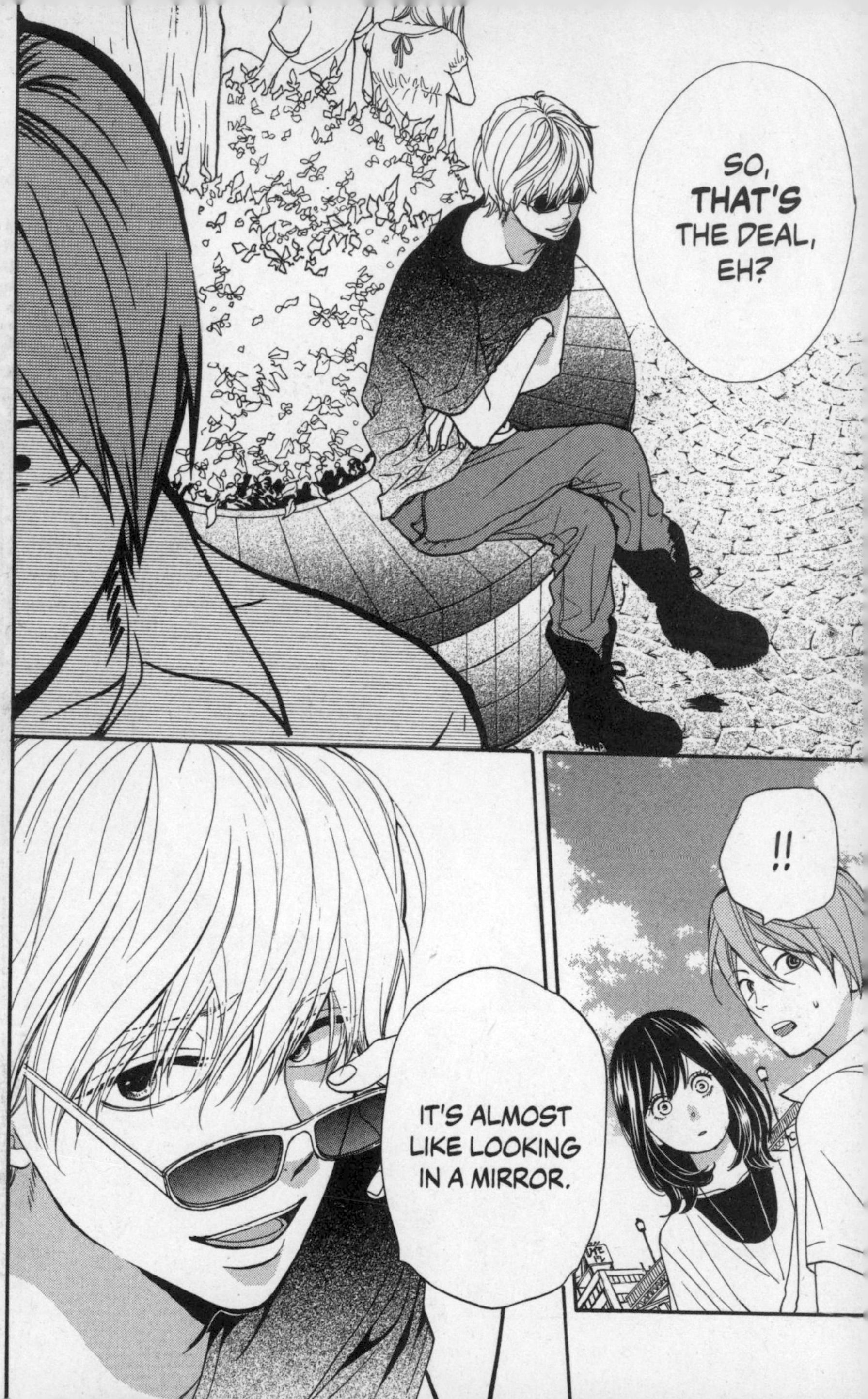
SO, THAT'S THE DEAL, EH?
!!
IT'S ALMOST LIKE LOOKING IN A MIRROR.

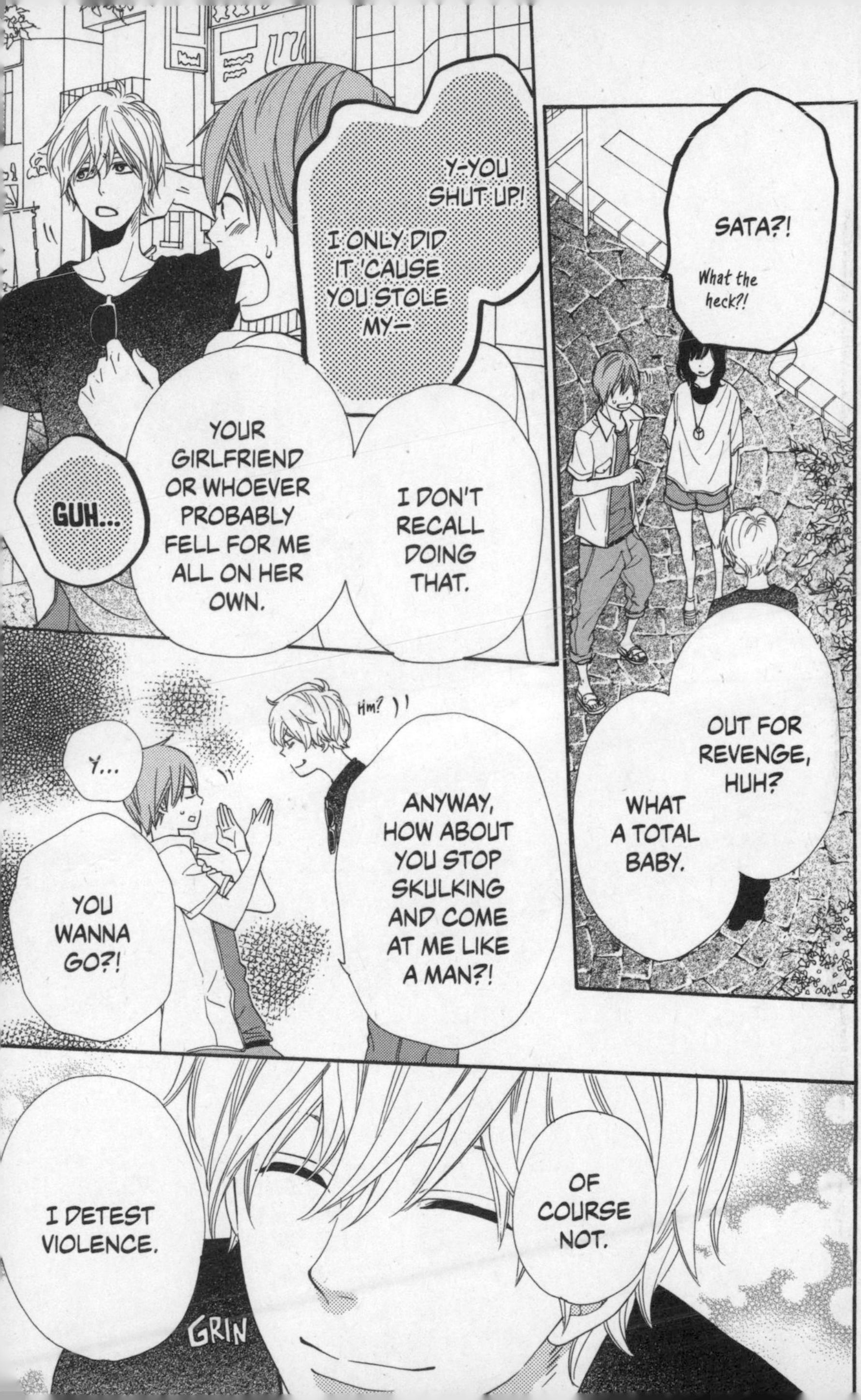
SATA?!
What the heck?!
OUT FOR REVENGE, HUH?
WHAT A TOTAL BABY.
Y-YOU SHUT UP!
I ONLY DID IT 'CAUSE YOU STOLE MY—
I DON'T RECALL DOING THAT.
YOUR GIRLFRIEND OR WHOEVER PROBABLY FELL FOR ME ALL ON HER OWN.
GUH...
Hm?
ANYWAY, HOW ABOUT YOU STOP SKULKING AND COME AT ME LIKE A MAN?!
Y...
YOU WANNA GO?!
OF COURSE NOT.
I DETEST VIOLENCE.
GRIN

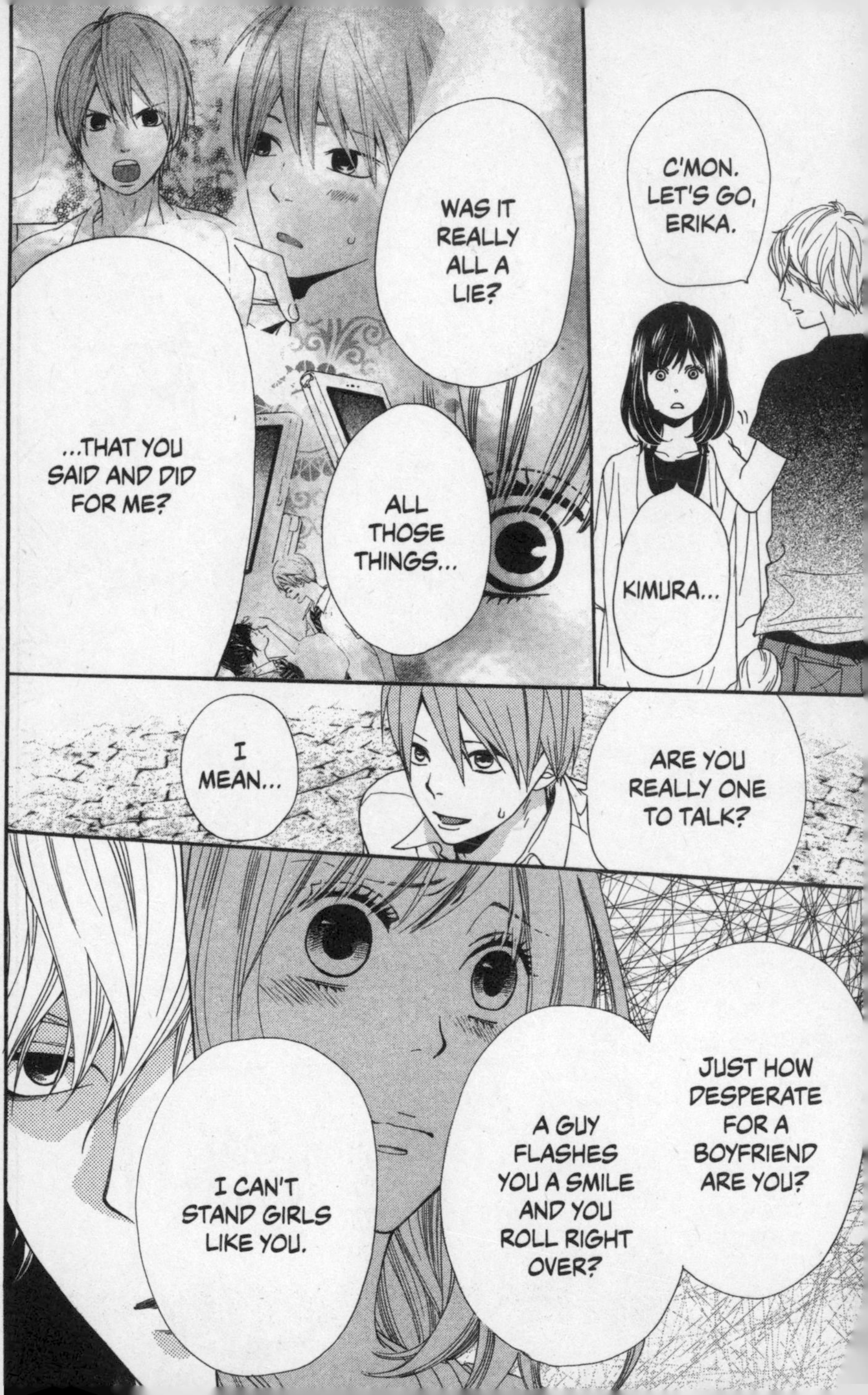
C'MON. LET'S GO, ERIKA.
KIMURA...
WAS IT REALLY ALL A LIE?
ALL THOSE THINGS...
...THAT YOU SAID AND DID FOR ME?
ARE YOU REALLY ONE TO TALK?
I MEAN...
JUST HOW DESPERATE FOR A BOYFRIEND ARE YOU?
A GUY FLASHES YOU A SMILE AND YOU ROLL RIGHT OVER?
I CAN'T STAND GIRLS LIKE YOU.

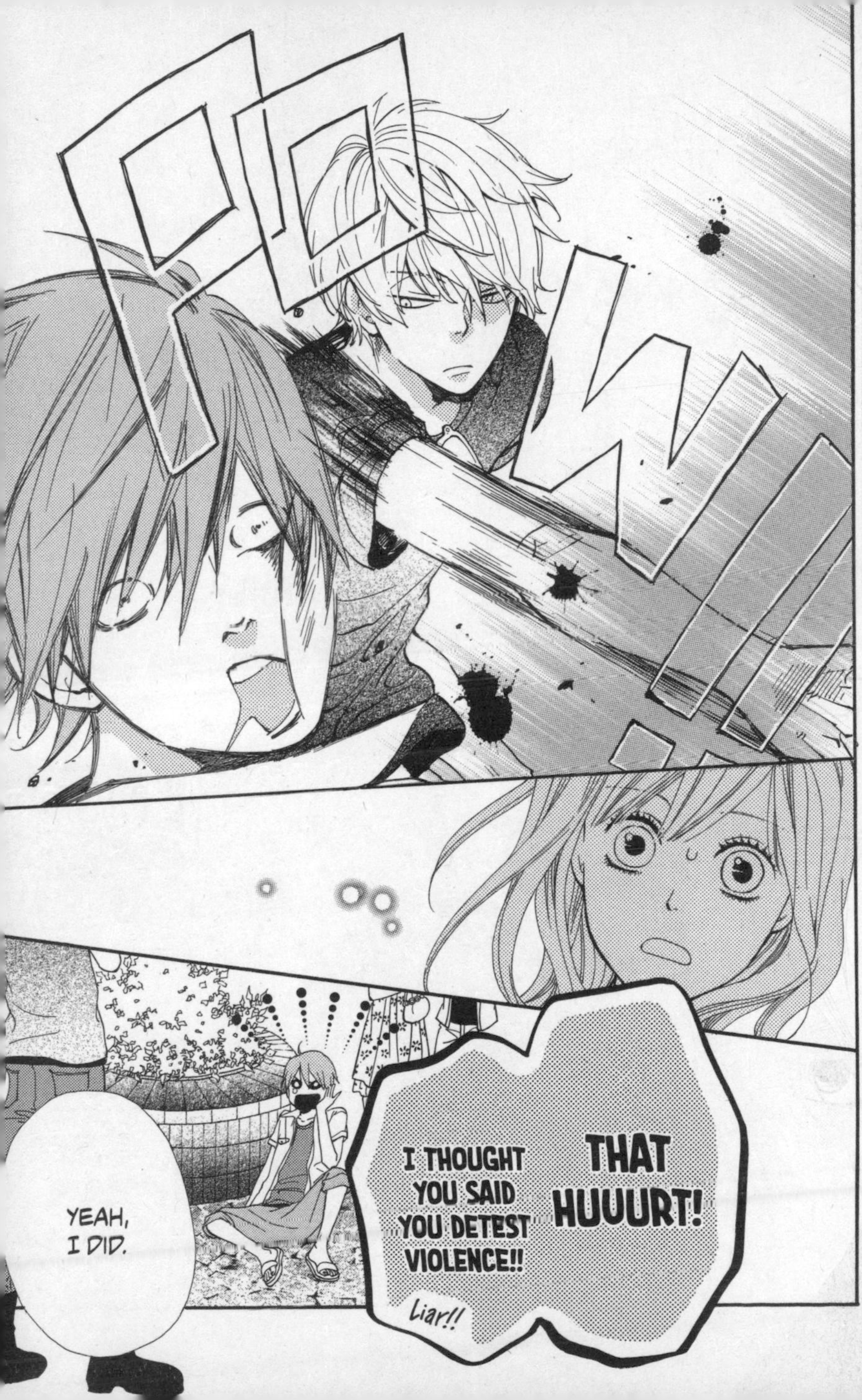
POW!!
THAT HUUURT!
I THOUGHT YOU SAID YOU DETEST VIOLENCE!!
Liar!!
YEAH, I DID.

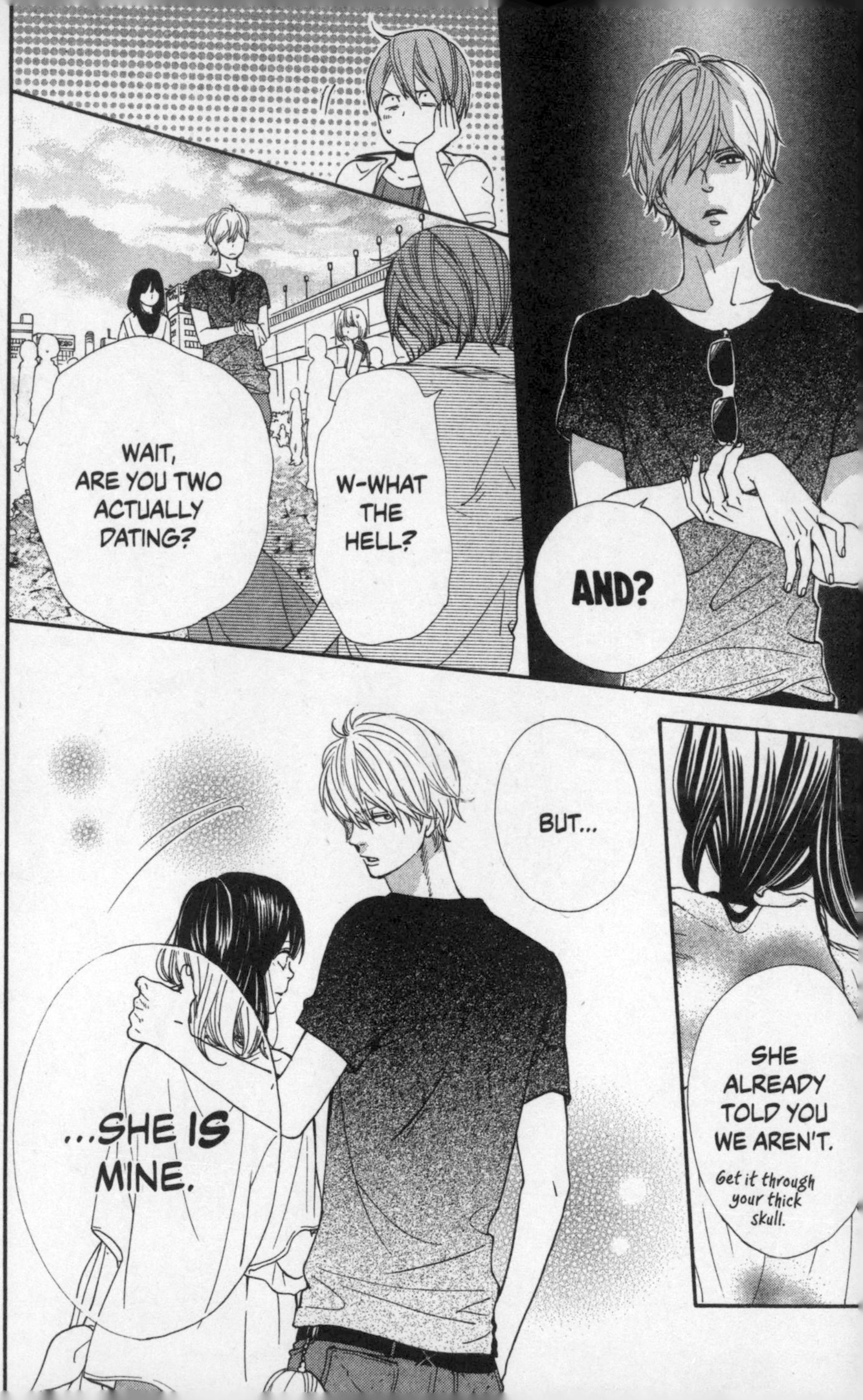
AND?
W-WHAT THE HELL?
WAIT, ARE YOU TWO ACTUALLY DATING?
SHE ALREADY TOLD YOU WE AREN'T.
Get it through your thick skull.
BUT...
...SHE IS MINE.

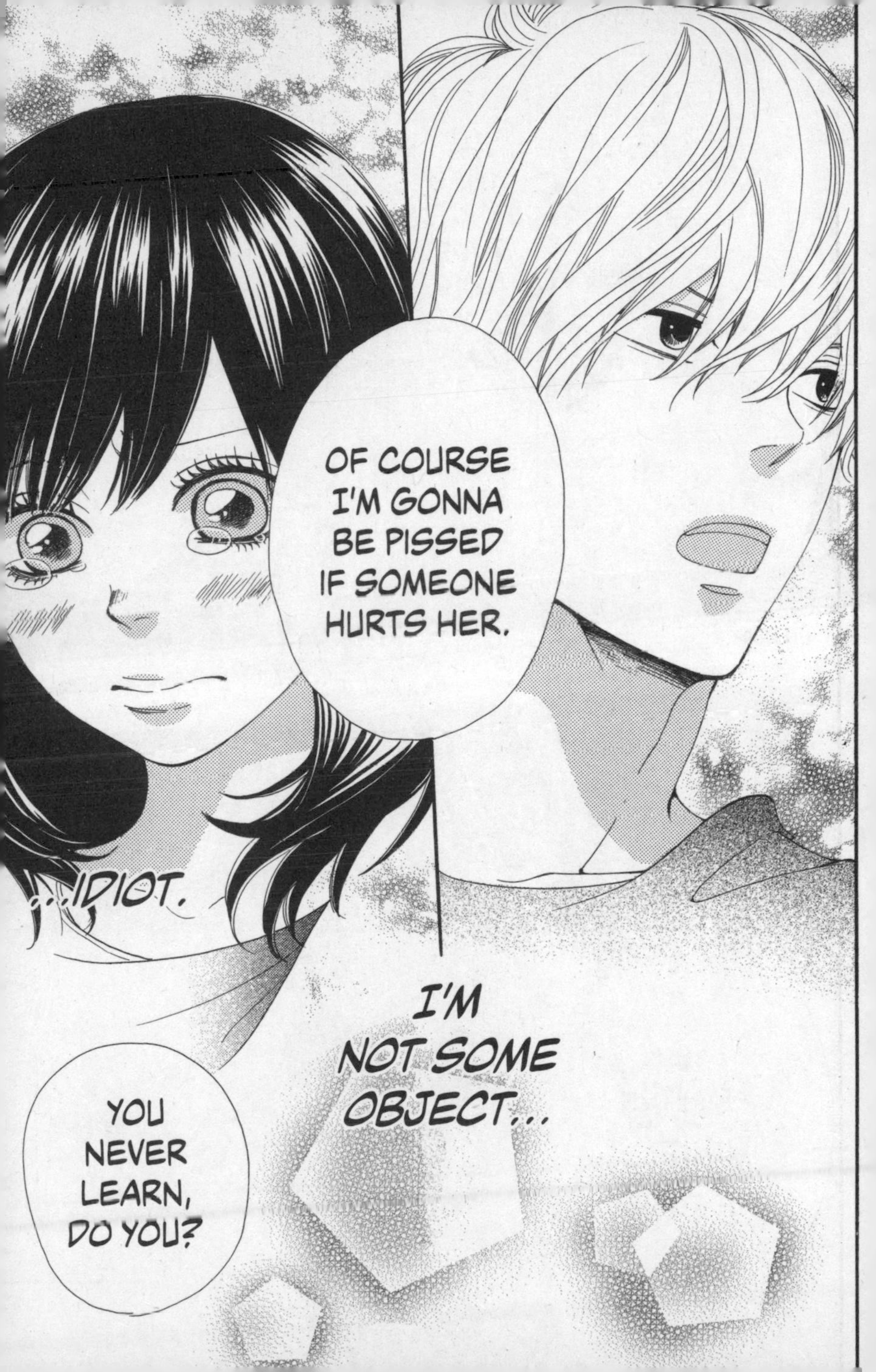
OF COURSE I'M GONNA BE PISSED IF SOMEONE HURTS HER.
...IDIOT.
I'M NOT SOME OBJECT...
YOU NEVER LEARN, DO YOU?

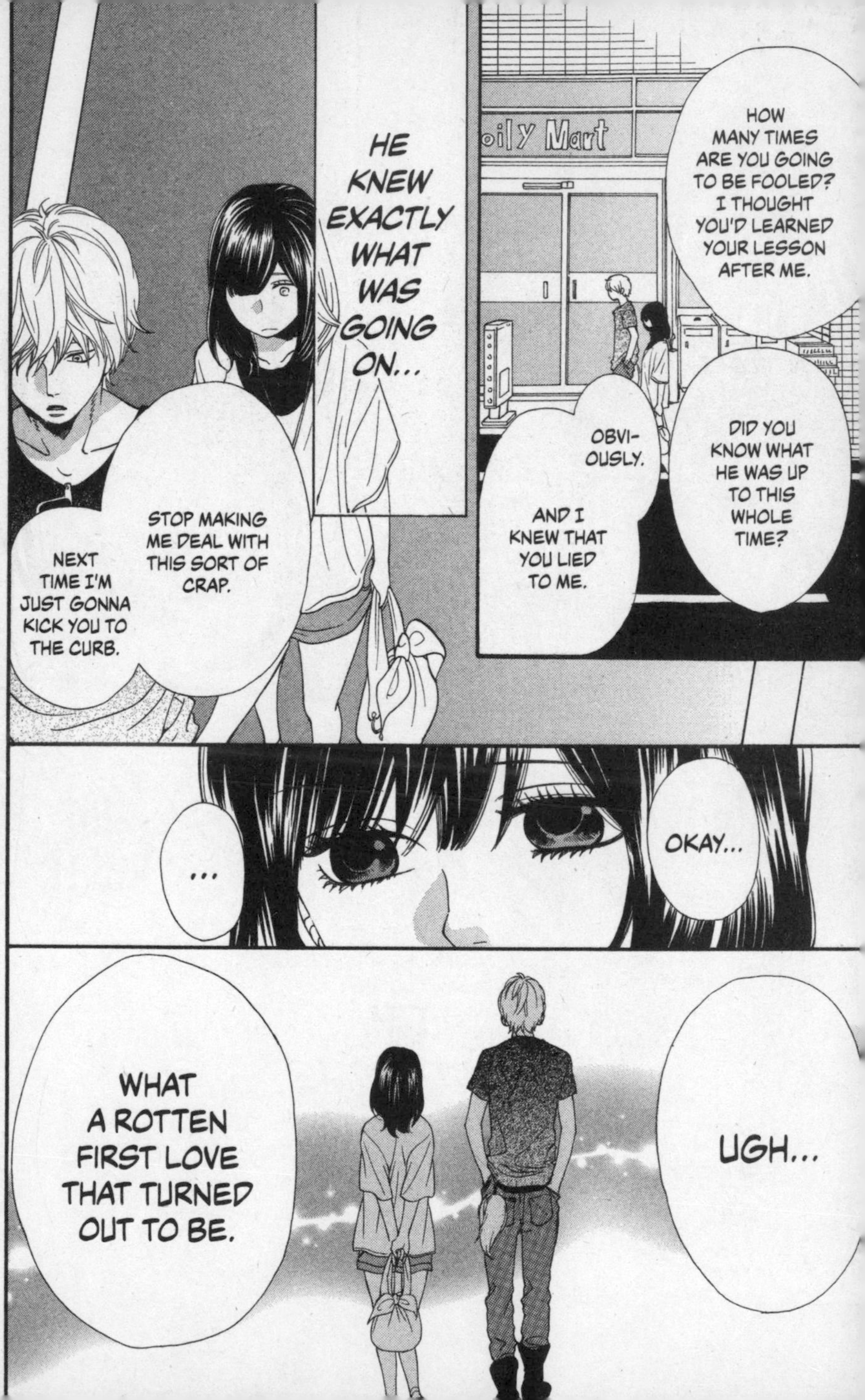
oily Mart
HOW MANY TIMES ARE YOU GOING TO BE FOOLED? I THOUGHT YOU'D LEARNED YOUR LESSON AFTER ME.
DID YOU KNOW WHAT HE WAS UP TO THIS WHOLE TIME?
OBVI-OUSLY.
AND I KNEW THAT YOU LIED TO ME.
HE KNEW EXACTLY WHAT WAS GOING ON...
STOP MAKING ME DEAL WITH THIS SORT OF CRAP.
NEXT TIME I'M JUST GONNA KICK YOU TO THE CURB.
OKAY...
...
UGH...
WHAT A ROTTEN FIRST LOVE THAT TURNED OUT TO BE.

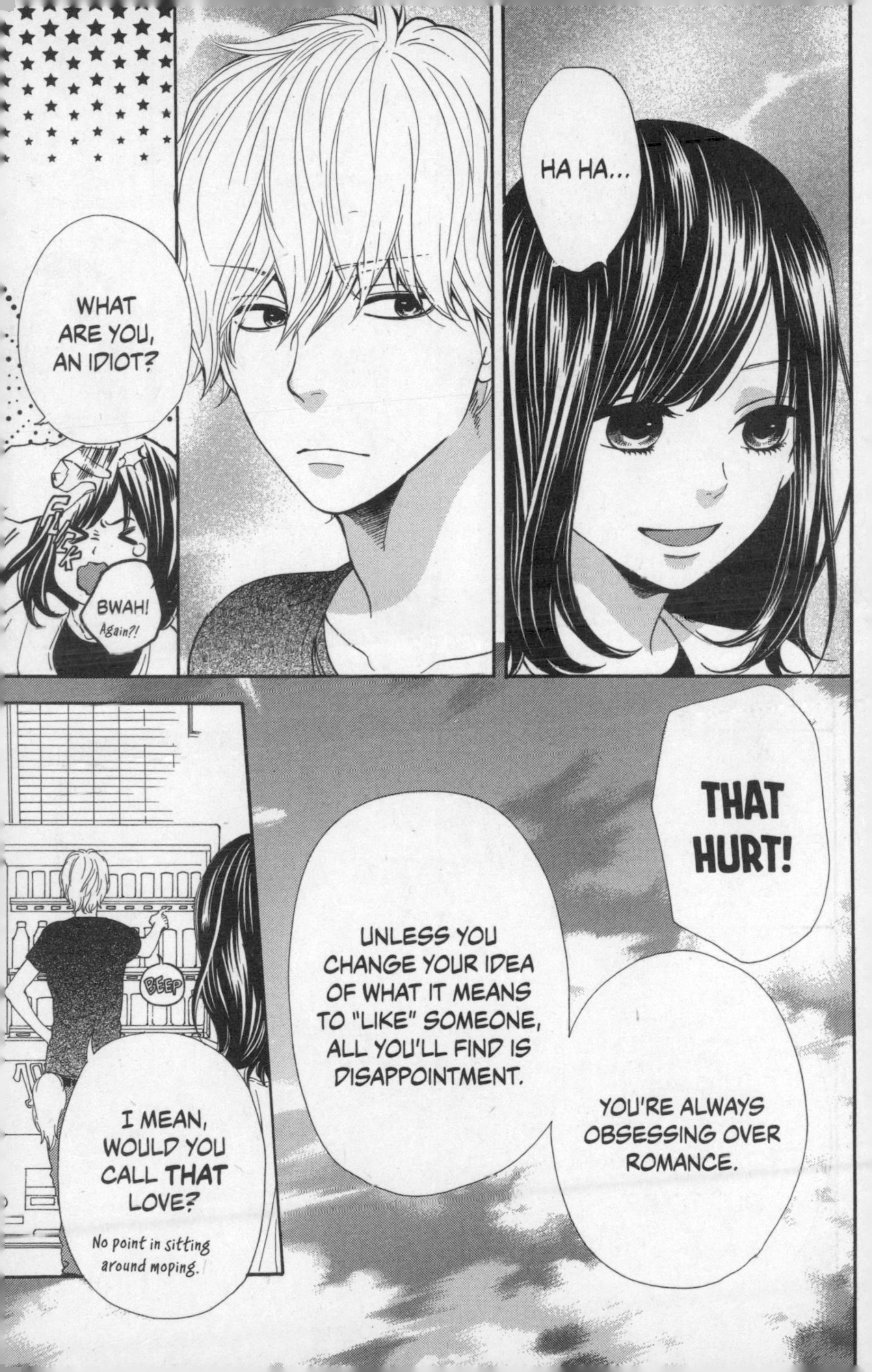
HA HA...
WHAT ARE YOU, AN IDIOT?
FLICK
BWAH!
Again?!
THAT HURT!
YOU'RE ALWAYS OBSESSING OVER ROMANCE.
UNLESS YOU CHANGE YOUR IDEA OF WHAT IT MEANS TO "LIKE" SOMEONE, ALL YOU'LL FIND IS DISAPPOINTMENT.
I MEAN, WOULD YOU CALL THAT LOVE?
No point in sitting around moping.
BEEP

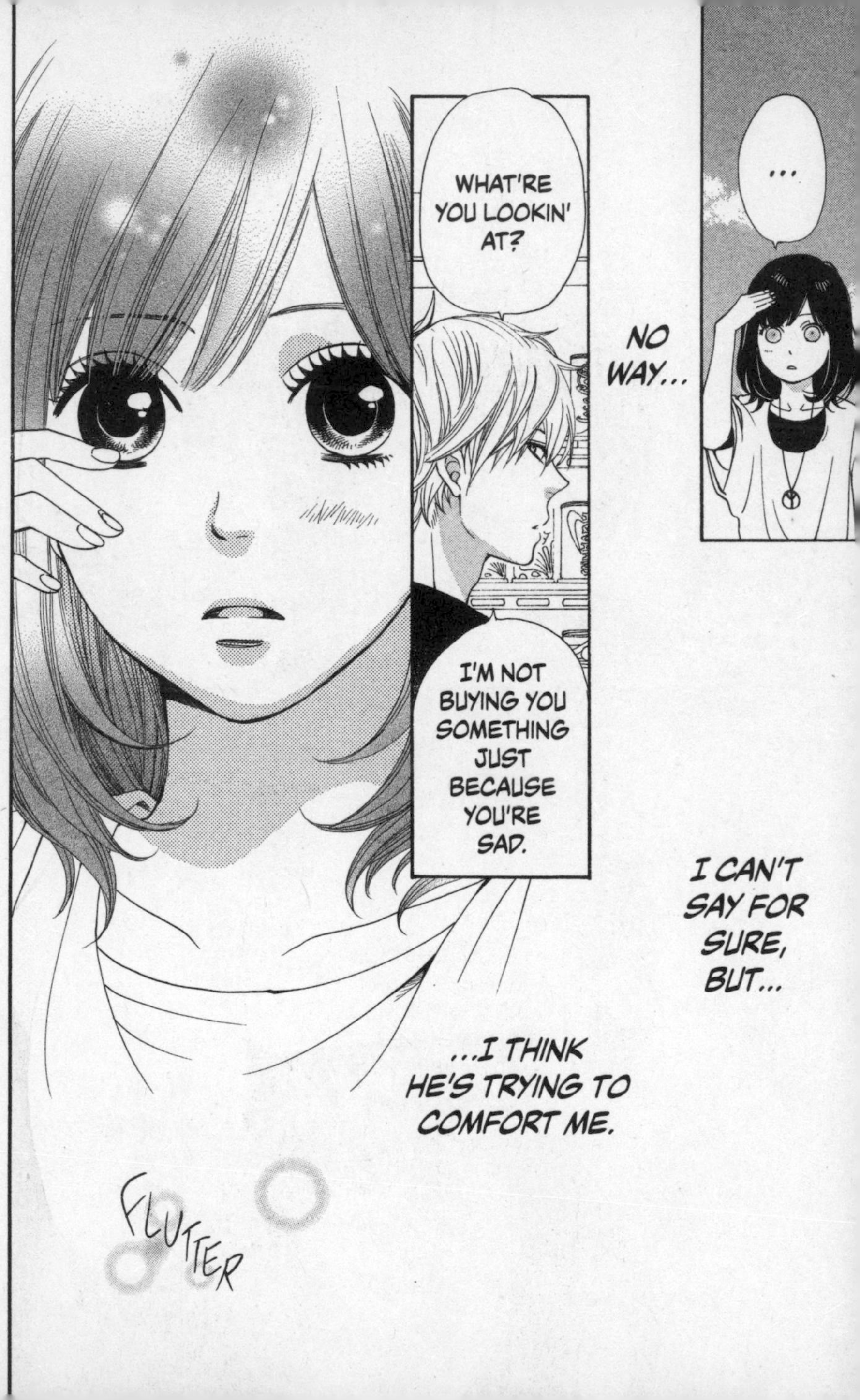
...
NO WAY...
WHAT'RE YOU LOOKIN' AT?
I'M NOT BUYING YOU SOMETHING JUST BECAUSE YOU'RE SAD.
I CAN'T SAY FOR SURE, BUT...
...I THINK HE'S TRYING TO COMFORT ME.
FLUTTER

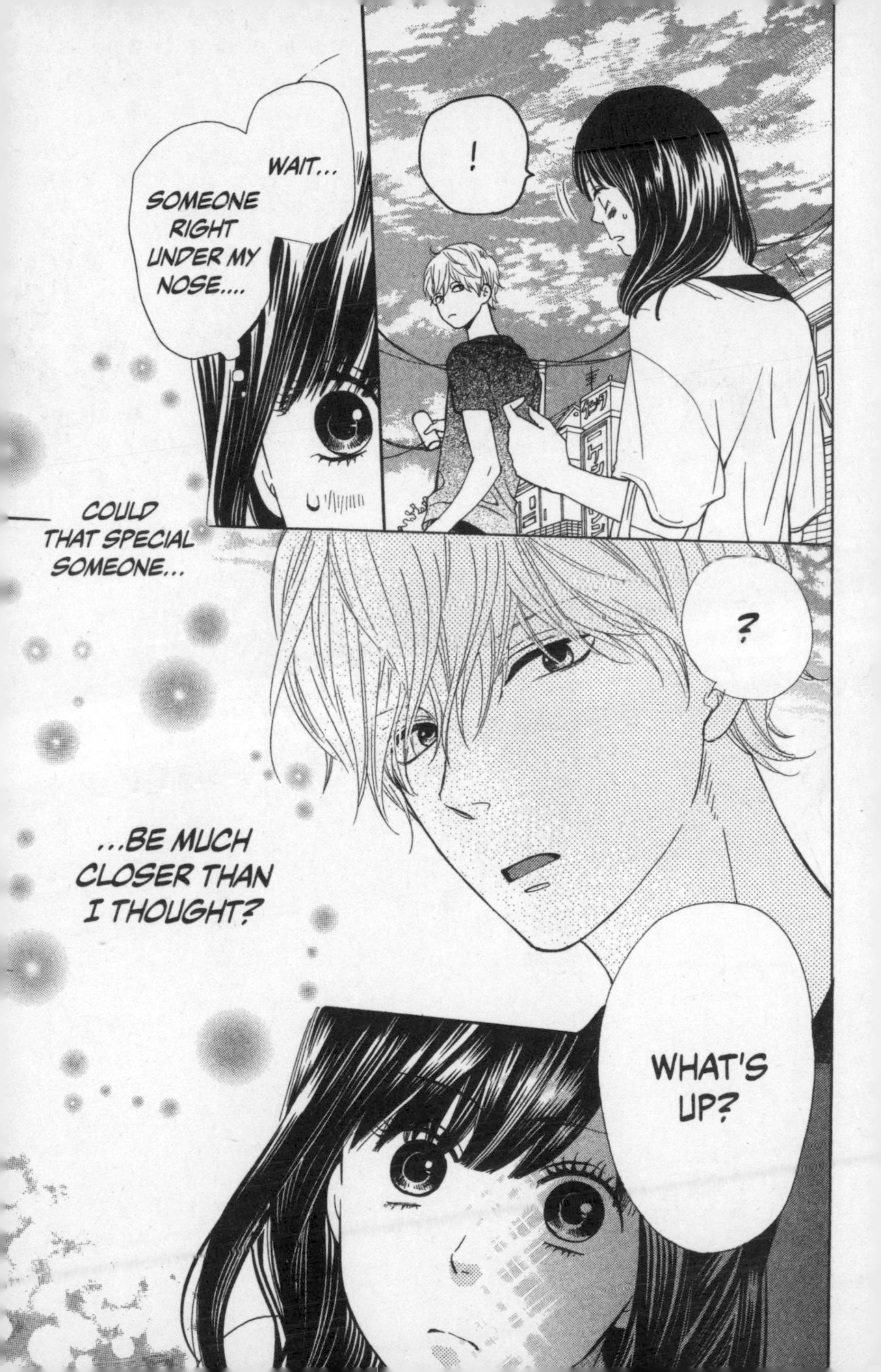
!
WAIT... SOMEONE RIGHT UNDER MY NOSE....
?
—COULD THAT SPECIAL SOMEONE...
...BE MUCH CLOSER THAN I THOUGHT?
WHAT'S UP?

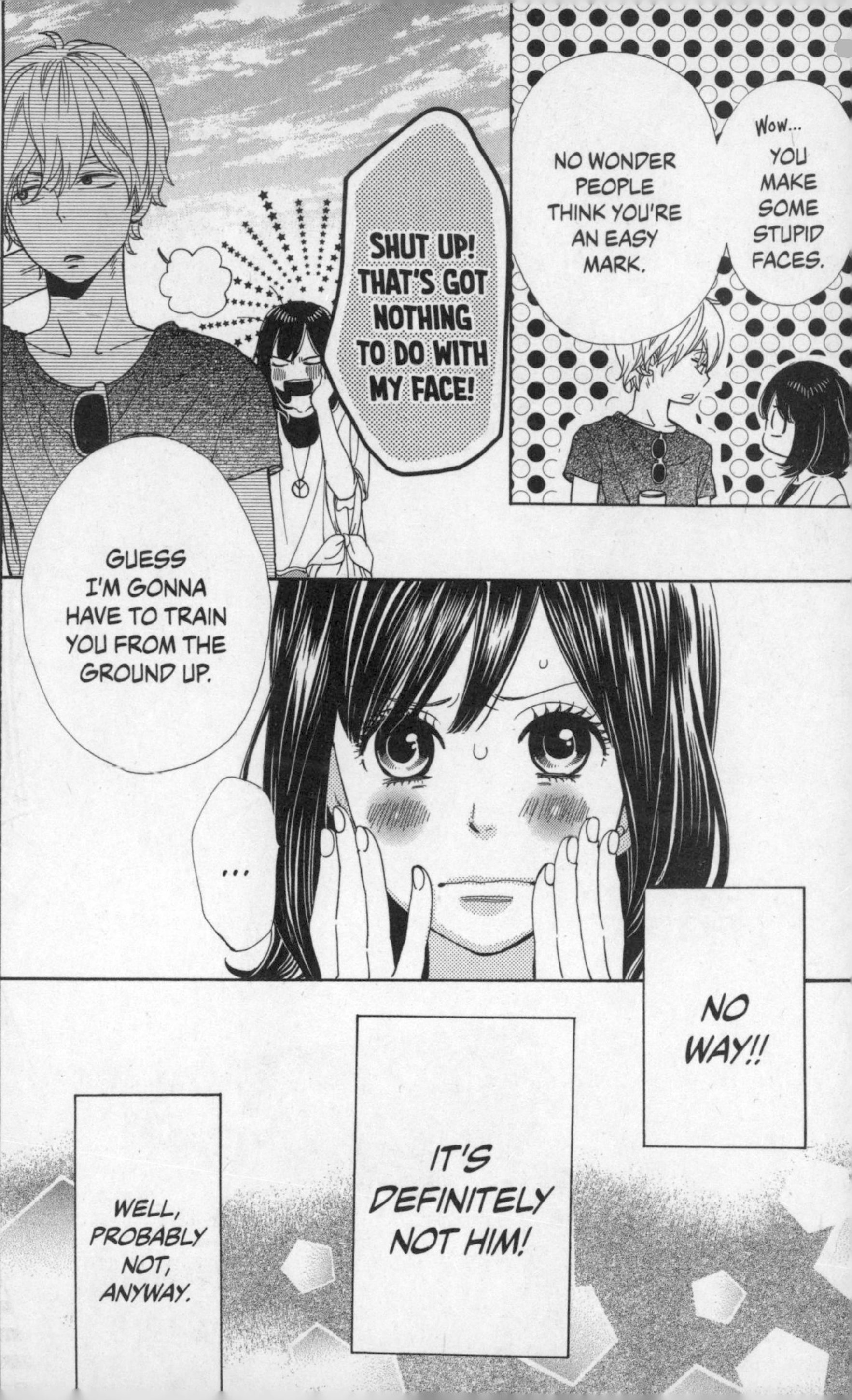
Wow... YOU MAKE SOME STUPID FACES.
NO WONDER PEOPLE THINK YOU'RE AN EASY MARK.
SHUT UP! THAT'S GOT NOTHING TO DO WITH MY FACE!
GUESS I'M GONNA HAVE TO TRAIN YOU FROM THE GROUND UP.
...
NO WAY!!
IT'S DEFINITELY NOT HIM!
WELL, PROBABLY NOT, ANYWAY.

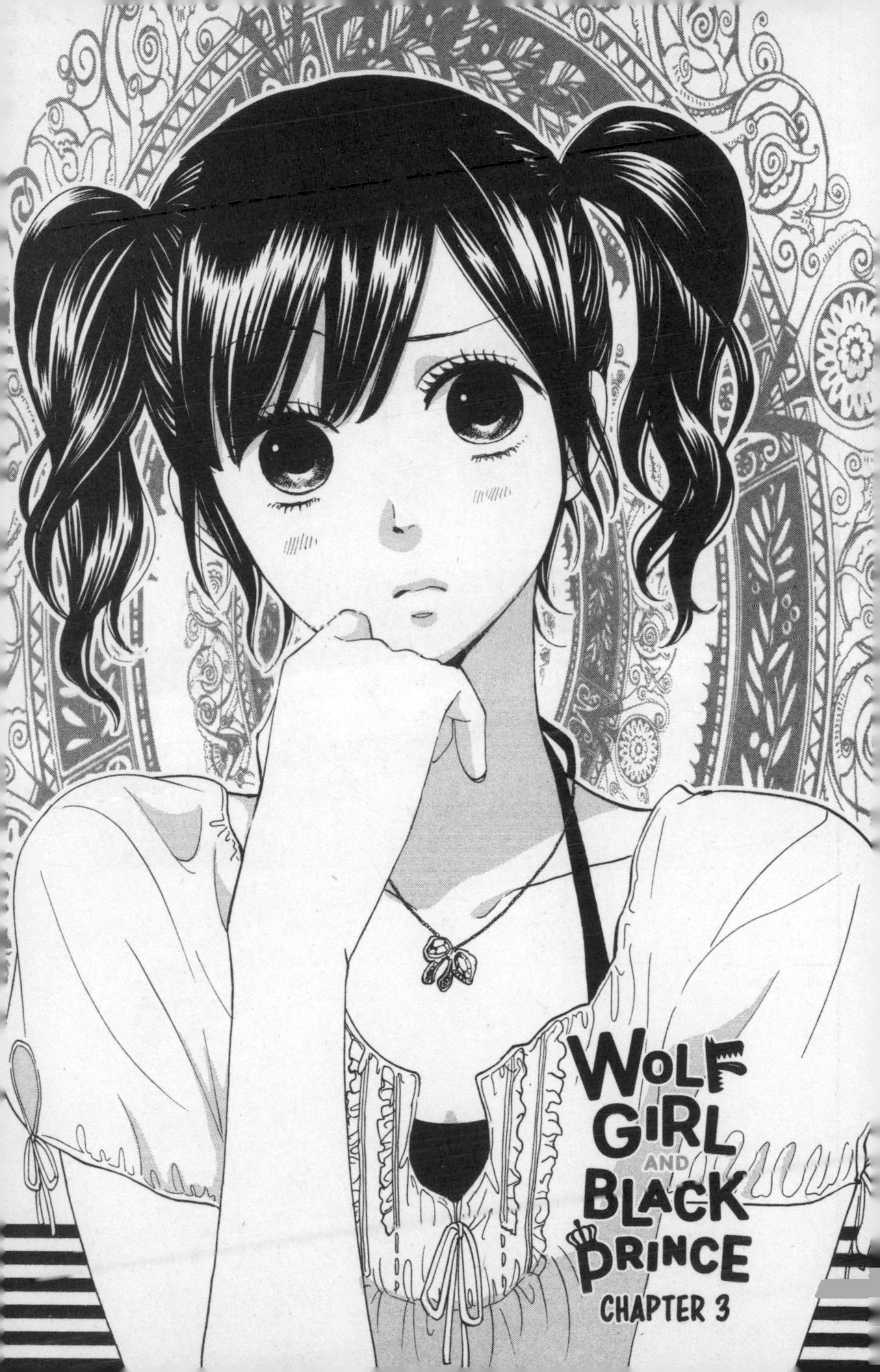
WOLF GIRL AND BLACK PRINCE
CHAPTER 3

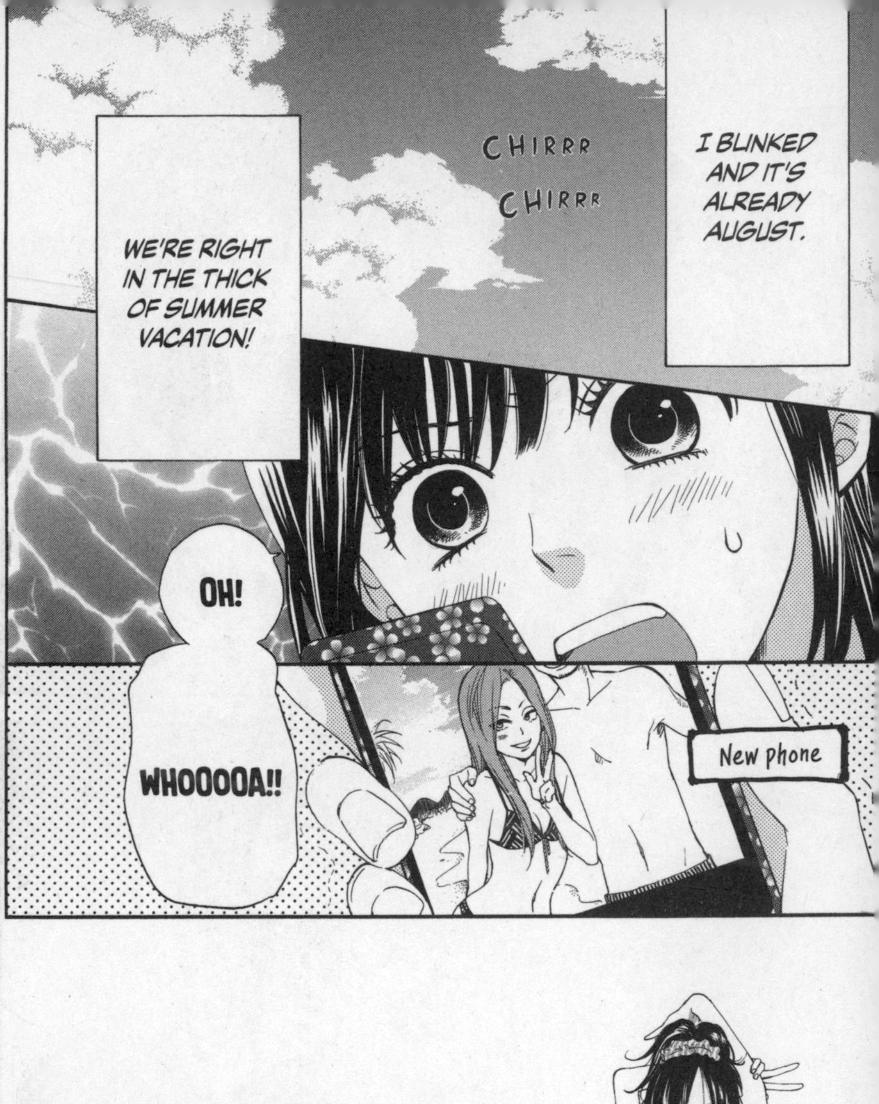
I BLINKED AND IT'S ALREADY AUGUST.
CHIRRR
CHIRRR
WE'RE RIGHT IN THE THICK OF SUMMER VACATION!
OH!
New phone
WHOOOOA!!

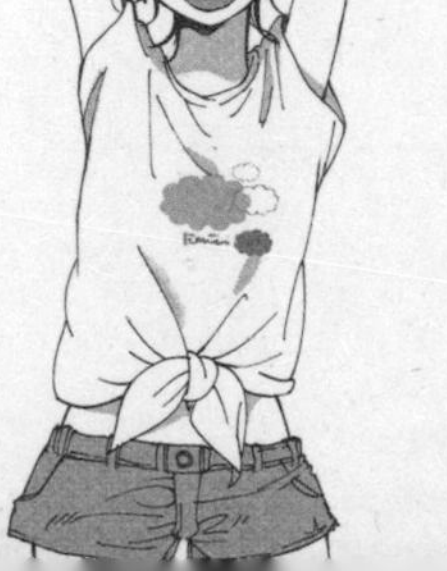

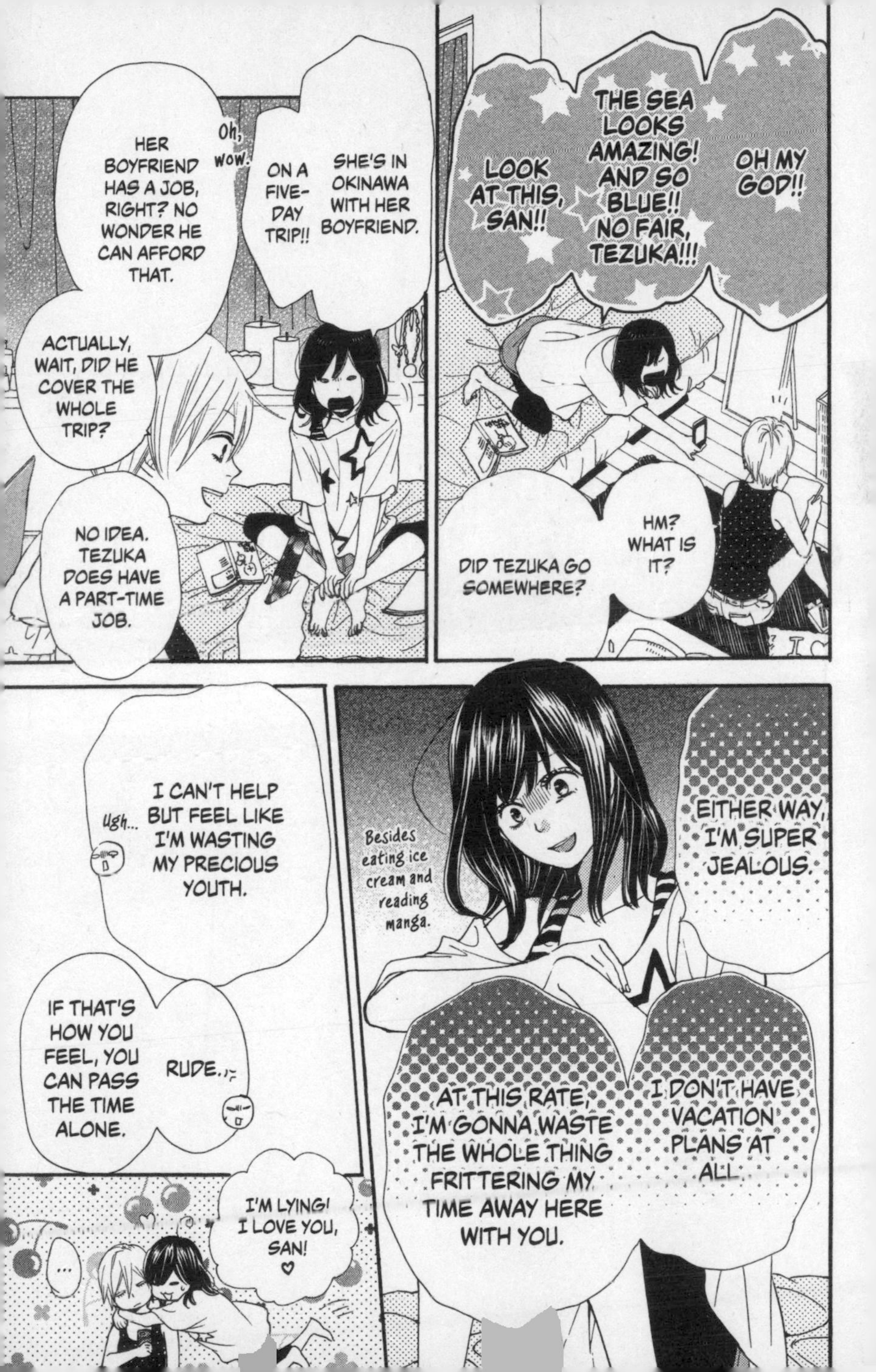
OH MY GOD!!
THE SEA LOOKS AMAZING! AND SO BLUE!! NO FAIR, TEZUKA!!!
LOOK AT THIS, SAN!!
HM? WHAT IS IT?
DID TEZUKA GO SOMEWHERE?
SHE'S IN OKINAWA WITH HER BOYFRIEND.
ON A FIVE-DAY TRIP!!
Oh, wow.
HER BOYFRIEND HAS A JOB, RIGHT? NO WONDER HE CAN AFFORD THAT.
ACTUALLY, WAIT, DID HE COVER THE WHOLE TRIP?
NO IDEA. TEZUKA DOES HAVE A PART-TIME JOB.
EITHER WAY, I'M SUPER JEALOUS.
I DON'T HAVE VACATION PLANS AT ALL.
AT THIS RATE, I'M GONNA WASTE THE WHOLE THING FRITTERING MY TIME AWAY HERE WITH YOU.
Besides eating ice cream and reading manga.
I CAN'T HELP BUT FEEL LIKE I'M WASTING MY PRECIOUS YOUTH.
Ugh...
IF THAT'S HOW YOU FEEL, YOU CAN PASS THE TIME ALONE.
RUDE.
I'M LYING! I LOVE YOU, SAN! ♡
...

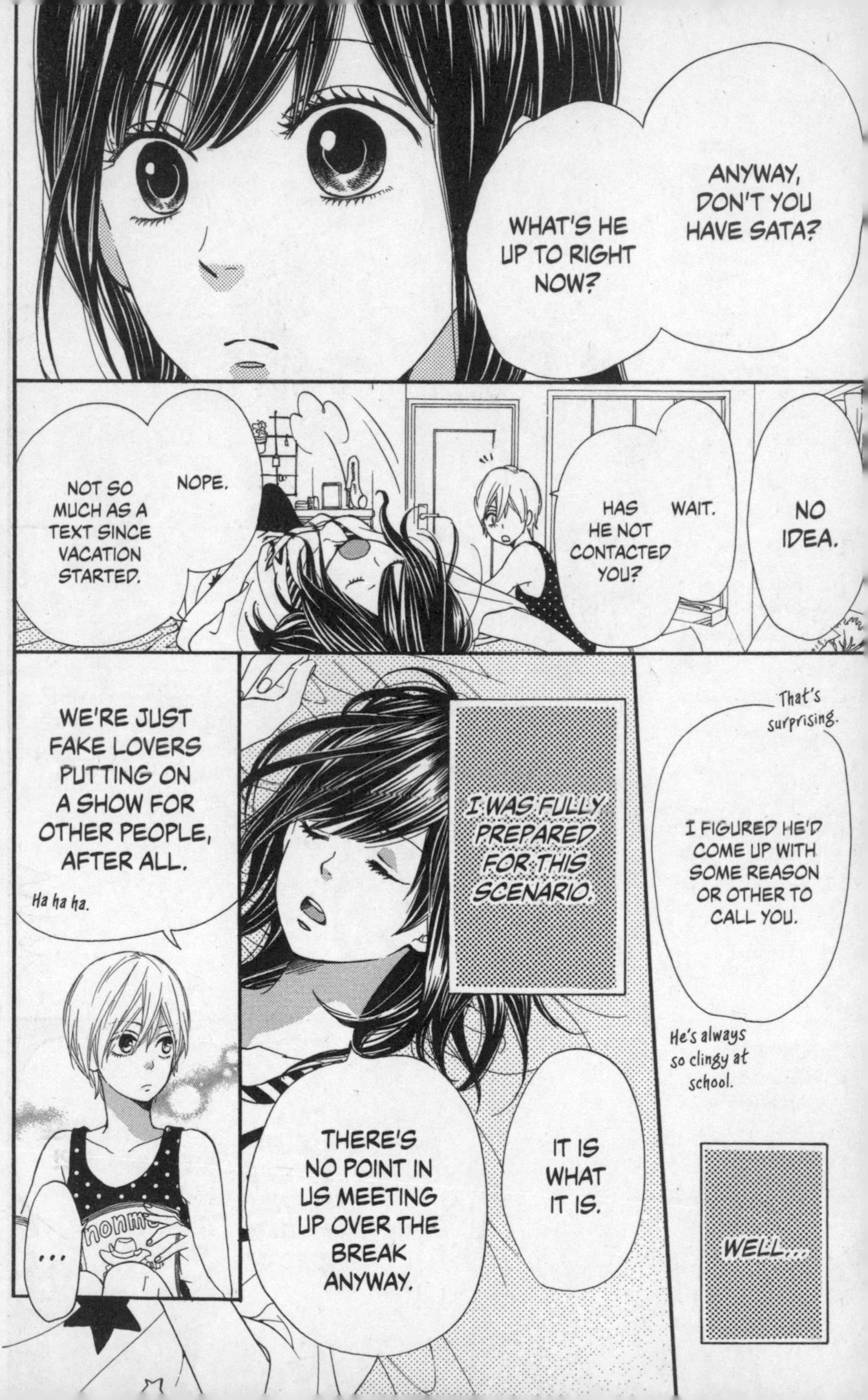
ANYWAY, DON'T YOU HAVE SATA?
WHAT'S HE UP TO RIGHT NOW?
NO IDEA.
WAIT.
HAS HE NOT CONTACTED YOU?
NOPE.
NOT SO MUCH AS A TEXT SINCE VACATION STARTED.
That's surprising.
I FIGURED HE'D COME UP WITH SOME REASON OR OTHER TO CALL YOU.
He's always so clingy at school.
WELL...
I WAS FULLY PREPARED FOR THIS SCENARIO.
IT IS WHAT IT IS.
THERE'S NO POINT IN US MEETING UP OVER THE BREAK ANYWAY.
WE'RE JUST FAKE LOVERS PUTTING ON A SHOW FOR OTHER PEOPLE, AFTER ALL.
Ha ha ha.
...

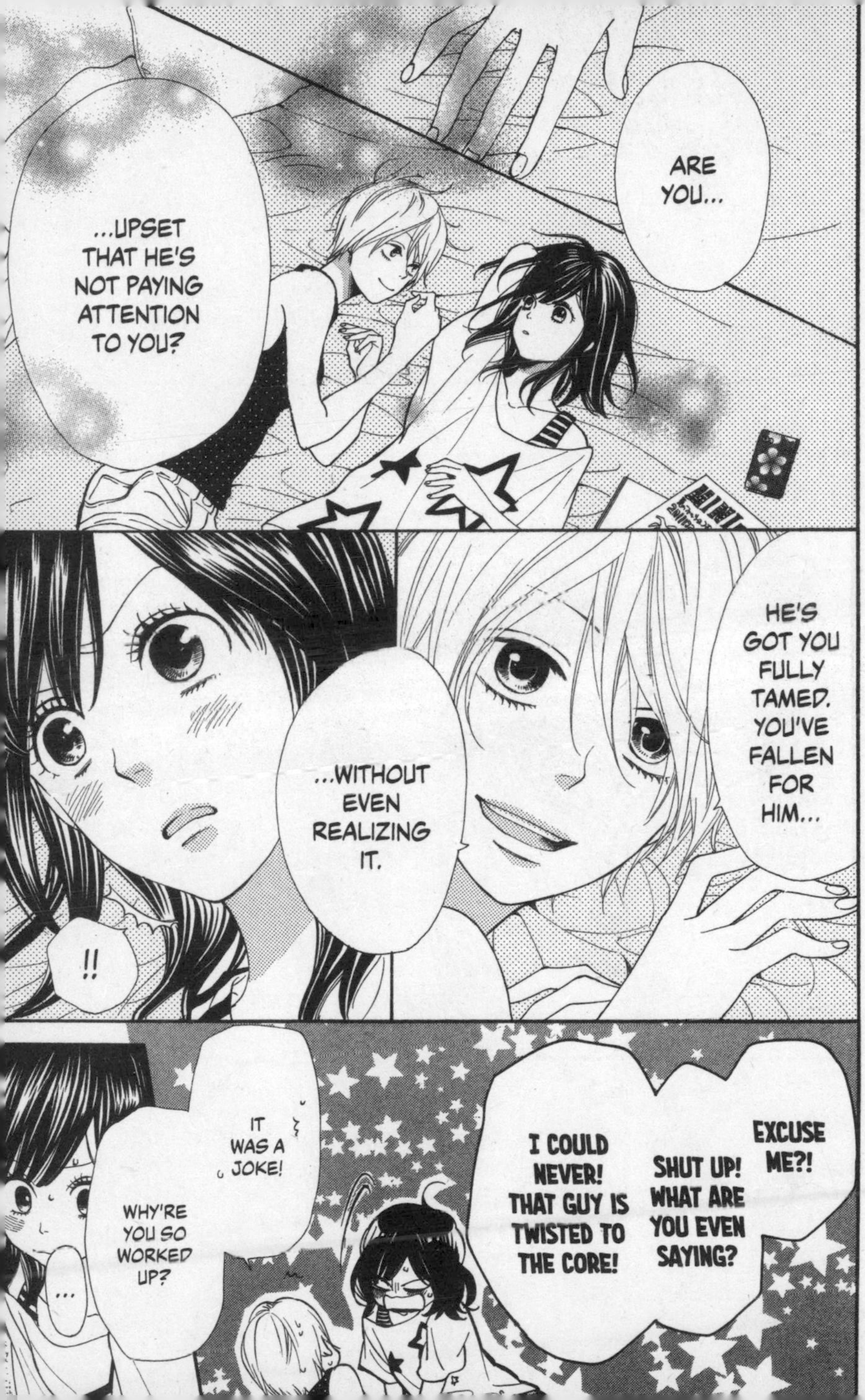
ARE YOU...
...UPSET THAT HE'S NOT PAYING ATTENTION TO YOU?
HE'S GOT YOU FULLY TAMED. YOU'VE FALLEN FOR HIM...
...WITHOUT EVEN REALIZING IT.
!!
EXCUSE ME?!
SHUT UP! WHAT ARE YOU EVEN SAYING?
I COULD NEVER! THAT GUY IS TWISTED TO THE CORE!
IT WAS A JOKE!
WHY'RE YOU SO WORKED UP?
...

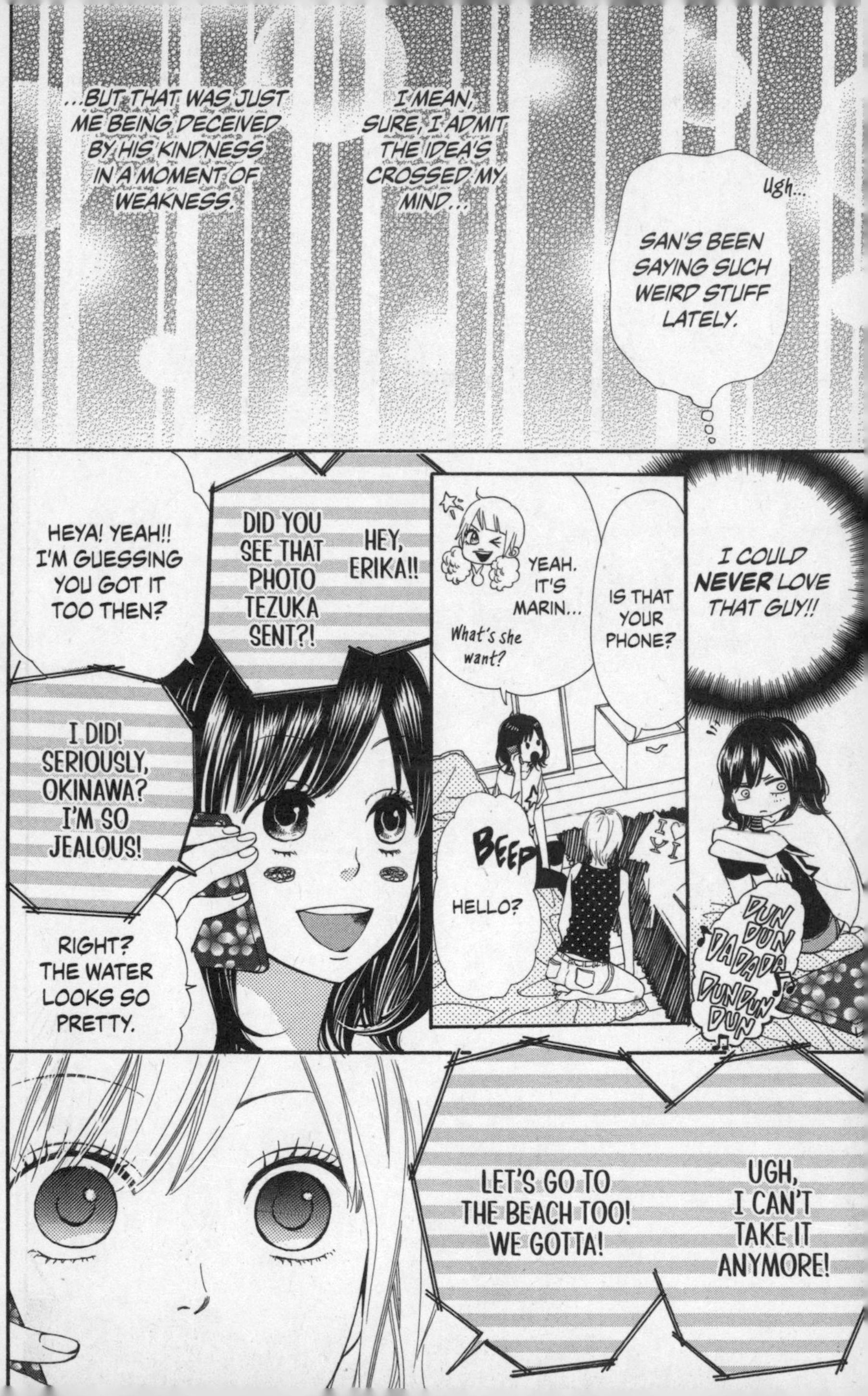
Ugh...
SAN'S BEEN SAYING SUCH WEIRD STUFF LATELY.
I MEAN, SURE, I ADMIT THE IDEA'S CROSSED MY MIND...
...BUT THAT WAS JUST ME BEING DECEIVED BY HIS KINDNESS IN A MOMENT OF WEAKNESS.
I COULD **NEVER** LOVE THAT GUY!!
DUN DUN DADADA DUNDUN DUN
IS THAT YOUR PHONE?
YEAH. IT'S MARIN...
What's she want?
BEEP
HELLO?
HEY, ERIKA!!
DID YOU SEE THAT PHOTO TEZUKA SENT?!
HEYA! YEAH!! I'M GUESSING YOU GOT IT TOO THEN?
I DID! SERIOUSLY, OKINAWA? I'M SO JEALOUS!
RIGHT? THE WATER LOOKS SO PRETTY.
UGH, I CAN'T TAKE IT ANYMORE!
LET'S GO TO THE BEACH TOO! WE GOTTA!

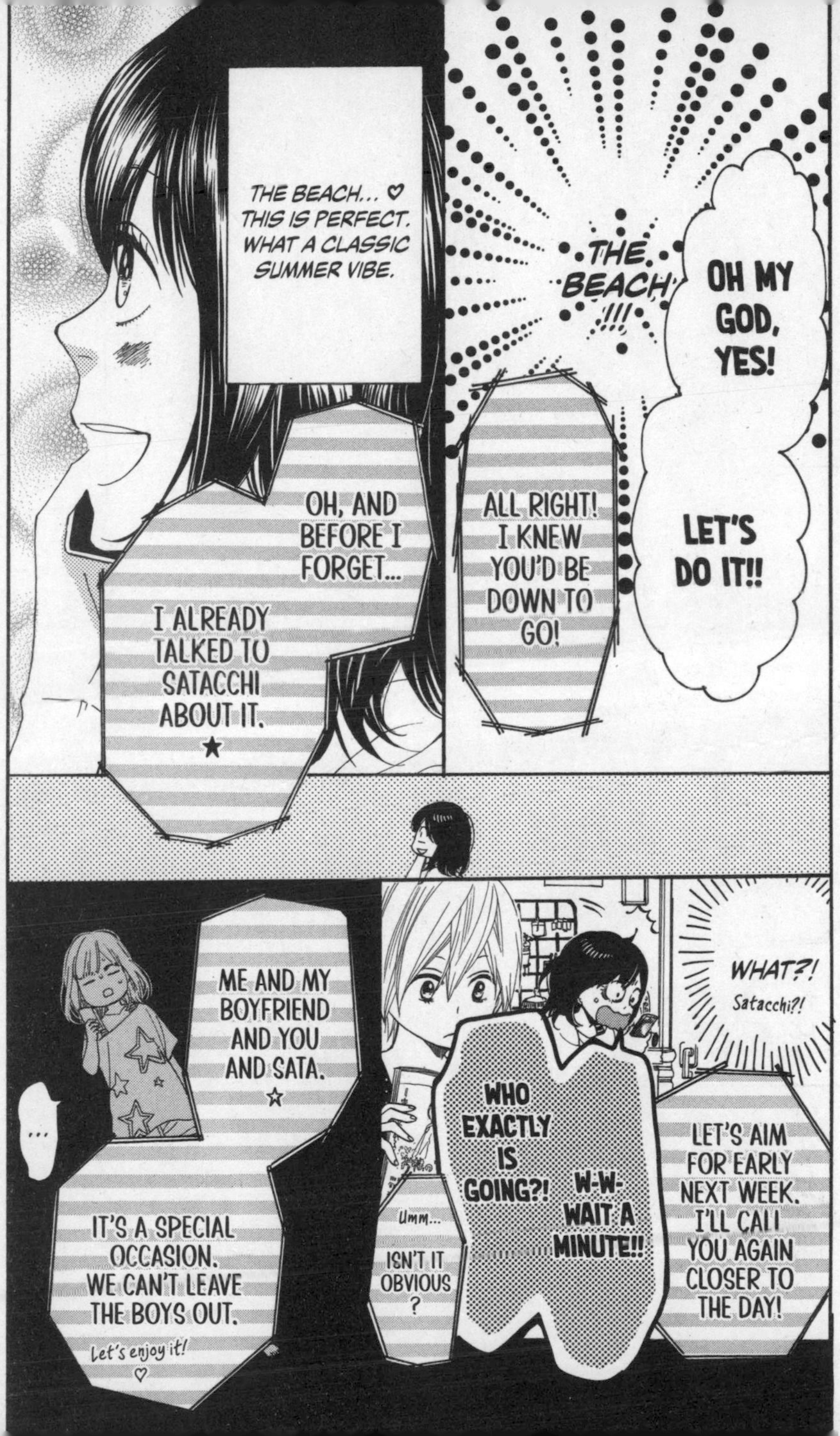
THE BEACH!!!
OH MY GOD, YES!
LET'S DO IT!!
ALL RIGHT! I KNEW YOU'D BE DOWN TO GO!
THE BEACH... ♡ THIS IS PERFECT. WHAT A CLASSIC SUMMER VIBE.
OH, AND BEFORE I FORGET...
I ALREADY TALKED TO SATACCHI ABOUT IT. ★
WHAT?! Satacchi?!
LET'S AIM FOR EARLY NEXT WEEK. I'LL CALL YOU AGAIN CLOSER TO THE DAY!
W-W-WAIT A MINUTE!!
WHO EXACTLY IS GOING?!
Umm... ISN'T IT OBVIOUS?
ME AND MY BOYFRIEND AND YOU AND SATA. ☆
...
IT'S A SPECIAL OCCASION. WE CAN'T LEAVE THE BOYS OUT. Let's enjoy it! ♡

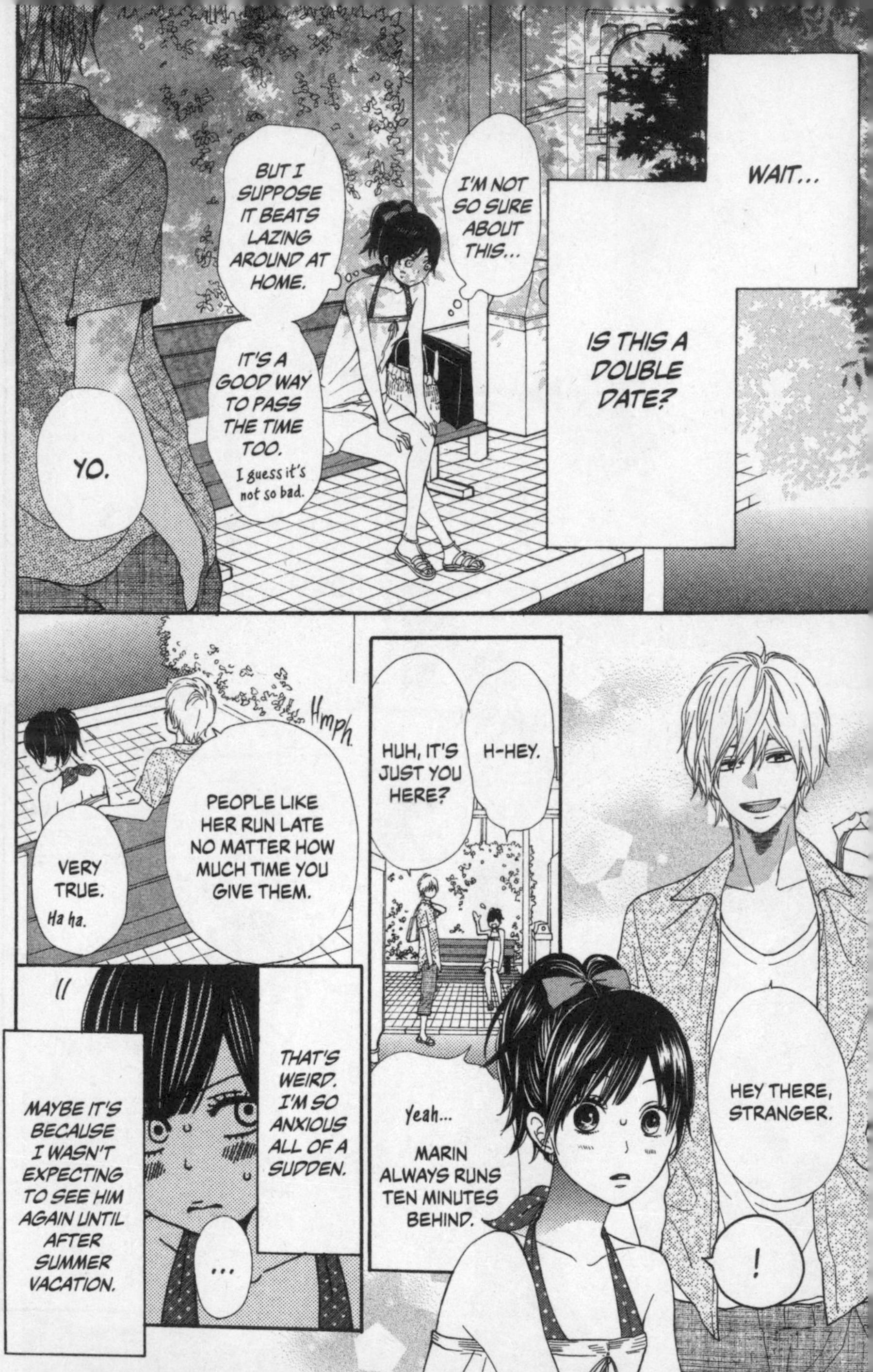
WAIT...
IS THIS A DOUBLE DATE?
I'M NOT SO SURE ABOUT THIS...
BUT I SUPPOSE IT BEATS LAZING AROUND AT HOME.
IT'S A GOOD WAY TO PASS THE TIME TOO.
I guess it's not so bad.
YO.
HEY THERE, STRANGER.
!
H-HEY.
HUH, IT'S JUST YOU HERE?
Yeah...
MARIN ALWAYS RUNS TEN MINUTES BEHIND.
Hmph
PEOPLE LIKE HER RUN LATE NO MATTER HOW MUCH TIME YOU GIVE THEM.
VERY TRUE.
Ha ha.
THAT'S WEIRD. I'M SO ANXIOUS ALL OF A SUDDEN.
MAYBE IT'S BECAUSE I WASN'T EXPECTING TO SEE HIM AGAIN UNTIL AFTER SUMMER VACATION.
...

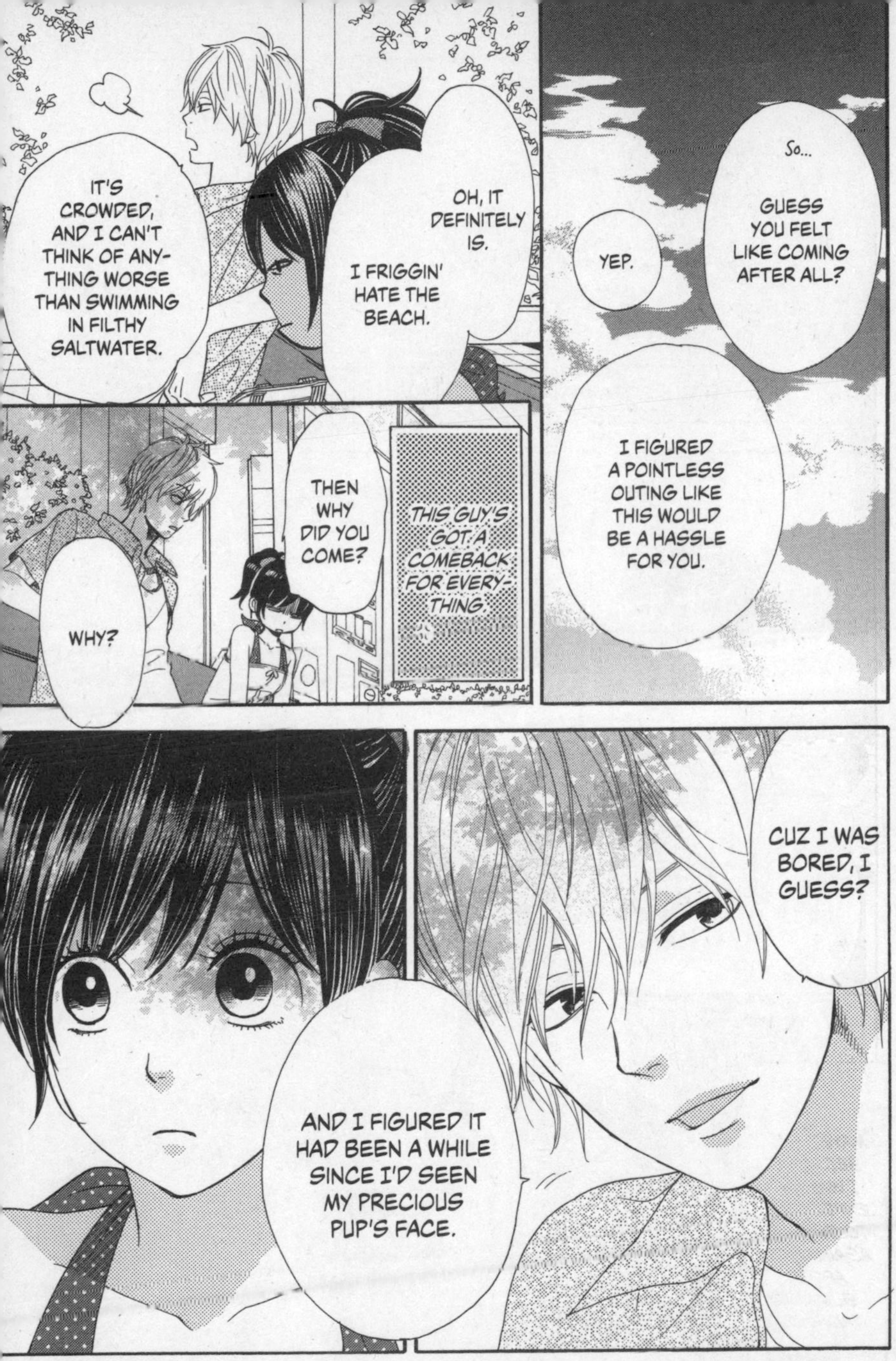
So...
GUESS YOU FELT LIKE COMING AFTER ALL?
YEP.
I FIGURED A POINTLESS OUTING LIKE THIS WOULD BE A HASSLE FOR YOU.
OH, IT DEFINITELY IS.
I FRIGGIN' HATE THE BEACH.
IT'S CROWDED, AND I CAN'T THINK OF ANY-THING WORSE THAN SWIMMING IN FILTHY SALTWATER.
THIS GUY'S GOT A COMEBACK FOR EVERY-THING.
THEN WHY DID YOU COME?
WHY?
CUZ I WAS BORED, I GUESS?
AND I FIGURED IT HAD BEEN A WHILE SINCE I'D SEEN MY PRECIOUS PUP'S FACE.

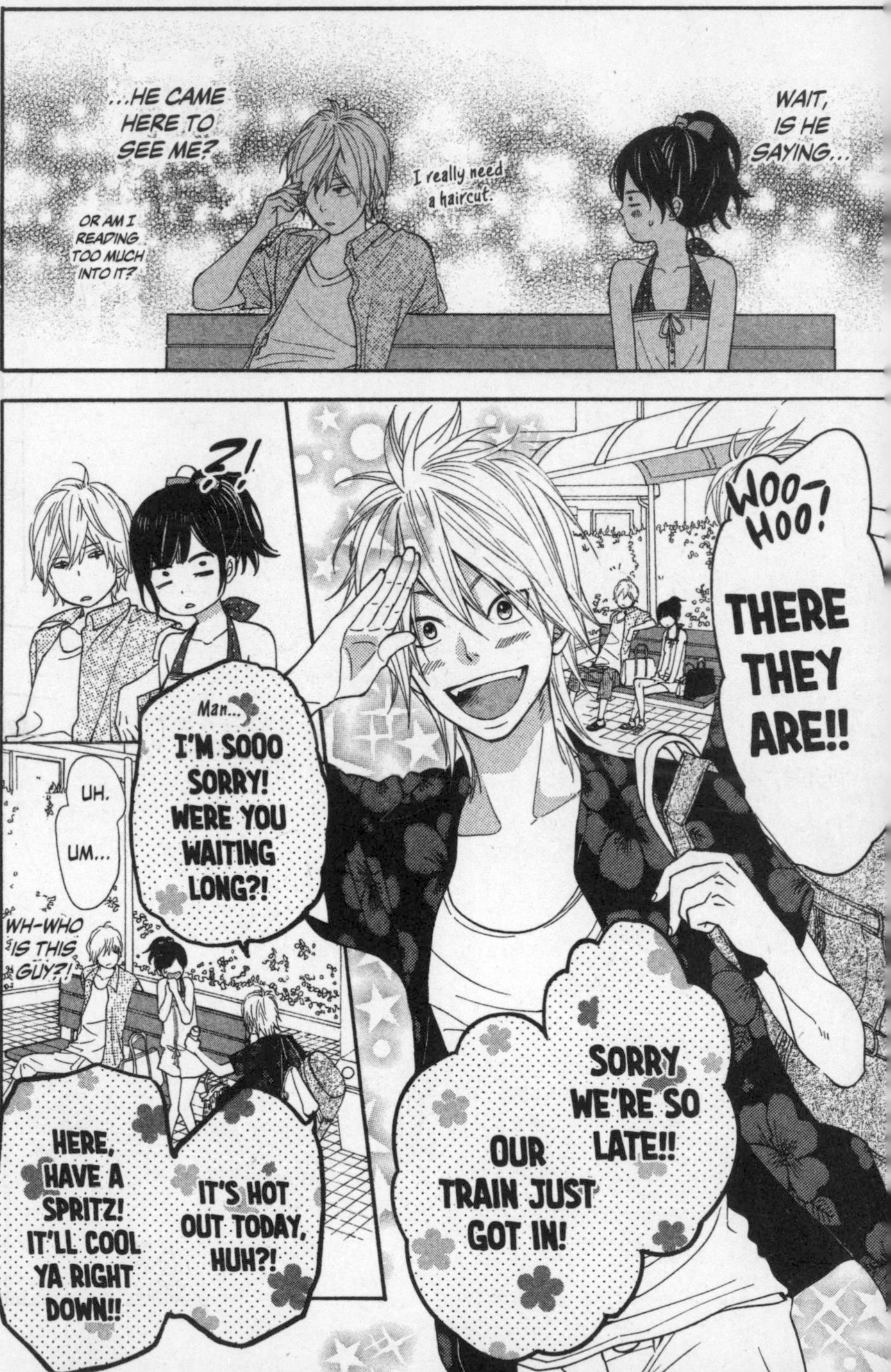
WAIT, IS HE SAYING...
...HE CAME HERE TO SEE ME?
OR AM I READING TOO MUCH INTO IT?
I really need a haircut.
WOO-HOO!
THERE THEY ARE!!
SORRY WE'RE SO LATE!!
OUR TRAIN JUST GOT IN!
Z?!
Man...
I'M SOOO SORRY! WERE YOU WAITING LONG?!
UH.
UM...
WH-WHO IS THIS GUY?!
IT'S HOT OUT TODAY, HUH?!
HERE, HAVE A SPRITZ! IT'LL COOL YA RIGHT DOWN!!

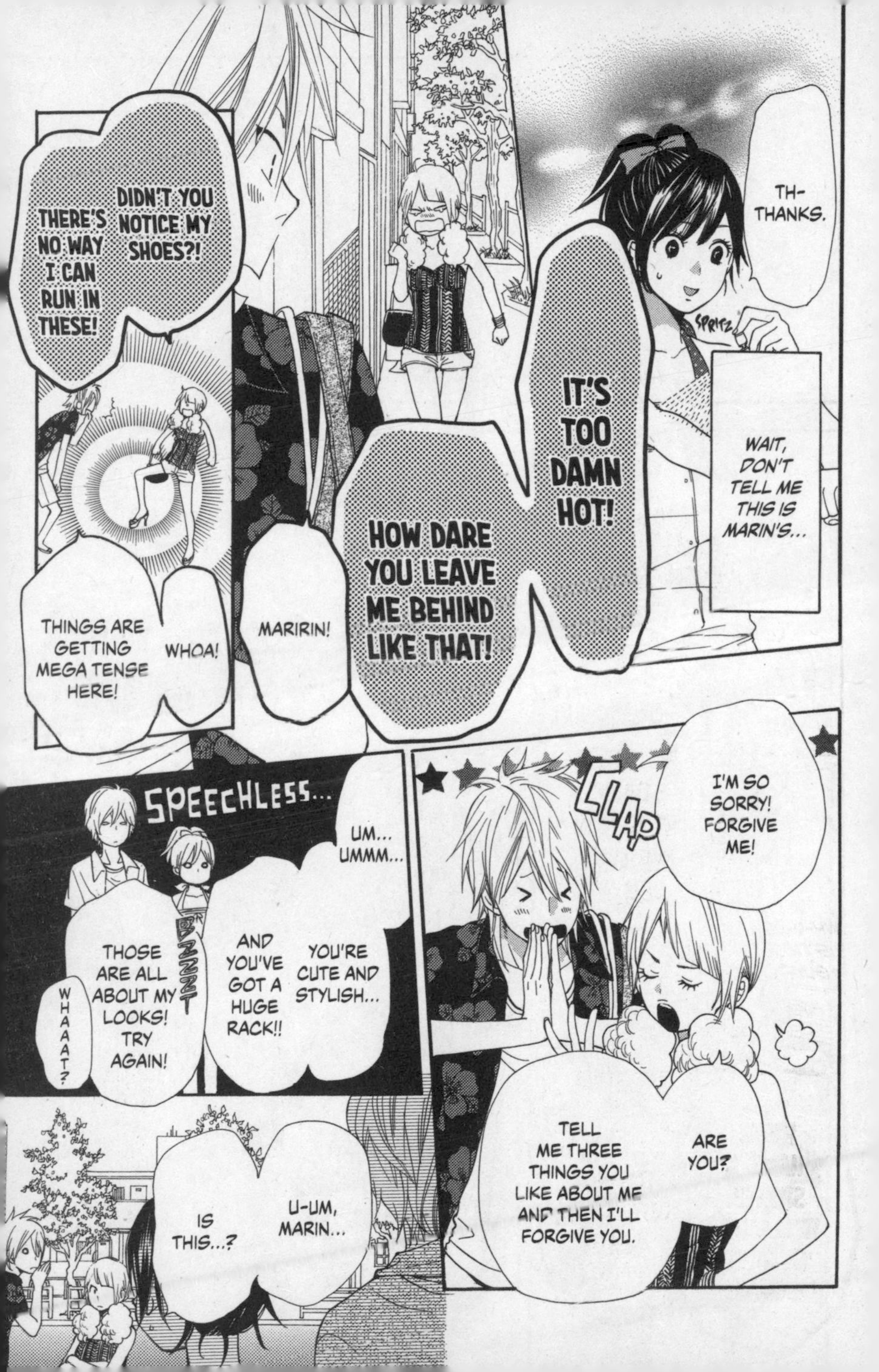
TH-THANKS.
SPRITZ
WAIT, DON'T TELL ME THIS IS MARIN'S...
IT'S TOO DAMN HOT!
HOW DARE YOU LEAVE ME BEHIND LIKE THAT!
MARIRIN!
DIDN'T YOU NOTICE MY SHOES?!
THERE'S NO WAY I CAN RUN IN THESE!
WHOA!
THINGS ARE GETTING MEGA TENSE HERE!
I'M SO SORRY! FORGIVE ME!
CLAP
ARE YOU?
TELL ME THREE THINGS YOU LIKE ABOUT ME AND THEN I'LL FORGIVE YOU.
SPEECHLESS...
UM... UMMM...
YOU'RE CUTE AND STYLISH...
AND YOU'VE GOT A HUGE RACK!!
BZZZT
THOSE ARE ALL ABOUT MY LOOKS! TRY AGAIN!
WHAAAT?
U-UM, MARIN...
IS THIS...?

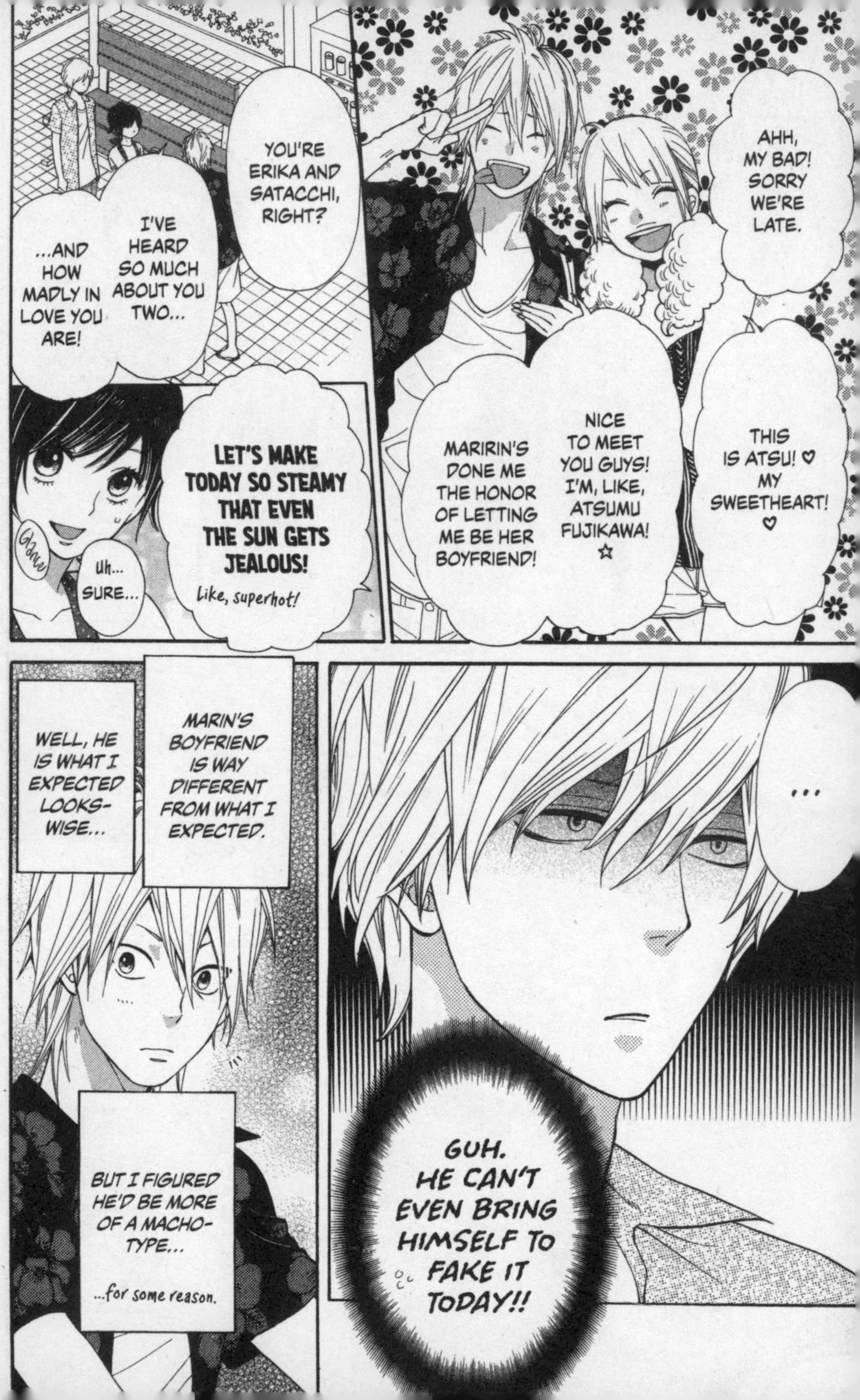
AHH, MY BAD! SORRY WE'RE LATE.
THIS IS ATSU! ♡ MY SWEETHEART! ♡
NICE TO MEET YOU GUYS! I'M, LIKE, ATSUMU FUJIKAWA! ☆
MARIRIN'S DONE ME THE HONOR OF LETTING ME BE HER BOYFRIEND!
YOU'RE ERIKA AND SATACCHI, RIGHT?
I'VE HEARD SO MUCH ABOUT YOU TWO...
...AND HOW MADLY IN LOVE YOU ARE!
LET'S MAKE TODAY SO STEAMY THAT EVEN THE SUN GETS JEALOUS!
Like, superhot!
Glance
Uh... SURE...
...
GUH. HE CAN'T EVEN BRING HIMSELF TO FAKE IT TODAY!!
MARIN'S BOYFRIEND IS WAY DIFFERENT FROM WHAT I EXPECTED.
WELL, HE IS WHAT I EXPECTED LOOKS-WISE...
BUT I FIGURED HE'D BE MORE OF A MACHO-TYPE...
...for some reason.

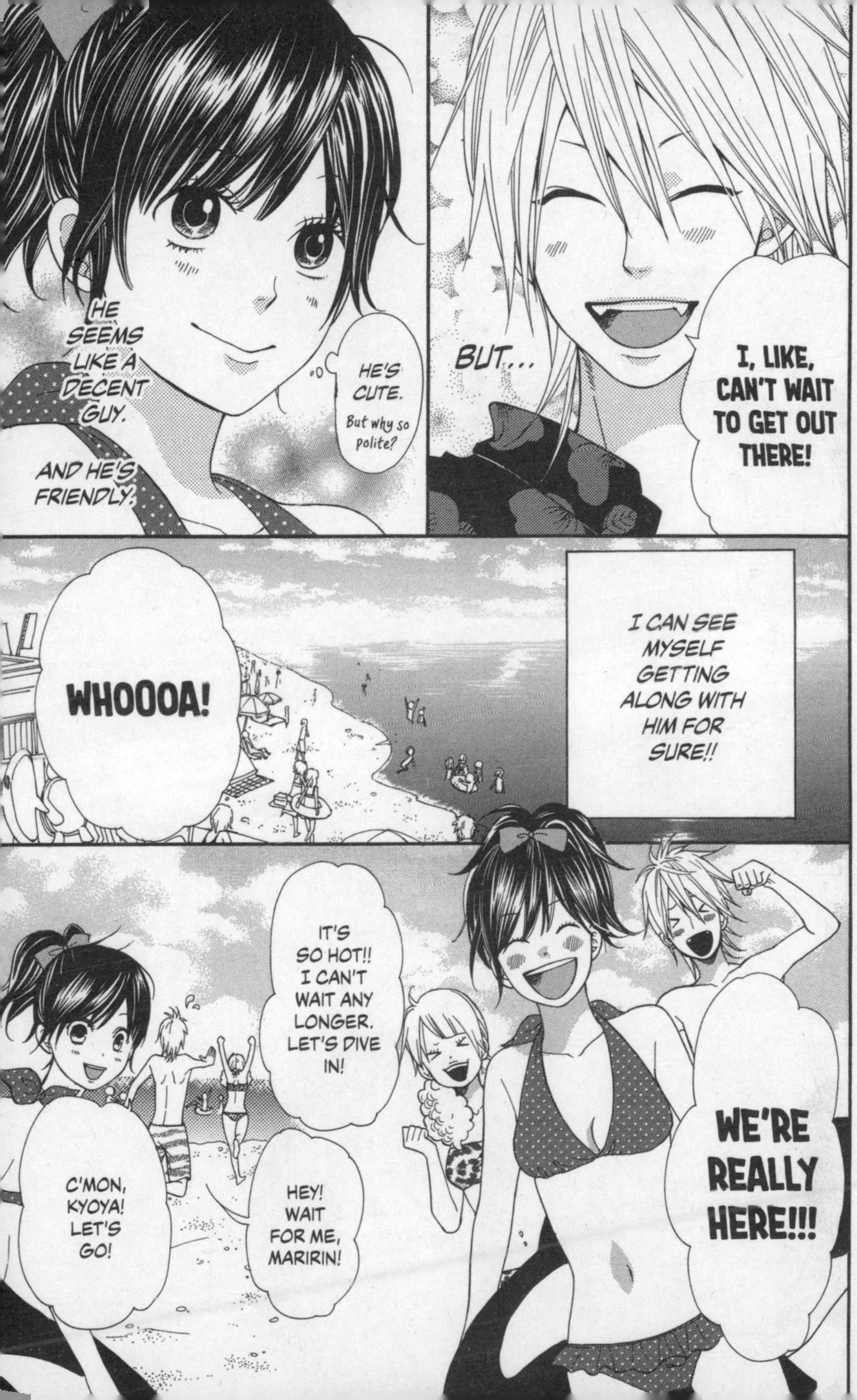
I, LIKE, CAN'T WAIT TO GET OUT THERE!
BUT...
HE'S CUTE.
But why so polite?
HE SEEMS LIKE A DECENT GUY.
AND HE'S FRIENDLY.
I CAN SEE MYSELF GETTING ALONG WITH HIM FOR SURE!!
WHOOOA!
WE'RE REALLY HERE!!!
IT'S SO HOT!! I CAN'T WAIT ANY LONGER. LET'S DIVE IN!
HEY! WAIT FOR ME, MARIRIN!
C'MON, KYOYA! LET'S GO!

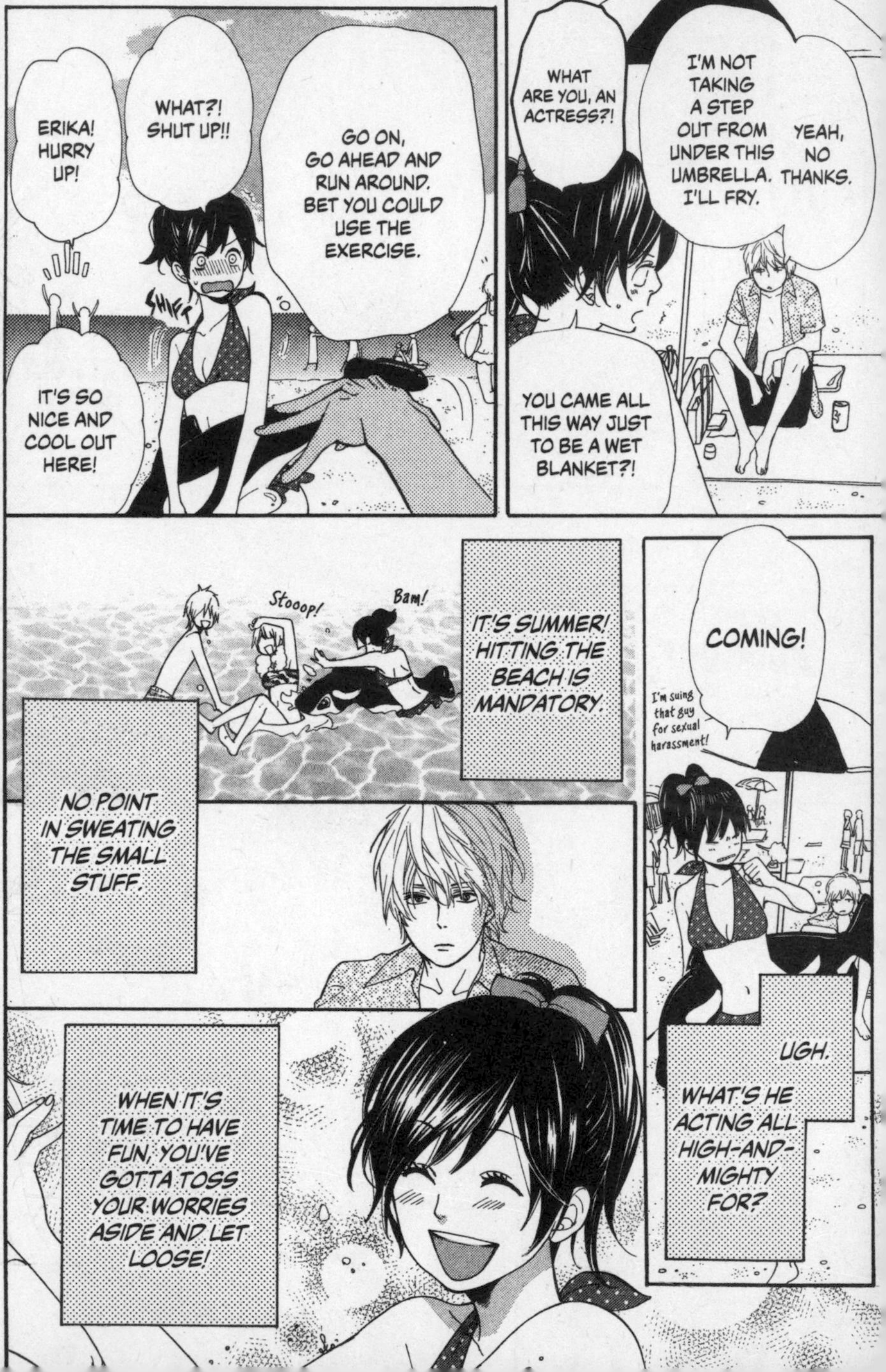

YEAH, NO THANKS.
I'M NOT TAKING A STEP OUT FROM UNDER THIS UMBRELLA. I'LL FRY.
WHAT ARE YOU, AN ACTRESS?!
YOU CAME ALL THIS WAY JUST TO BE A WET BLANKET?!
GO ON, GO AHEAD AND RUN AROUND. BET YOU COULD USE THE EXERCISE.
WHAT?! SHUT UP!!
ERIKA! HURRY UP!
SHIFT
IT'S SO NICE AND COOL OUT HERE!
COMING!
I'm suing that guy for sexual harassment!
UGH. WHAT'S HE ACTING ALL HIGH-AND-MIGHTY FOR?
IT'S SUMMER! HITTING THE BEACH IS MANDATORY.
Bam!
Stooop!
NO POINT IN SWEATING THE SMALL STUFF.
WHEN IT'S TIME TO HAVE FUN, YOU'VE GOTTA TOSS YOUR WORRIES ASIDE AND LET LOOSE!

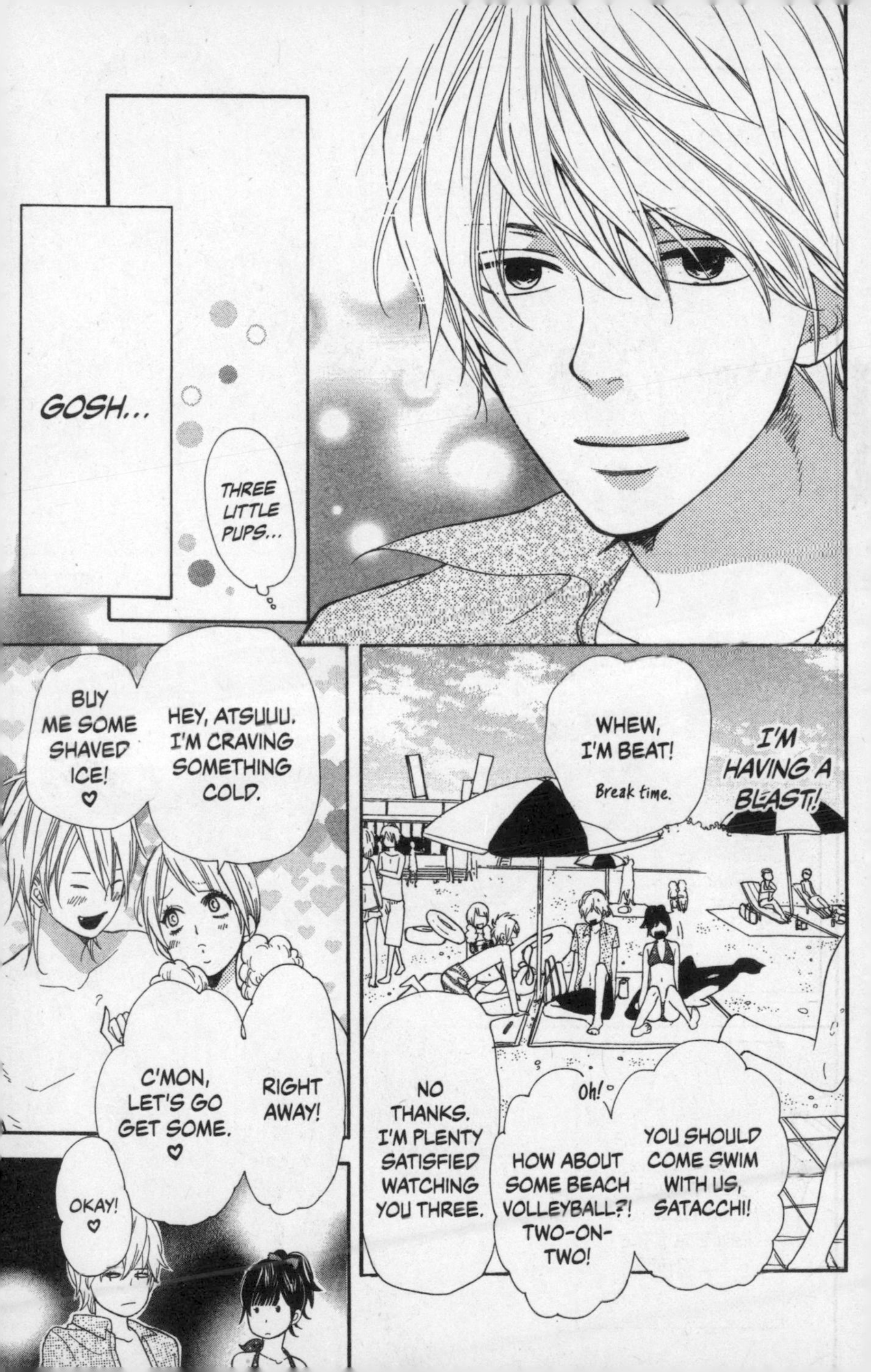
THREE LITTLE PUPS...
GOSH...
WHEW, I'M BEAT!
Break time.
I'M HAVING A BLAST!
YOU SHOULD COME SWIM WITH US, SATACCHI!
Oh!
HOW ABOUT SOME BEACH VOLLEYBALL?! TWO-ON-TWO!
NO THANKS. I'M PLENTY SATISFIED WATCHING YOU THREE.
HEY, ATSUUU. I'M CRAVING SOMETHING COLD.
BUY ME SOME SHAVED ICE! ♡
RIGHT AWAY!
C'MON, LET'S GO GET SOME. ♡
OKAY! ♡

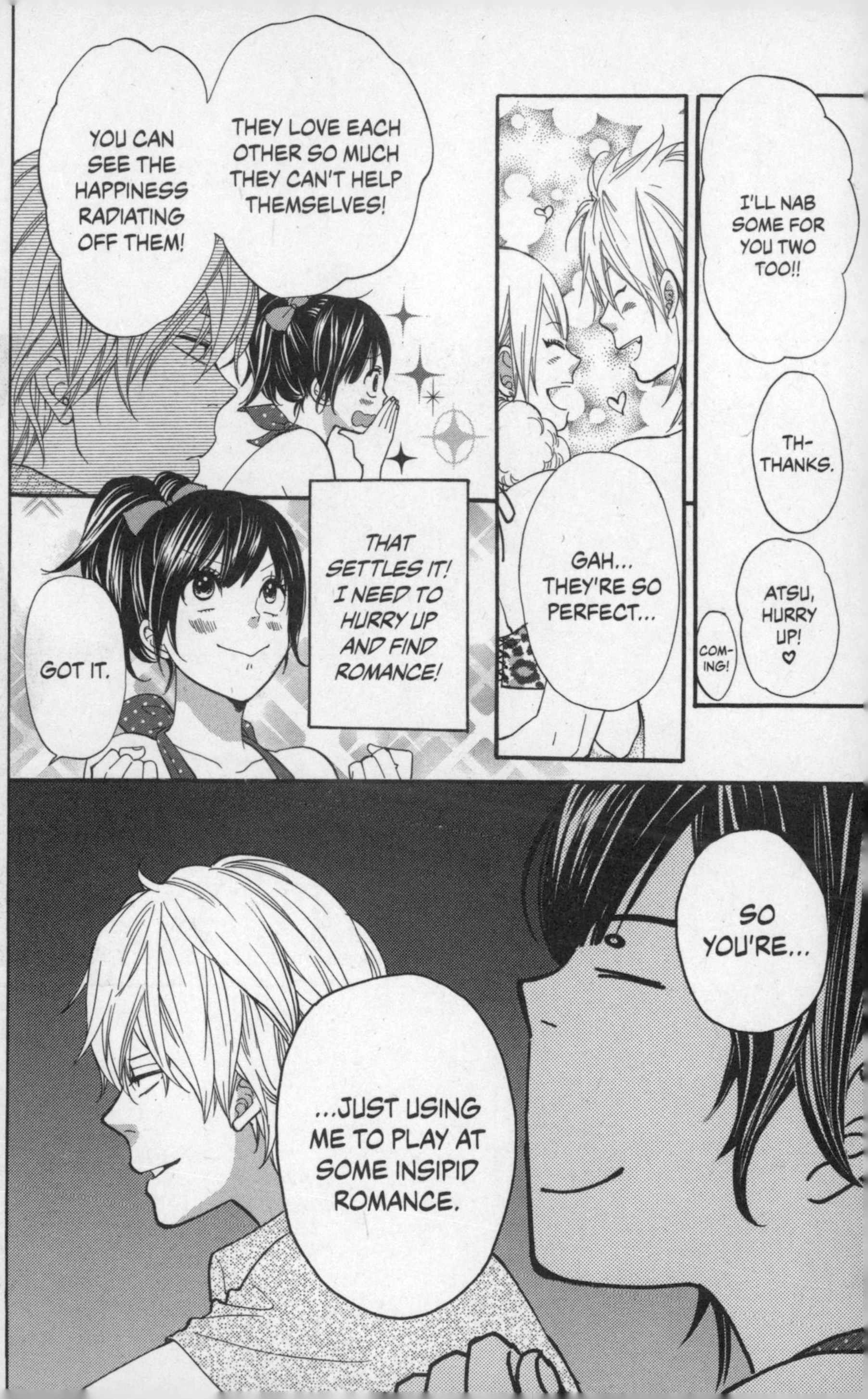
I'LL NAB SOME FOR YOU TWO TOO!!
TH- THANKS.
ATSU, HURRY UP! ♡
COMING!
GAH... THEY'RE SO PERFECT...
THEY LOVE EACH OTHER SO MUCH THEY CAN'T HELP THEMSELVES!
YOU CAN SEE THE HAPPINESS RADIATING OFF THEM!
THAT SETTLES IT! I NEED TO HURRY UP AND FIND ROMANCE!
GOT IT.
SO YOU'RE...
...JUST USING ME TO PLAY AT SOME INSIPID ROMANCE.

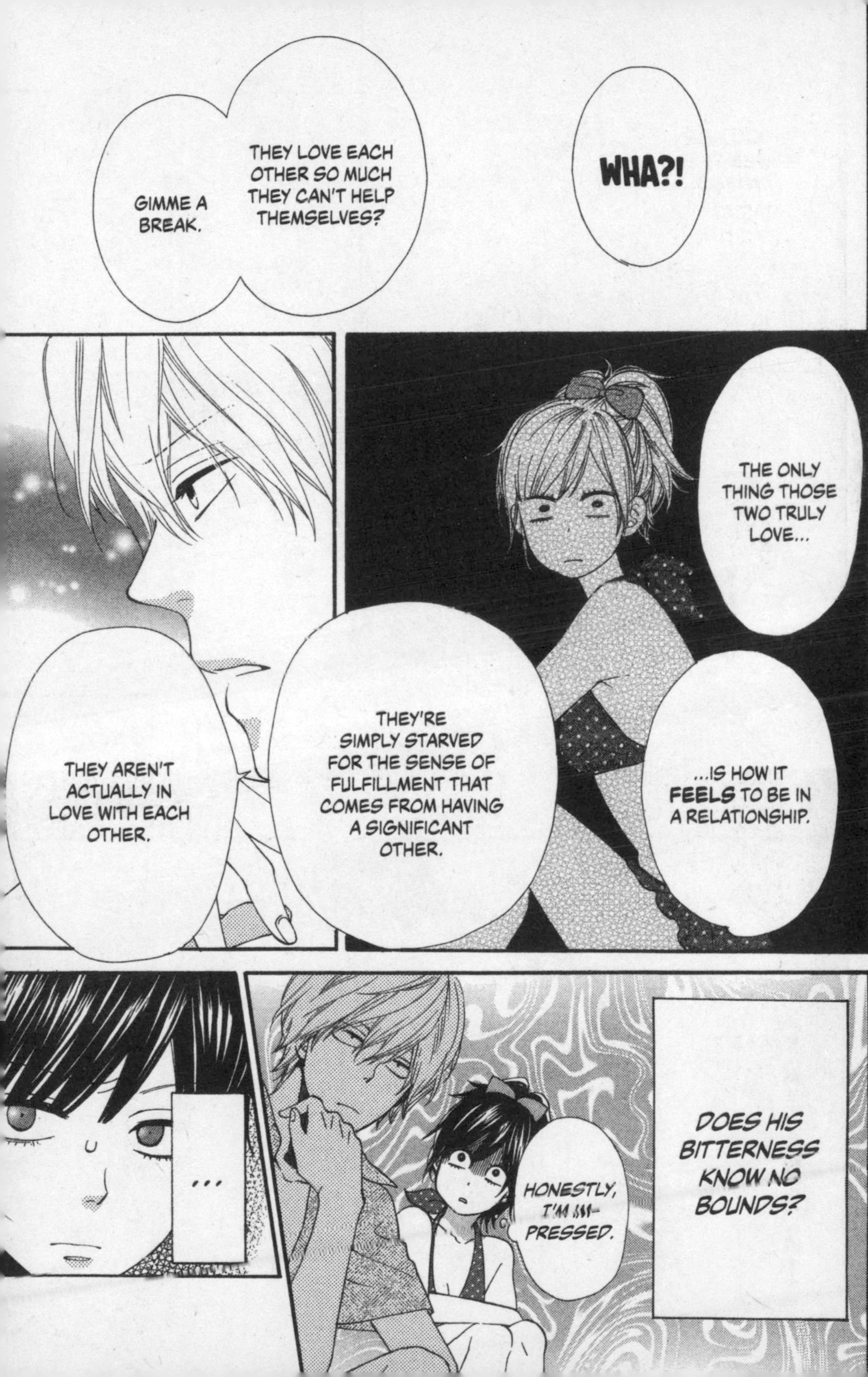
WHA?!
THEY LOVE EACH OTHER SO MUCH THEY CAN'T HELP THEMSELVES?
GIMME A BREAK.
THE ONLY THING THOSE TWO TRULY LOVE...
...IS HOW IT FEELS TO BE IN A RELATIONSHIP.
THEY'RE SIMPLY STARVED FOR THE SENSE OF FULFILLMENT THAT COMES FROM HAVING A SIGNIFICANT OTHER.
THEY AREN'T ACTUALLY IN LOVE WITH EACH OTHER.
DOES HIS BITTERNESS KNOW NO BOUNDS?
HONESTLY, I'M IM-PRESSED.
...

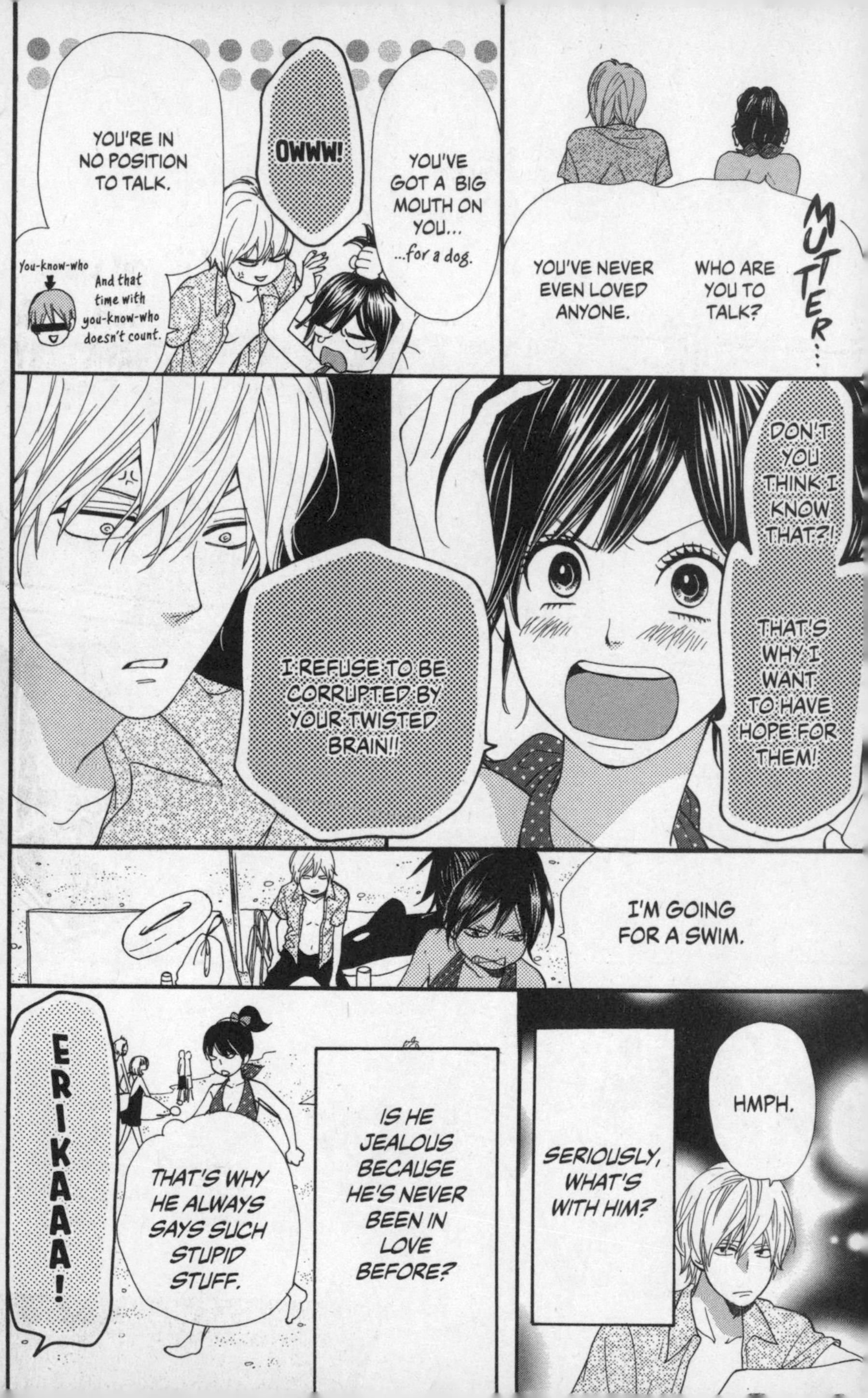
MUTTER...
WHO ARE YOU TO TALK?
YOU'VE NEVER EVEN LOVED ANYONE.
YOU'VE GOT A BIG MOUTH ON YOU... ...for a dog.
OWWW!
YOU'RE IN NO POSITION TO TALK.
You-know-who
And that time with you-know-who doesn't count.
DON'T YOU THINK I KNOW THAT?!
THAT'S WHY I WANT TO HAVE HOPE FOR THEM!
I REFUSE TO BE CORRUPTED BY YOUR TWISTED BRAIN!!
I'M GOING FOR A SWIM.
HMPH.
SERIOUSLY, WHAT'S WITH HIM?
IS HE JEALOUS BECAUSE HE'S NEVER BEEN IN LOVE BEFORE?
THAT'S WHY HE ALWAYS SAYS SUCH STUPID STUFF.
ERIKAAA!

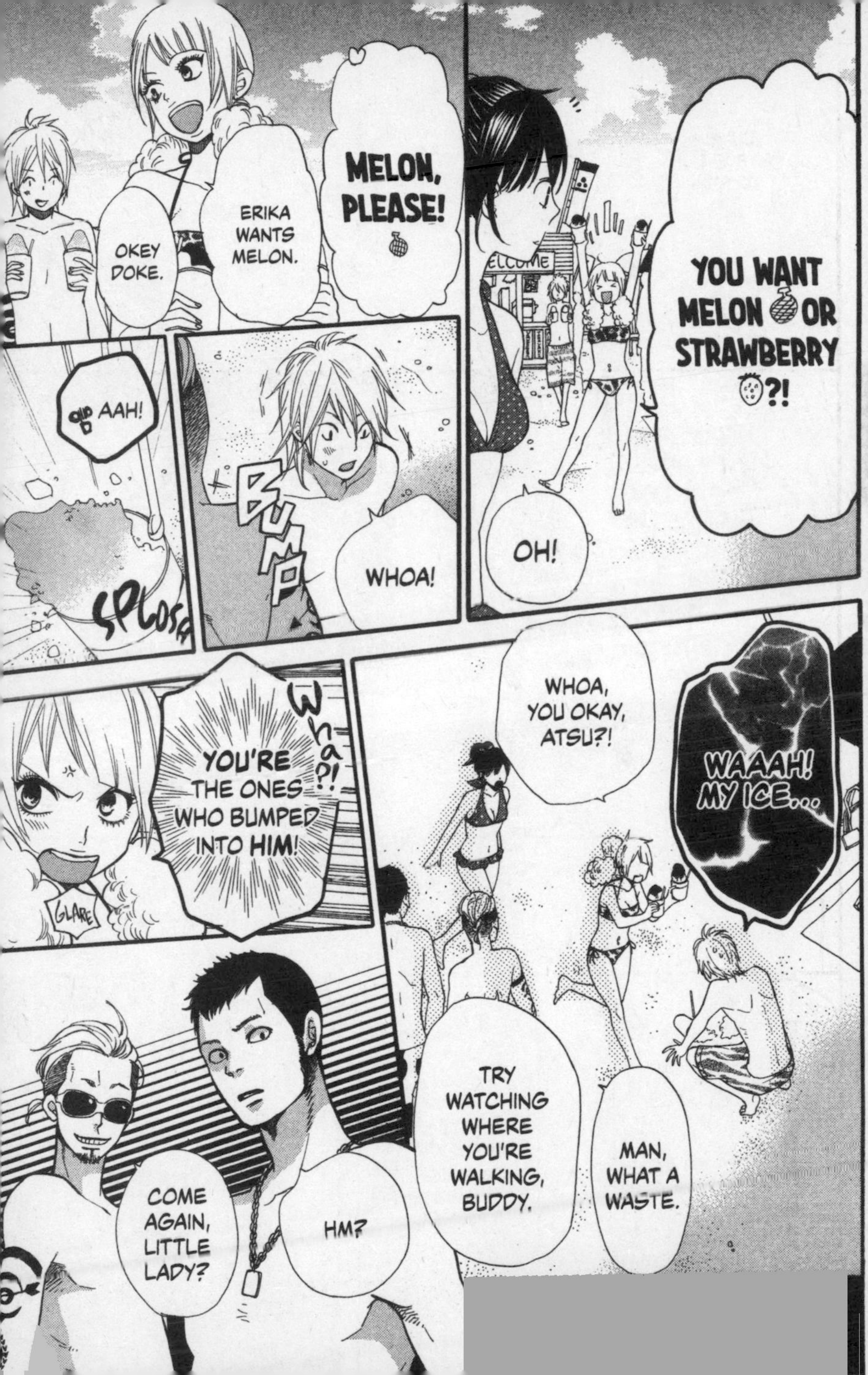
YOU WANT MELON OR STRAWBERRY?!
OH!
MELON, PLEASE!
ERIKA WANTS MELON.
OKEY DOKE.
WHOA!
BUMP
AAH!
SPLOSH
WAAAH! MY ICE...
WHOA, YOU OKAY, ATSU?!
MAN, WHAT A WASTE.
TRY WATCHING WHERE YOU'RE WALKING, BUDDY.
YOU'RE THE ONES WHO BUMPED INTO HIM!
Wha?!
GLARE
HM?
COME AGAIN, LITTLE LADY?

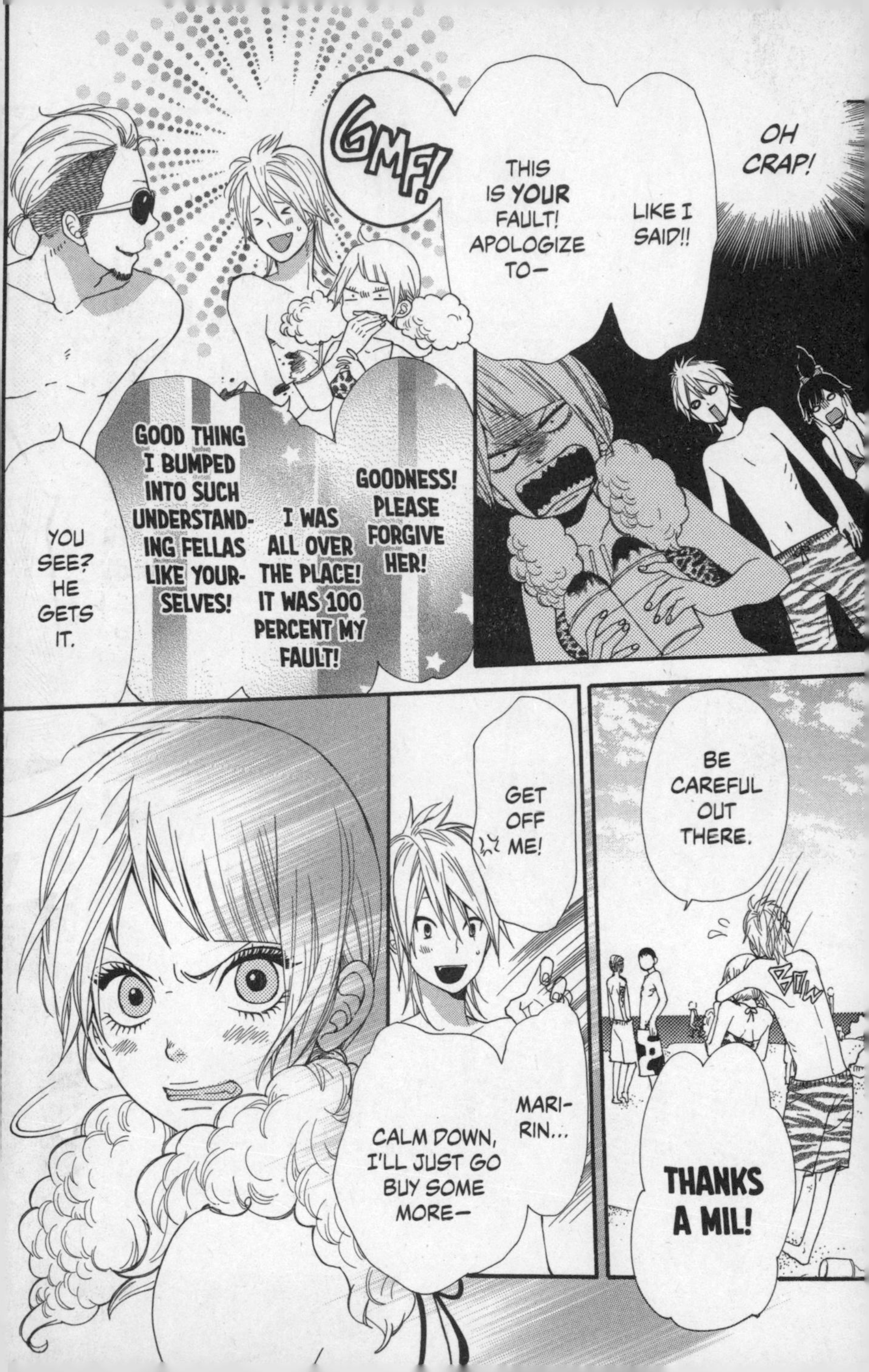
OH CRAP!
LIKE I SAID!!
THIS IS YOUR FAULT! APOLOGIZE TO—
GMF!
GOODNESS! PLEASE FORGIVE HER!
I WAS ALL OVER THE PLACE! IT WAS 100 PERCENT MY FAULT!
GOOD THING I BUMPED INTO SUCH UNDERSTAND-ING FELLAS LIKE YOUR-SELVES!
YOU SEE? HE GETS IT.
BE CAREFUL OUT THERE.
THANKS A MIL!
GET OFF ME!
MARI-RIN...
CALM DOWN, I'LL JUST GO BUY SOME MORE—

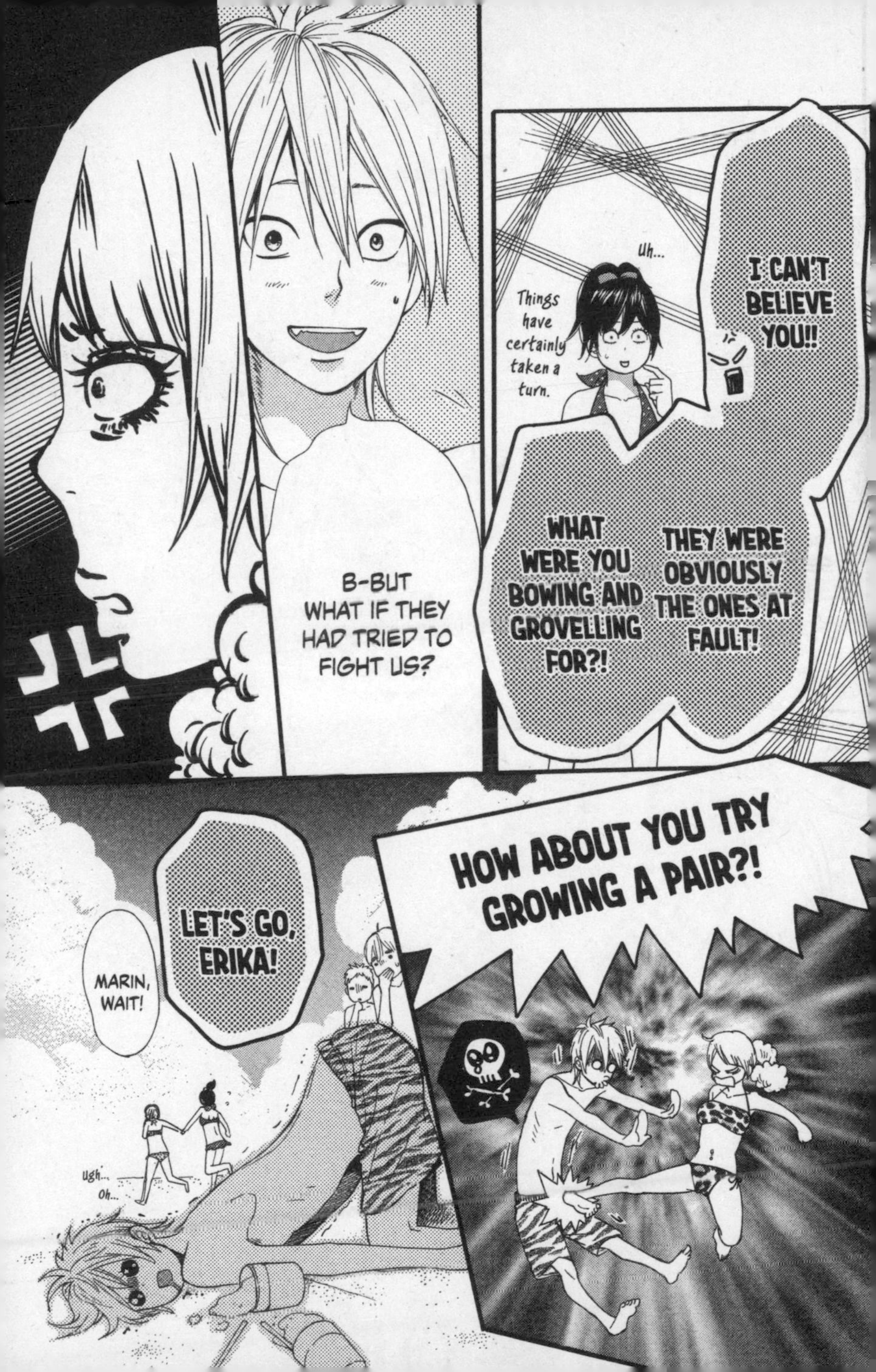

I CAN'T BELIEVE YOU!!
Uh...
Things have certainly taken a turn.
THEY WERE OBVIOUSLY THE ONES AT FAULT!
WHAT WERE YOU BOWING AND GROVELLING FOR?!
B-BUT WHAT IF THEY HAD TRIED TO FIGHT US?
HOW ABOUT YOU TRY GROWING A PAIR?!
LET'S GO, ERIKA!
MARIN, WAIT!
Ugh... Oh...

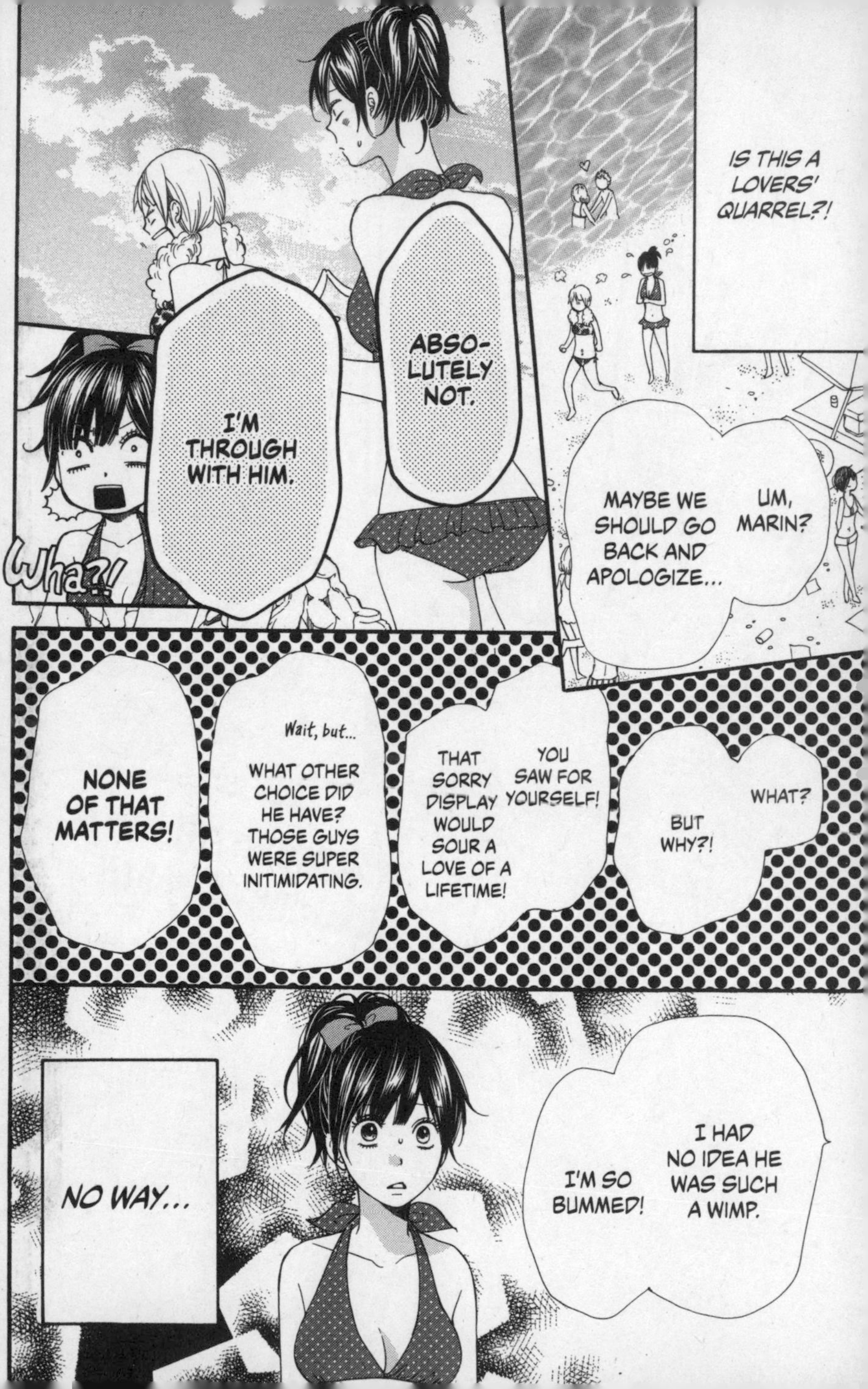
IS THIS A LOVERS' QUARREL?!
UM, MARIN?
MAYBE WE SHOULD GO BACK AND APOLOGIZE...
ABSO-LUTELY NOT.
I'M THROUGH WITH HIM.
Wha?!
WHAT?
BUT WHY?!
YOU SAW FOR YOURSELF!
THAT SORRY DISPLAY WOULD SOUR A LOVE OF A LIFETIME!
Wait, but...
WHAT OTHER CHOICE DID HE HAVE? THOSE GUYS WERE SUPER INITIMIDATING.
NONE OF THAT MATTERS!
I HAD NO IDEA HE WAS SUCH A WIMP.
I'M SO BUMMED!
NO WAY...

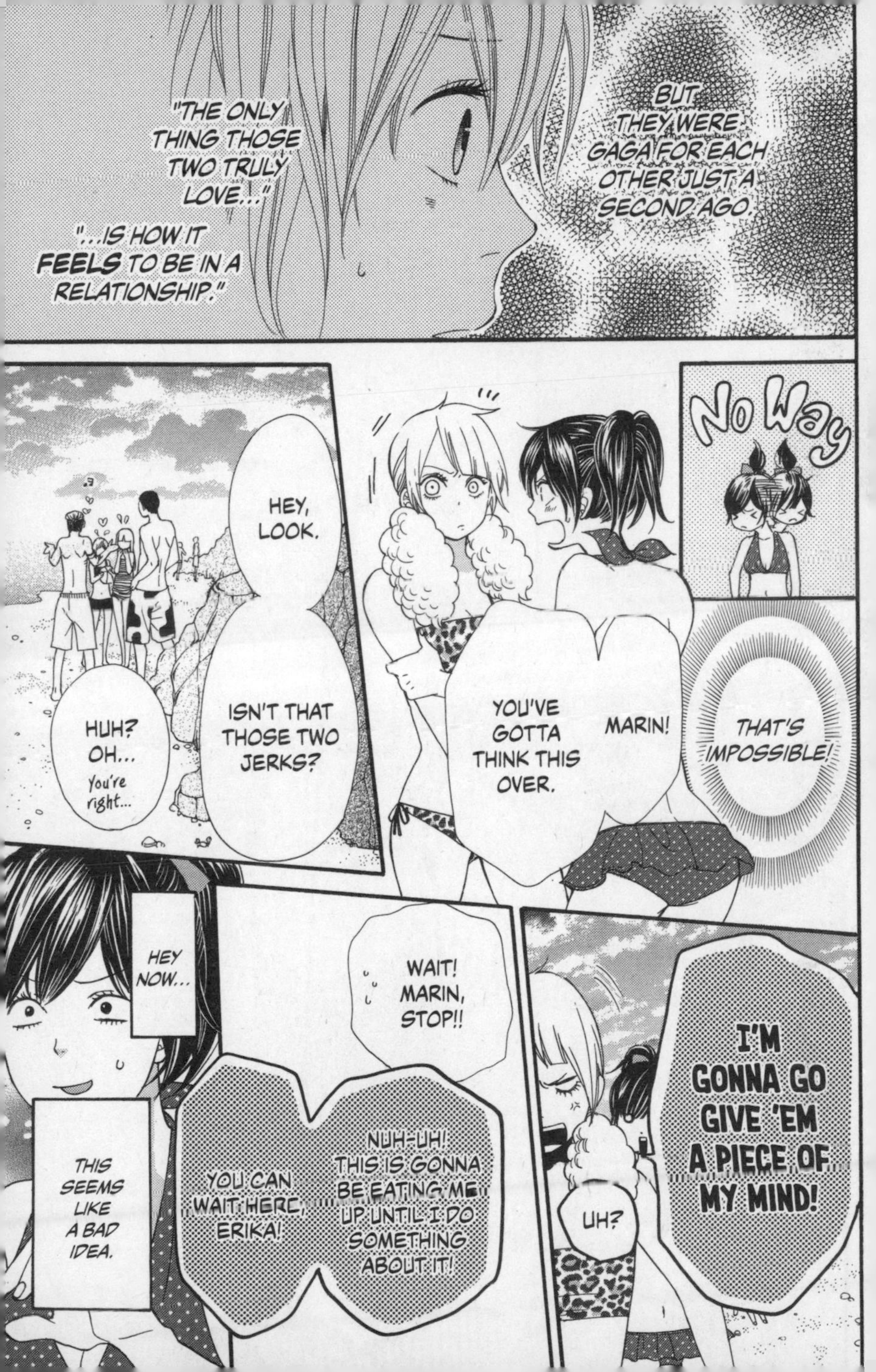
BUT THEY WERE GAGA FOR EACH OTHER JUST A SECOND AGO.
"THE ONLY THING THOSE TWO TRULY LOVE..."
"...IS HOW IT FEELS TO BE IN A RELATIONSHIP."
No Way
THAT'S IMPOSSIBLE!
MARIN!
YOU'VE GOTTA THINK THIS OVER.
HEY, LOOK.
ISN'T THAT THOSE TWO JERKS?
HUH? OH... You're right...
I'M GONNA GO GIVE 'EM A PIECE OF MY MIND!
UH?
WAIT! MARIN, STOP!!
NUH-UH! THIS IS GONNA BE EATING ME UP UNTIL I DO SOMETHING ABOUT IT!
YOU CAN WAIT HERE, ERIKA!
HEY NOW...
THIS SEEMS LIKE A BAD IDEA.

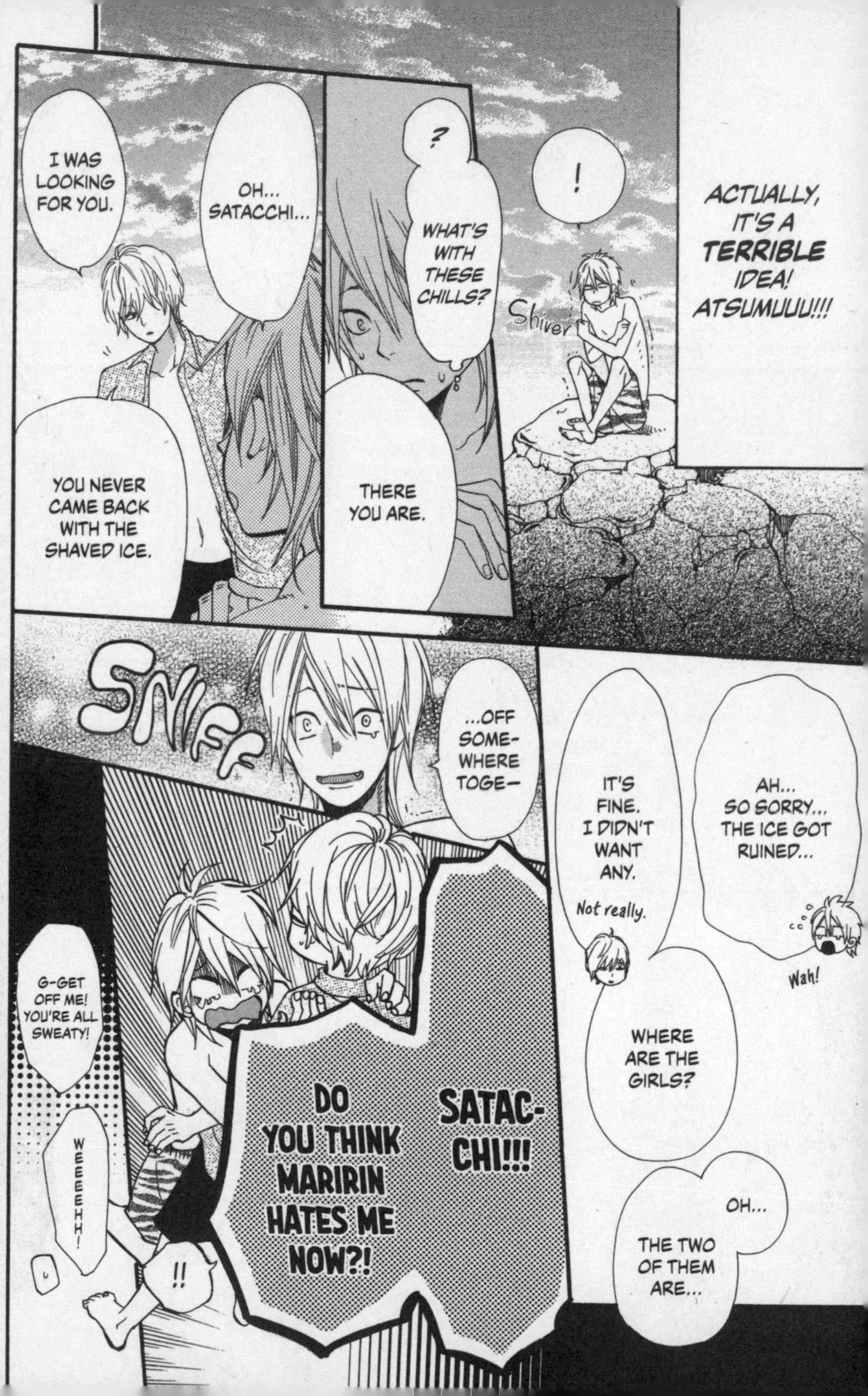
ACTUALLY, IT'S A TERRIBLE IDEA! ATSUMUUU!!!
!
Shiver
?
WHAT'S WITH THESE CHILLS?
THERE YOU ARE.
OH... SATACCHI...
I WAS LOOKING FOR YOU.
YOU NEVER CAME BACK WITH THE SHAVED ICE.
AH... SO SORRY... THE ICE GOT RUINED...
Wah!
IT'S FINE. I DIDN'T WANT ANY.
Not really.
WHERE ARE THE GIRLS?
OH...
THE TWO OF THEM ARE...
...OFF SOME-WHERE TOGE—
SNIFF
SATAC-CHI!!!
DO YOU THINK MARIRIN HATES ME NOW?!
G-GET OFF ME! YOU'RE ALL SWEATY!
WEEEEEHH!
!!

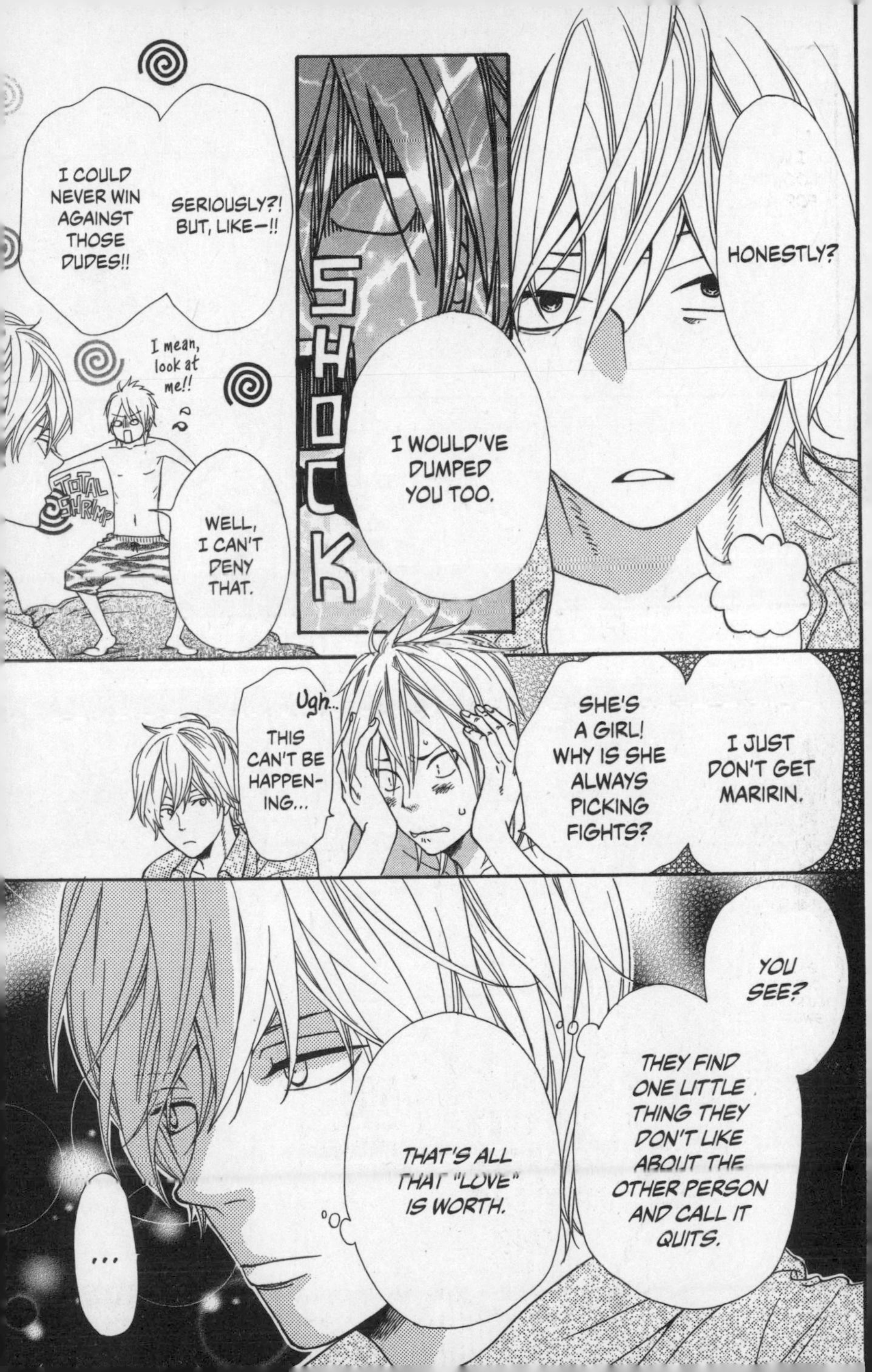
HONESTLY?
I WOULD'VE DUMPED YOU TOO.
SHOCK
SERIOUSLY?! BUT, LIKE—!!
I COULD NEVER WIN AGAINST THOSE DUDES!!
I mean, look at me!!
TOTAL SHRIMP
WELL, I CAN'T DENY THAT.
I JUST DON'T GET MARIRIN.
SHE'S A GIRL! WHY IS SHE ALWAYS PICKING FIGHTS?
Ugh...
THIS CAN'T BE HAPPENING...
YOU SEE?
THEY FIND ONE LITTLE THING THEY DON'T LIKE ABOUT THE OTHER PERSON AND CALL IT QUITS.
THAT'S ALL "LOVE" IS WORTH.
...

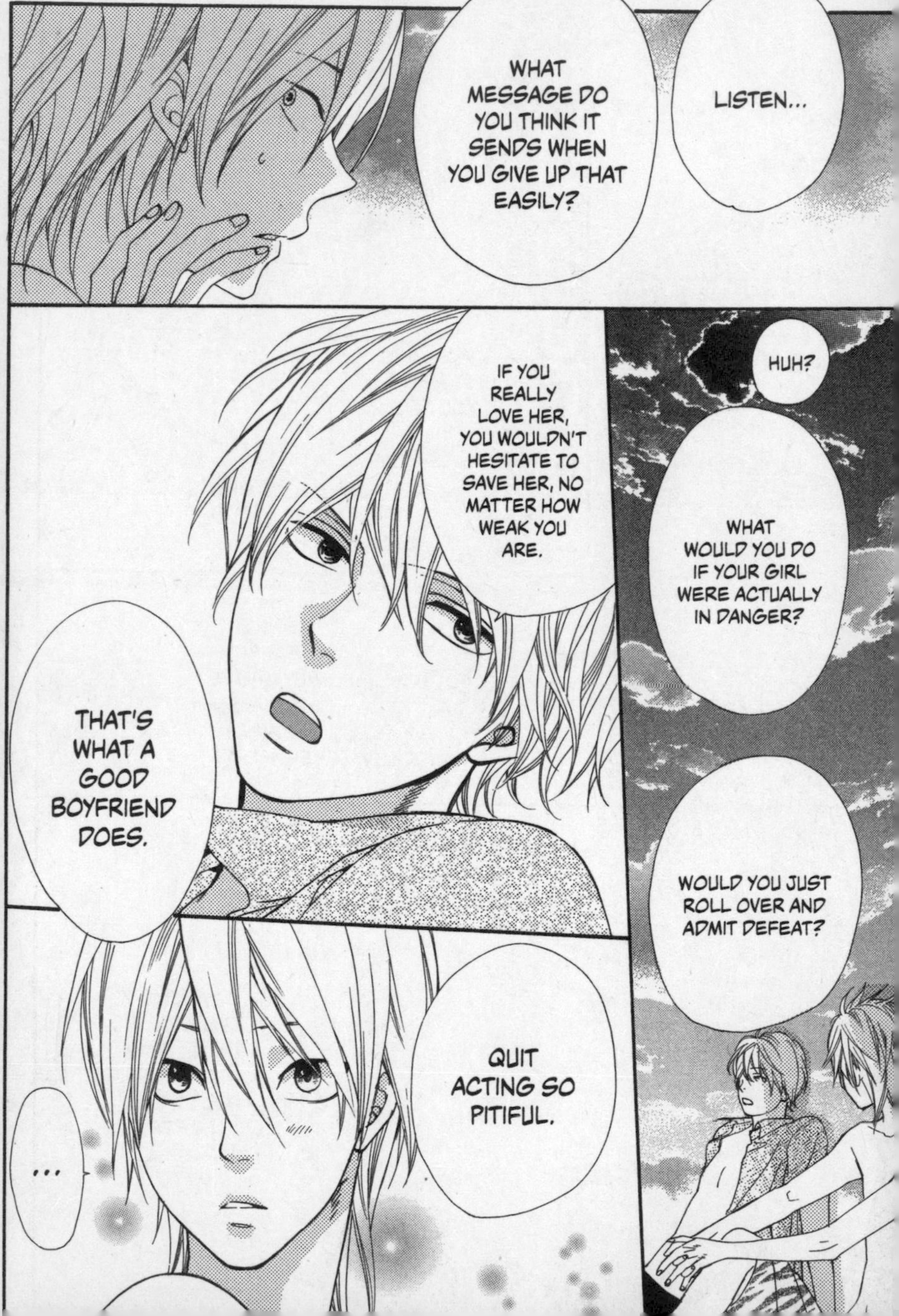
LISTEN...
WHAT MESSAGE DO YOU THINK IT SENDS WHEN YOU GIVE UP THAT EASILY?
HUH?
WHAT WOULD YOU DO IF YOUR GIRL WERE ACTUALLY IN DANGER?
WOULD YOU JUST ROLL OVER AND ADMIT DEFEAT?
IF YOU REALLY LOVE HER, YOU WOULDN'T HESITATE TO SAVE HER, NO MATTER HOW WEAK YOU ARE.
THAT'S WHAT A GOOD BOYFRIEND DOES.
QUIT ACTING SO PITIFUL.
...

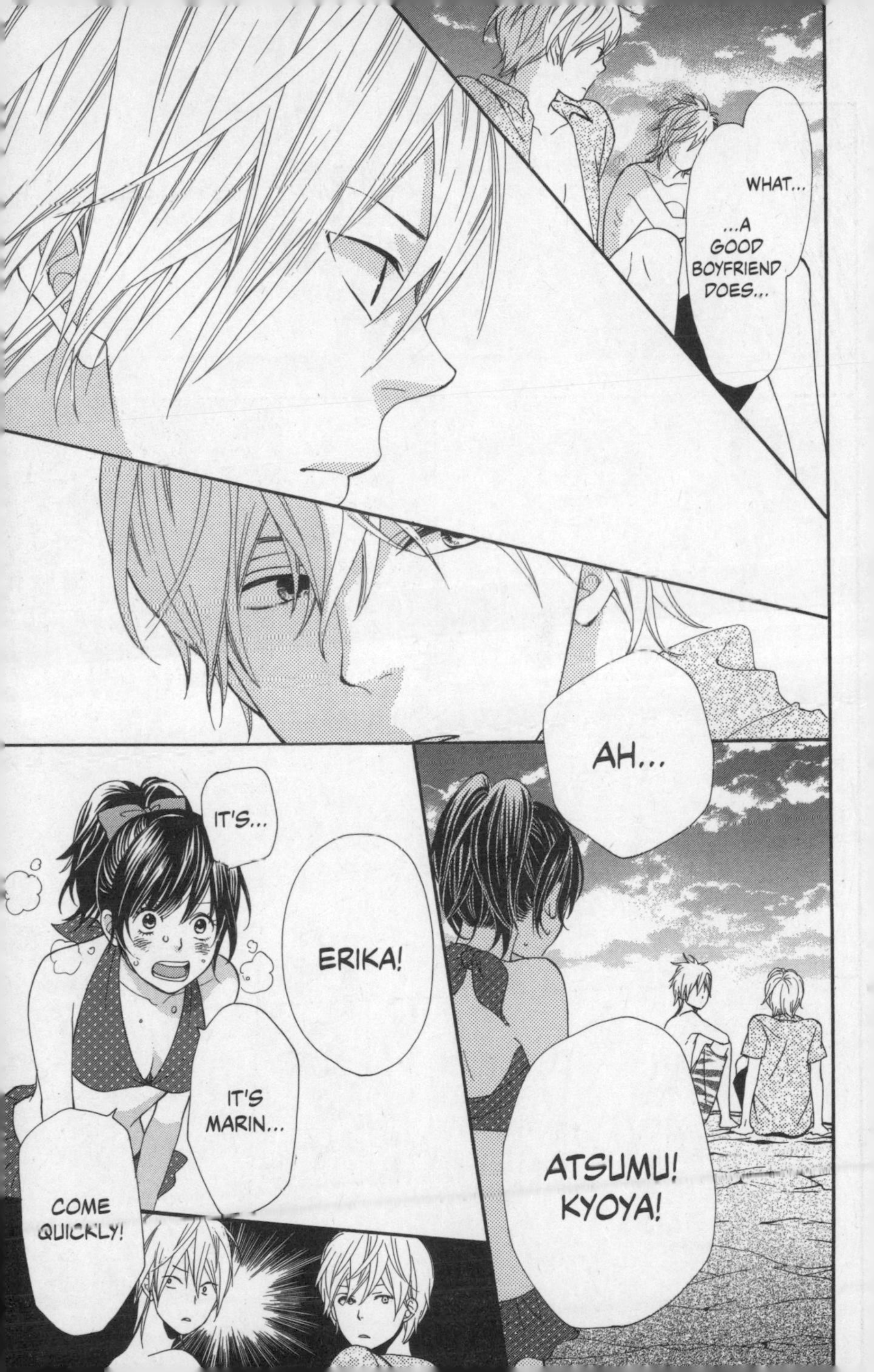
WHAT...
...A GOOD BOYFRIEND DOES...
AH...
ATSUMU! KYOYA!
IT'S...
ERIKA!
IT'S MARIN...
COME QUICKLY!

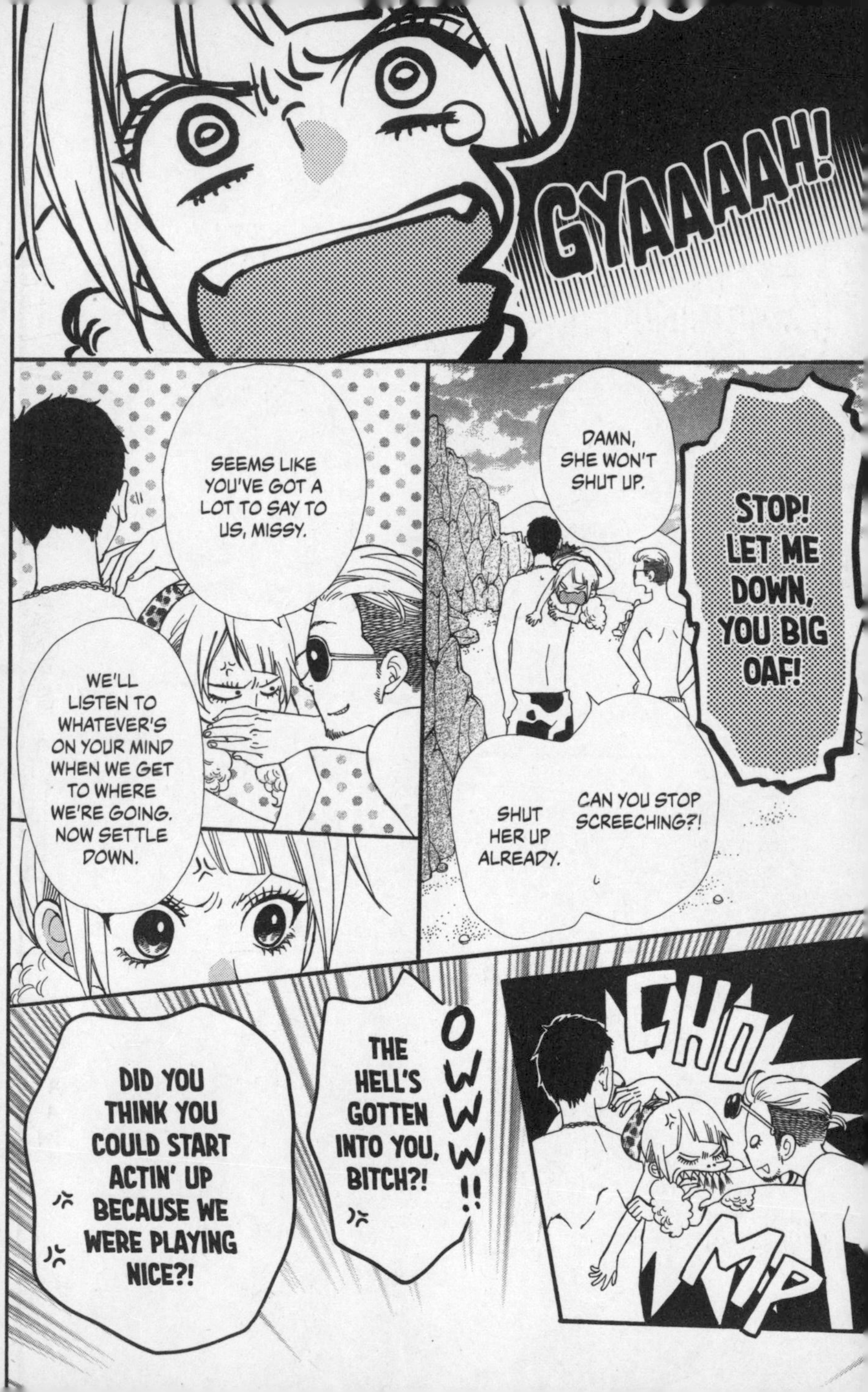
GYAAAAH!
STOP! LET ME DOWN, YOU BIG OAF!
DAMN, SHE WON'T SHUT UP.
CAN YOU STOP SCREECHING?!
SHUT HER UP ALREADY.
SEEMS LIKE YOU'VE GOT A LOT TO SAY TO US, MISSY.
WE'LL LISTEN TO WHATEVER'S ON YOUR MIND WHEN WE GET TO WHERE WE'RE GOING. NOW SETTLE DOWN.
CHOMP
OWWW!!
THE HELL'S GOTTEN INTO YOU, BITCH?!
DID YOU THINK YOU COULD START ACTIN' UP BECAUSE WE WERE PLAYING NICE?!

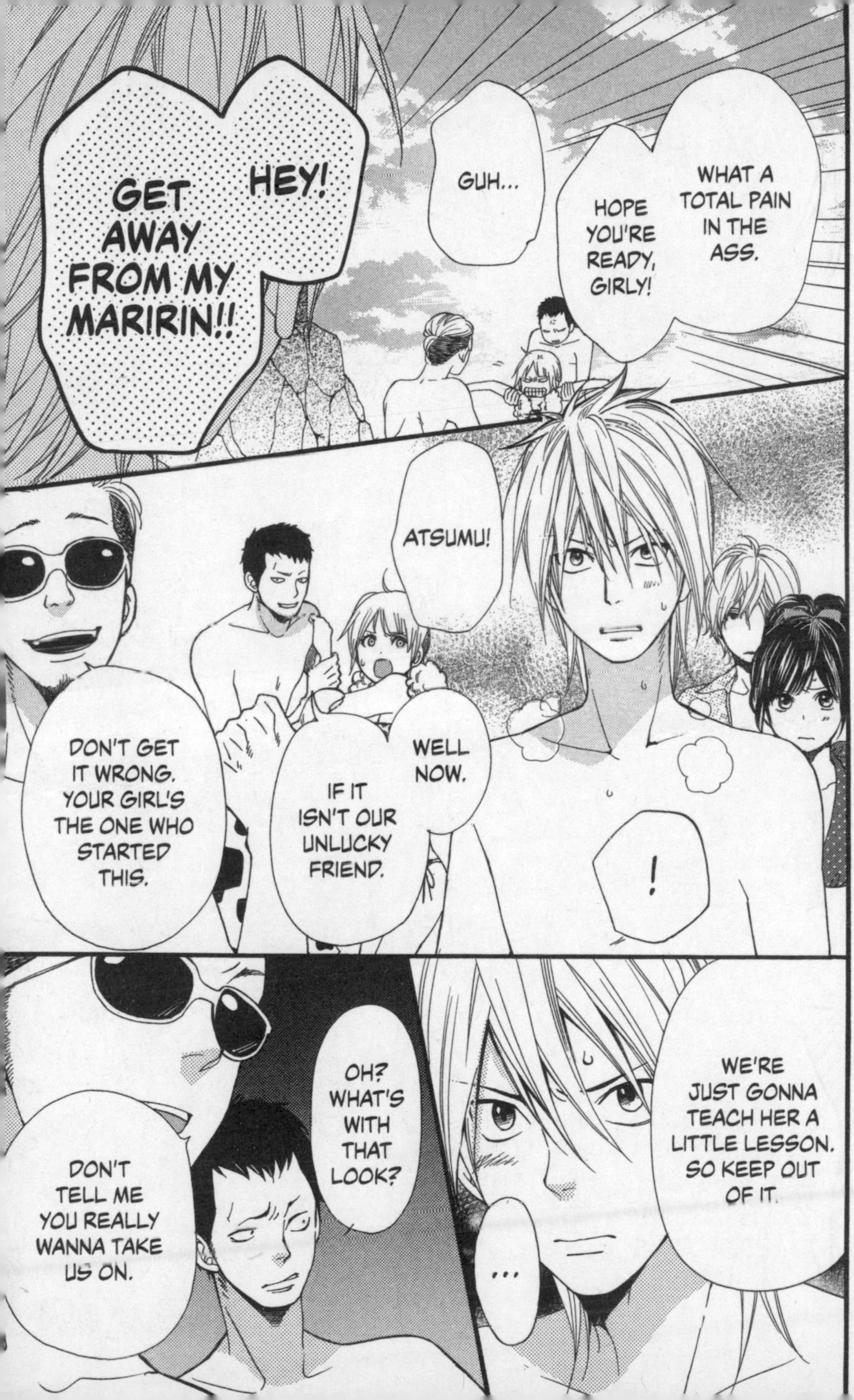
WHAT A TOTAL PAIN IN THE ASS.
HOPE YOU'RE READY, GIRLY!
GUH...
HEY! GET AWAY FROM MY MARIRIN!!
ATSUMU!
!
WELL NOW. IF IT ISN'T OUR UNLUCKY FRIEND.
DON'T GET IT WRONG. YOUR GIRL'S THE ONE WHO STARTED THIS.
WE'RE JUST GONNA TEACH HER A LITTLE LESSON. SO KEEP OUT OF IT.
...
OH? WHAT'S WITH THAT LOOK?
DON'T TELL ME YOU REALLY WANNA TAKE US ON.

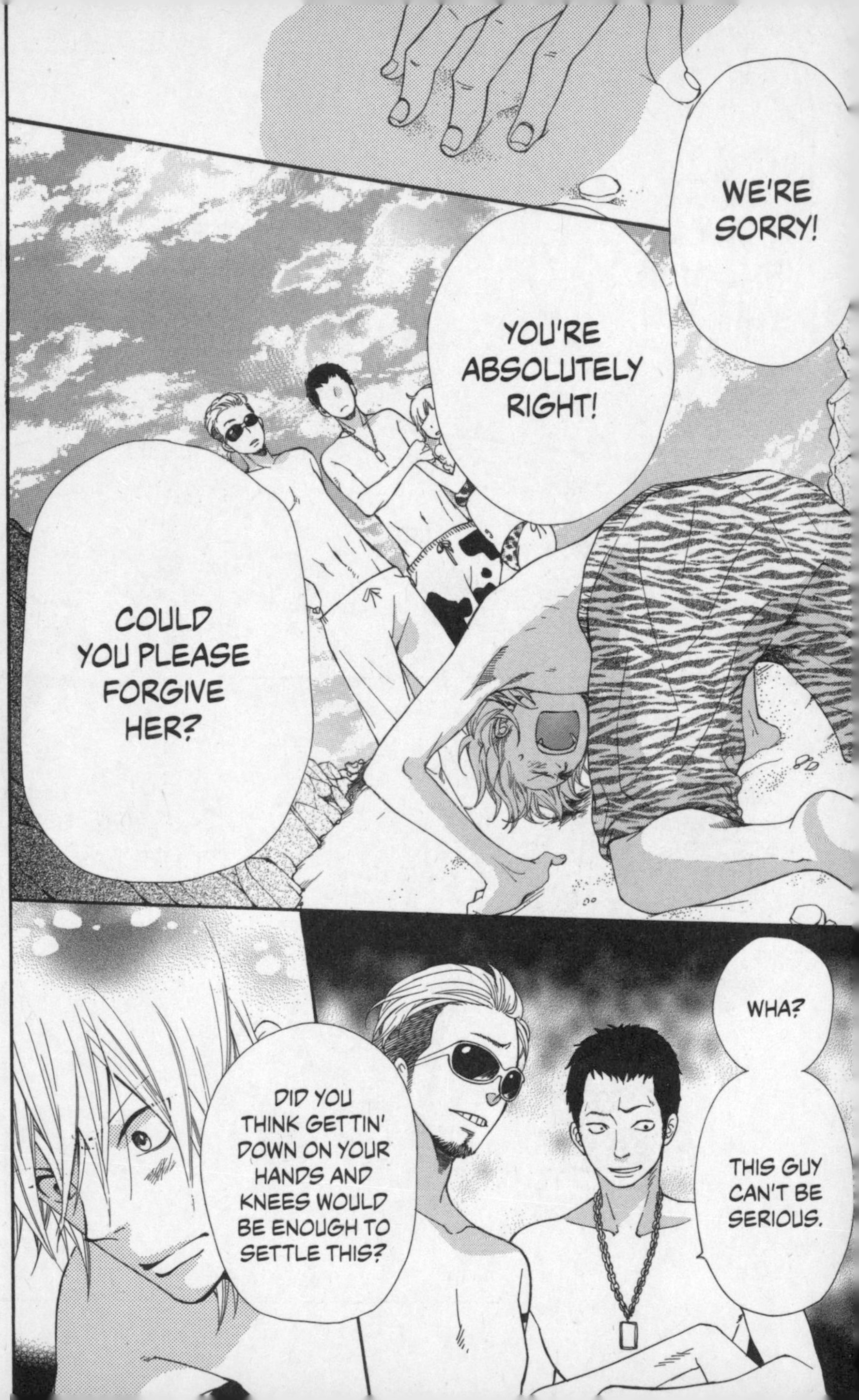
WE'RE SORRY!
YOU'RE ABSOLUTELY RIGHT!
COULD YOU PLEASE FORGIVE HER?
WHA?
THIS GUY CAN'T BE SERIOUS.
DID YOU THINK GETTIN' DOWN ON YOUR HANDS AND KNEES WOULD BE ENOUGH TO SETTLE THIS?

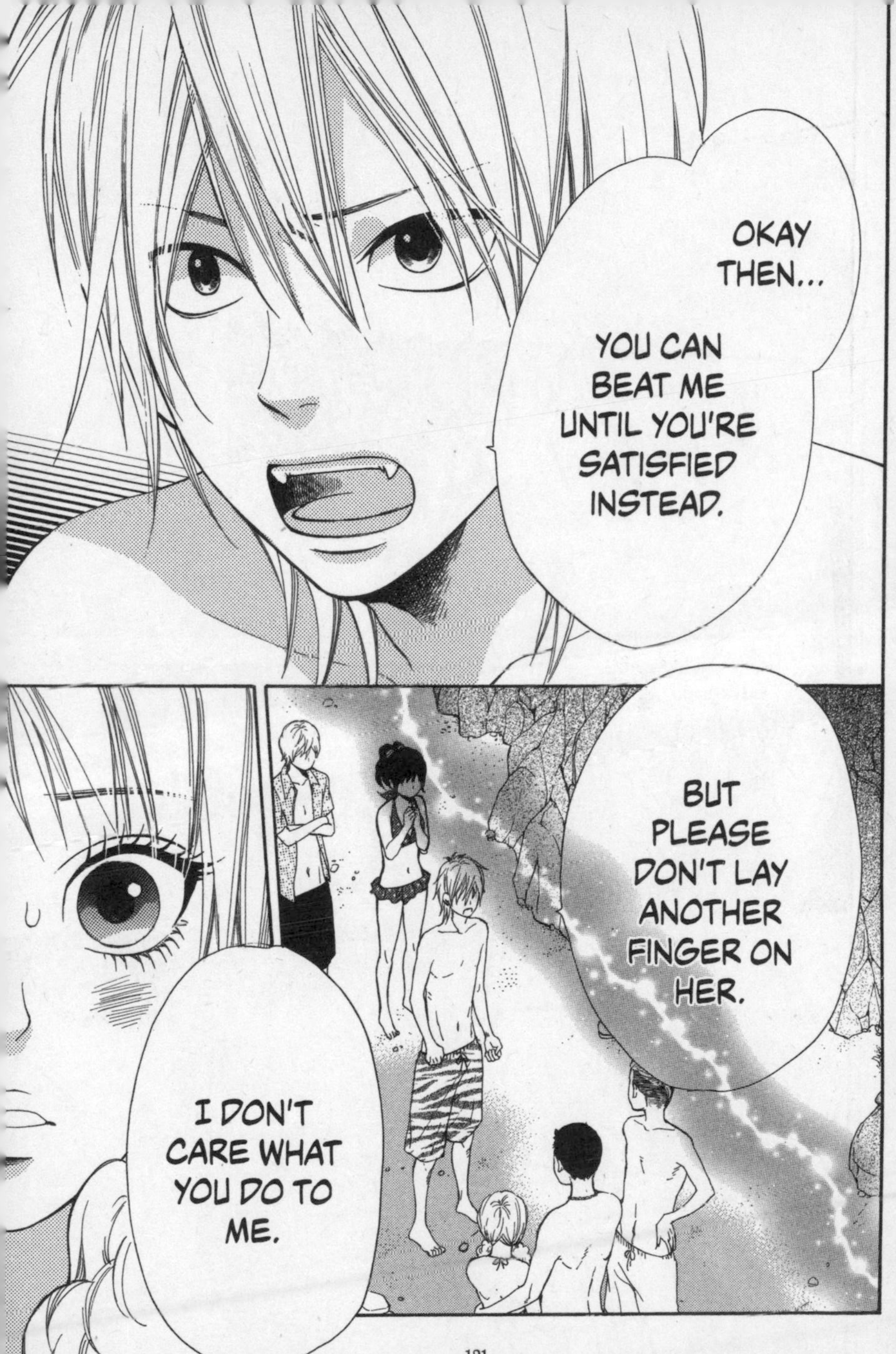
OKAY THEN...
YOU CAN BEAT ME UNTIL YOU'RE SATISFIED INSTEAD.
BUT PLEASE DON'T LAY ANOTHER FINGER ON HER.
I DON'T CARE WHAT YOU DO TO ME.

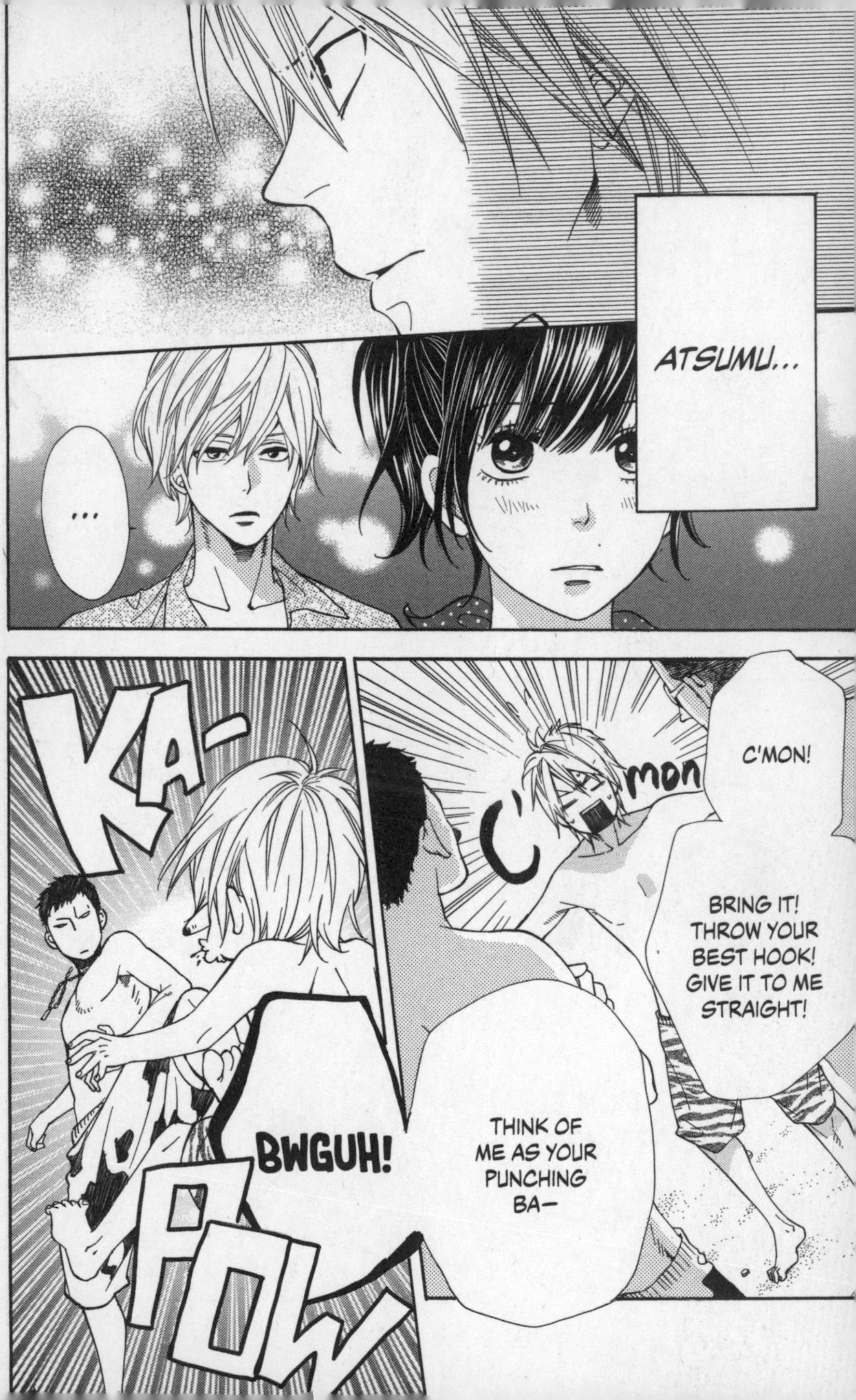
ATSUMU...
...
C'MON!
C'mon
BRING IT! THROW YOUR BEST HOOK! GIVE IT TO ME STRAIGHT!
THINK OF ME AS YOUR PUNCHING BA—
KA-POW
BWGUH!

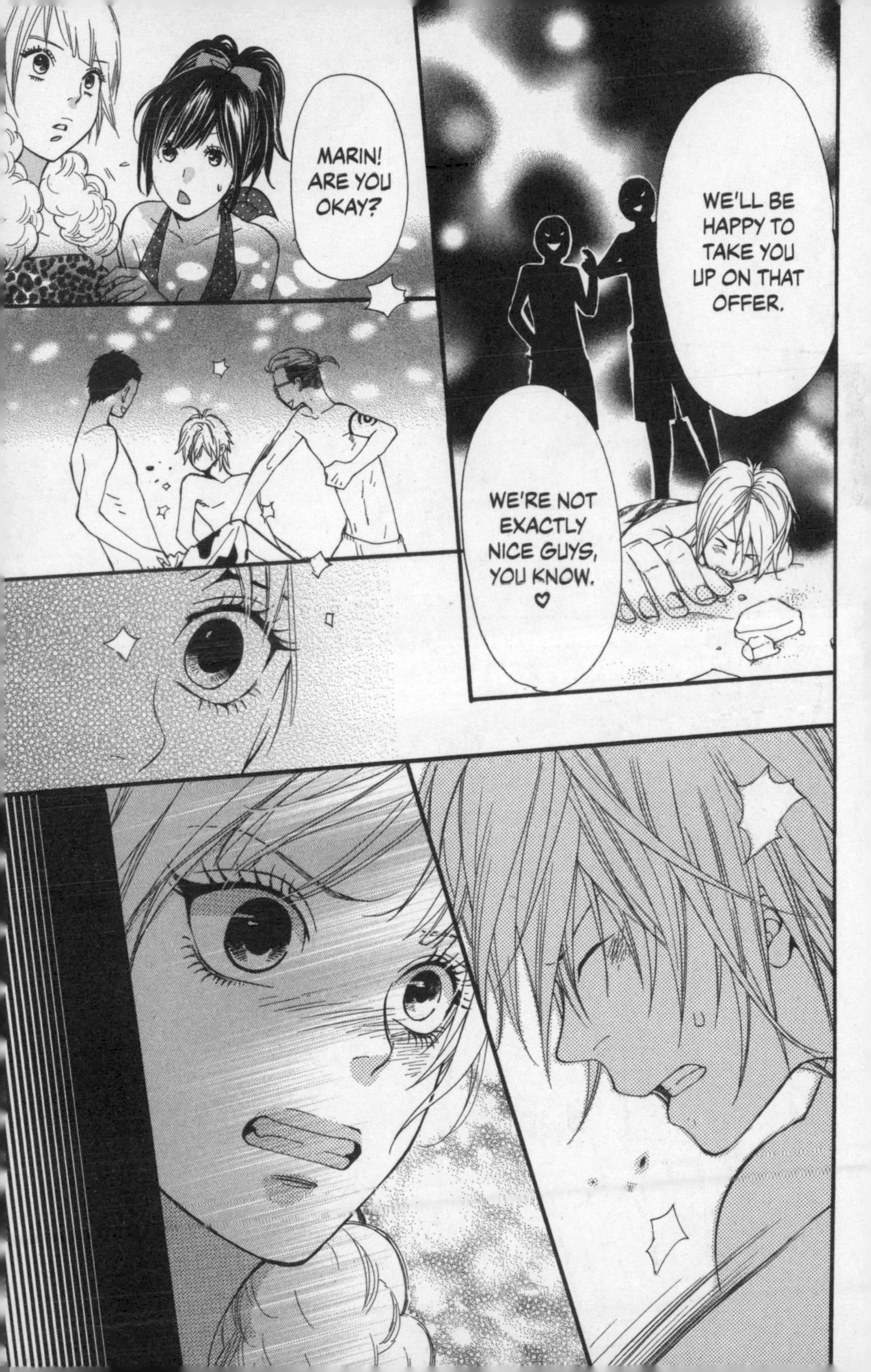
WE'LL BE HAPPY TO TAKE YOU UP ON THAT OFFER.
WE'RE NOT EXACTLY NICE GUYS, YOU KNOW. ♡
MARIN! ARE YOU OKAY?

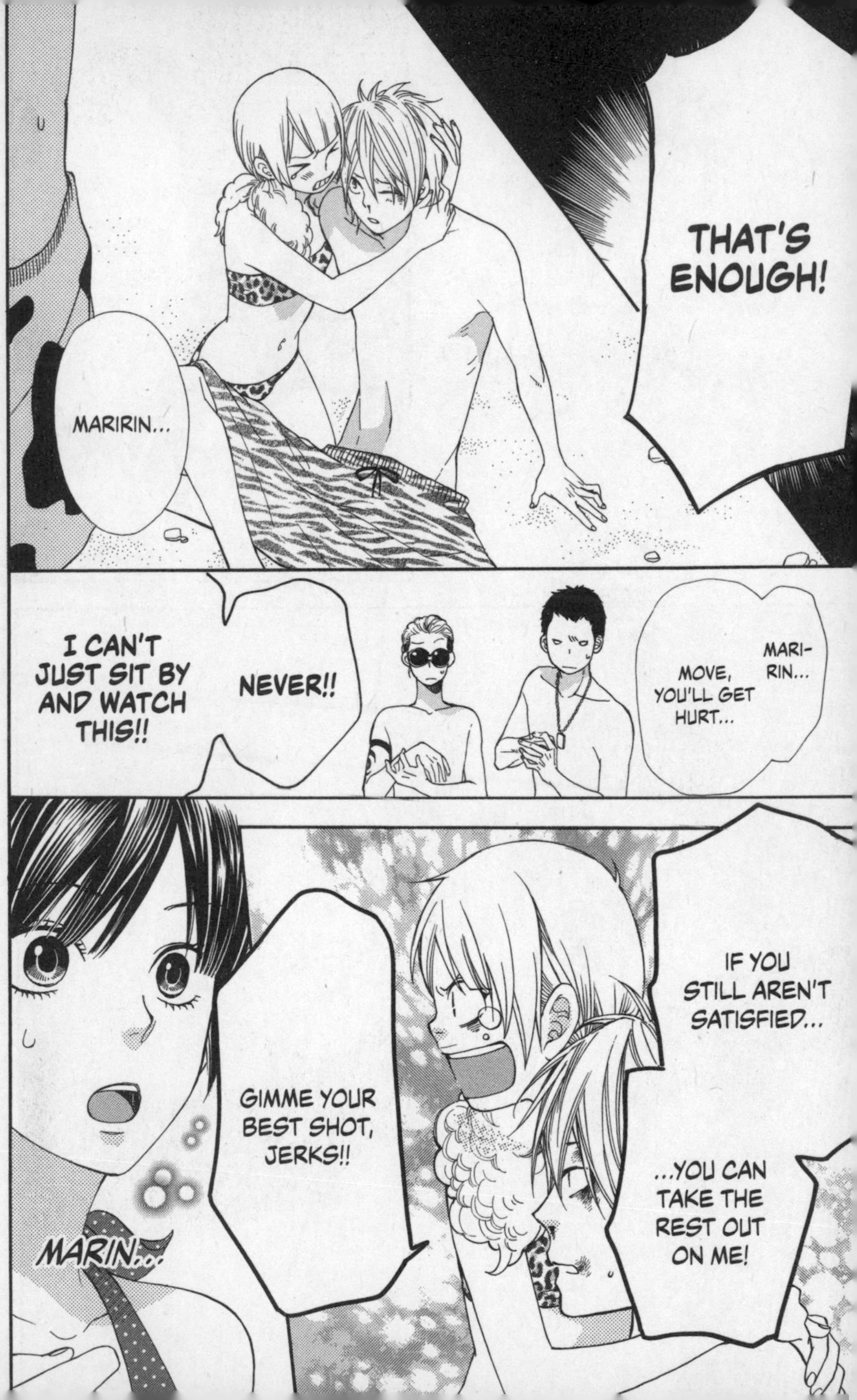
THAT'S ENOUGH!
MARIRIN...
MARI-RIN... MOVE, YOU'LL GET HURT...
NEVER!!
I CAN'T JUST SIT BY AND WATCH THIS!!
IF YOU STILL AREN'T SATISFIED...
...YOU CAN TAKE THE REST OUT ON ME!
GIMME YOUR BEST SHOT, JERKS!!
MARIN...

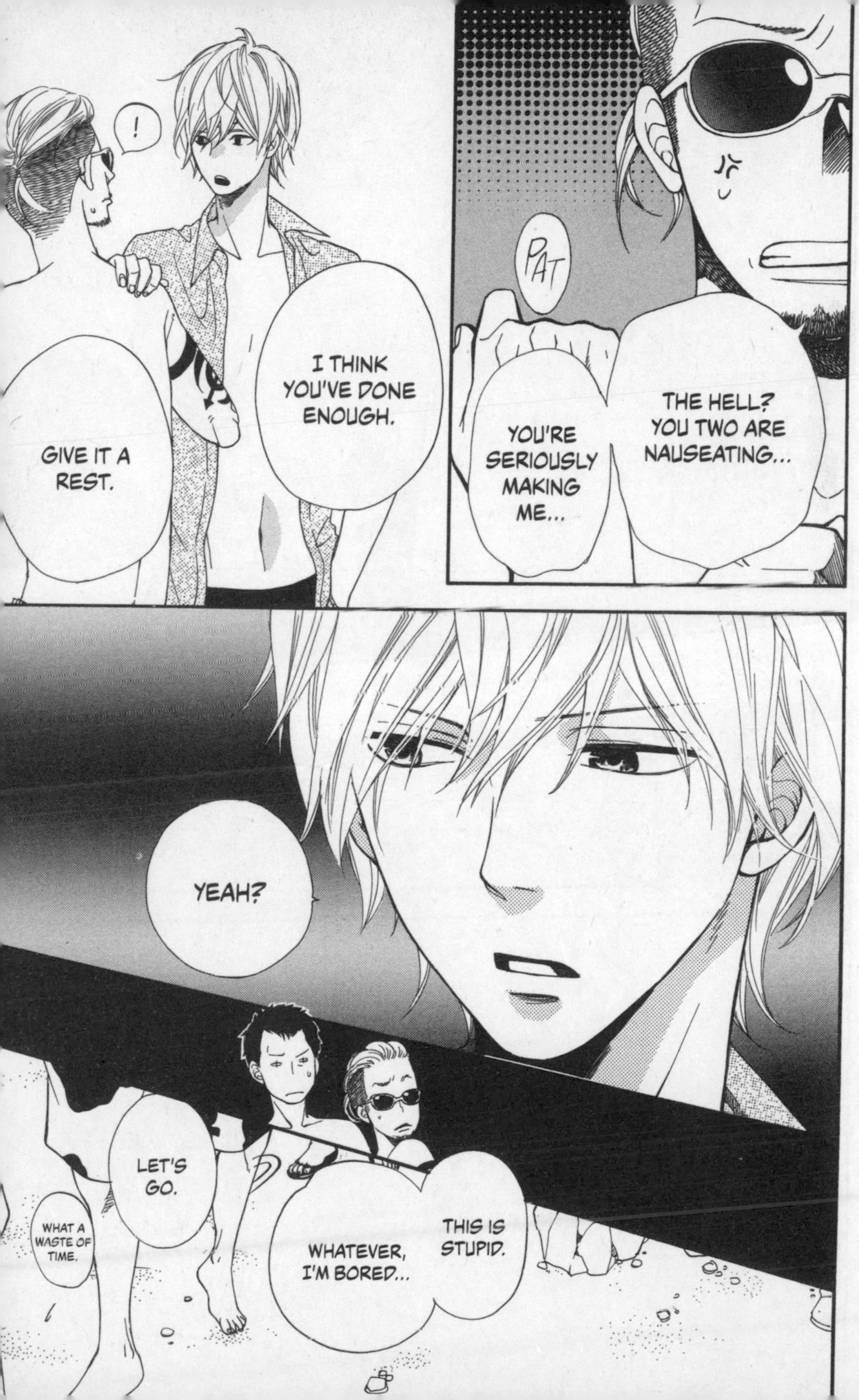
PAT
THE HELL? YOU TWO ARE NAUSEATING...
YOU'RE SERIOUSLY MAKING ME...
!
I THINK YOU'VE DONE ENOUGH.
GIVE IT A REST.
YEAH?
THIS IS STUPID.
WHATEVER, I'M BORED...
LET'S GO.
WHAT A WASTE OF TIME.

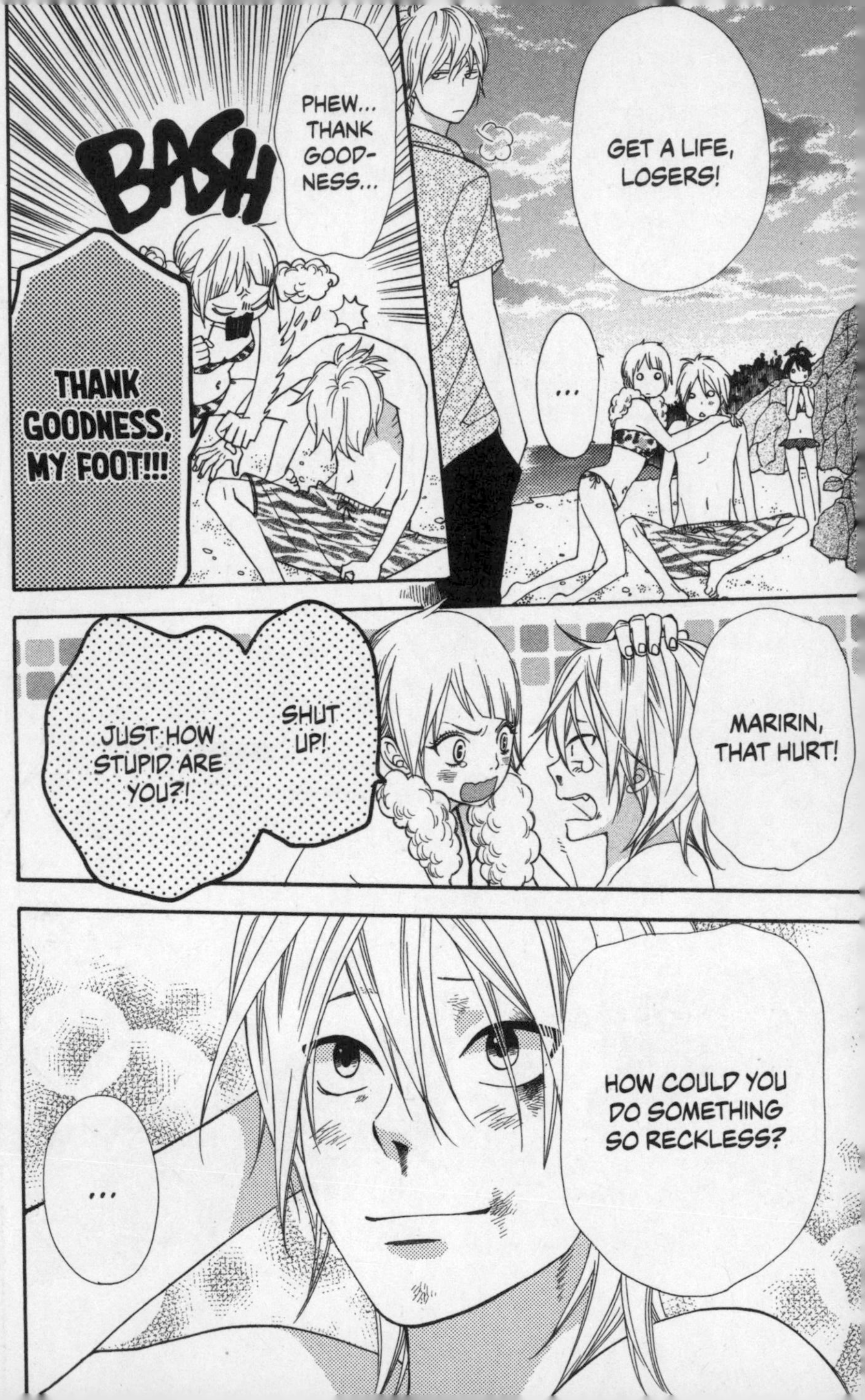
GET A LIFE, LOSERS!
...
PHEW... THANK GOOD-NESS...
BASH
THANK GOODNESS, MY FOOT!!!
MARIRIN, THAT HURT!
SHUT UP!
JUST HOW STUPID ARE YOU?!
HOW COULD YOU DO SOMETHING SO RECKLESS?
...

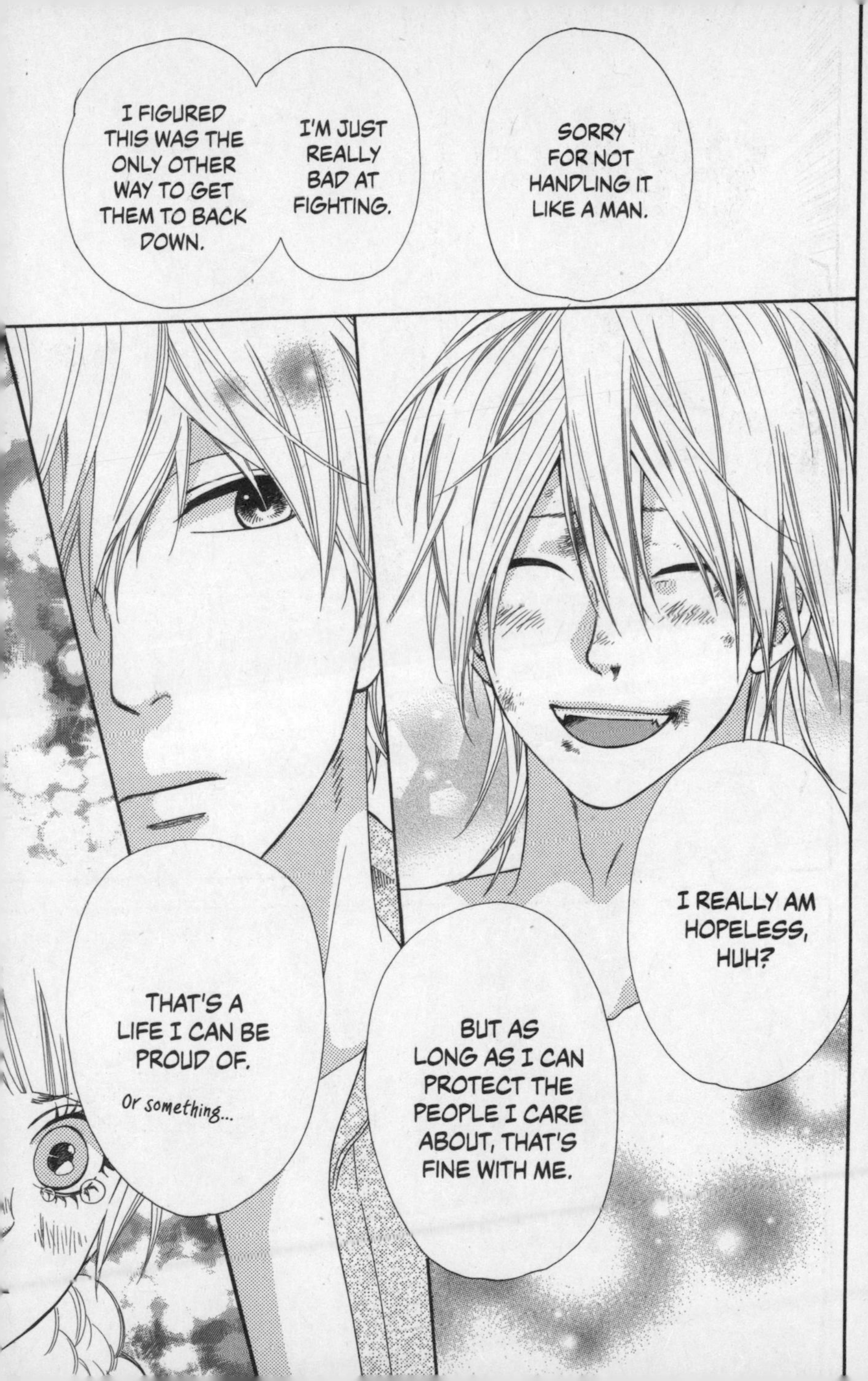
SORRY FOR NOT HANDLING IT LIKE A MAN.
I'M JUST REALLY BAD AT FIGHTING.
I FIGURED THIS WAS THE ONLY OTHER WAY TO GET THEM TO BACK DOWN.
I REALLY AM HOPELESS, HUH?
BUT AS LONG AS I CAN PROTECT THE PEOPLE I CARE ABOUT, THAT'S FINE WITH ME.
THAT'S A LIFE I CAN BE PROUD OF.
Or something...

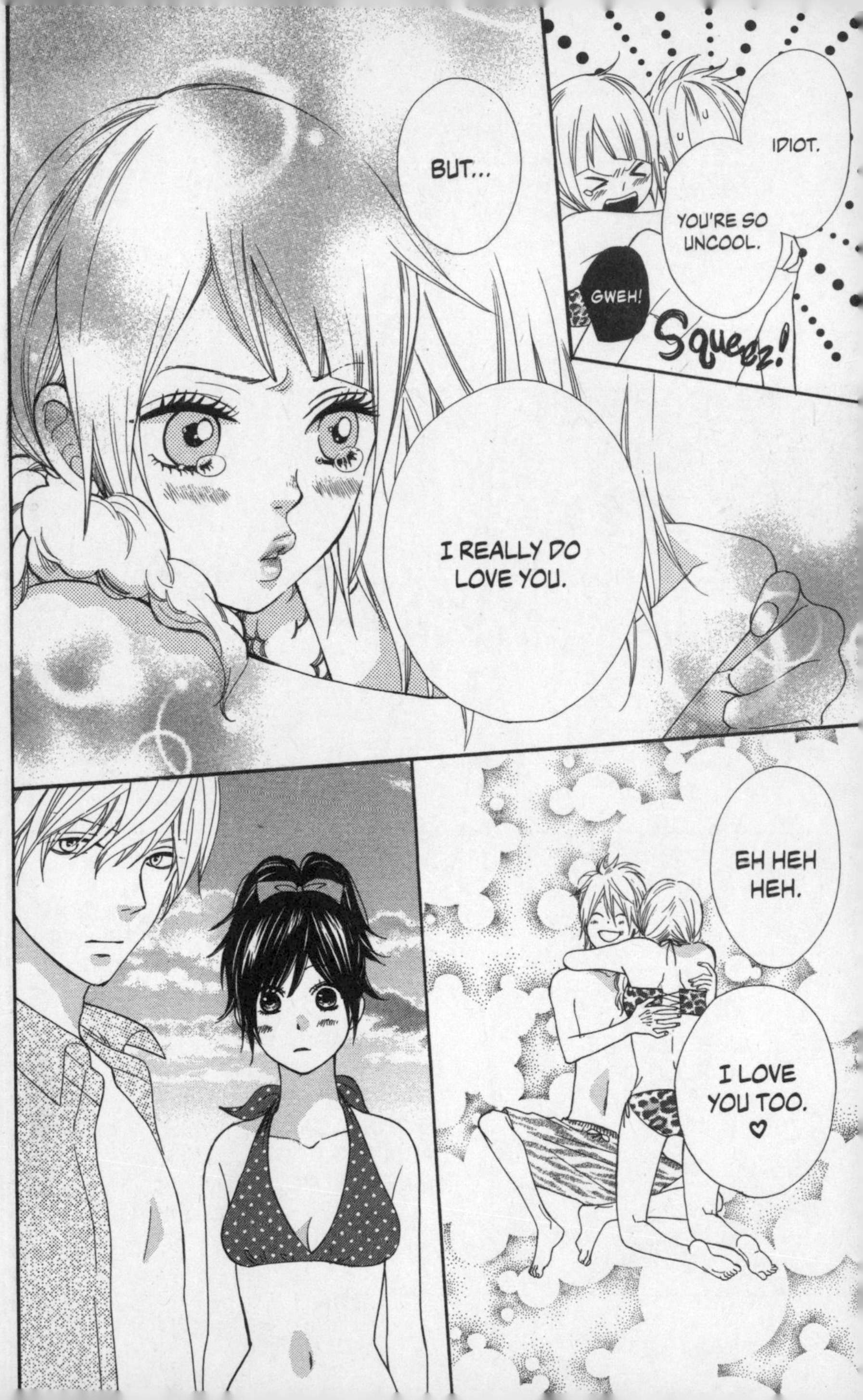
BUT...
I REALLY DO LOVE YOU.
IDIOT.
YOU'RE SO UNCOOL.
GWEH!
Squeez!
EH HEH HEH.
I LOVE YOU TOO. ♡

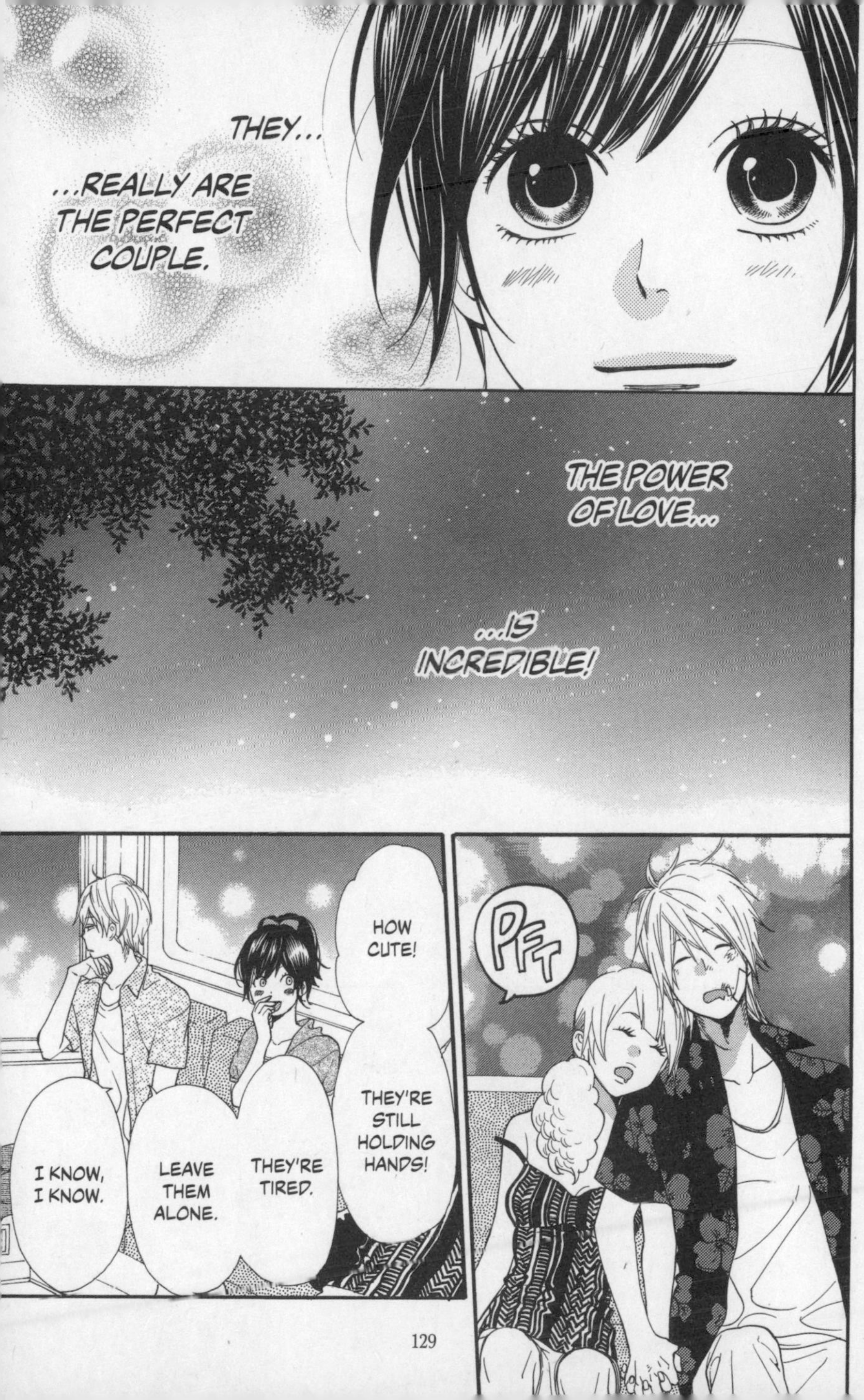
THEY...
...REALLY ARE THE PERFECT COUPLE.
THE POWER OF LOVE...
...IS INCREDIBLE!
PFFT
HOW CUTE!
THEY'RE STILL HOLDING HANDS!
THEY'RE TIRED.
LEAVE THEM ALONE.
I KNOW, I KNOW.

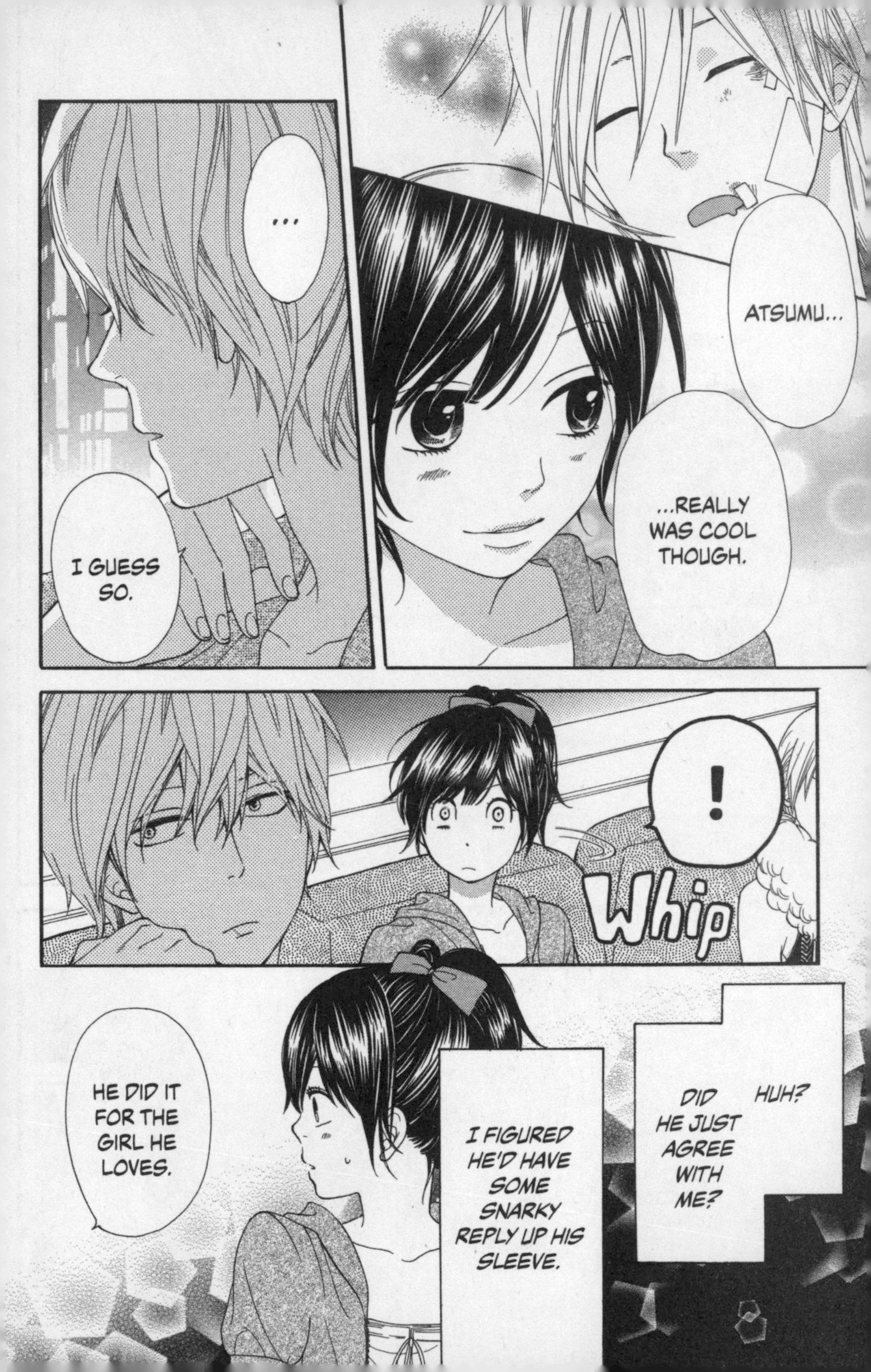
ATSUMU...
...REALLY WAS COOL THOUGH.
...
I GUESS SO.
!
Whip
HUH?
DID HE JUST AGREE WITH ME?
I FIGURED HE'D HAVE SOME SNARKY REPLY UP HIS SLEEVE.
HE DID IT FOR THE GIRL HE LOVES.

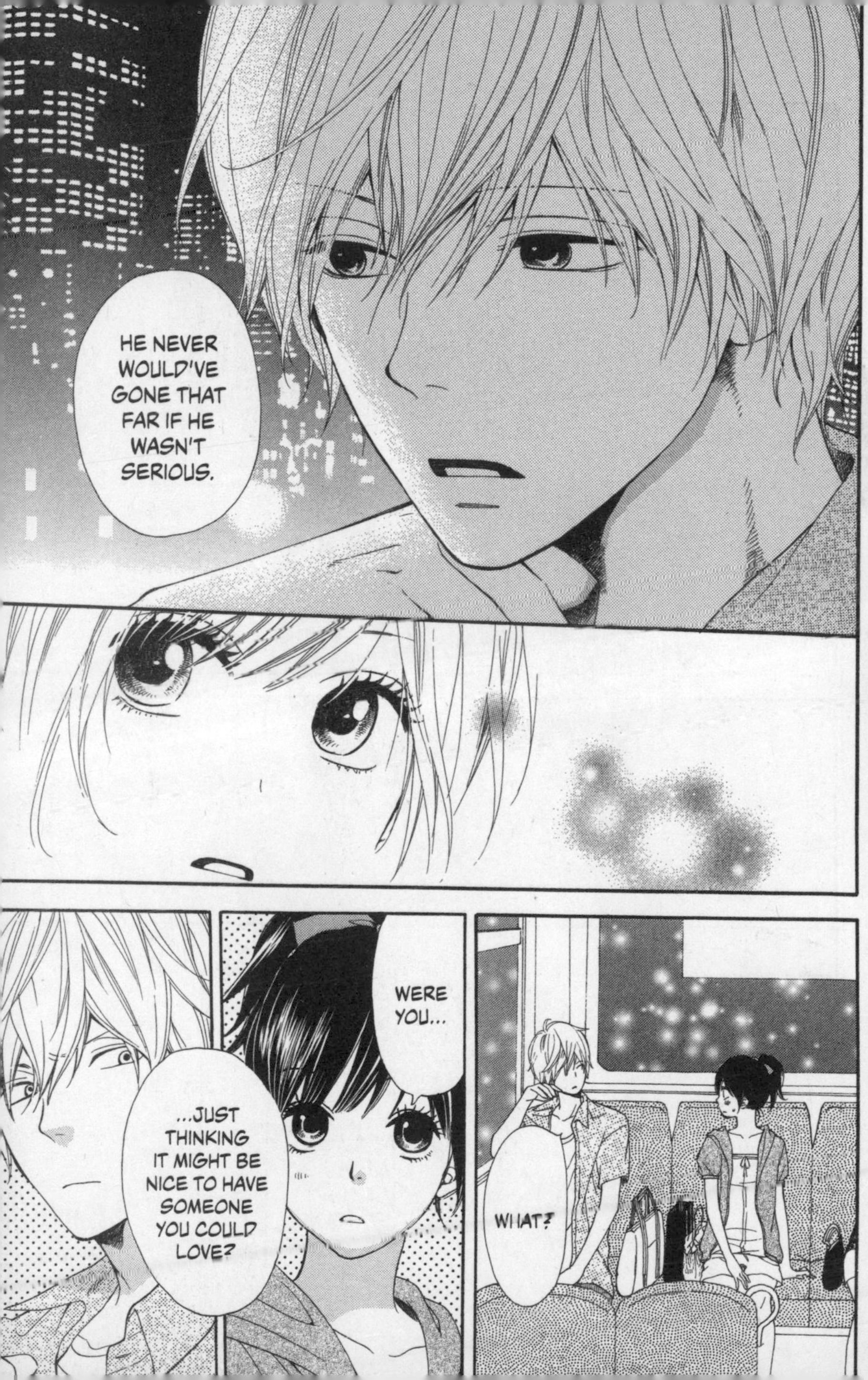
HE NEVER WOULD'VE GONE THAT FAR IF HE WASN'T SERIOUS.
WHAT?
WERE YOU...
...JUST THINKING IT MIGHT BE NICE TO HAVE SOMEONE YOU COULD LOVE?

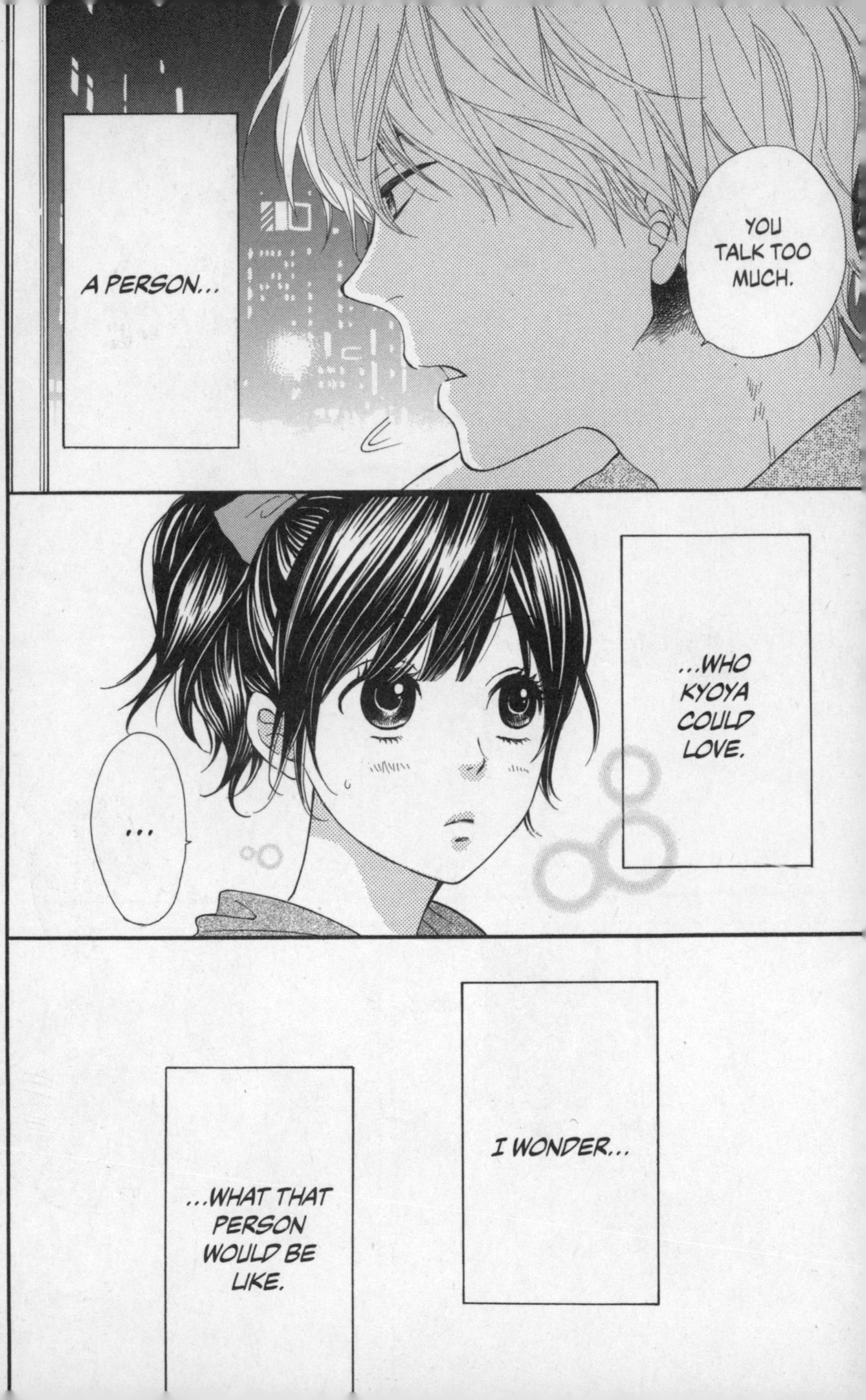
YOU TALK TOO MUCH.
A PERSON...
...WHO KYOYA COULD LOVE.
...
I WONDER...
...WHAT THAT PERSON WOULD BE LIKE.

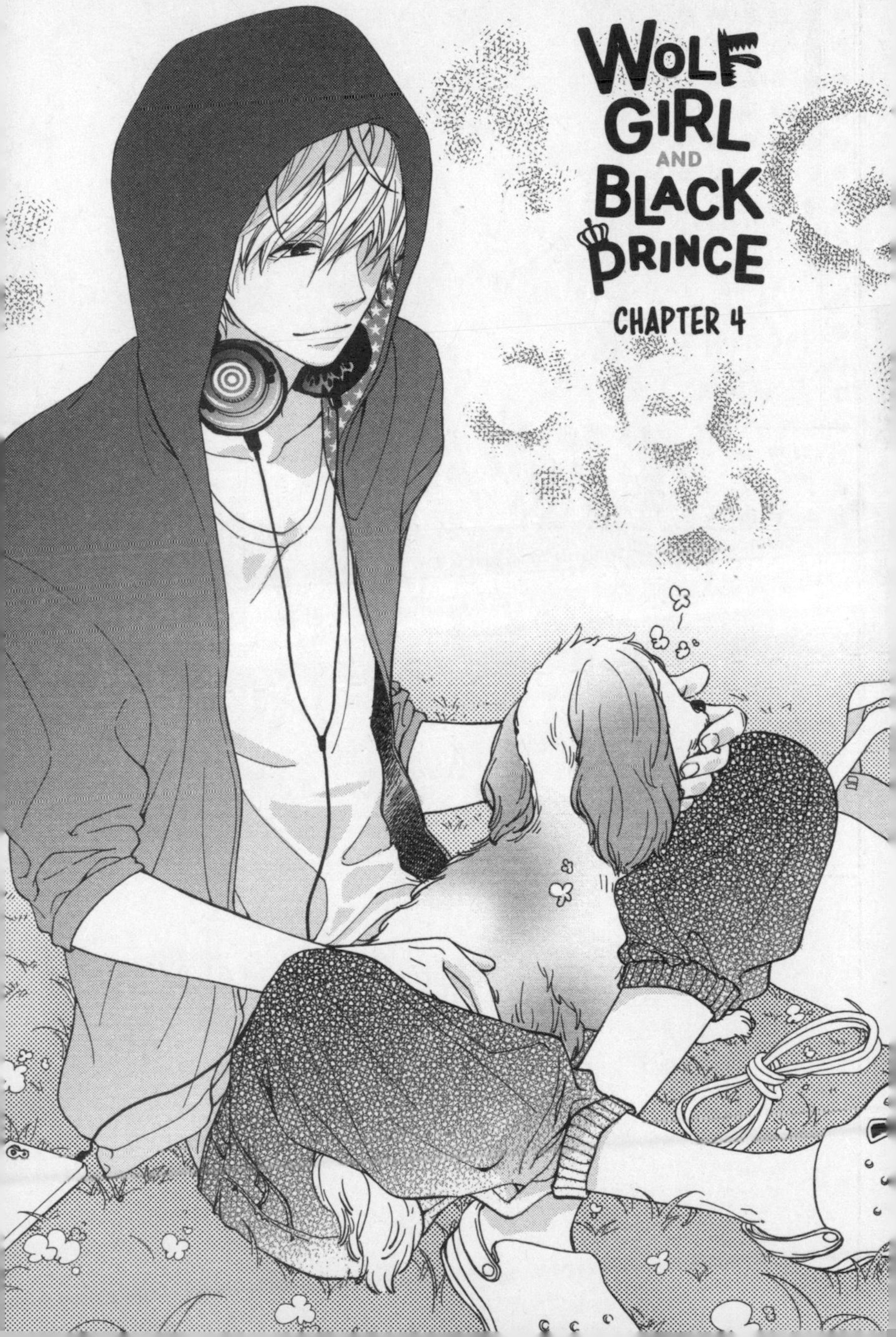
WOLF GIRL AND BLACK PRINCE
CHAPTER 4

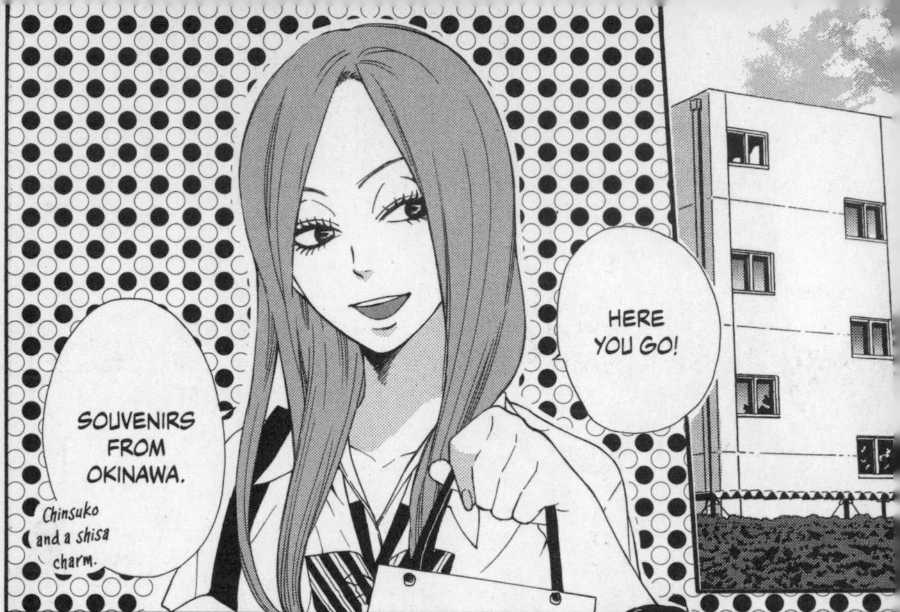
HERE YOU GO!
SOUVENIRS FROM OKINAWA.
Chinsuko and a shisa charm.

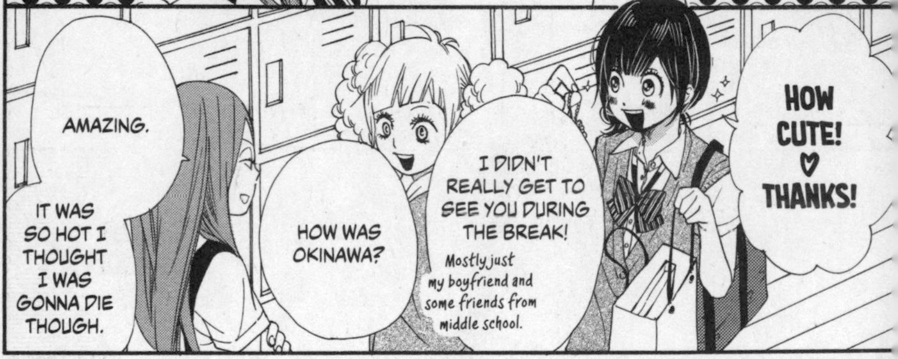
HOW CUTE! ♡ THANKS!
I DIDN'T REALLY GET TO SEE YOU DURING THE BREAK!
Mostly just my boyfriend and some friends from middle school.
HOW WAS OKINAWA?
AMAZING.
IT WAS SO HOT I THOUGHT I WAS GONNA DIE THOUGH.

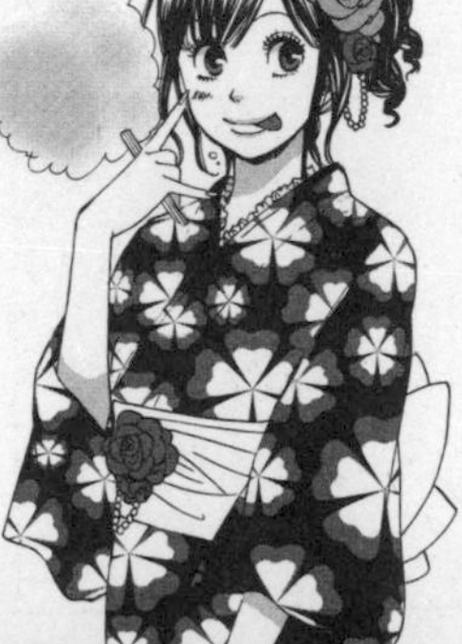

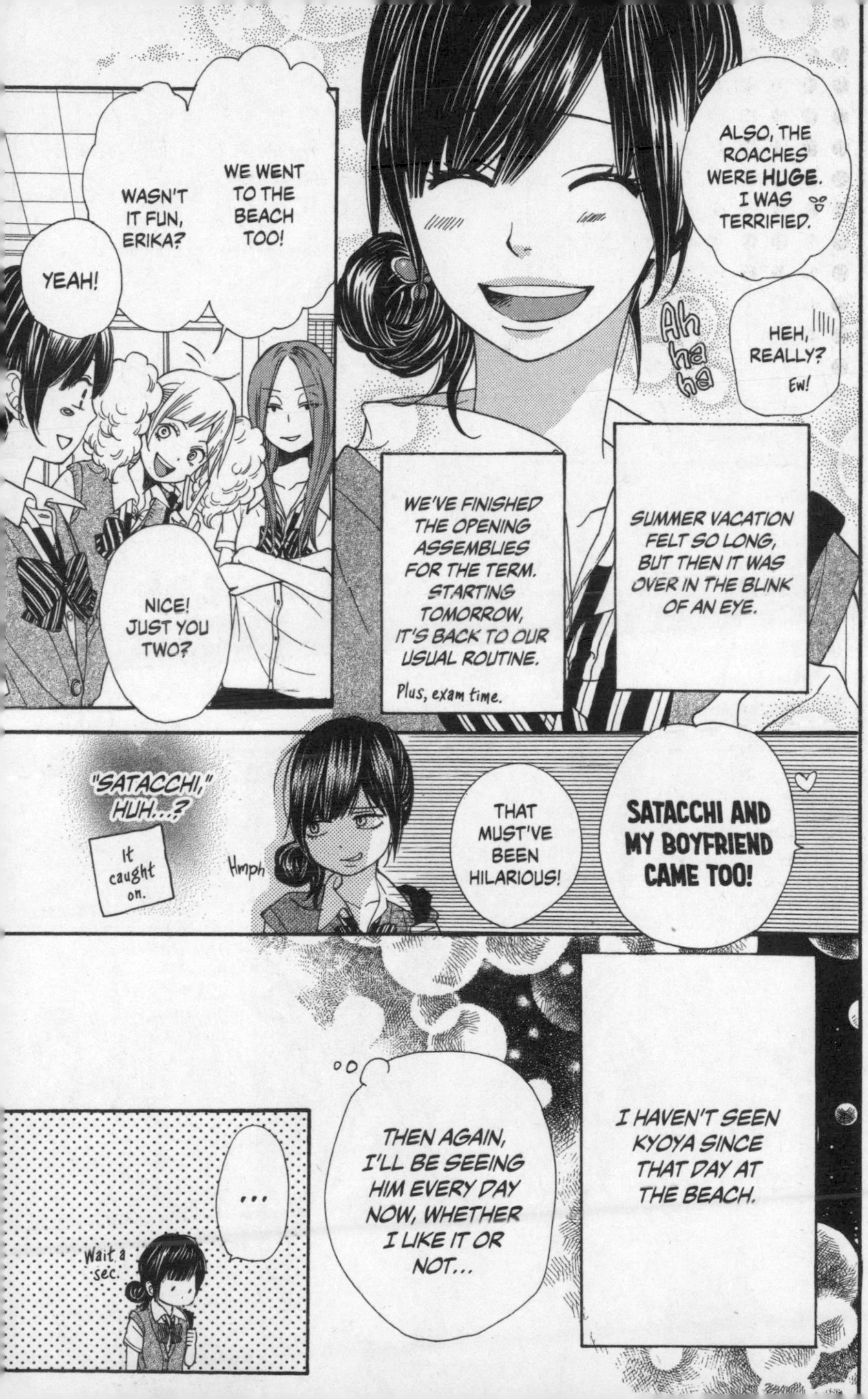
ALSO, THE ROACHES WERE HUGE. I WAS TERRIFIED.
Ah ha ha
HEH, REALLY?
Ew!
SUMMER VACATION FELT SO LONG, BUT THEN IT WAS OVER IN THE BLINK OF AN EYE.
WE'VE FINISHED THE OPENING ASSEMBLIES FOR THE TERM. STARTING TOMORROW, IT'S BACK TO OUR USUAL ROUTINE.
Plus, exam time.
WE WENT TO THE BEACH TOO!
WASN'T IT FUN, ERIKA?
YEAH!
NICE! JUST YOU TWO?
SATACCHI AND MY BOYFRIEND CAME TOO!
THAT MUST'VE BEEN HILARIOUS!
Hmph
"SATACCHI," HUH...?
It caught on.
I HAVEN'T SEEN KYOYA SINCE THAT DAY AT THE BEACH.
THEN AGAIN, I'LL BE SEEING HIM EVERY DAY NOW, WHETHER I LIKE IT OR NOT...
...
Wait a sec.

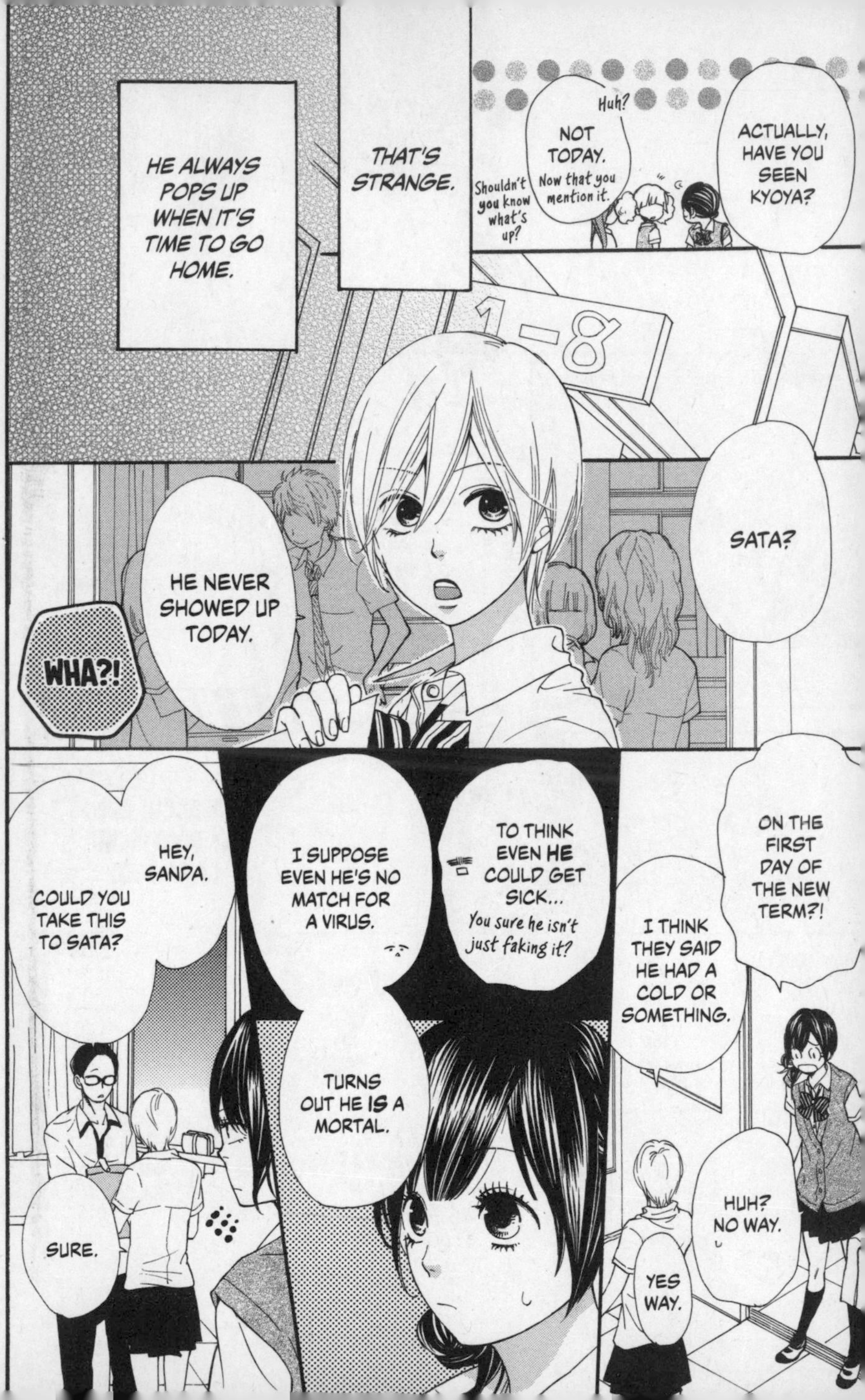
ACTUALLY, HAVE YOU SEEN KYOYA?
Huh?
NOT TODAY.
Now that you mention it.
Shouldn't you know what's up?
THAT'S STRANGE.
HE ALWAYS POPS UP WHEN IT'S TIME TO GO HOME.
SATA?
HE NEVER SHOWED UP TODAY.
WHA?!
ON THE FIRST DAY OF THE NEW TERM?!
I THINK THEY SAID HE HAD A COLD OR SOMETHING.
HUH? NO WAY.
YES WAY.
TO THINK EVEN **HE** COULD GET SICK...
You sure he isn't just faking it?
I SUPPOSE EVEN HE'S NO MATCH FOR A VIRUS.
TURNS OUT HE **IS** A MORTAL.
HEY, SANDA.
COULD YOU TAKE THIS TO SATA?
SURE.

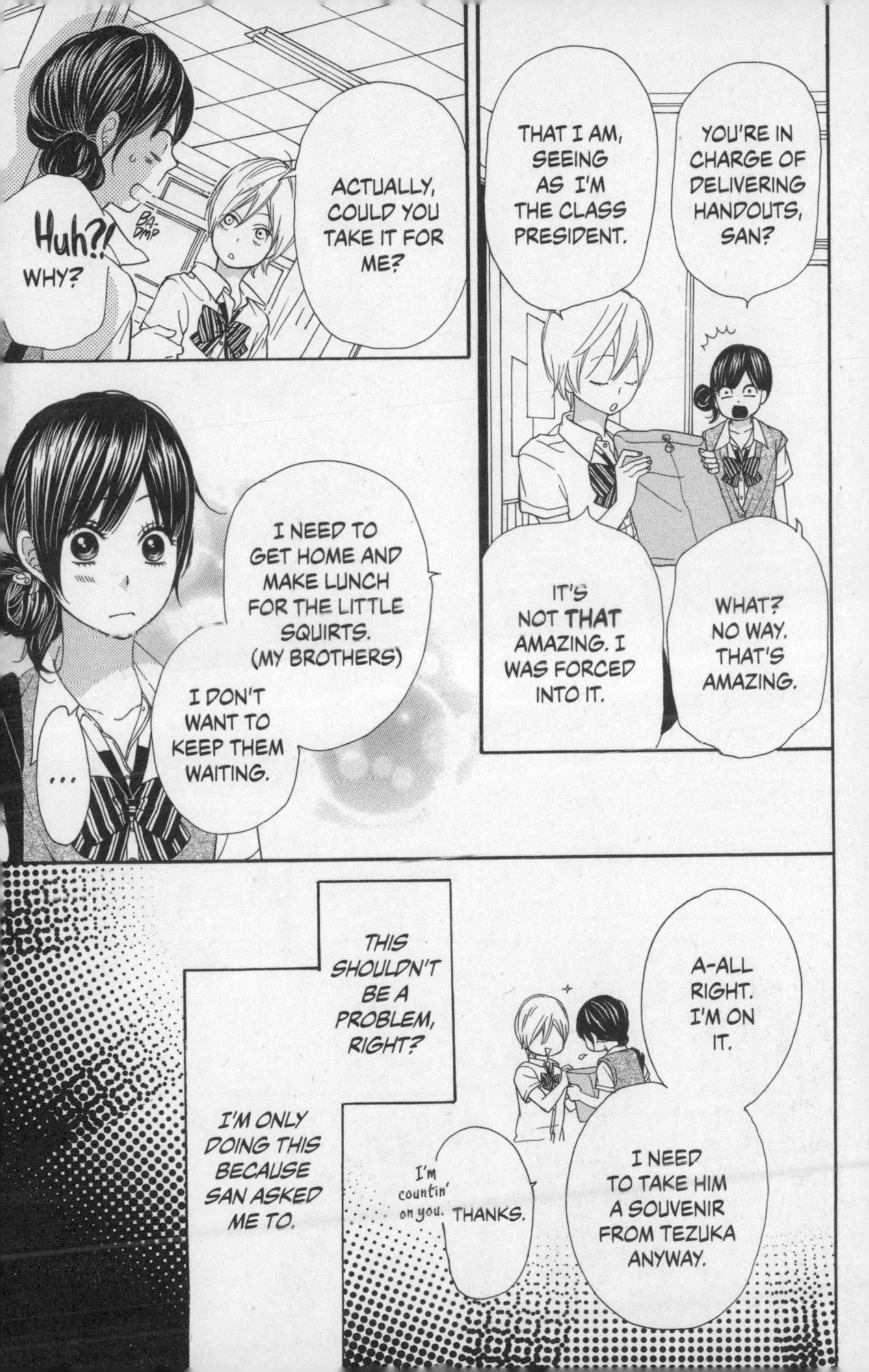
YOU'RE IN CHARGE OF DELIVERING HANDOUTS, SAN?
THAT I AM, SEEING AS I'M THE CLASS PRESIDENT.
WHAT? NO WAY. THAT'S AMAZING.
IT'S NOT THAT AMAZING. I WAS FORCED INTO IT.
ACTUALLY, COULD YOU TAKE IT FOR ME?
BA-DMP
Huh?! WHY?
I NEED TO GET HOME AND MAKE LUNCH FOR THE LITTLE SQUIRTS. (MY BROTHERS)
I DON'T WANT TO KEEP THEM WAITING.
...
A-ALL RIGHT. I'M ON IT.
I NEED TO TAKE HIM A SOUVENIR FROM TEZUKA ANYWAY.
THANKS.
I'm countin' on you.
THIS SHOULDN'T BE A PROBLEM, RIGHT?
I'M ONLY DOING THIS BECAUSE SAN ASKED ME TO.

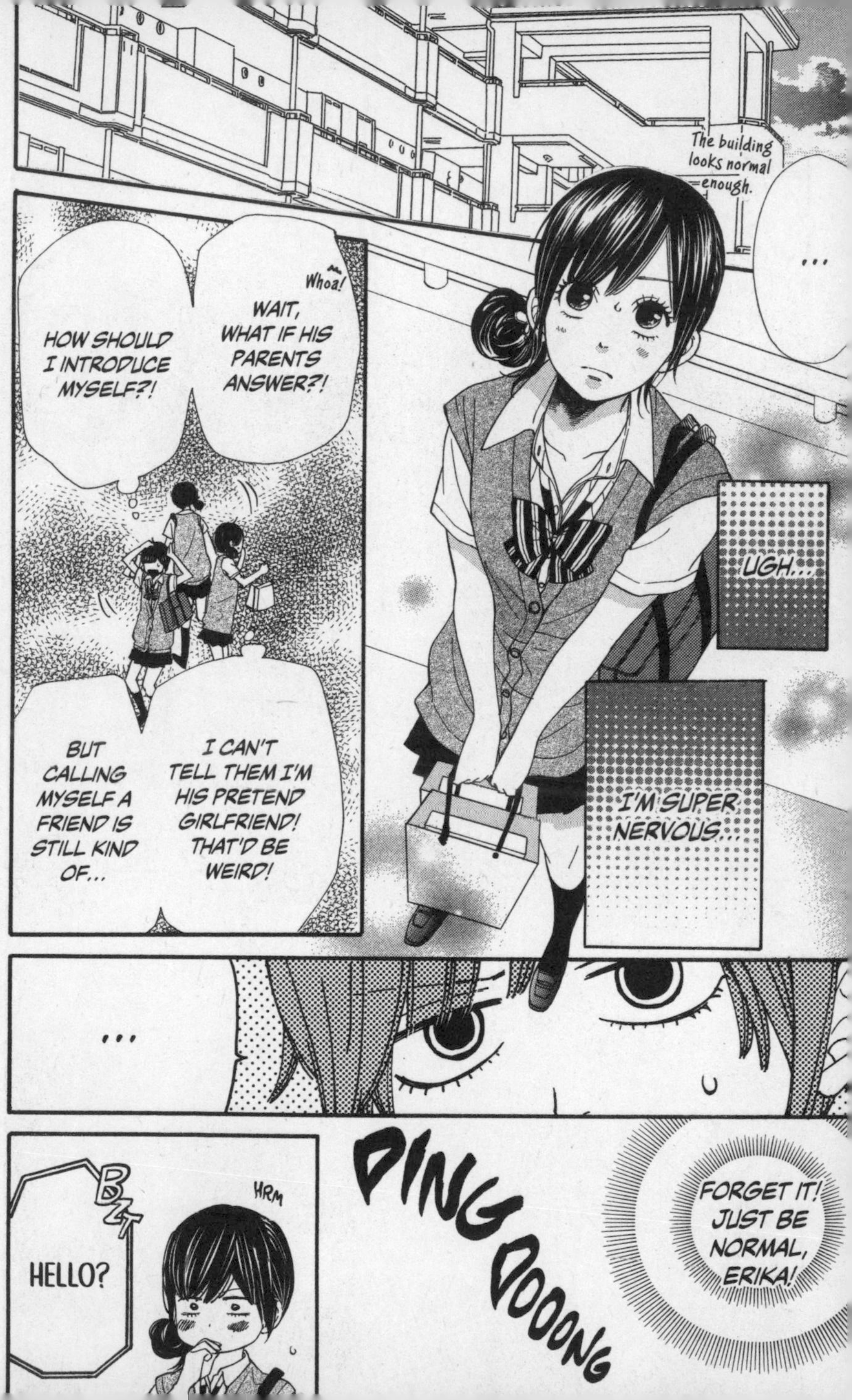
The building looks normal enough.
...
UGH...
I'M SUPER NERVOUS...
Whoa!
WAIT, WHAT IF HIS PARENTS ANSWER?!
HOW SHOULD I INTRODUCE MYSELF?!
I CAN'T TELL THEM I'M HIS PRETEND GIRLFRIEND! THAT'D BE WEIRD!
BUT CALLING MYSELF A FRIEND IS STILL KIND OF...
...
FORGET IT! JUST BE NORMAL, ERIKA!
DING DOOONG
HRM
BZT
HELLO?

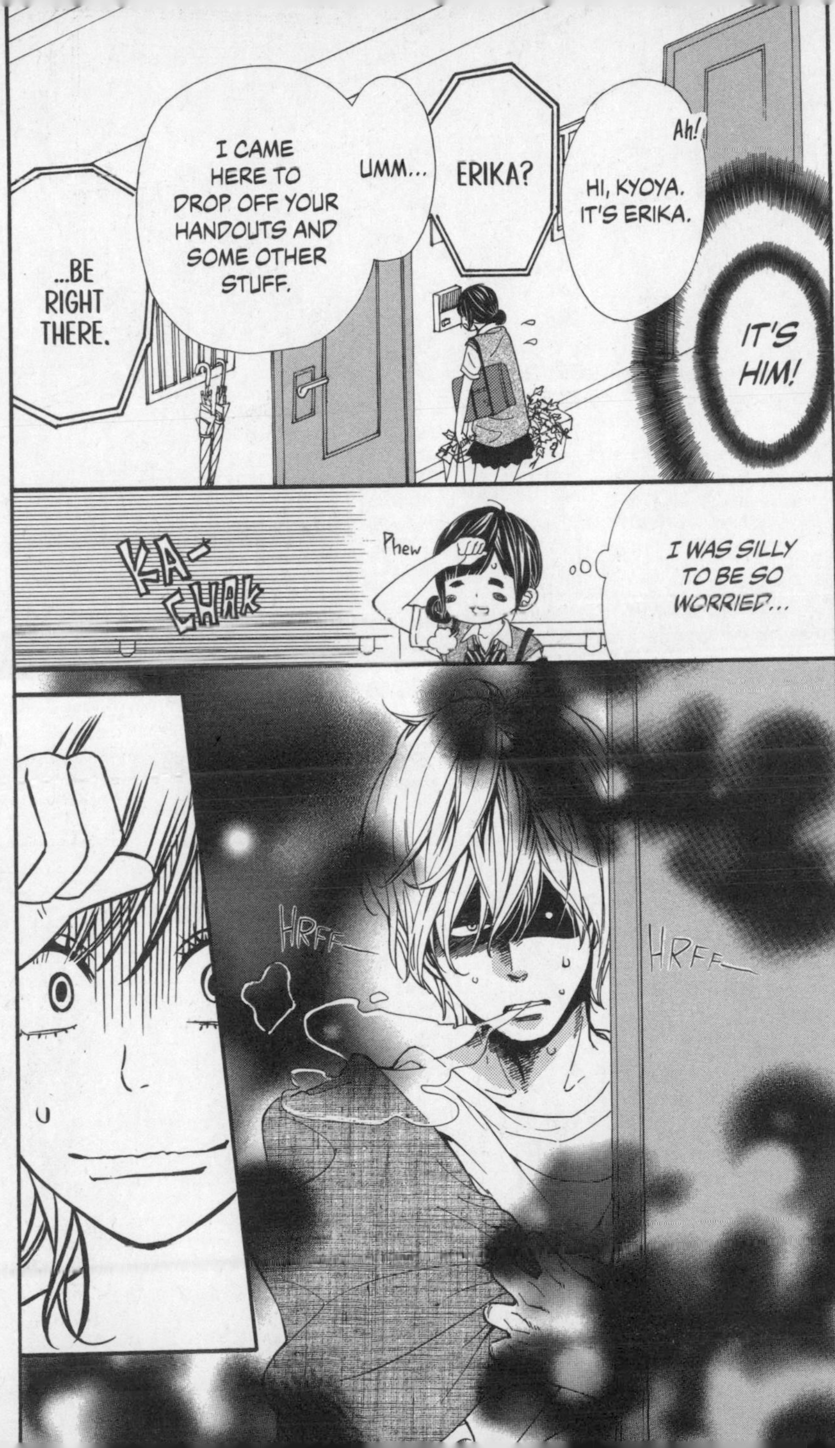
Ah!
HI, KYOYA. IT'S ERIKA.
IT'S HIM!
ERIKA?
UMM...
I CAME HERE TO DROP OFF YOUR HANDOUTS AND SOME OTHER STUFF.
...BE RIGHT THERE.
I WAS SILLY TO BE SO WORRIED...
Phew
KA-CHAK
HRFF—
HRFF—

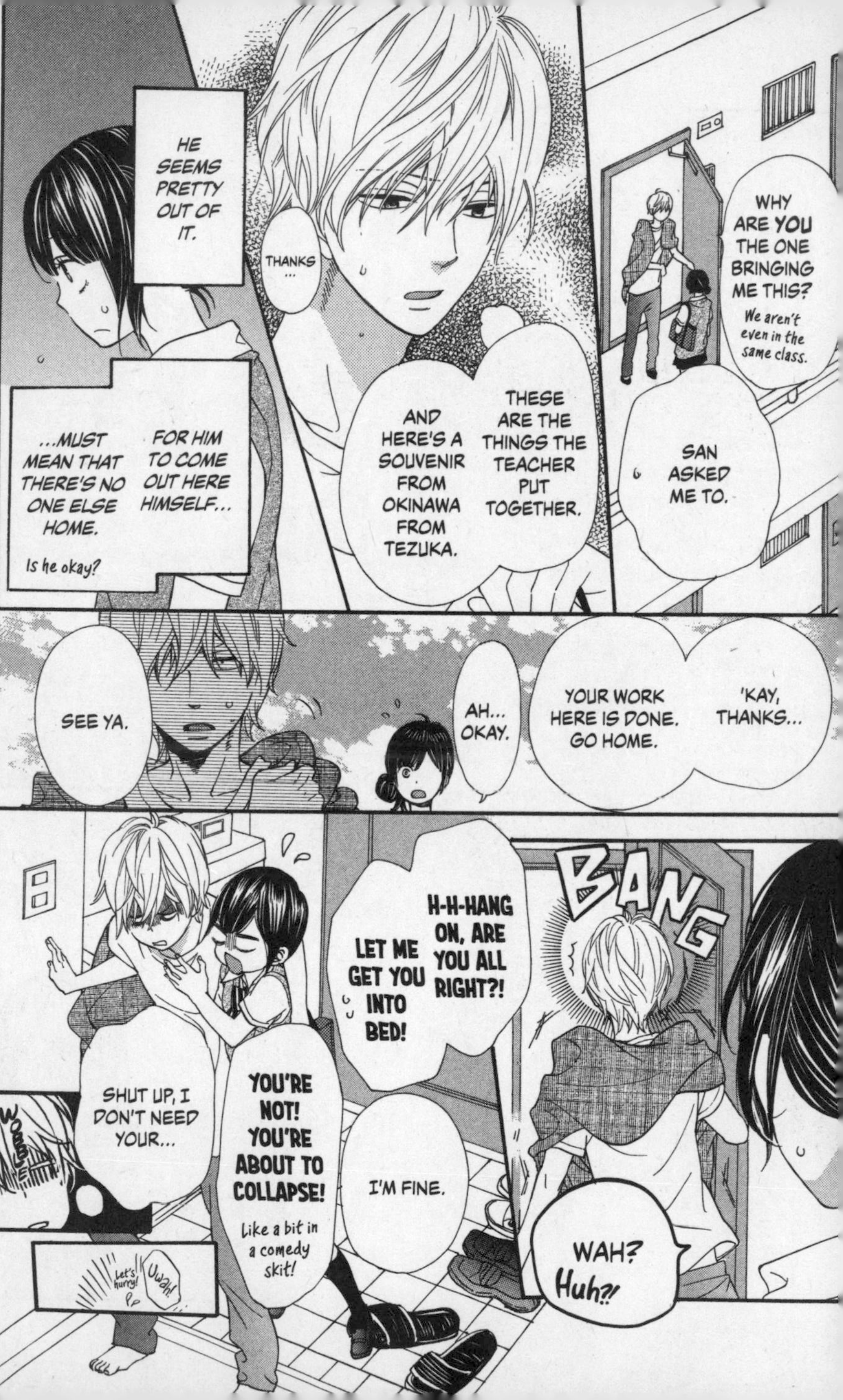
WHY ARE YOU THE ONE BRINGING ME THIS?
We aren't even in the same class.
SAN ASKED ME TO.
THESE ARE THE THINGS THE TEACHER PUT TOGETHER.
AND HERE'S A SOUVENIR FROM OKINAWA FROM TEZUKA.
THANKS...
HE SEEMS PRETTY OUT OF IT.
FOR HIM TO COME OUT HERE HIMSELF...
...MUST MEAN THAT THERE'S NO ONE ELSE HOME.
Is he okay?
'KAY, THANKS...
YOUR WORK HERE IS DONE. GO HOME.
AH... OKAY.
SEE YA.
BANG
WAH? Huh?!
H-H-HANG ON, ARE YOU ALL RIGHT?!
LET ME GET YOU INTO BED!
I'M FINE.
YOU'RE NOT! YOU'RE ABOUT TO COLLAPSE!
Like a bit in a comedy skit!
SHUT UP, I DON'T NEED YOUR...
WOBBLE
Uwah!
Let's hurry!

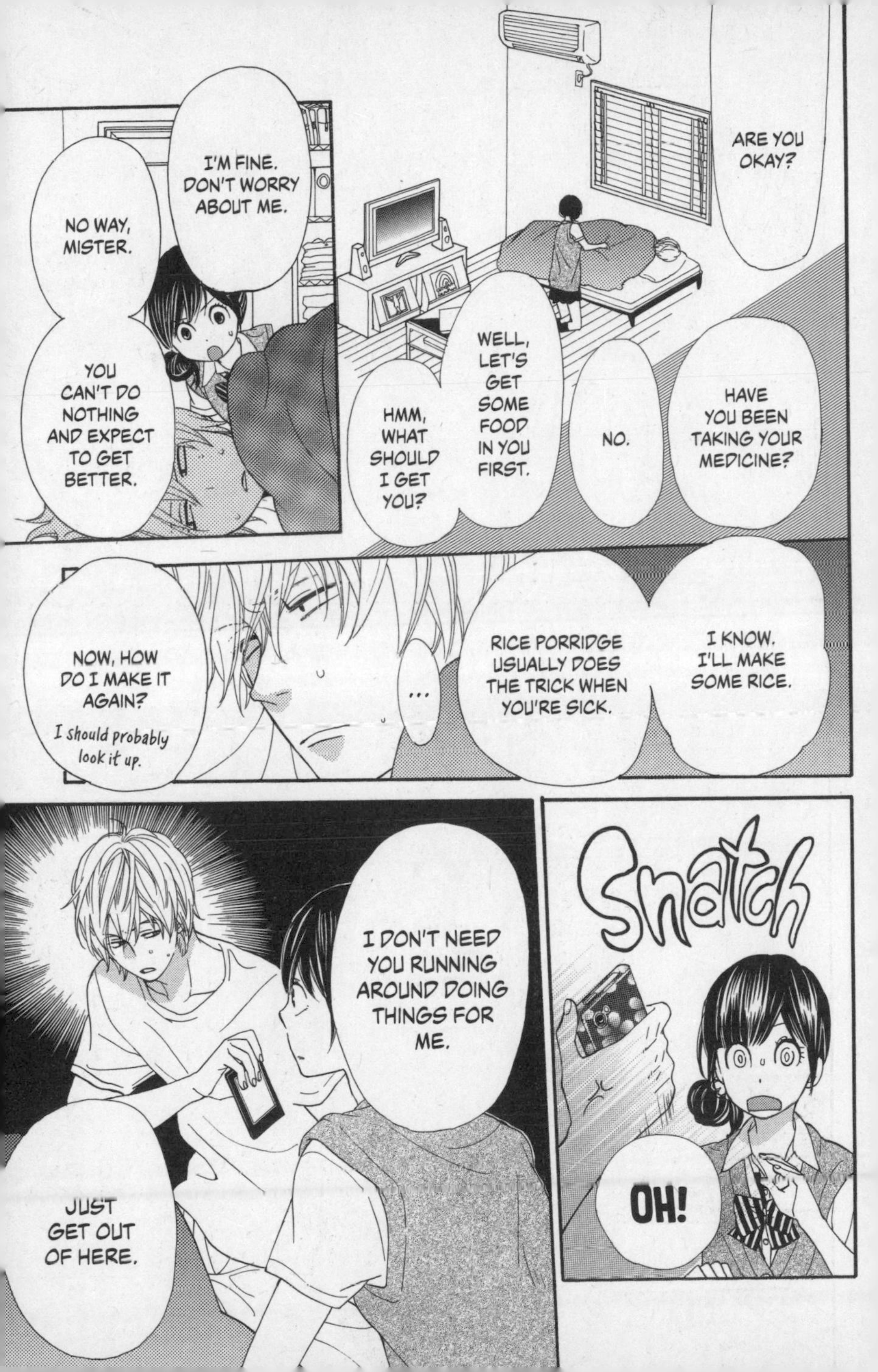
ARE YOU OKAY?
HAVE YOU BEEN TAKING YOUR MEDICINE?
NO.
WELL, LET'S GET SOME FOOD IN YOU FIRST.
HMM, WHAT SHOULD I GET YOU?
I'M FINE. DON'T WORRY ABOUT ME.
NO WAY, MISTER.
YOU CAN'T DO NOTHING AND EXPECT TO GET BETTER.
I KNOW. I'LL MAKE SOME RICE.
RICE PORRIDGE USUALLY DOES THE TRICK WHEN YOU'RE SICK.
...
NOW, HOW DO I MAKE IT AGAIN?
I should probably look it up.
Snatch
OH!
I DON'T NEED YOU RUNNING AROUND DOING THINGS FOR ME.
JUST GET OUT OF HERE.

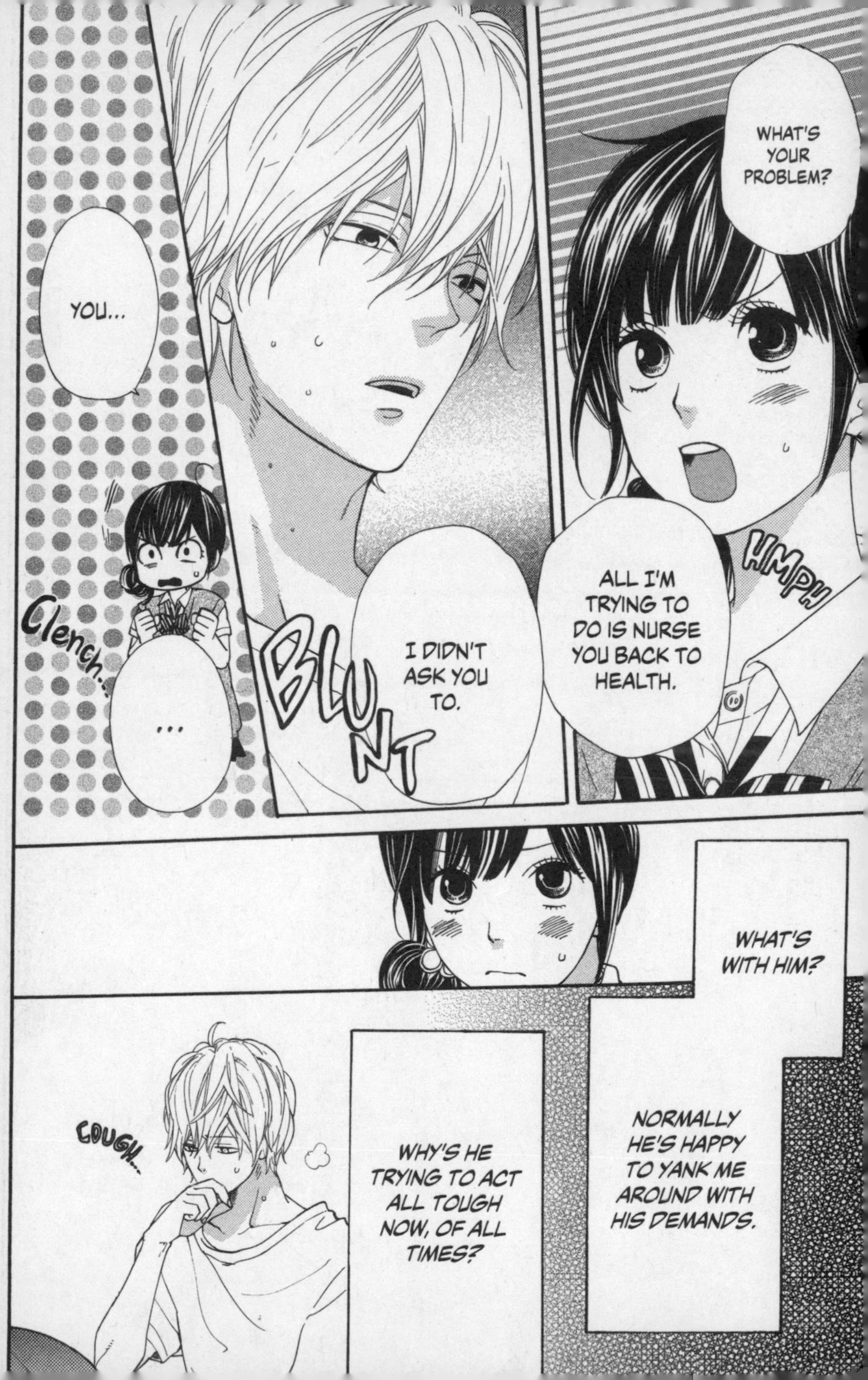
WHAT'S YOUR PROBLEM?
HMPH
ALL I'M TRYING TO DO IS NURSE YOU BACK TO HEALTH.
I DIDN'T ASK YOU TO.
BLUNT
YOU...
Clench...
...
WHAT'S WITH HIM?
NORMALLY HE'S HAPPY TO YANK ME AROUND WITH HIS DEMANDS.
WHY'S HE TRYING TO ACT ALL TOUGH NOW, OF ALL TIMES?
COUGH...

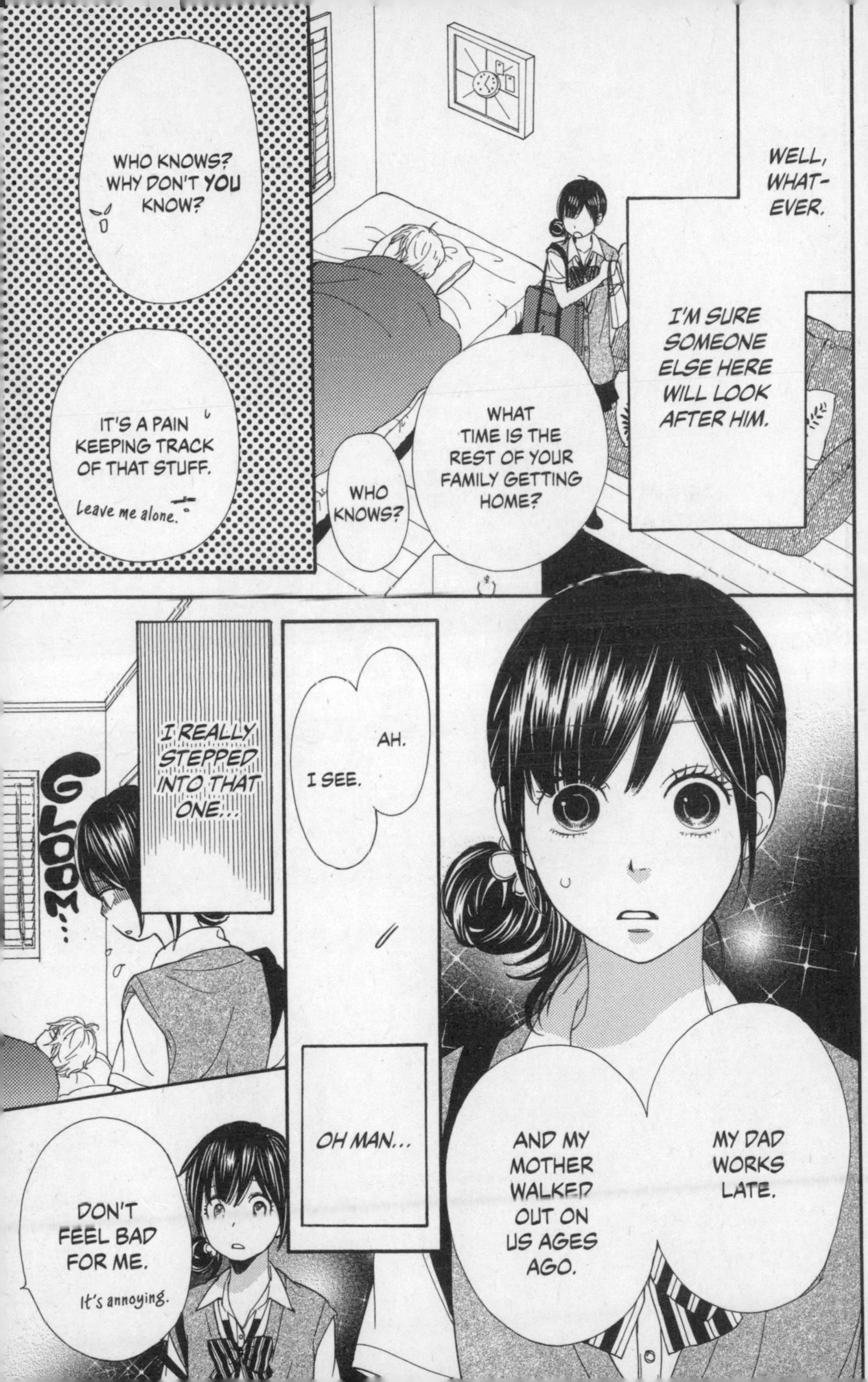
WELL, WHAT-EVER.
I'M SURE SOMEONE ELSE HERE WILL LOOK AFTER HIM.
WHAT TIME IS THE REST OF YOUR FAMILY GETTING HOME?
WHO KNOWS?
WHO KNOWS? WHY DON'T YOU KNOW?
IT'S A PAIN KEEPING TRACK OF THAT STUFF.
Leave me alone.
MY DAD WORKS LATE.
AND MY MOTHER WALKED OUT ON US AGES AGO.
AH.
I SEE.
OH MAN...
I REALLY STEPPED INTO THAT ONE...
GLOOM...
DON'T FEEL BAD FOR ME.
It's annoying.

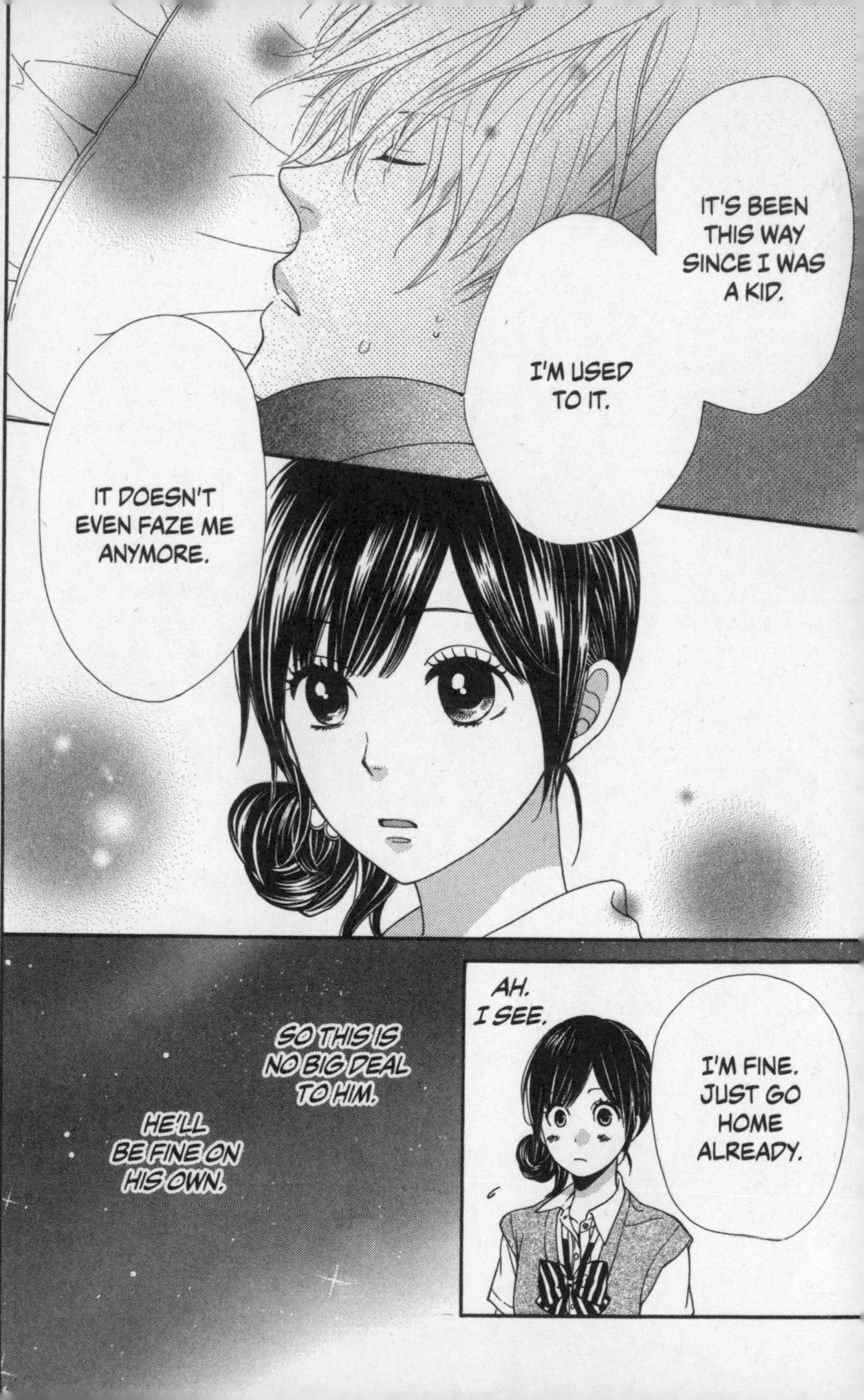
IT'S BEEN THIS WAY SINCE I WAS A KID.
I'M USED TO IT.
IT DOESN'T EVEN FAZE ME ANYMORE.
AH. I SEE.
I'M FINE. JUST GO HOME ALREADY.
SO THIS IS NO BIG DEAL TO HIM.
HE'LL BE FINE ON HIS OWN.

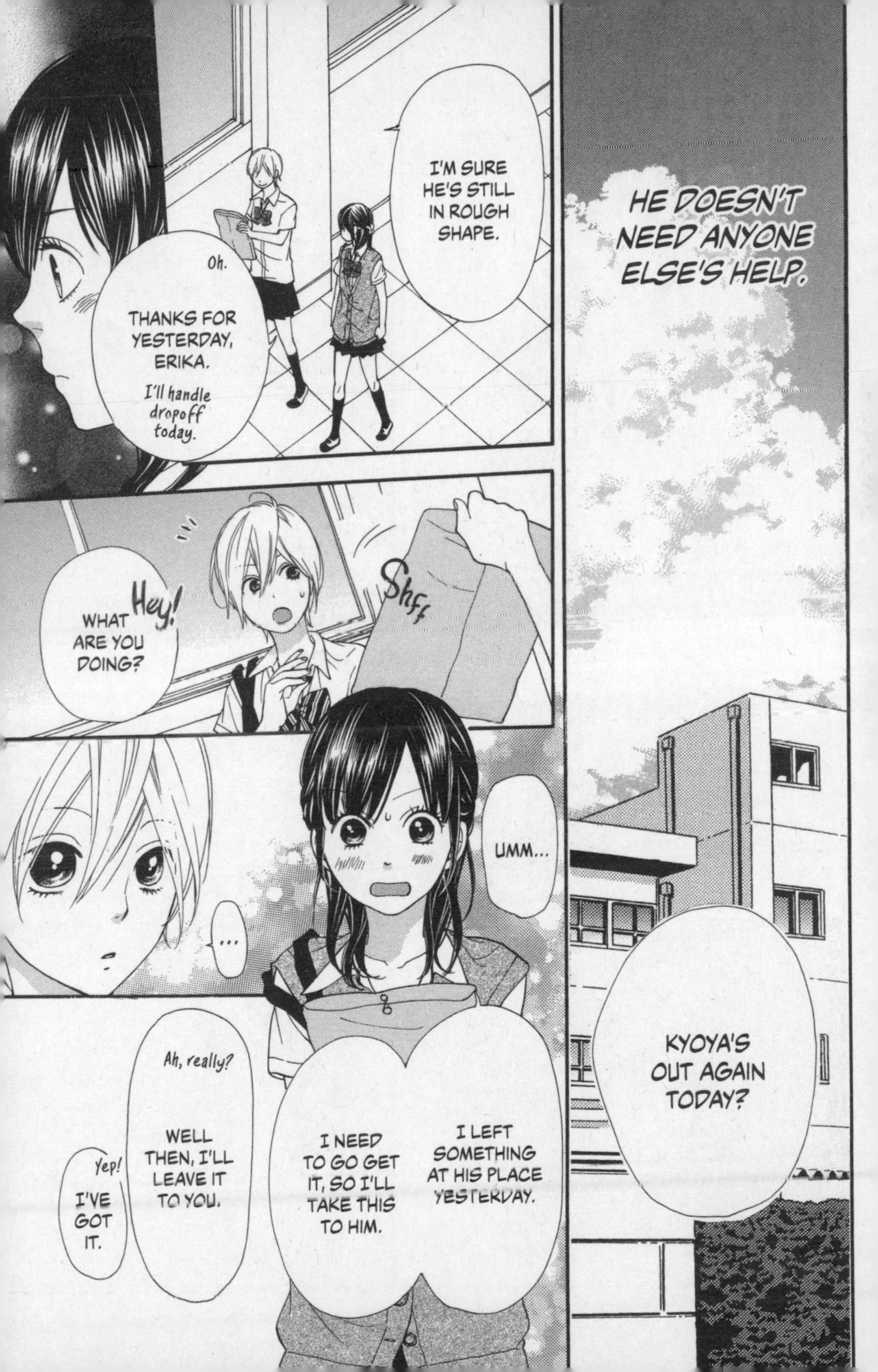
HE DOESN'T NEED ANYONE ELSE'S HELP.
KYOYA'S OUT AGAIN TODAY?
I'M SURE HE'S STILL IN ROUGH SHAPE.
Oh.
THANKS FOR YESTERDAY, ERIKA.
I'll handle dropoff today.
Shff
Hey!
WHAT ARE YOU DOING?
UMM...
...
I LEFT SOMETHING AT HIS PLACE YESTERDAY.
I NEED TO GO GET IT, SO I'LL TAKE THIS TO HIM.
Ah, really?
WELL THEN, I'LL LEAVE IT TO YOU.
Yep!
I'VE GOT IT.

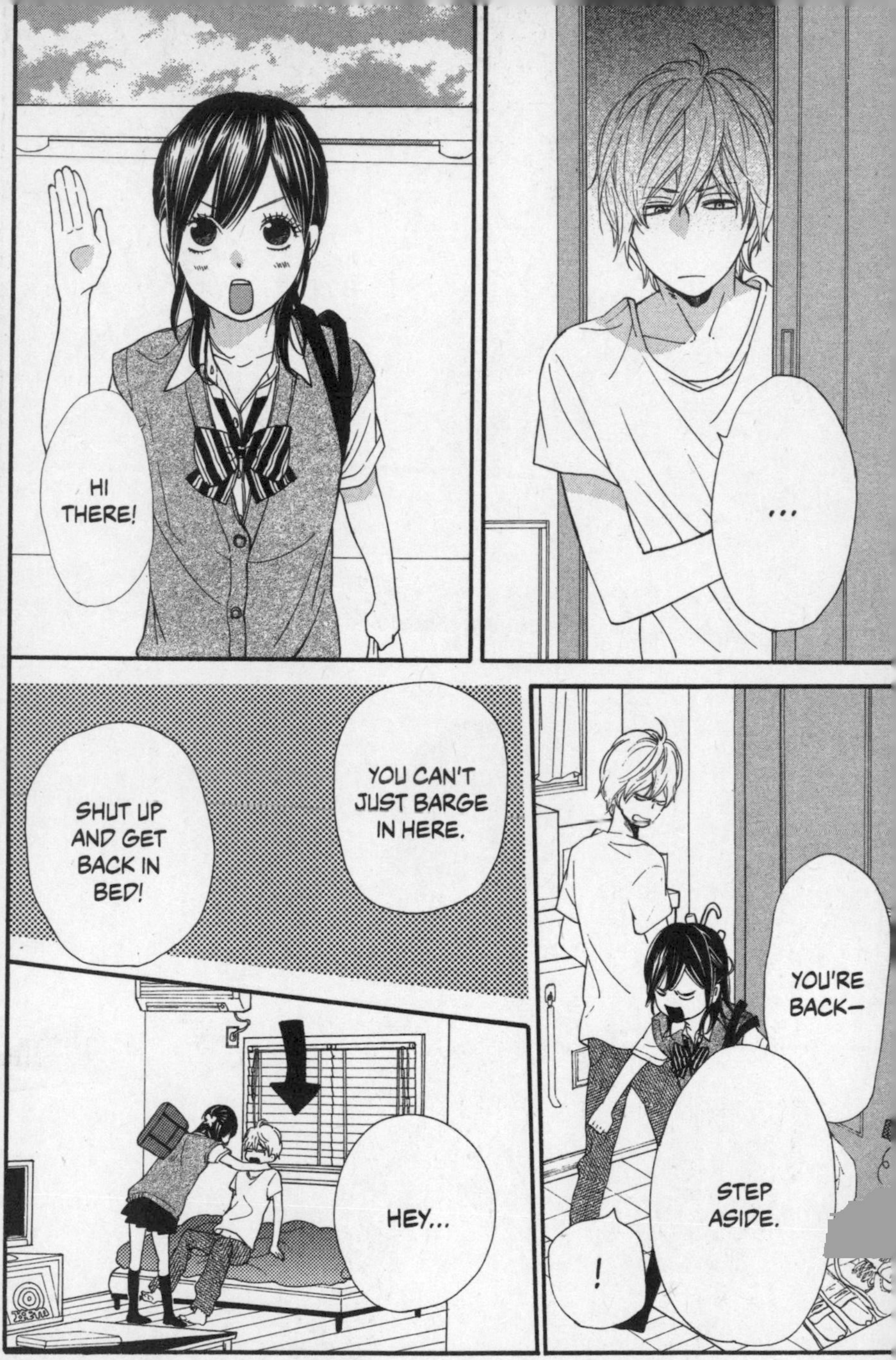
...
HI THERE!
YOU'RE BACK—
STEP ASIDE.
!
YOU CAN'T JUST BARGE IN HERE.
SHUT UP AND GET BACK IN BED!
HEY...

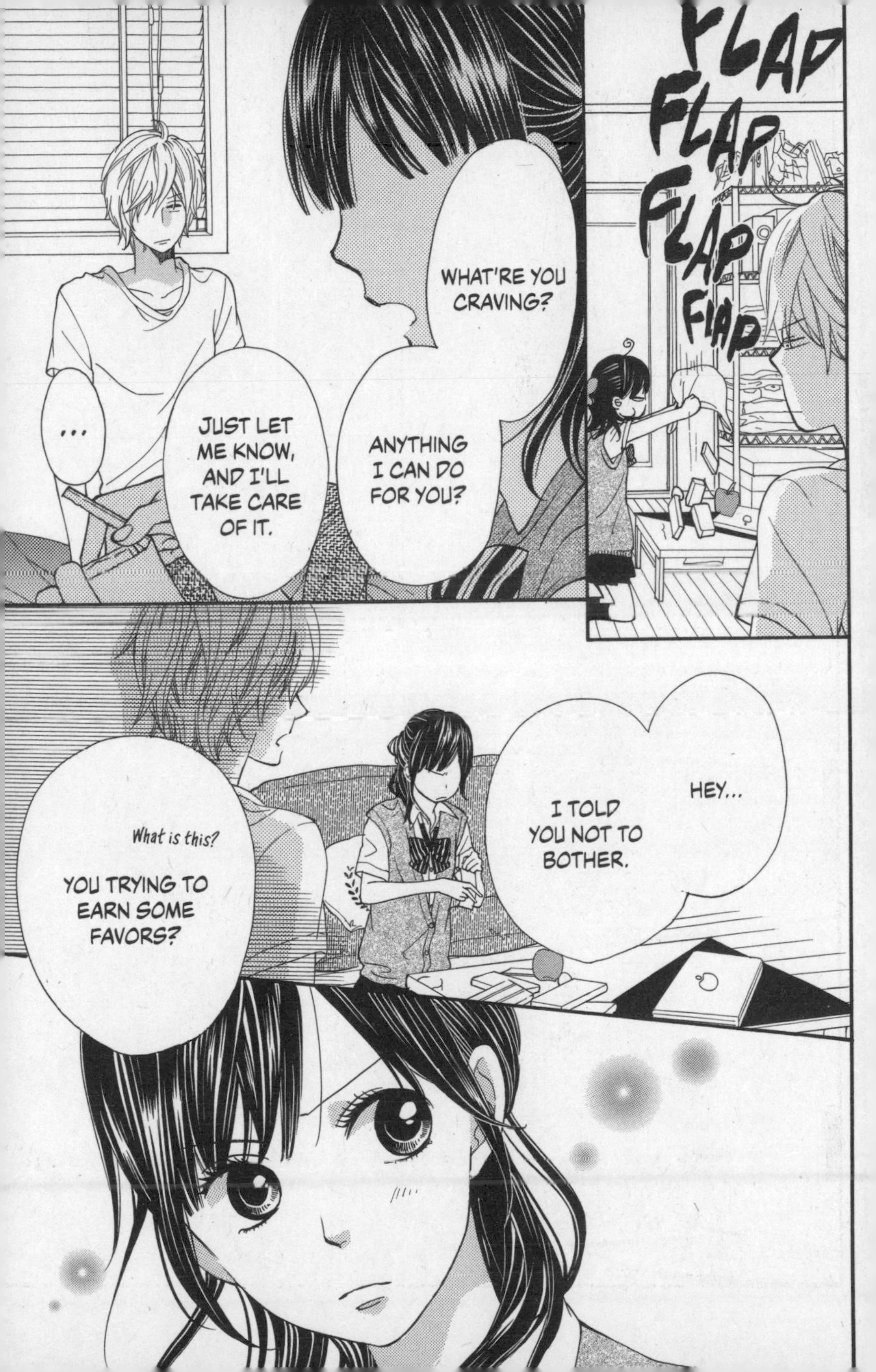

FLAP FLAP FLAP FLAP
WHAT'RE YOU CRAVING?
ANYTHING I CAN DO FOR YOU?
JUST LET ME KNOW, AND I'LL TAKE CARE OF IT.
...
HEY...
I TOLD YOU NOT TO BOTHER.
What is this?
YOU TRYING TO EARN SOME FAVORS?

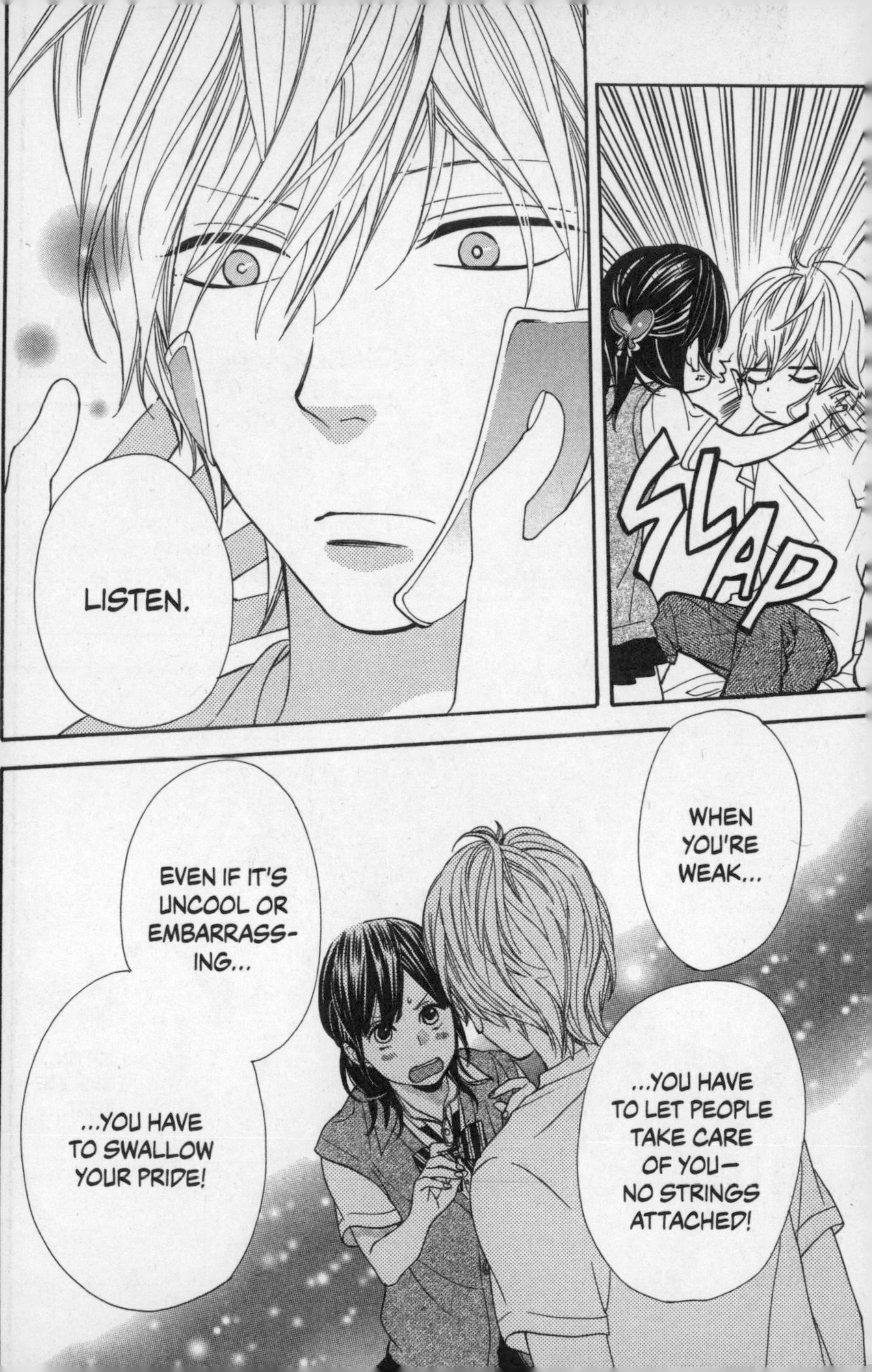
SLAP
LISTEN.
WHEN YOU'RE WEAK...
...YOU HAVE TO LET PEOPLE TAKE CARE OF YOU—NO STRINGS ATTACHED!
EVEN IF IT'S UNCOOL OR EMBARRASS-ING...
...YOU HAVE TO SWALLOW YOUR PRIDE!

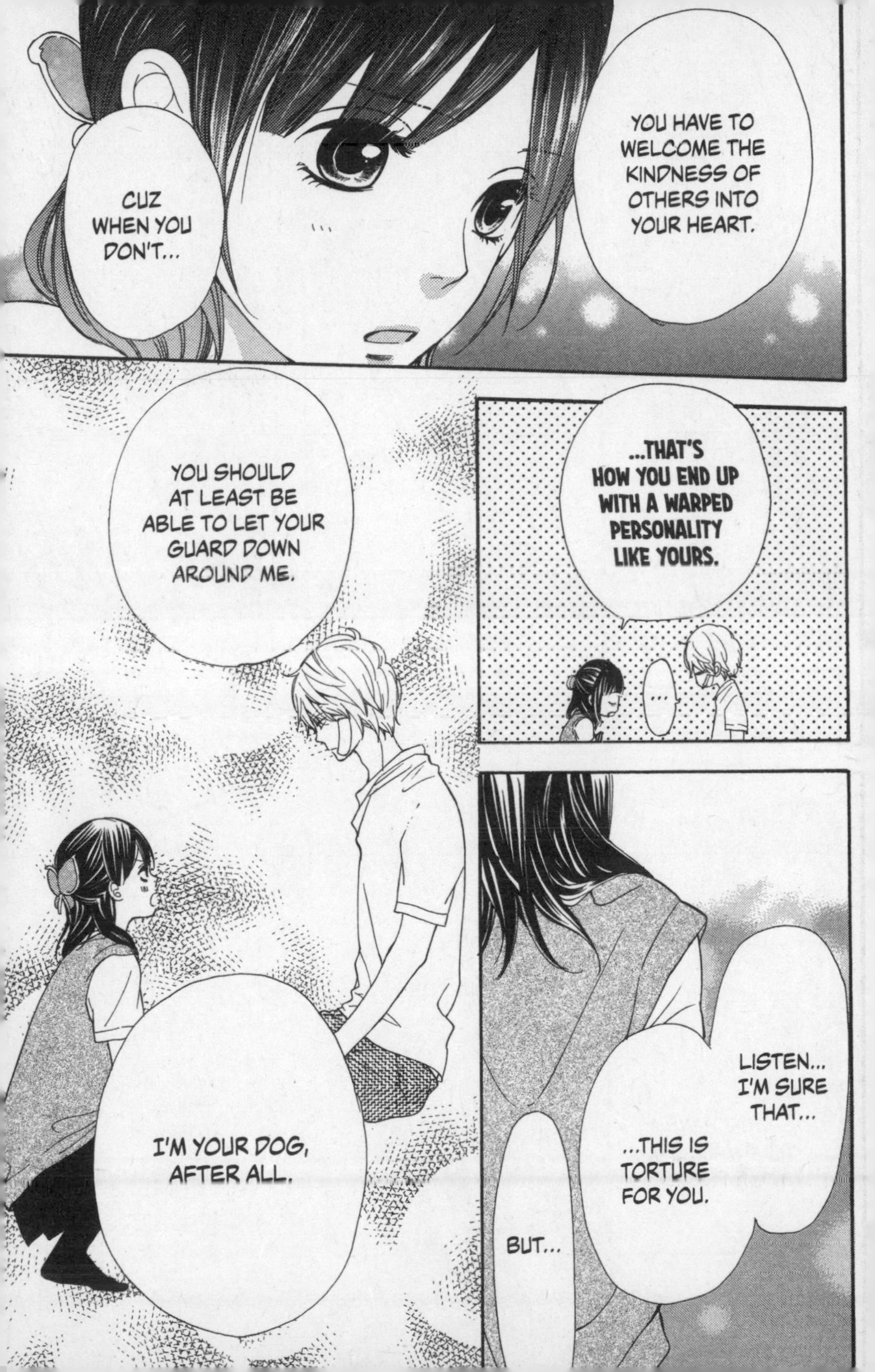
YOU HAVE TO WELCOME THE KINDNESS OF OTHERS INTO YOUR HEART.
CUZ WHEN YOU DON'T...
...THAT'S HOW YOU END UP WITH A WARPED PERSONALITY LIKE YOURS.
...
LISTEN... I'M SURE THAT...
...THIS IS TORTURE FOR YOU.
BUT...
YOU SHOULD AT LEAST BE ABLE TO LET YOUR GUARD DOWN AROUND ME.
I'M YOUR DOG, AFTER ALL.

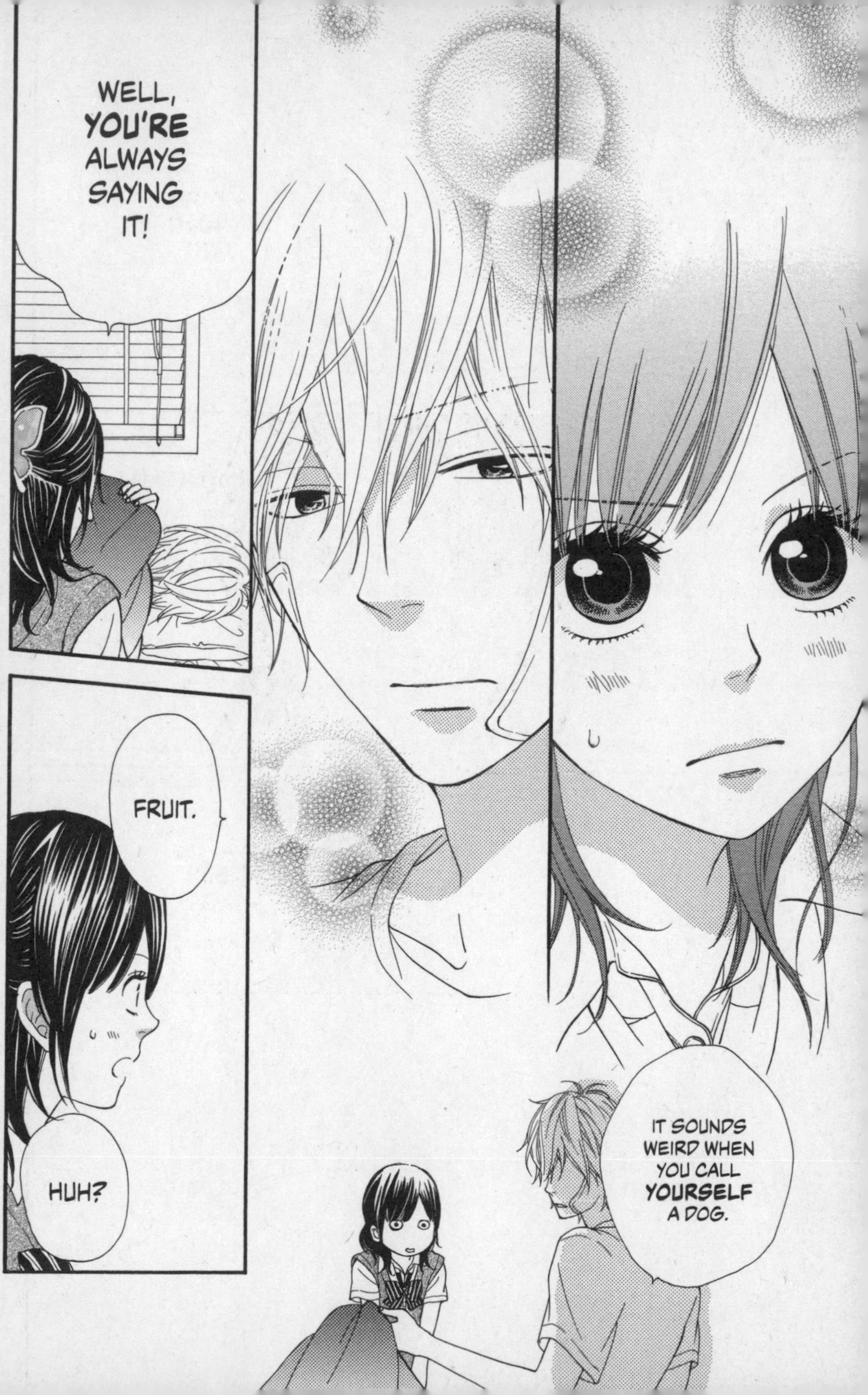
IT SOUNDS WEIRD WHEN YOU CALL YOURSELF A DOG.
WELL, YOU'RE ALWAYS SAYING IT!
FRUIT.
HUH?

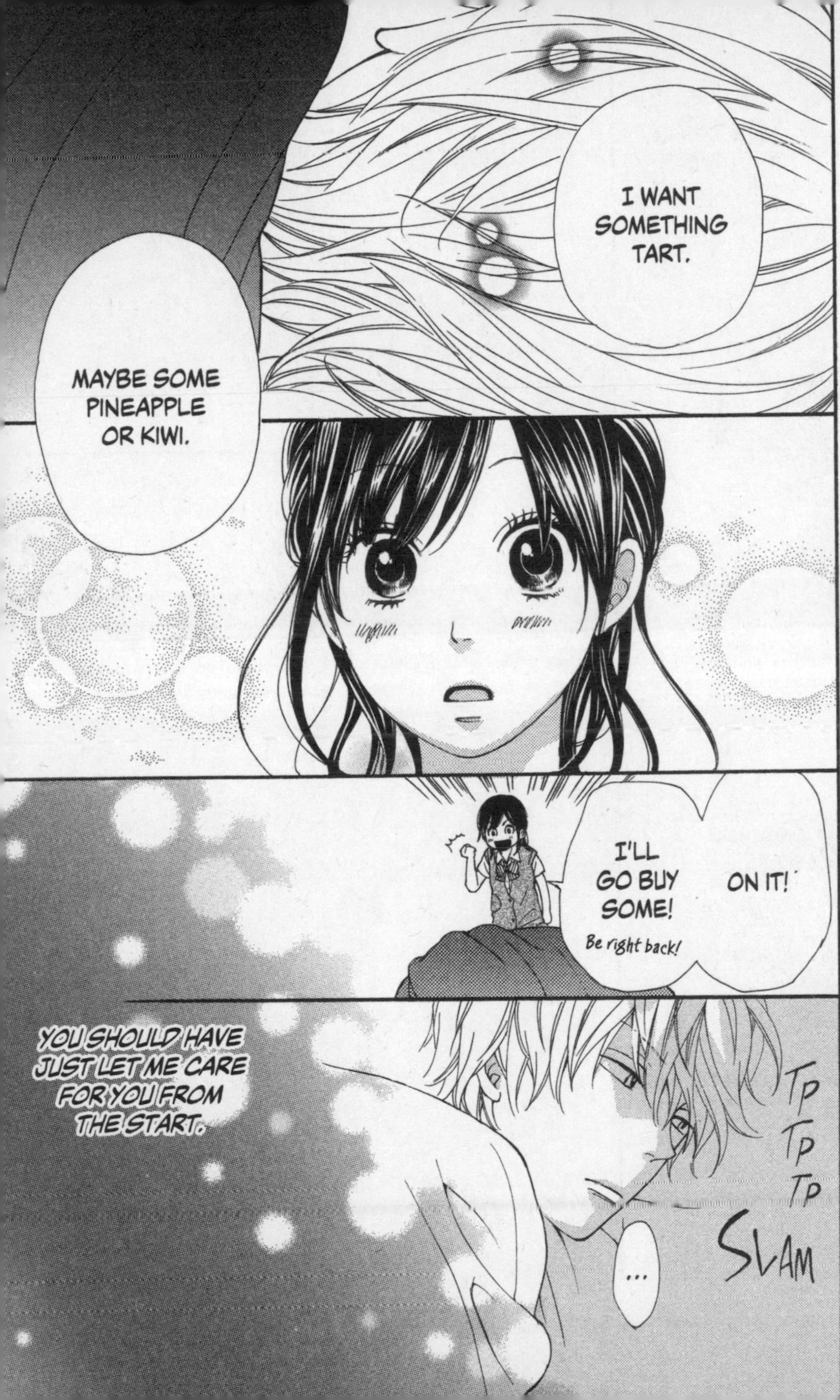
I WANT SOMETHING TART.
MAYBE SOME PINEAPPLE OR KIWI.
ON IT!
I'LL GO BUY SOME!
Be right back!
TP TP TP
SLAM
...
YOU SHOULD HAVE JUST LET ME CARE FOR YOU FROM THE START.

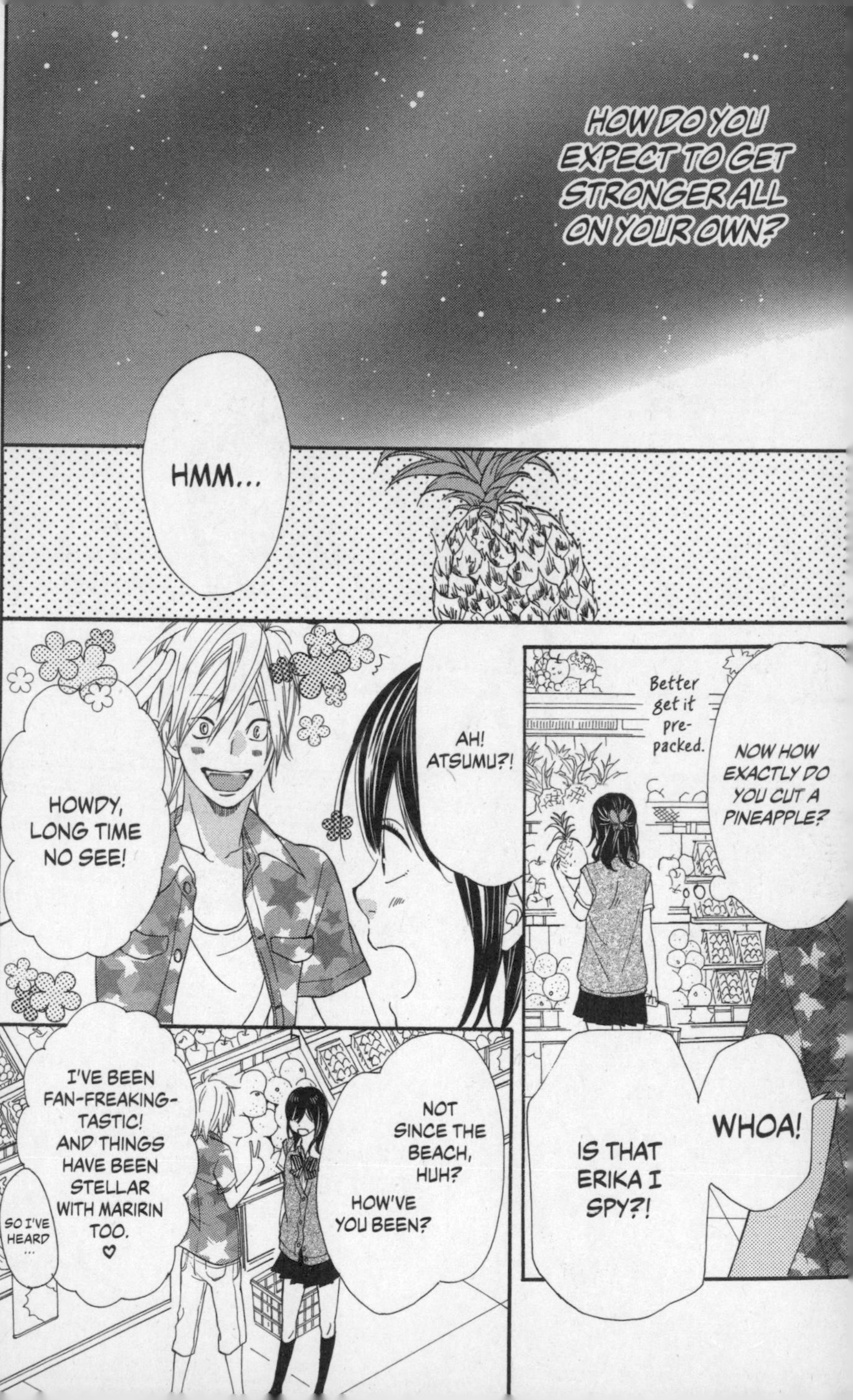
HOW DO YOU EXPECT TO GET STRONGER ALL ON YOUR OWN?
HMM...
NOW HOW EXACTLY DO YOU CUT A PINEAPPLE?
Better get it pre-packed.
WHOA!
IS THAT ERIKA I SPY?!
AH! ATSUMU?!
HOWDY, LONG TIME NO SEE!
NOT SINCE THE BEACH, HUH?
HOW'VE YOU BEEN?
I'VE BEEN FAN-FREAKING-TASTIC! AND THINGS HAVE BEEN STELLAR WITH MARIRIN TOO. ♡
SO I'VE HEARD...

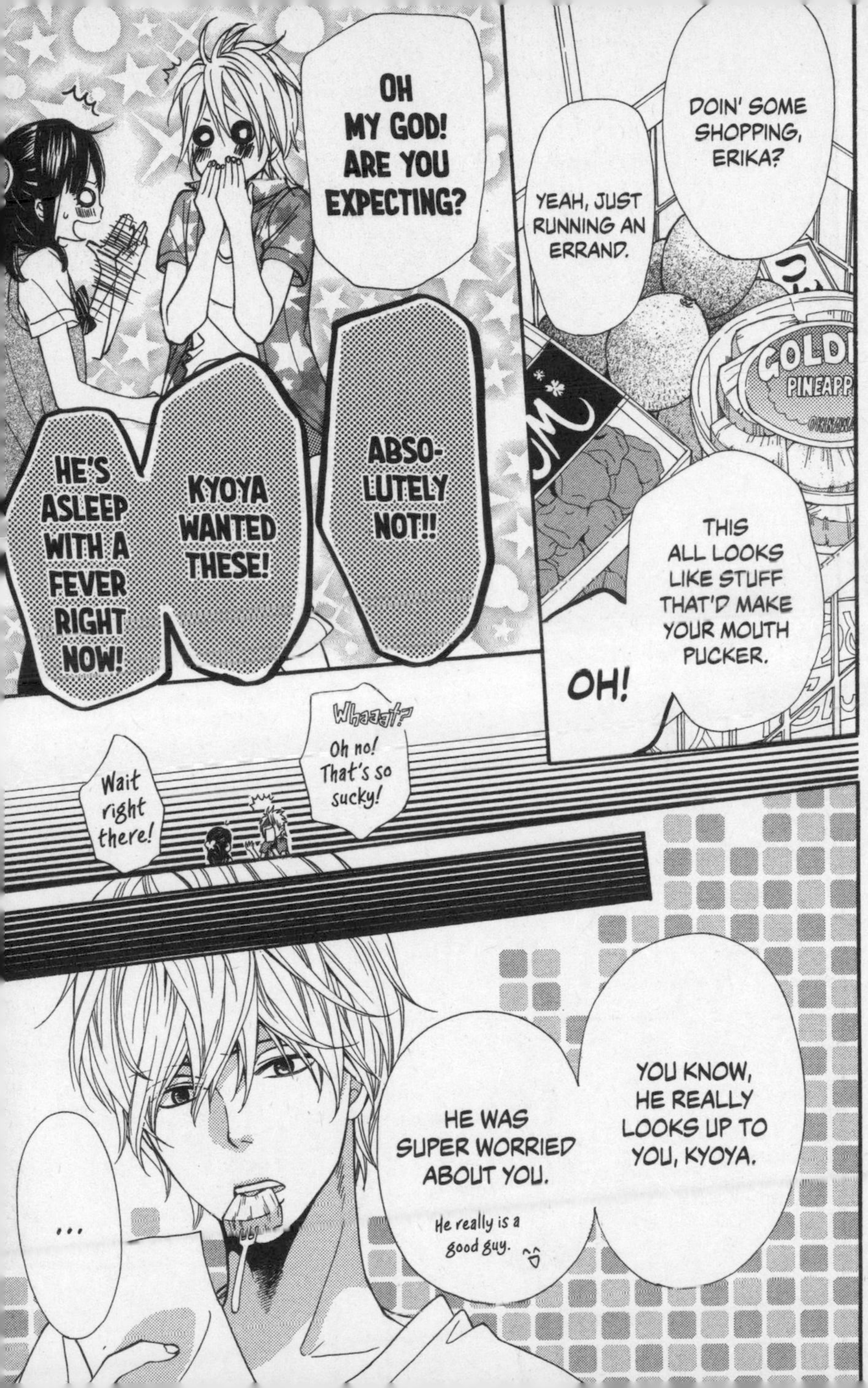
DOIN' SOME SHOPPING, ERIKA?
YEAH, JUST RUNNING AN ERRAND.
THIS ALL LOOKS LIKE STUFF THAT'D MAKE YOUR MOUTH PUCKER.
OH!
OH MY GOD! ARE YOU EXPECTING?
ABSO-LUTELY NOT!!
KYOYA WANTED THESE!
HE'S ASLEEP WITH A FEVER RIGHT NOW!
Whaaat? Oh no! That's so sucky!
Wait right there!
YOU KNOW, HE REALLY LOOKS UP TO YOU, KYOYA.
HE WAS SUPER WORRIED ABOUT YOU.
He really is a good guy.
...

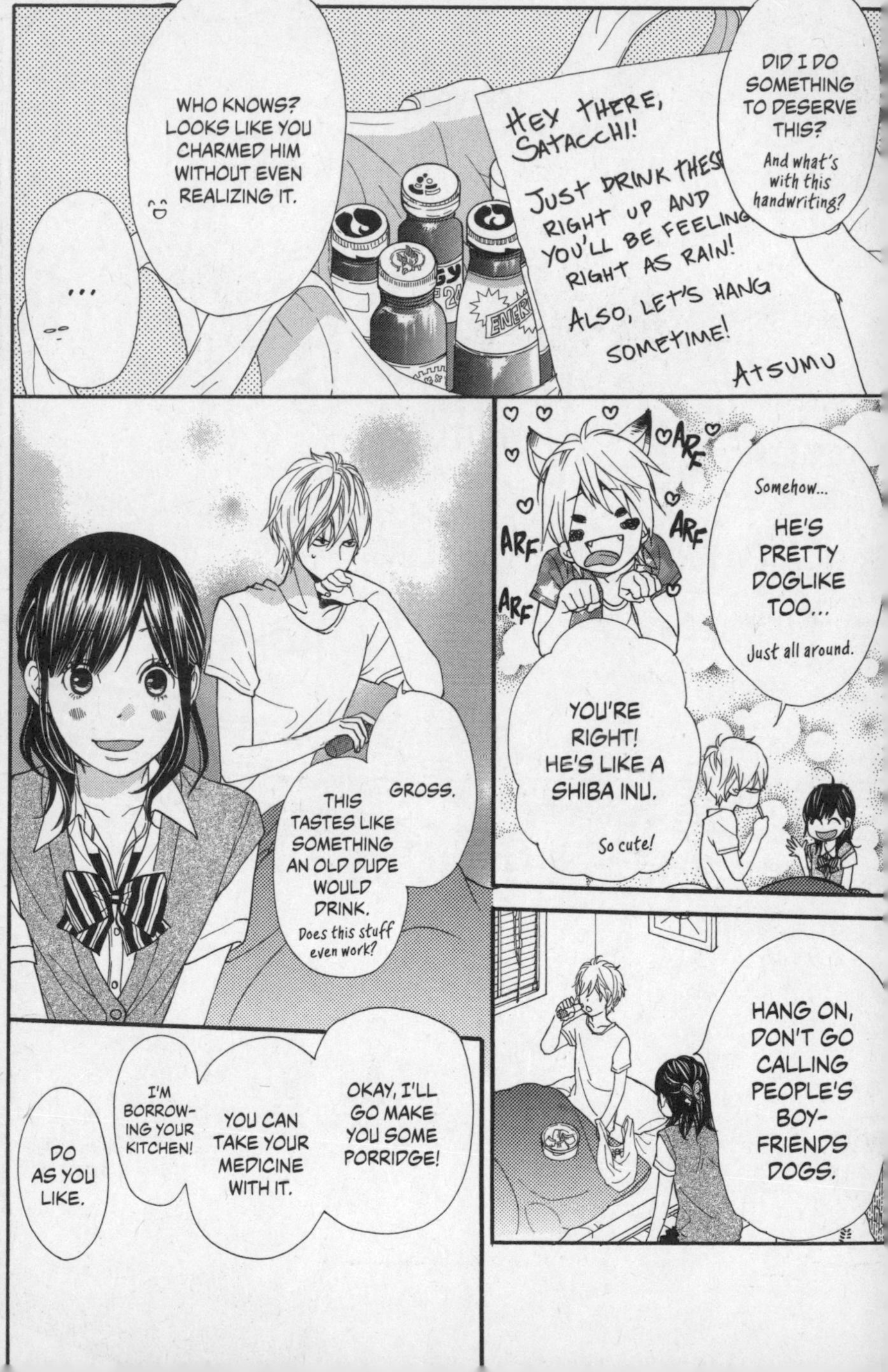
DID I DO SOMETHING TO DESERVE THIS?
And what's with this handwriting?
Hey there, Satacchi! Just drink these right up and you'll be feeling right as rain! Also, let's hang sometime! Atsumu
WHO KNOWS? LOOKS LIKE YOU CHARMED HIM WITHOUT EVEN REALIZING IT.
...
Somehow... HE'S PRETTY DOGLIKE TOO... Just all around.
ARF
ARF
ARF
ARF
YOU'RE RIGHT! HE'S LIKE A SHIBA INU.
So cute!
HANG ON, DON'T GO CALLING PEOPLE'S BOY-FRIENDS DOGS.
GROSS.
THIS TASTES LIKE SOMETHING AN OLD DUDE WOULD DRINK.
Does this stuff even work?
OKAY, I'LL GO MAKE YOU SOME PORRIDGE!
YOU CAN TAKE YOUR MEDICINE WITH IT.
I'M BORROW-ING YOUR KITCHEN!
DO AS YOU LIKE.

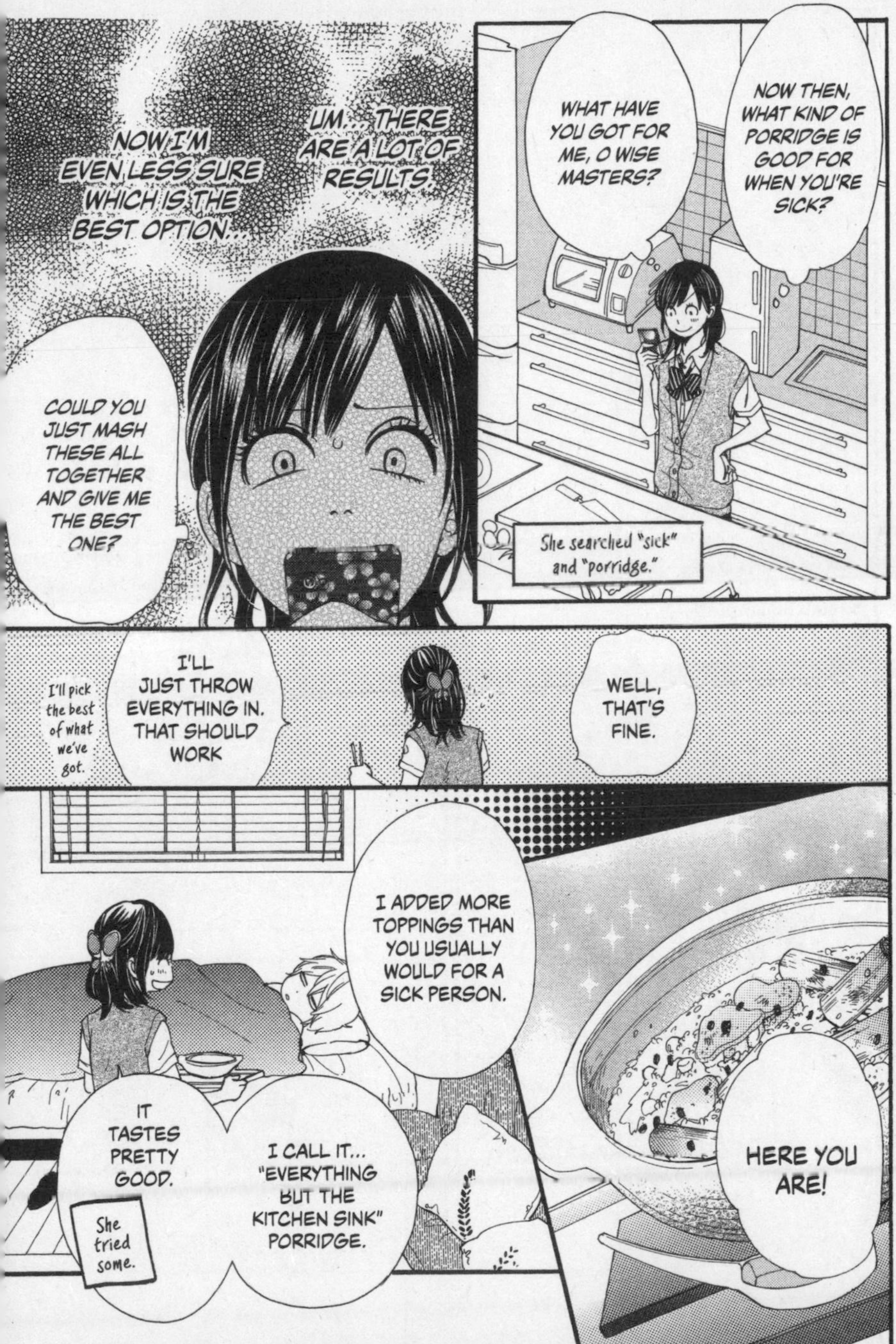
NOW THEN, WHAT KIND OF PORRIDGE IS GOOD FOR WHEN YOU'RE SICK?
WHAT HAVE YOU GOT FOR ME, O WISE MASTERS?
She searched "sick" and "porridge."
UM... THERE ARE A LOT OF RESULTS.
NOW I'M EVEN LESS SURE WHICH IS THE BEST OPTION...
COULD YOU JUST MASH THESE ALL TOGETHER AND GIVE ME THE BEST ONE?
WELL, THAT'S FINE.
I'LL JUST THROW EVERYTHING IN. THAT SHOULD WORK
I'll pick the best of what we've got.
HERE YOU ARE!
I ADDED MORE TOPPINGS THAN YOU USUALLY WOULD FOR A SICK PERSON.
I CALL IT... "EVERYTHING BUT THE KITCHEN SINK" PORRIDGE.
IT TASTES PRETTY GOOD.
She tried some.

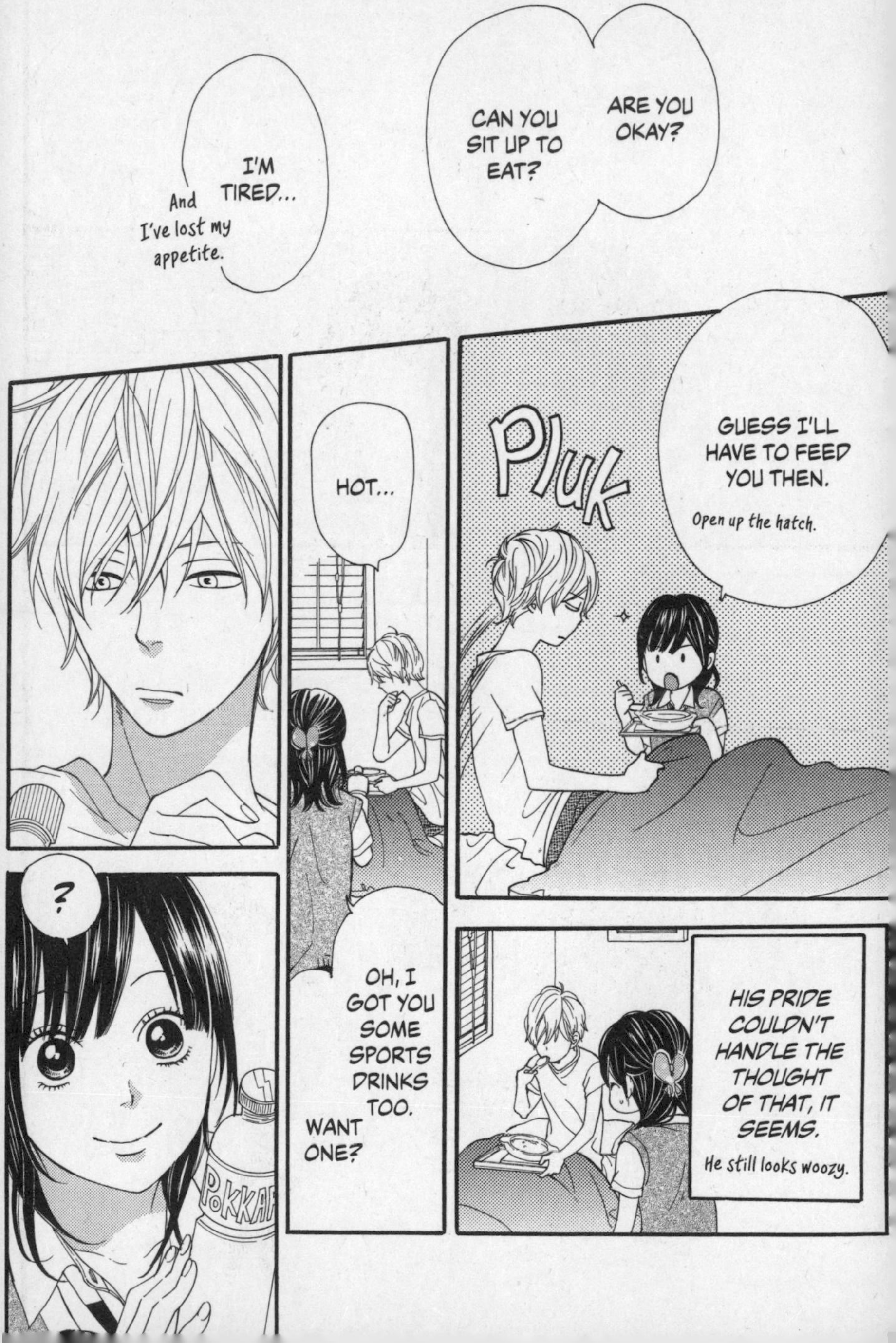
ARE YOU OKAY?
CAN YOU SIT UP TO EAT?
I'M TIRED...
And I've lost my appetite.
Pluk
GUESS I'LL HAVE TO FEED YOU THEN.
Open up the hatch.
HIS PRIDE COULDN'T HANDLE THE THOUGHT OF THAT, IT SEEMS.
He still looks woozy.
HOT...
OH, I GOT YOU SOME SPORTS DRINKS TOO.
WANT ONE?
?

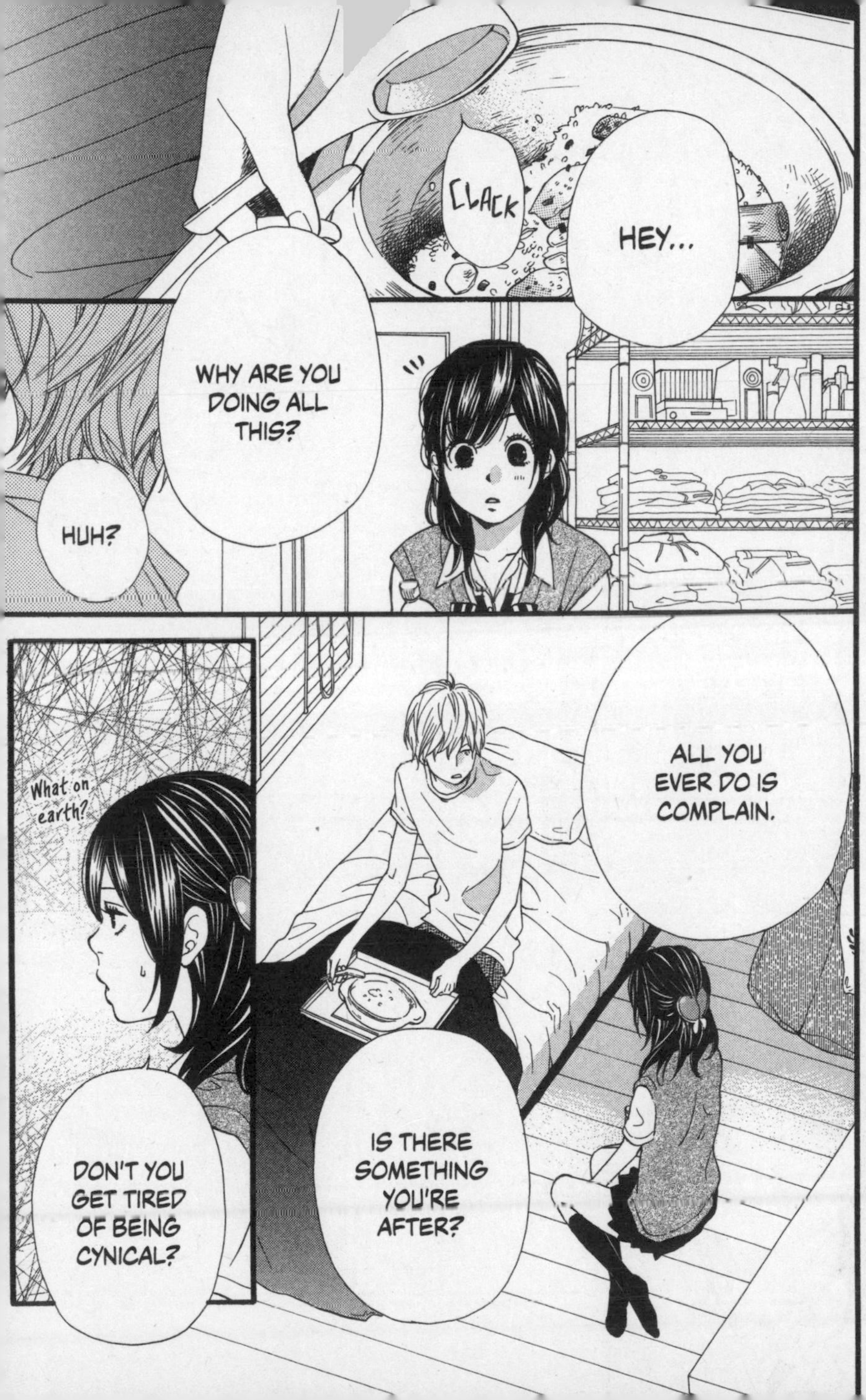
HEY...
CLACK
WHY ARE YOU DOING ALL THIS?
HUH?
ALL YOU EVER DO IS COMPLAIN.
IS THERE SOMETHING YOU'RE AFTER?
What on earth?
DON'T YOU GET TIRED OF BEING CYNICAL?

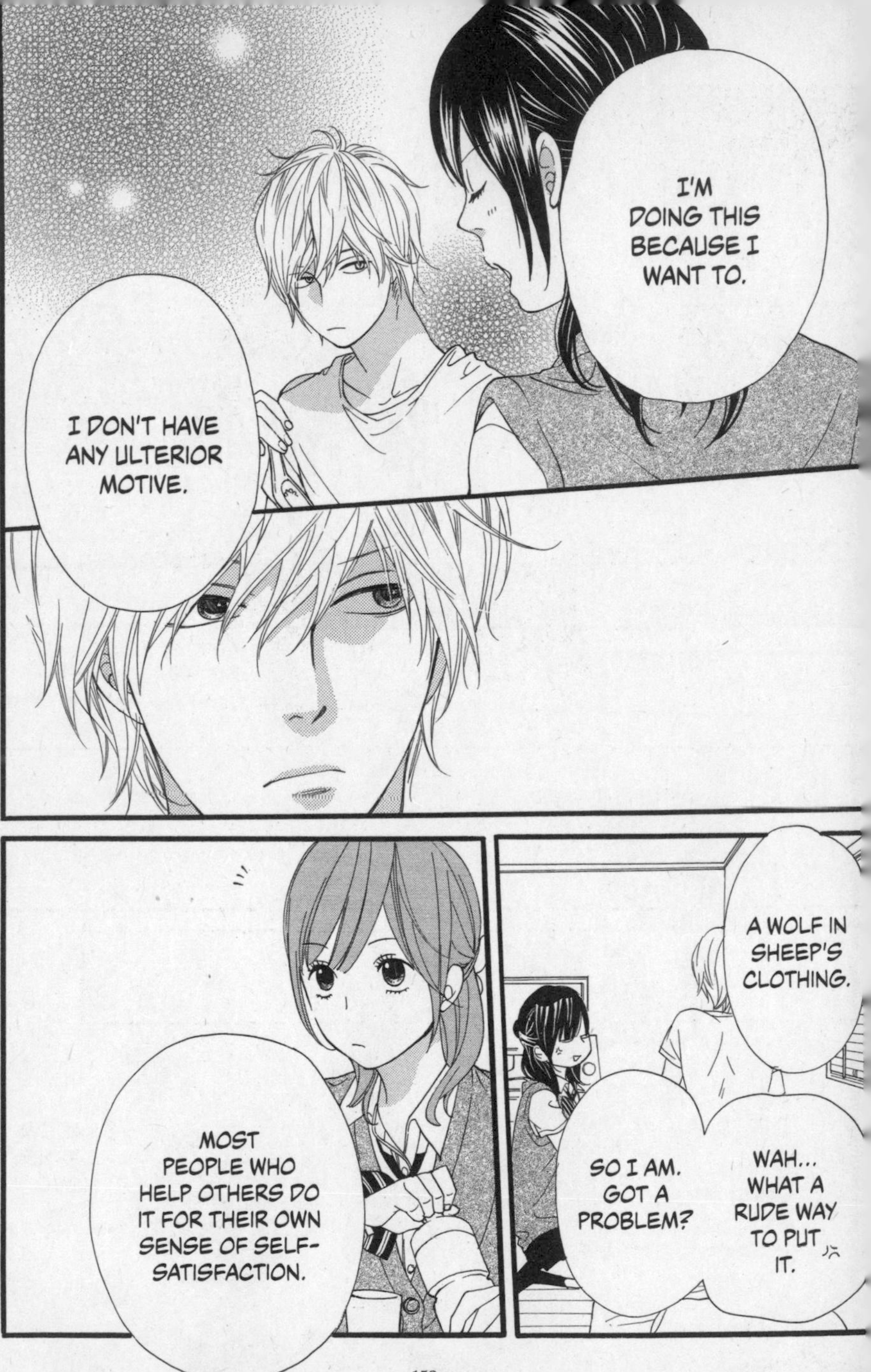
I'M DOING THIS BECAUSE I WANT TO.
I DON'T HAVE ANY ULTERIOR MOTIVE.
A WOLF IN SHEEP'S CLOTHING.
WAH... WHAT A RUDE WAY TO PUT IT.
SO I AM. GOT A PROBLEM?
MOST PEOPLE WHO HELP OTHERS DO IT FOR THEIR OWN SENSE OF SELF-SATISFACTION.

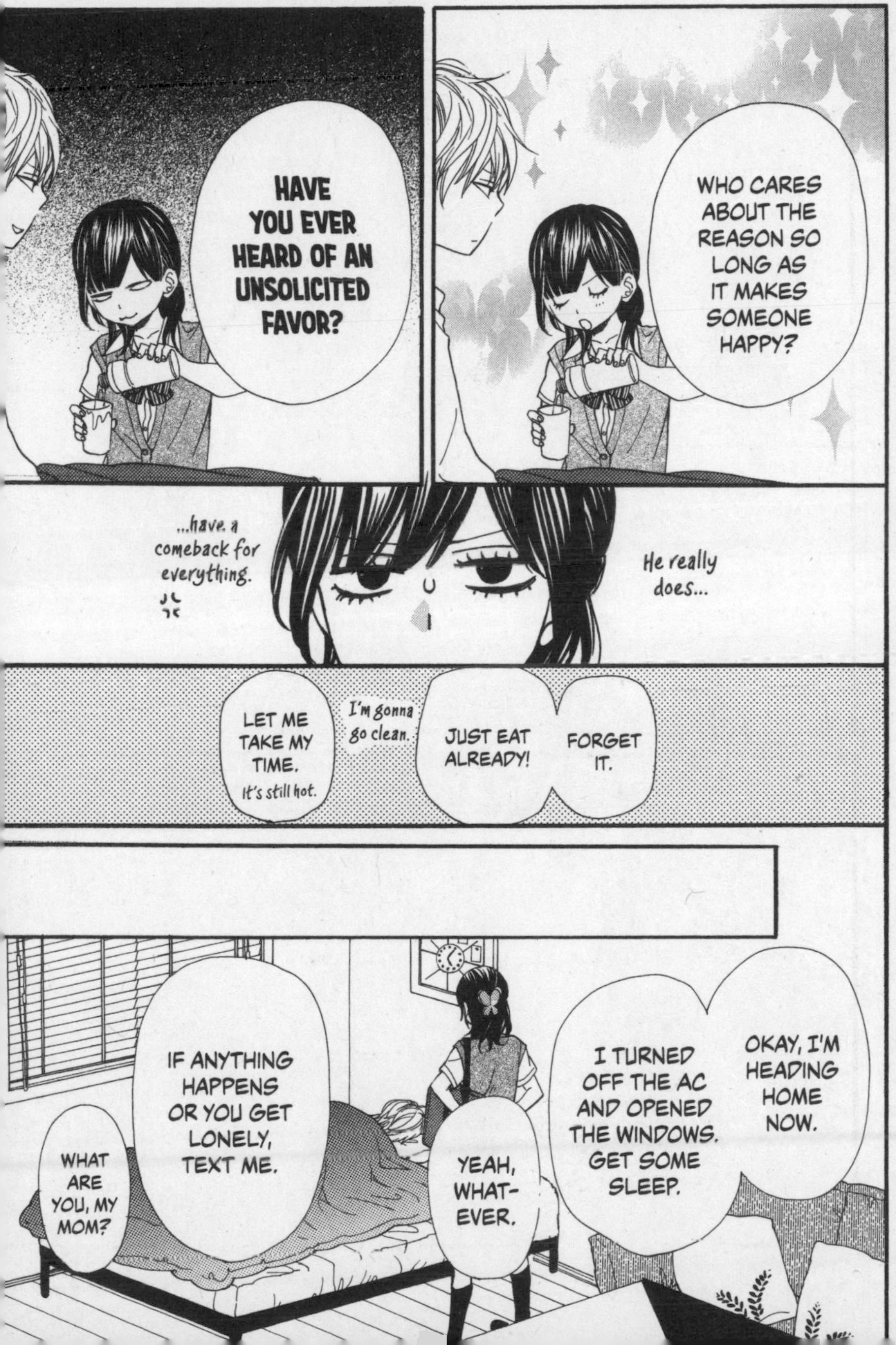
WHO CARES ABOUT THE REASON SO LONG AS IT MAKES SOMEONE HAPPY?
HAVE YOU EVER HEARD OF AN UNSOLICITED FAVOR?
He really does...
...have a comeback for everything.
FORGET IT.
JUST EAT ALREADY!
I'm gonna go clean.
LET ME TAKE MY TIME.
It's still hot.
OKAY, I'M HEADING HOME NOW.
I TURNED OFF THE AC AND OPENED THE WINDOWS. GET SOME SLEEP.
YEAH, WHATEVER.
IF ANYTHING HAPPENS OR YOU GET LONELY, TEXT ME.
WHAT ARE YOU, MY MOM?

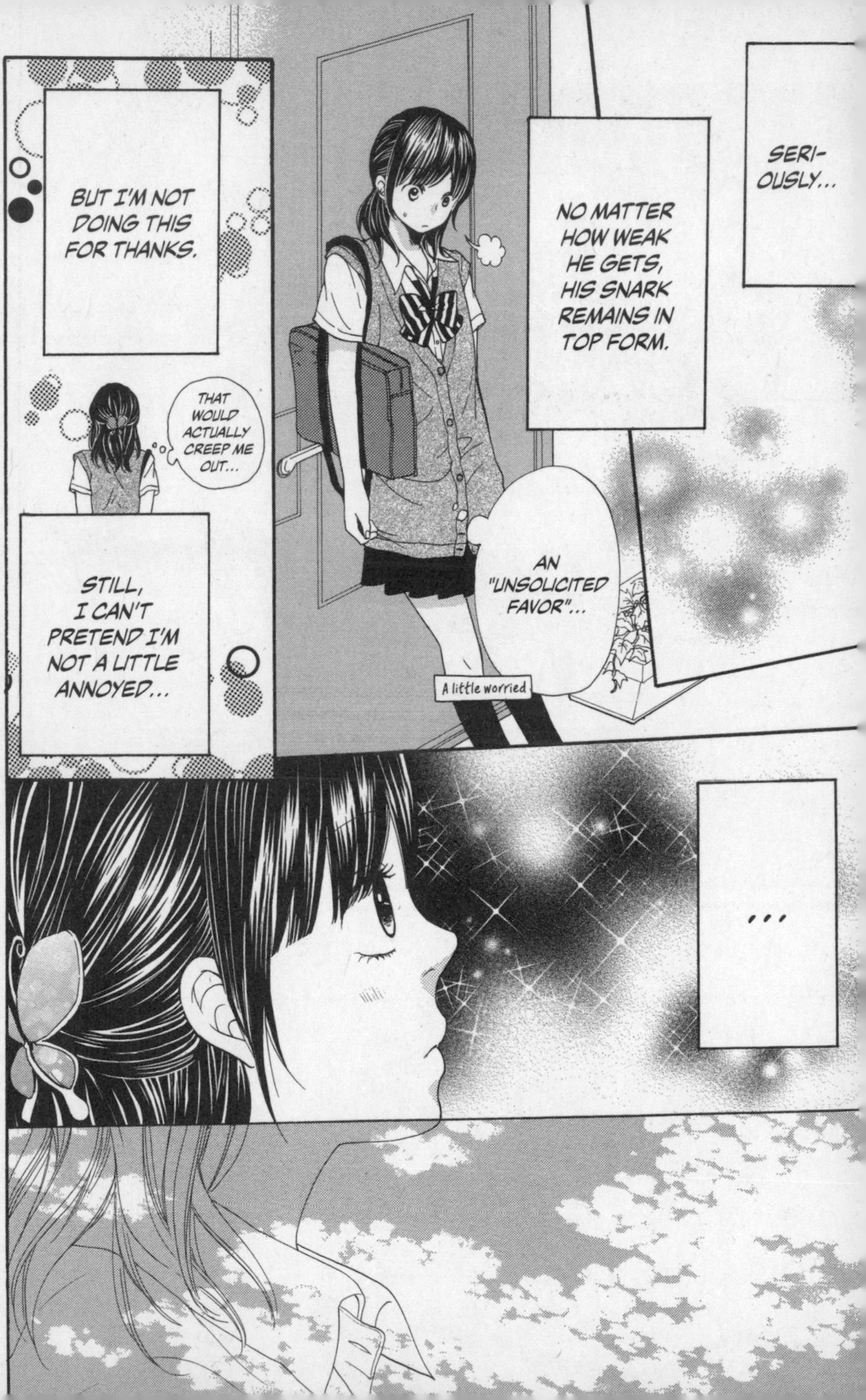
SERI-OUSLY...
NO MATTER HOW WEAK HE GETS, HIS SNARK REMAINS IN TOP FORM.
AN "UNSOLICITED FAVOR"...
A little worried
BUT I'M NOT DOING THIS FOR THANKS.
THAT WOULD ACTUALLY CREEP ME OUT...
STILL, I CAN'T PRETEND I'M NOT A LITTLE ANNOYED...
...

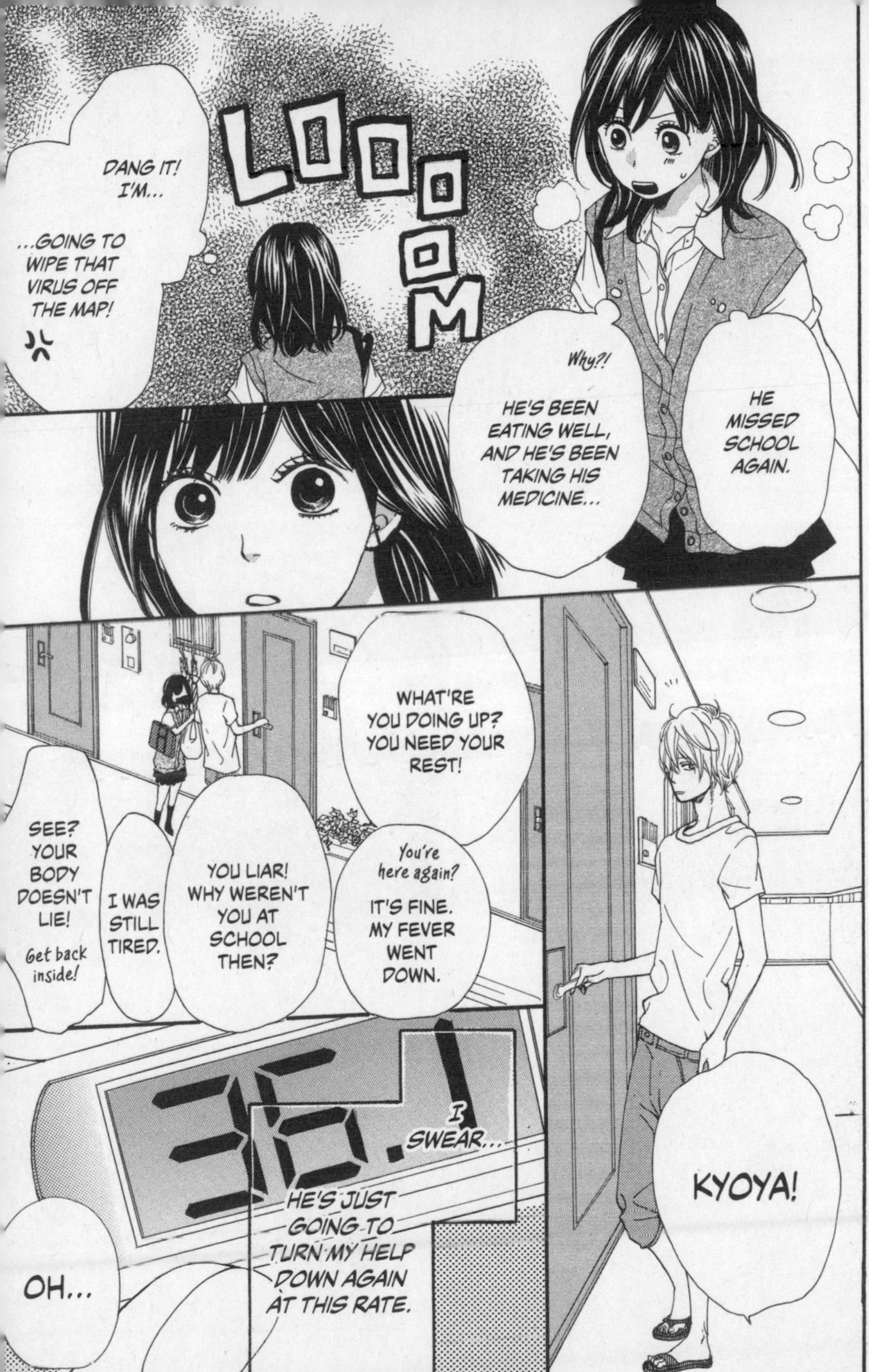
HE MISSED SCHOOL AGAIN.
Why?! HE'S BEEN EATING WELL, AND HE'S BEEN TAKING HIS MEDICINE...
LOOOOOM
DANG IT! I'M...
...GOING TO WIPE THAT VIRUS OFF THE MAP!
KYOYA!
WHAT'RE YOU DOING UP? YOU NEED YOUR REST!
You're here again? IT'S FINE. MY FEVER WENT DOWN.
YOU LIAR! WHY WEREN'T YOU AT SCHOOL THEN?
I WAS STILL TIRED.
SEE? YOUR BODY DOESN'T LIE! Get back inside!
36.1
I SWEAR...
HE'S JUST GOING TO TURN MY HELP DOWN AGAIN AT THIS RATE.
OH...

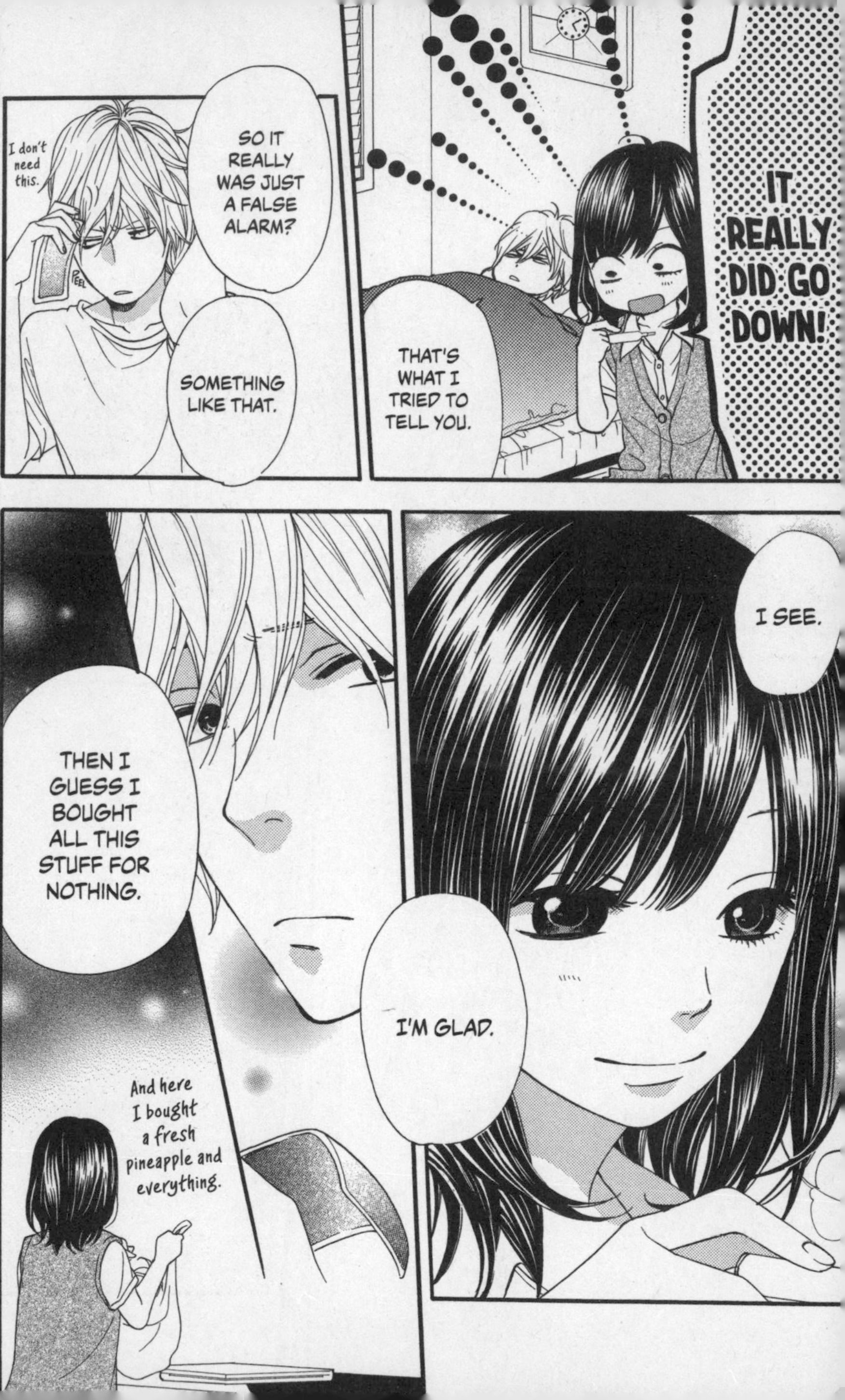
IT REALLY DID GO DOWN!
THAT'S WHAT I TRIED TO TELL YOU.
SO IT REALLY WAS JUST A FALSE ALARM?
I don't need this.
PEEL
SOMETHING LIKE THAT.
I SEE.
I'M GLAD.
THEN I GUESS I BOUGHT ALL THIS STUFF FOR NOTHING.
And here I bought a fresh pineapple and everything.

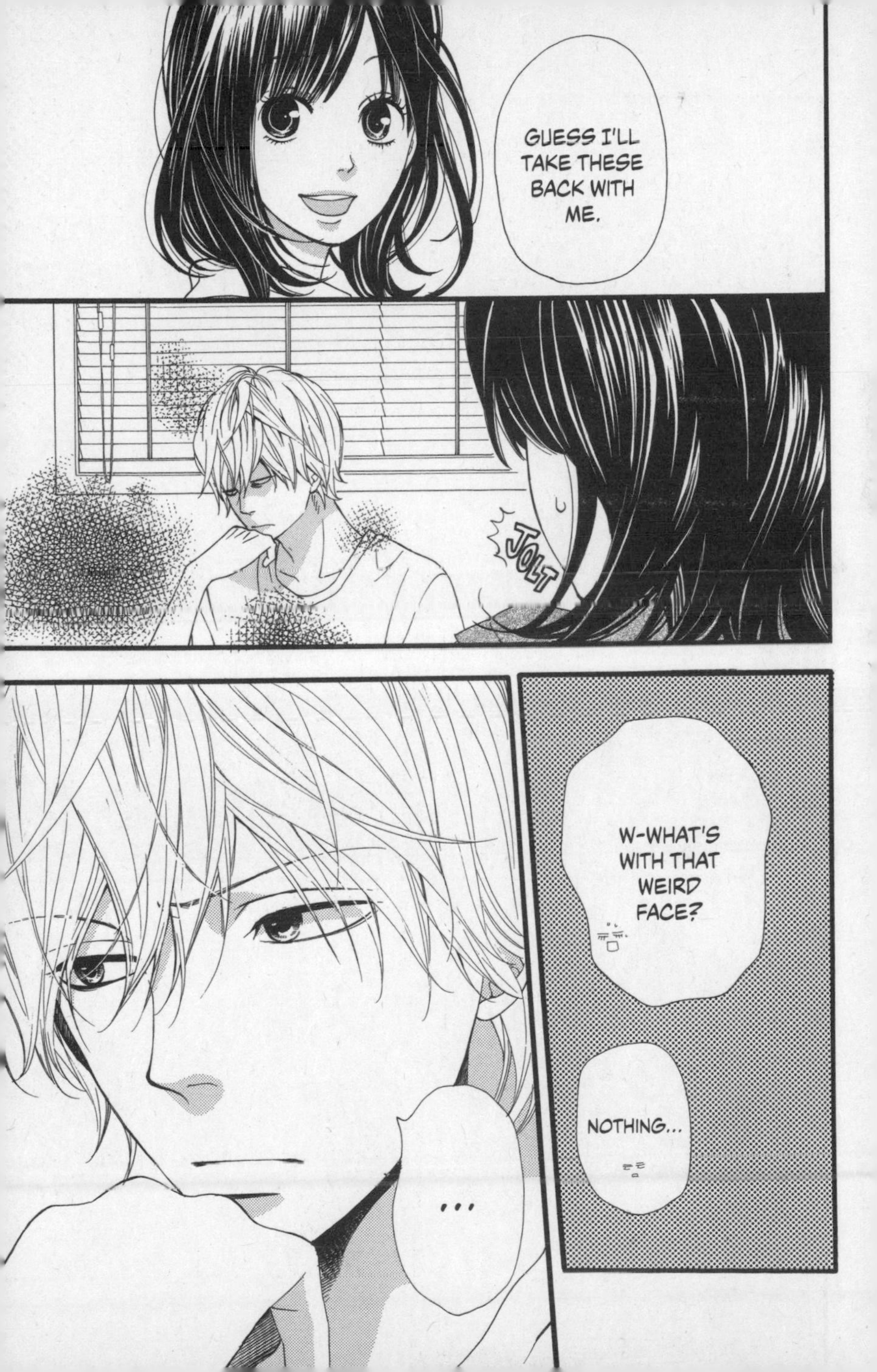
GUESS I'LL TAKE THESE BACK WITH ME.
JOLT
W-WHAT'S WITH THAT WEIRD FACE?
NOTHING...
...

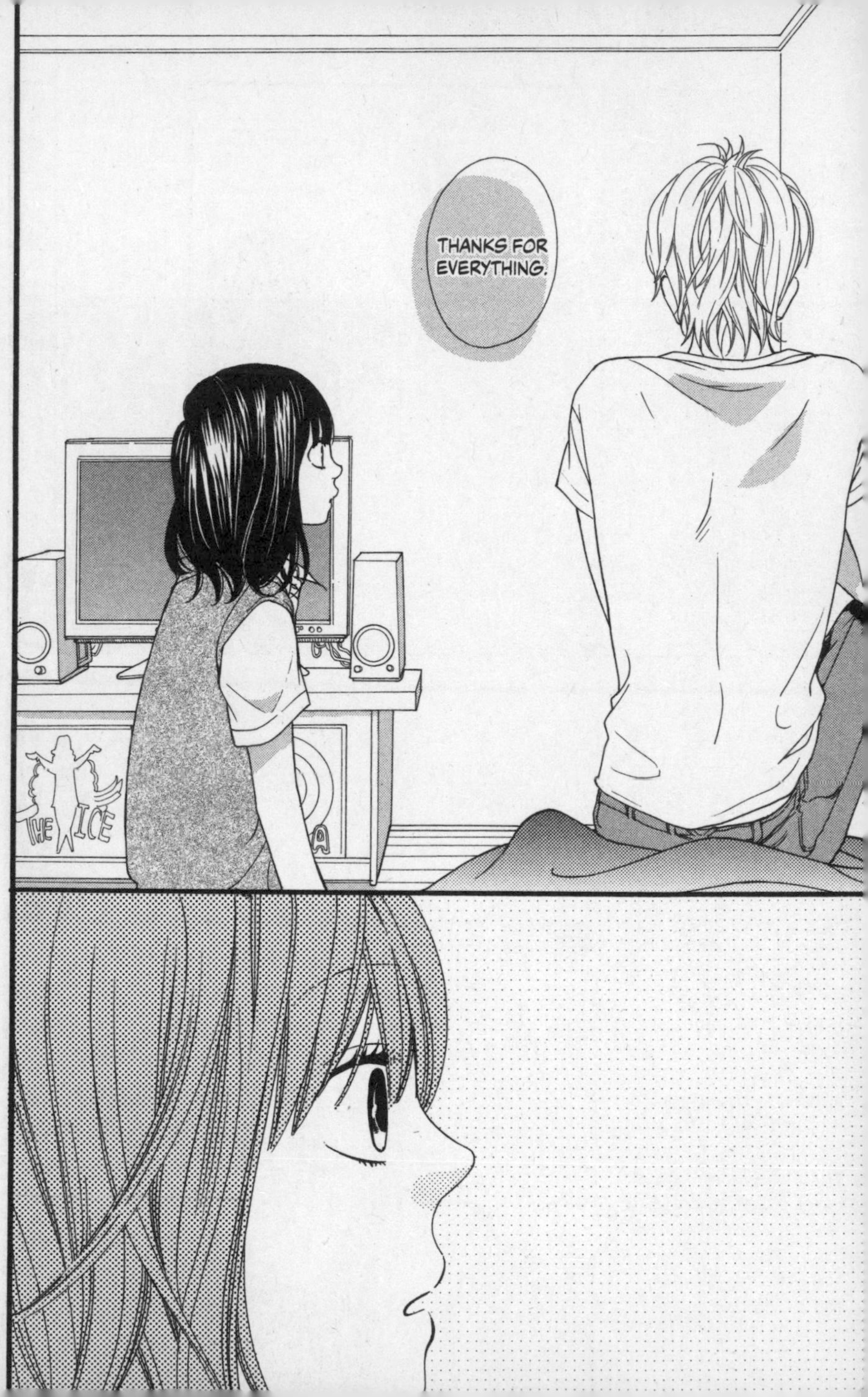
THANKS FOR EVERYTHING.
THE ICE

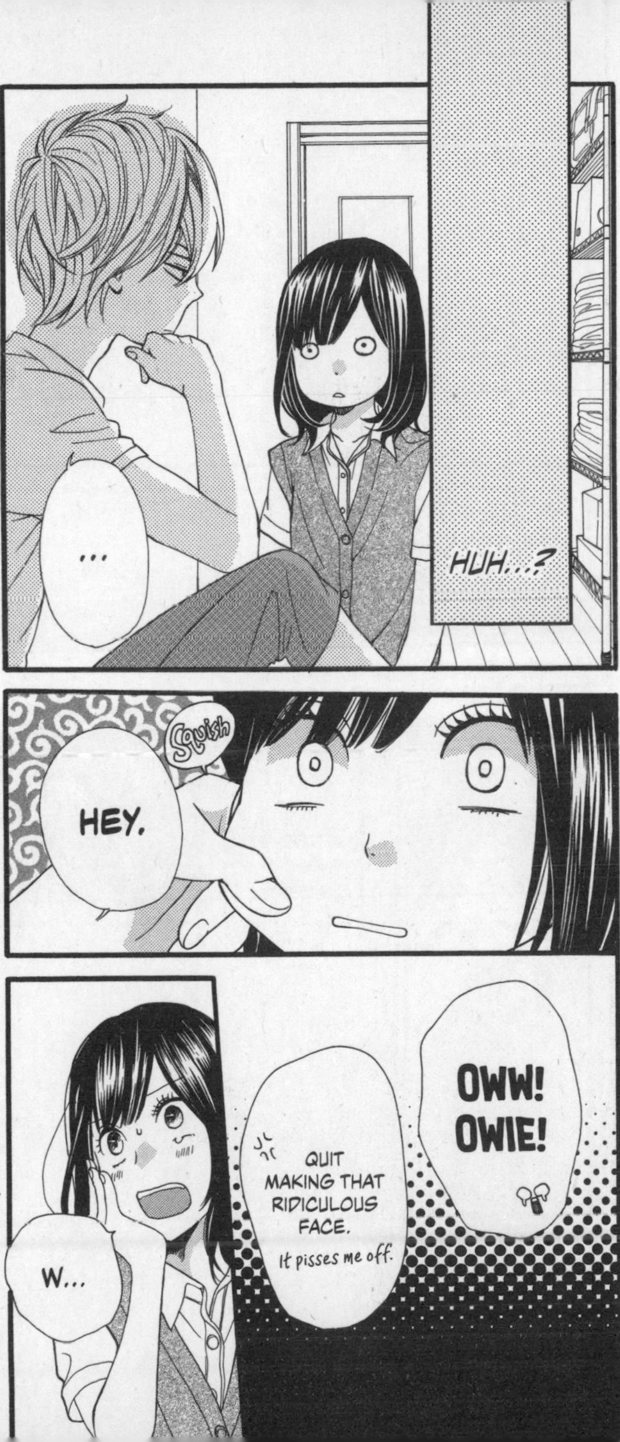
HUH...?
...
Squish
HEY.
OWW! OWIE!
QUIT MAKING THAT RIDICULOUS FACE.
It pisses me off.
W...

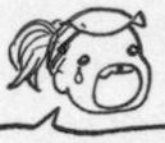

I chipped my front tooth.

Picking up where I left off... Whenever I go to the salon, I get the staff to let me draw caricatures of them. Of course, I only go once every six months, so there's always someone new there. They stick the portraits up in the front of the shop. They're pretty good, if I dare say so myself.

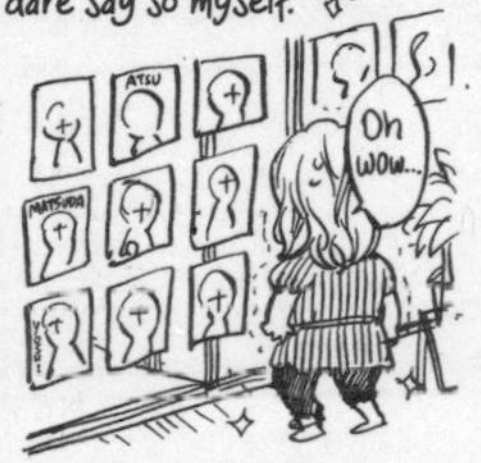
Oh wow...

Should you ever see them, I hope you think, "Oh, so this is the swanky place where Hatta gets her hair cut." Hee hee. I love drawing caricatures. When I graduated from high school and quit my part-time job, I was broke. So I started drawing "pay what you like" caricatures on a hikkake-bashi bridge in Shinsaibashi in Osaka. The ladies dragging around their host boyfriends would usually give me around 2,000 yen (about $20). There were also a lot of grandparents who wanted me to draw their grandkids. And couples. Dang it! Gosh dang it! I was so jealous... It was nice to get to talk to and draw so many different people. Though the cops did take me in one time. (I got off with a warning.) I'd do it again if I ever had the chance.

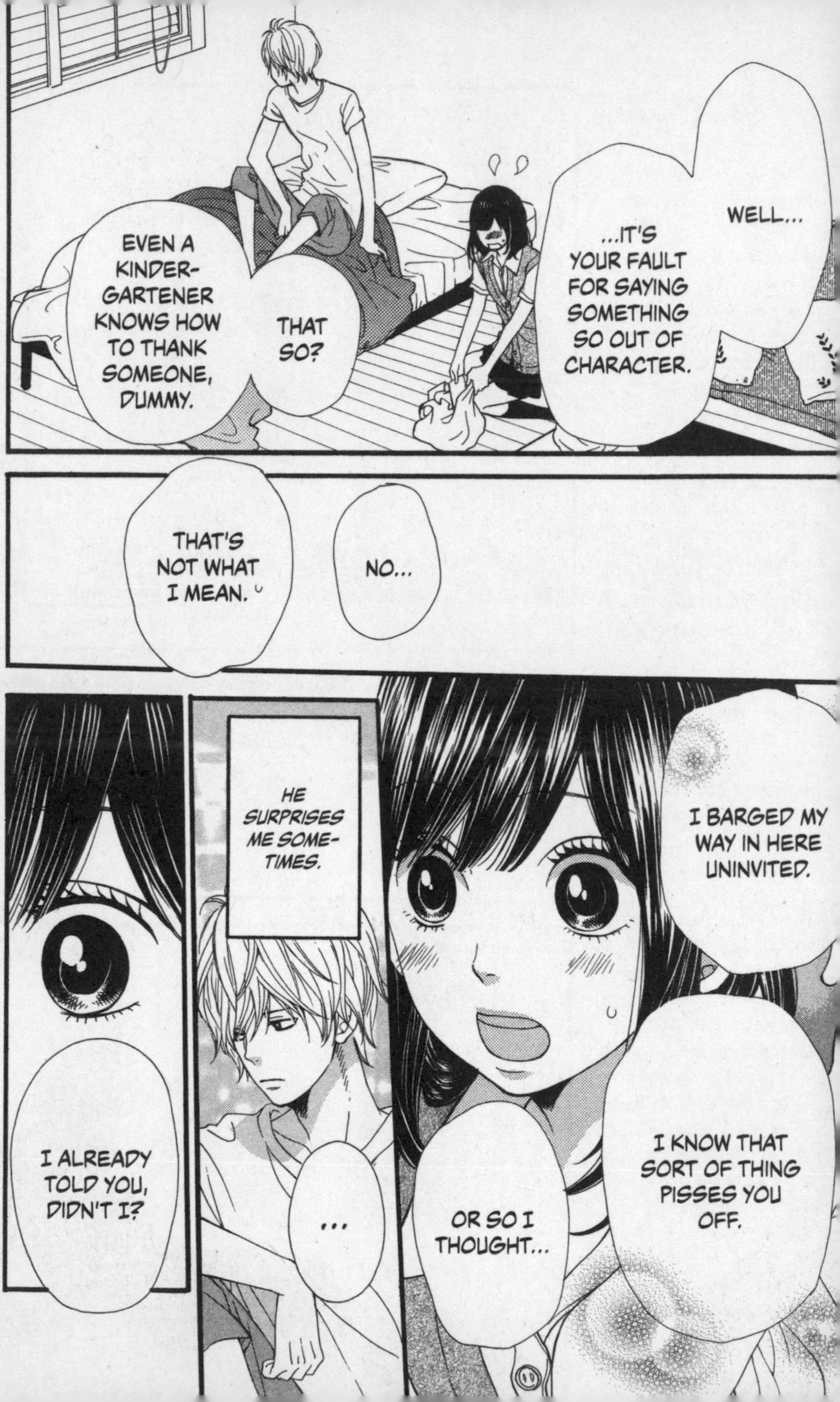
WELL...
...IT'S YOUR FAULT FOR SAYING SOMETHING SO OUT OF CHARACTER.
THAT SO?
EVEN A KINDER-GARTENER KNOWS HOW TO THANK SOMEONE, DUMMY.
NO...
THAT'S NOT WHAT I MEAN.
I BARGED MY WAY IN HERE UNINVITED.
I KNOW THAT SORT OF THING PISSES YOU OFF.
OR SO I THOUGHT...
HE SURPRISES ME SOME-TIMES.
...
I ALREADY TOLD YOU, DIDN'T I?

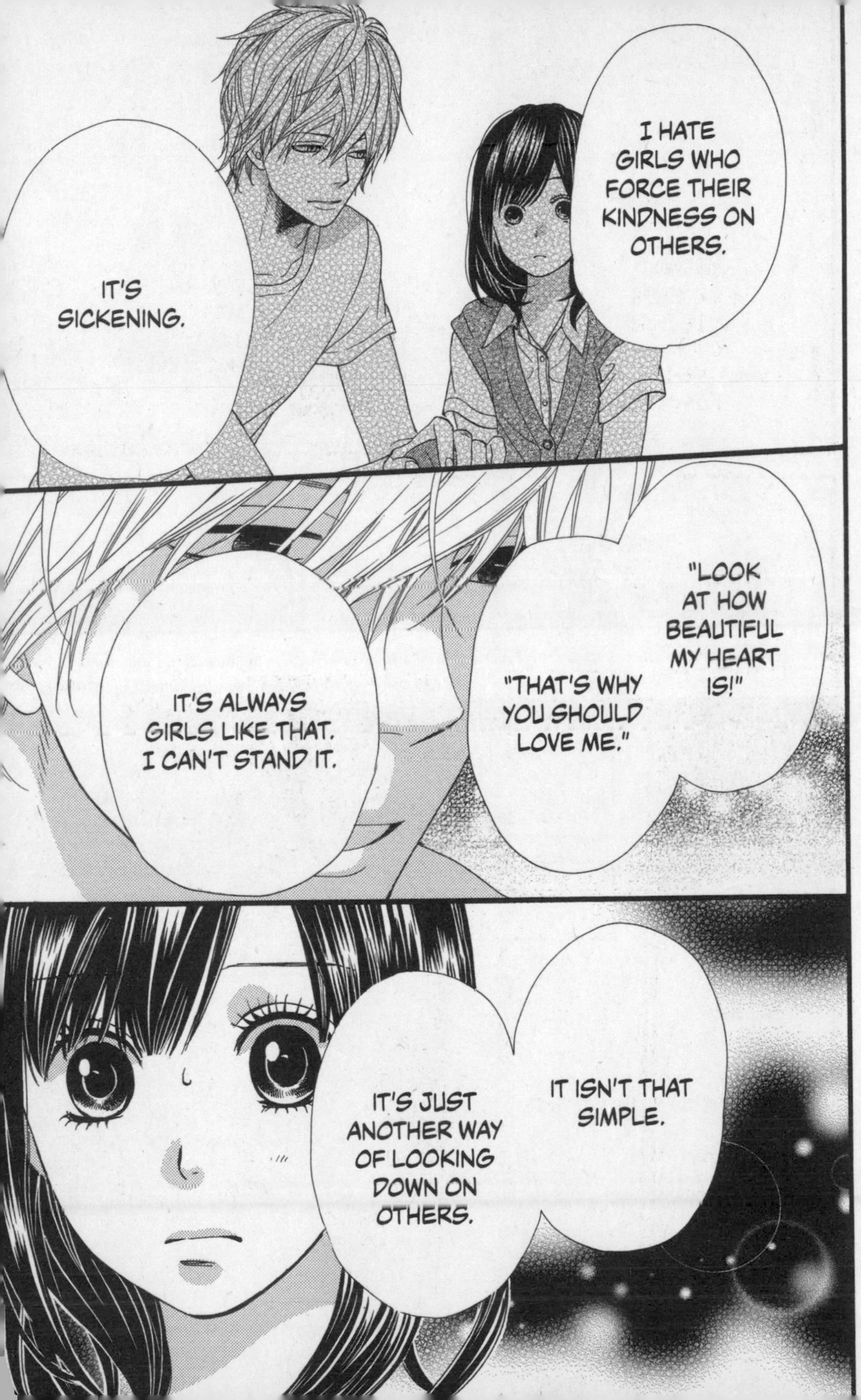
I HATE GIRLS WHO FORCE THEIR KINDNESS ON OTHERS.
IT'S SICKENING.
"LOOK AT HOW BEAUTIFUL MY HEART IS!"
"THAT'S WHY YOU SHOULD LOVE ME."
IT'S ALWAYS GIRLS LIKE THAT. I CAN'T STAND IT.
IT ISN'T THAT SIMPLE.
IT'S JUST ANOTHER WAY OF LOOKING DOWN ON OTHERS.

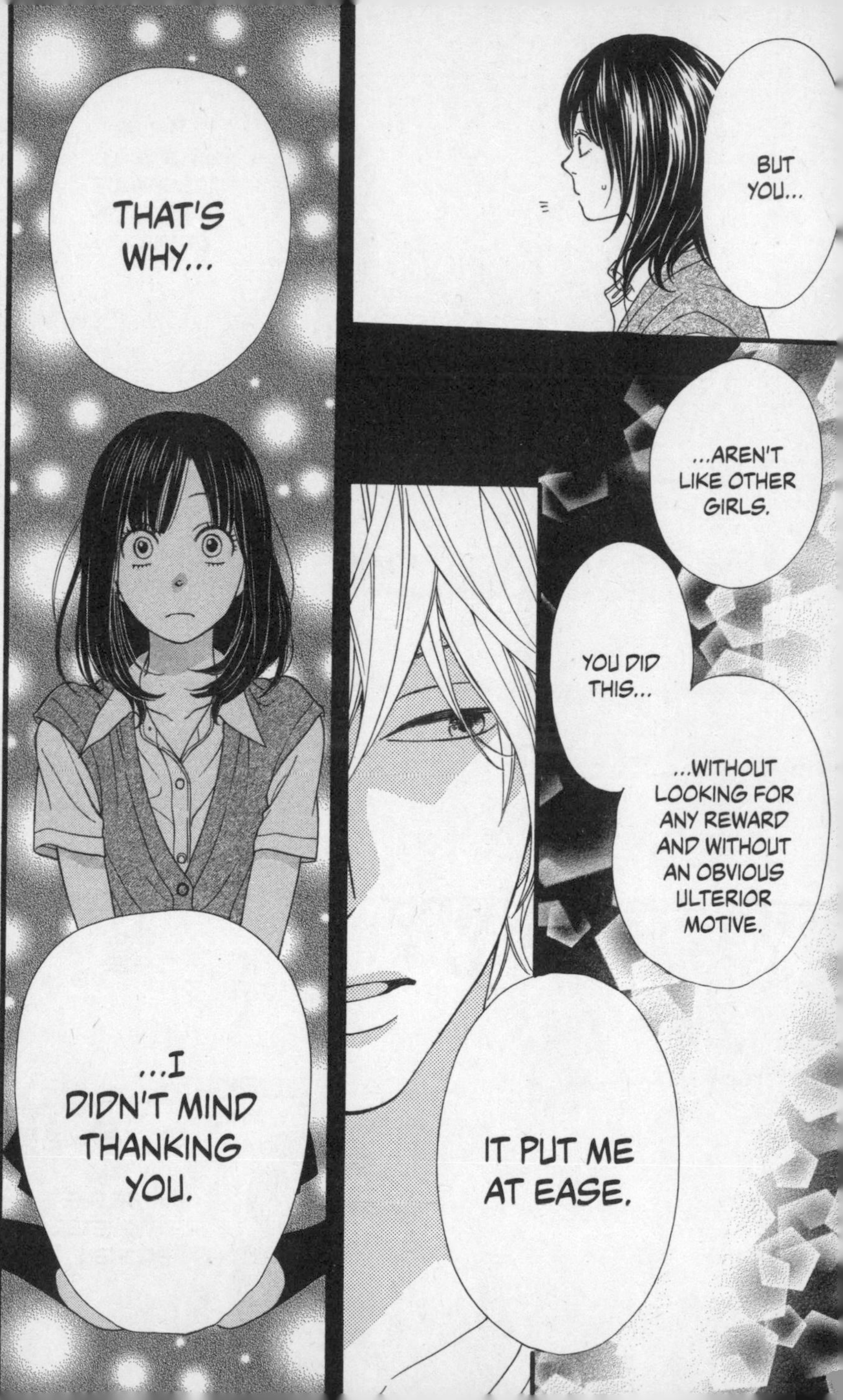
BUT YOU...
...AREN'T LIKE OTHER GIRLS.
YOU DID THIS...
...WITHOUT LOOKING FOR ANY REWARD AND WITHOUT AN OBVIOUS ULTERIOR MOTIVE.
IT PUT ME AT EASE.
THAT'S WHY...
...I DIDN'T MIND THANKING YOU.

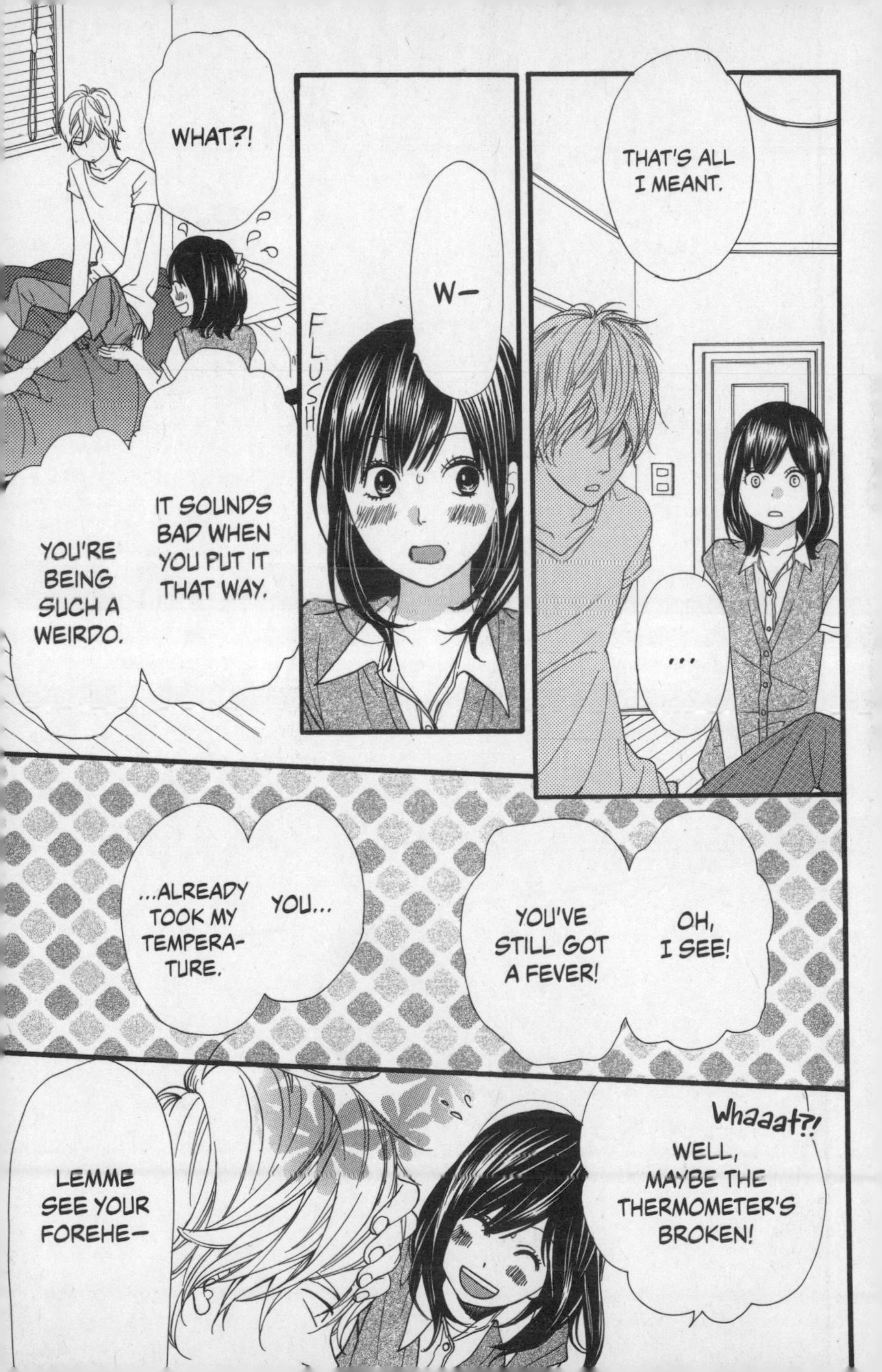
THAT'S ALL I MEANT.
...
W-
FLUSH
WHAT?!
IT SOUNDS BAD WHEN YOU PUT IT THAT WAY.
YOU'RE BEING SUCH A WEIRDO.
OH, I SEE!
YOU'VE STILL GOT A FEVER!
YOU...
...ALREADY TOOK MY TEMPERA-TURE.
Whaaat?!
WELL, MAYBE THE THERMOMETER'S BROKEN!
LEMME SEE YOUR FOREHE-

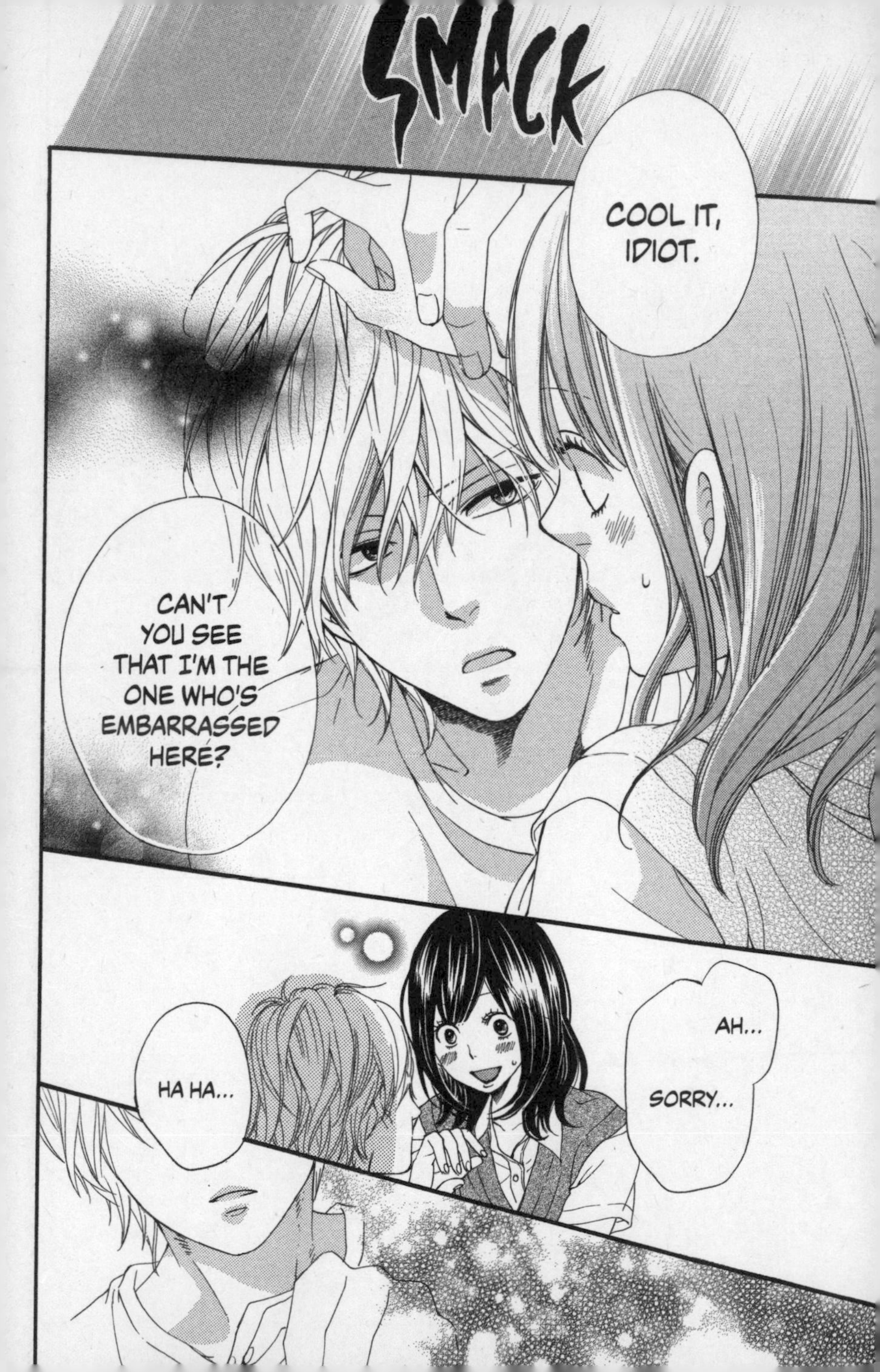
SMACK
COOL IT, IDIOT.
CAN'T YOU SEE THAT I'M THE ONE WHO'S EMBARRASSED HERE?
AH...
SORRY...
HA HA...

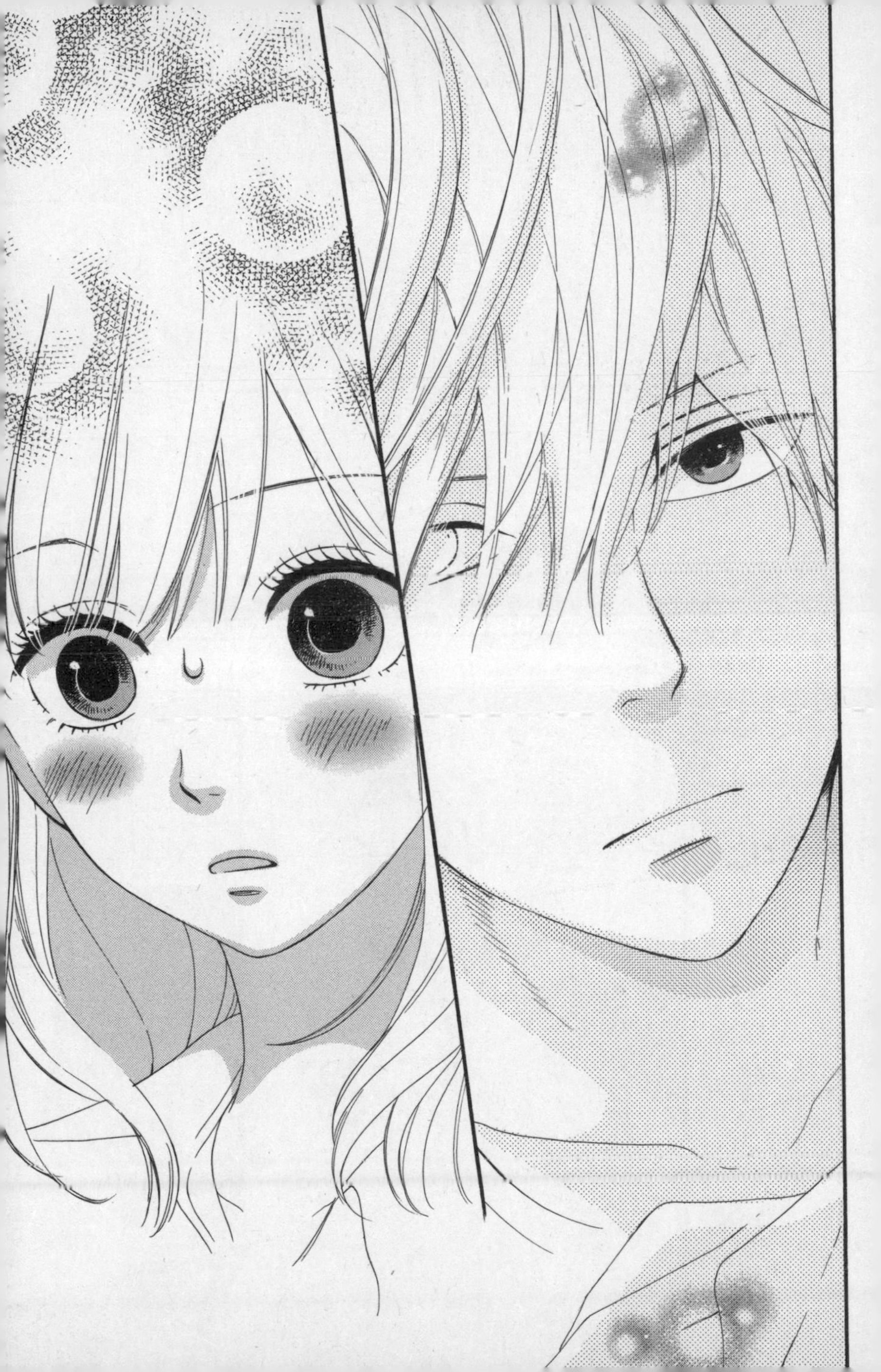

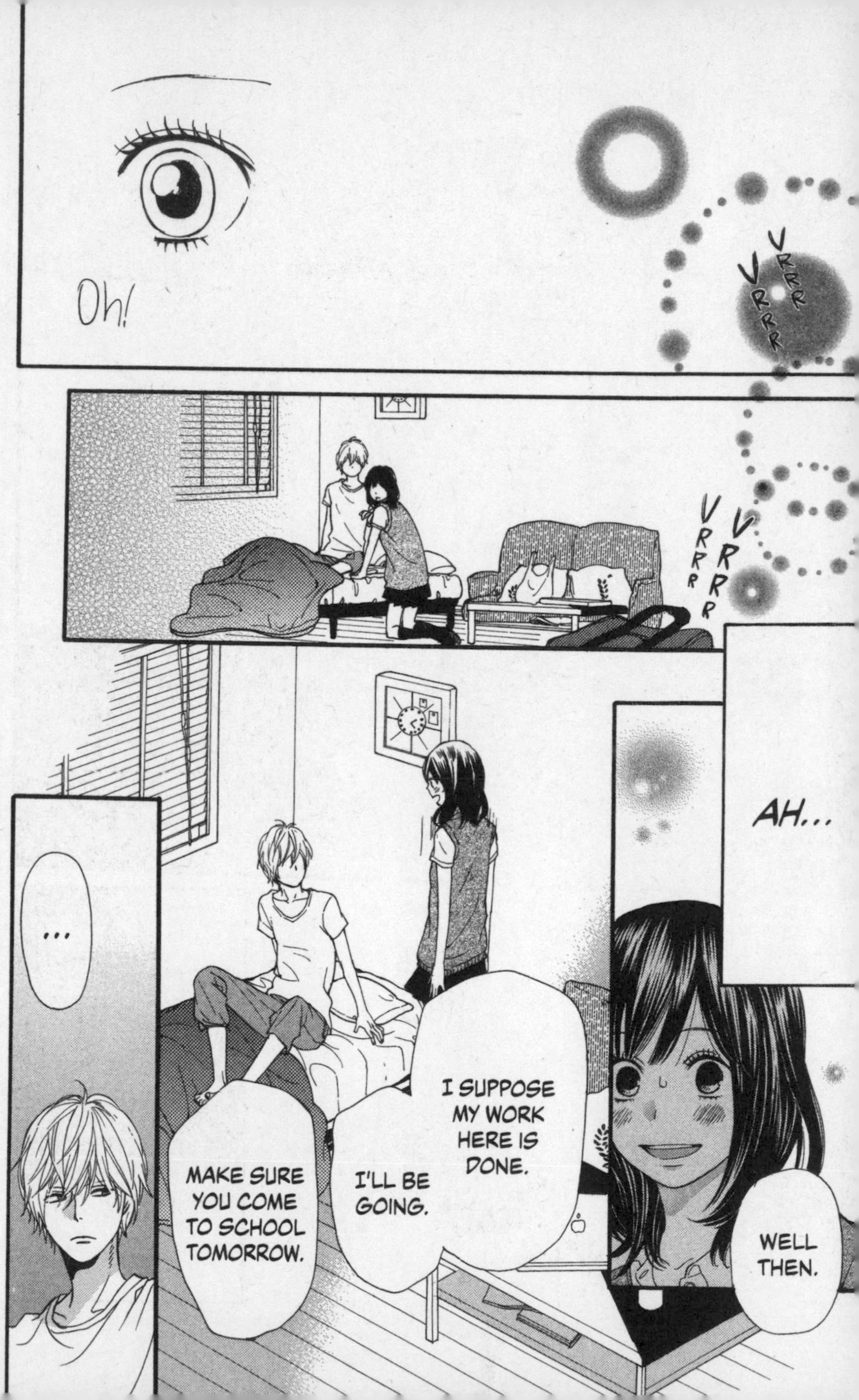
VRRRR
VRRR
Oh!
VRRRR
VRRR
AH...
WELL THEN.
I SUPPOSE MY WORK HERE IS DONE.
I'LL BE GOING.
MAKE SURE YOU COME TO SCHOOL TOMORROW.
...

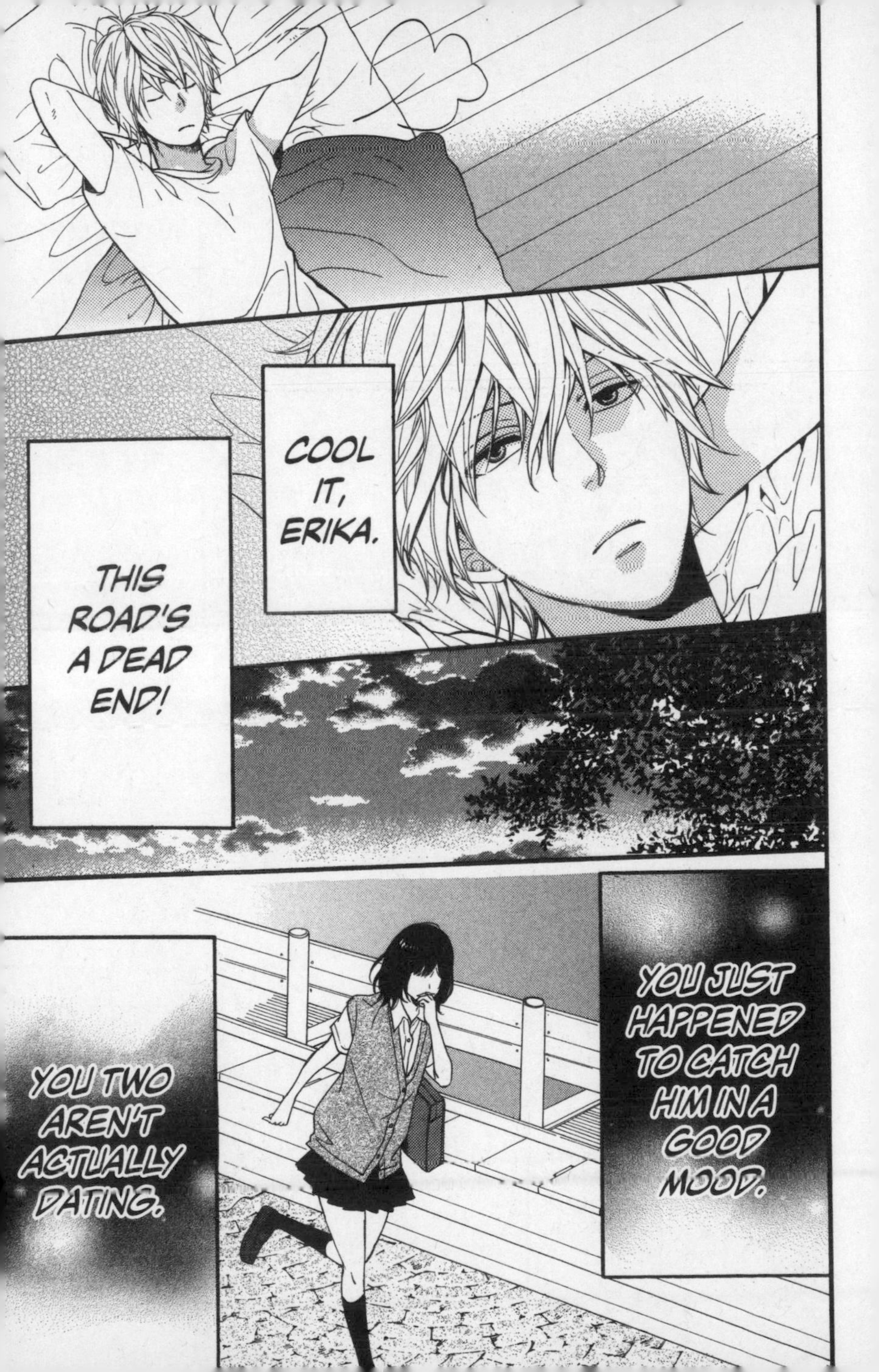
COOL IT, ERIKA.
THIS ROAD'S A DEAD END!
YOU JUST HAPPENED TO CATCH HIM IN A GOOD MOOD.
YOU TWO AREN'T ACTUALLY DATING.

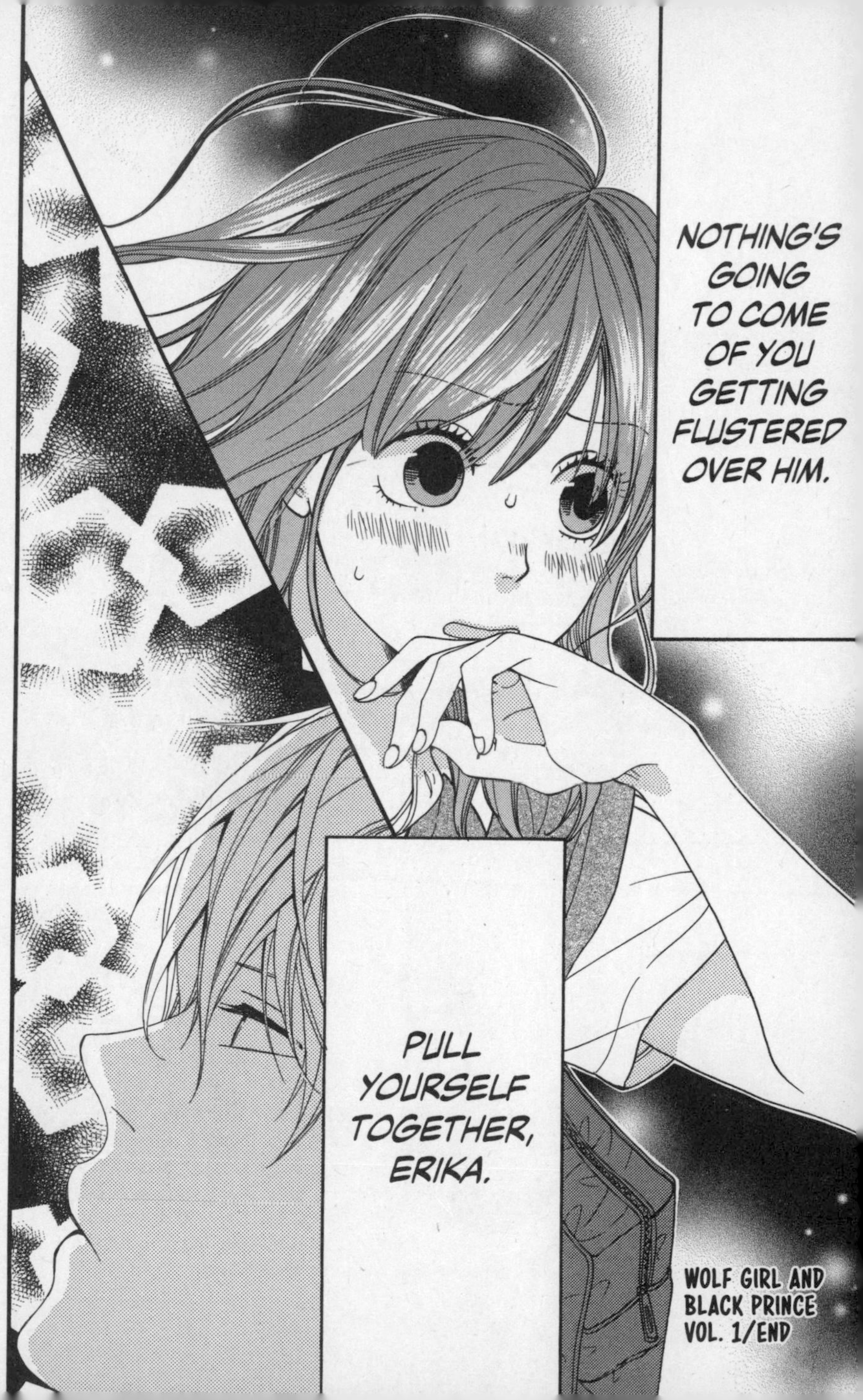
NOTHING'S GOING TO COME OF YOU GETTING FLUSTERED OVER HIM.
PULL YOURSELF TOGETHER, ERIKA.
WOLF GIRL AND BLACK PRINCE VOL. 1/END

I only put on makeup a few times a year, so I'm still using the foundation I bought in high school. It's ten years old…and it's nowhere near empty. It's starting to smell kind of weird though. Could it be…mold? No, that can't be it. I'm sure using it isn't the best thing for my skin, but I don't really feel like buying more.

— AYUKO HATTA

Ayuko Hatta resides in the Kansai region of Japan. In 2007, she began her shojo manga career in *Deluxe Margaret* with *Order wa Boku de Yoroshii desu ka?* (Am I All You Wish to Order?). Since then, she has gone on to publish numerous works, including *Bye-Bye Liberty*, *Haibara-kun wa Gokigen Naname* (Haibara Is in a Bad Mood), and the popular hit series *Wolf Girl and Black Prince*. Her series *Ima Koi: Now I'm in Love* began serialization in 2019. She loves playing games and is generally acknowledged by those around her to be an innate gamer. She's also good at cooking and drawing caricatures.

WOLF GIRL AND BLACK PRINCE

VOLUME

SHOJO BEAT EDITION

STORY AND ART BY

Ayuko Hatta

TRANSLATION — Diana Taylor
TOUCH-UP ART & LETTERING — Aidan Clarke
DESIGN — Alice Lewis
EDITOR — Karla Clark

OOKAMI SHOJO TO KURO OHJI © 2011 by Ayuko Hatta
All rights reserved.
First published in Japan in 2011 by SHUEISHA Inc., Tokyo.
English translation rights arranged by SHUEISHA Inc.

The stories, characters, and incidents mentioned in this publication are entirely fictional.

Printed in Canada

Published by VIZ Media, LLC
P.O. Box 77010
San Francisco, CA 94107

10 9 8 7 6 5 4 3 2 1
First printing, May 2023

VIZ MEDIA
viz.com

Shojo Beat
shojobeat.com

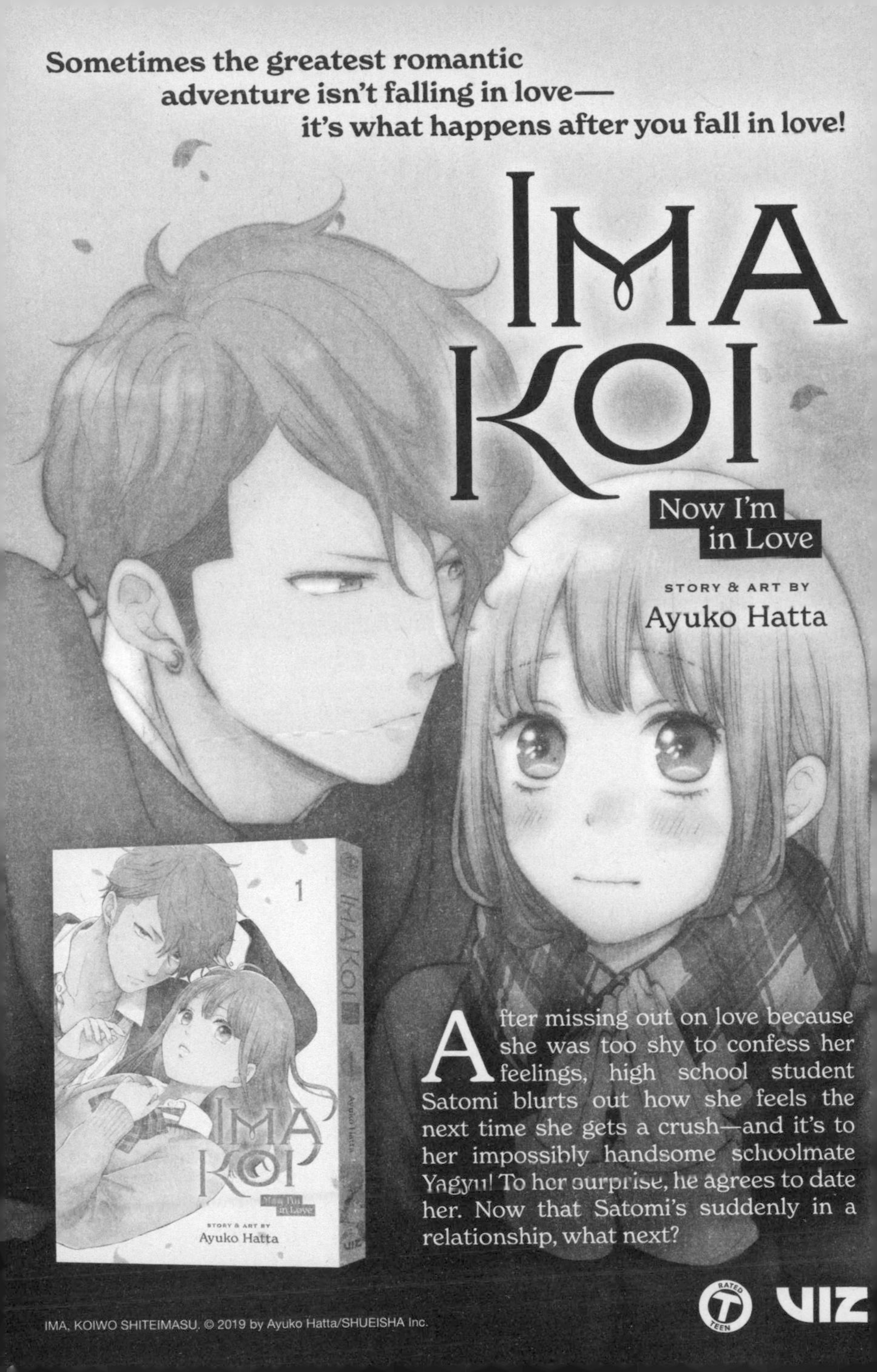
Sometimes the greatest romantic adventure isn't falling in love— it's what happens after you fall in love!
IMA KOI
Now I'm in Love
STORY & ART BY
Ayuko Hatta
1
IMA KOI
STORY & ART BY
Ayuko Hatta
After missing out on love because she was too shy to confess her feelings, high school student Satomi blurts out how she feels the next time she gets a crush—and it's to her impossibly handsome schoolmate Yagyu! To her surprise, he agrees to date her. Now that Satomi's suddenly in a relationship, what next?
RATED T TEEN
VIZ
IMA, KOIWO SHITEIMASU. © 2019 by Ayuko Hatta/SHUEISHA Inc.

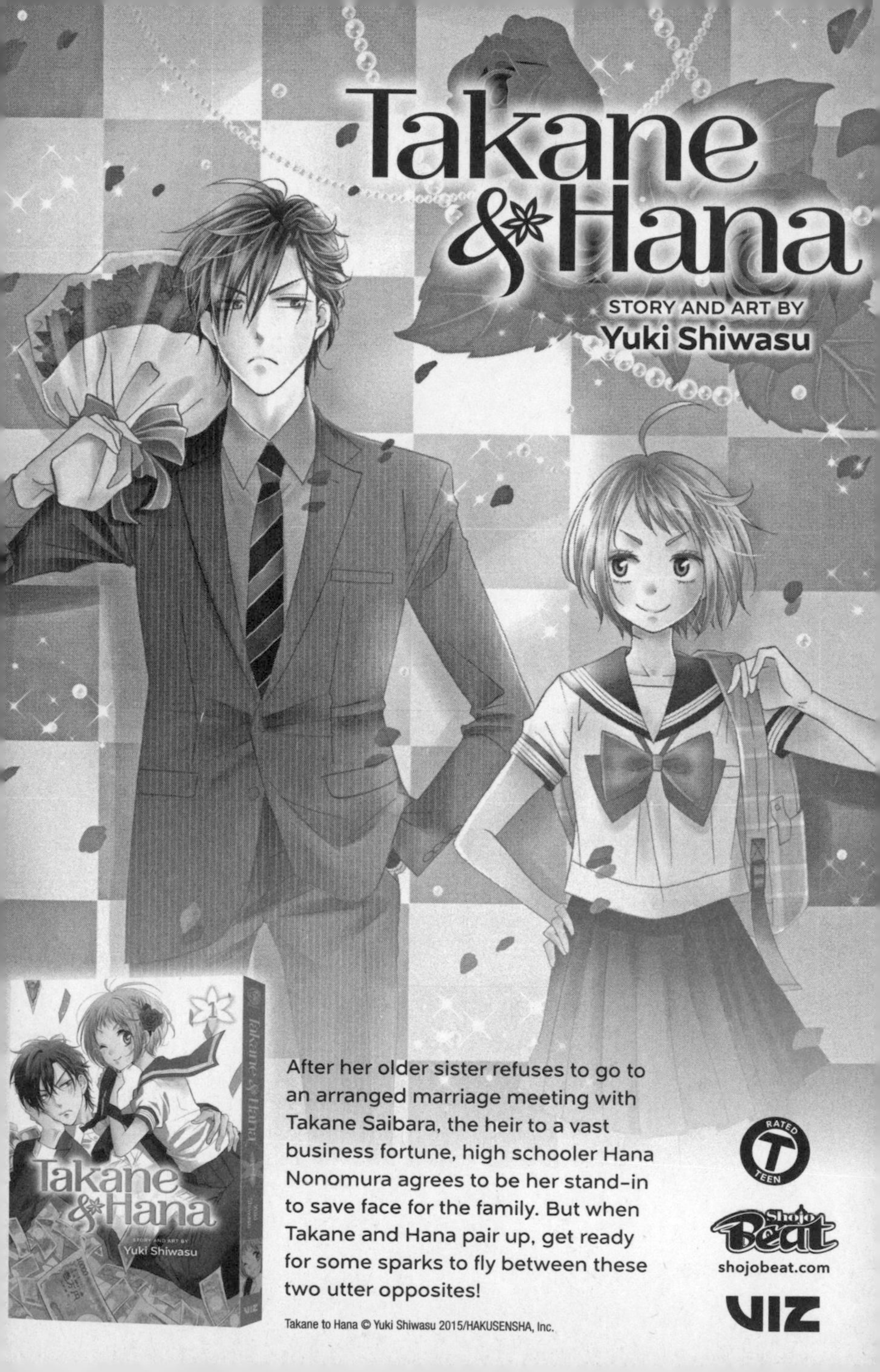
Takane & Hana
STORY AND ART BY
Yuki Shiwasu
Takane & Hana
1
STORY AND ART BY
Yuki Shiwasu
VIZ
After her older sister refuses to go to an arranged marriage meeting with Takane Saibara, the heir to a vast business fortune, high schooler Hana Nonomura agrees to be her stand-in to save face for the family. But when Takane and Hana pair up, get ready for some sparks to fly between these two utter opposites!
RATED T TEEN
Shojo Beat
shojobeat.com
VIZ
Takane to Hana © Yuki Shiwasu 2015/HAKUSENSHA, Inc.

SHORTCAKE CAKE

STORY AND ART BY
suu Morishita

An unflappable girl and a cast of
lovable roommates at a boardinghouse
create bonds of friendship and romance!

When Ten moves out of her parents' home
in the mountains to live in a boardinghouse,
she finds herself becoming fast friends with
her male roommates. But can love and
romance be far behind?

RATED
T
TEEN

VIZ

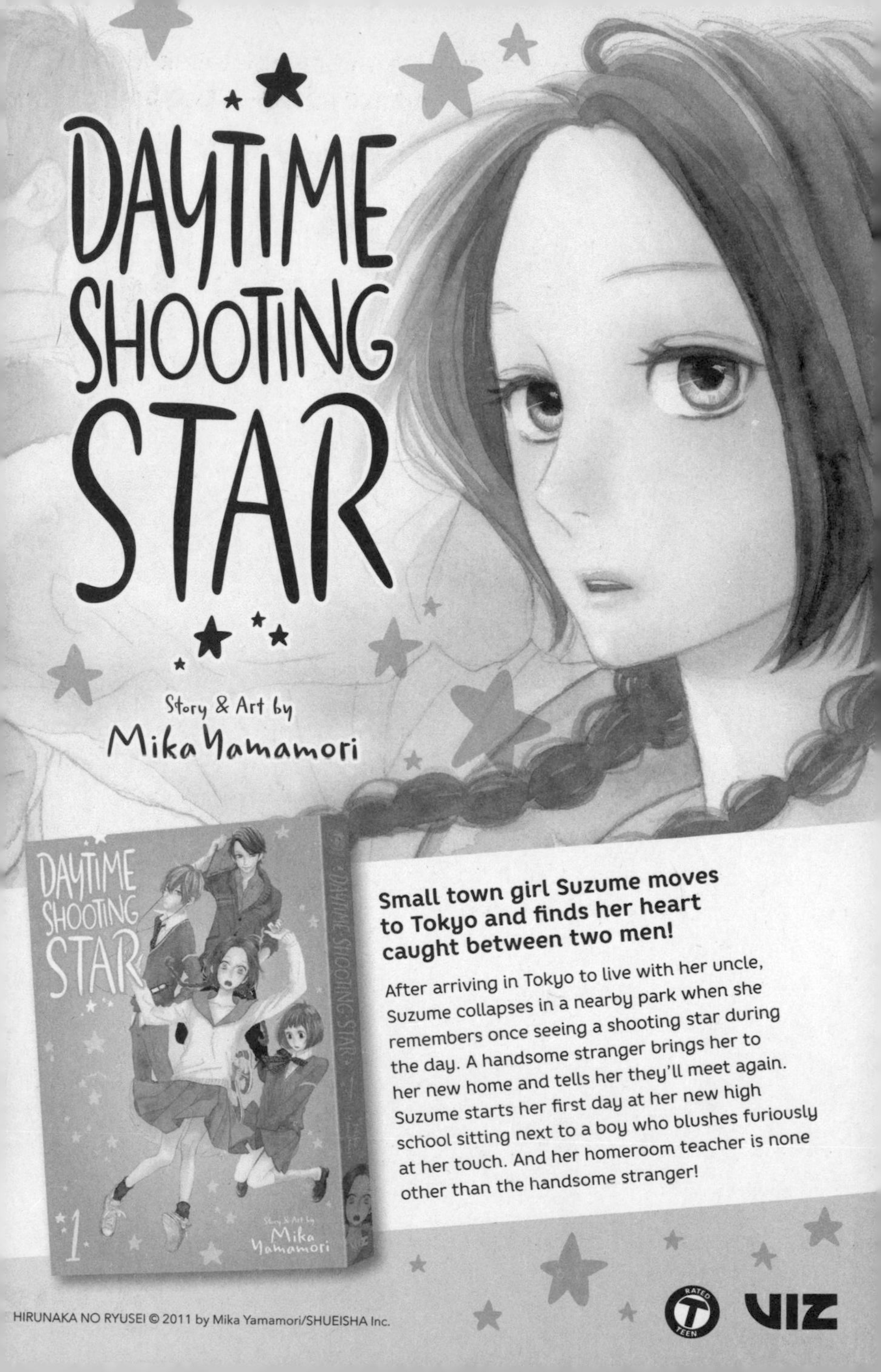
DAYTIME SHOOTING STAR
Story & Art by
Mika Yamamori
DAYTIME SHOOTING STAR
1
Story & Art by
Mika Yamamori
Small town girl Suzume moves to Tokyo and finds her heart caught between two men!
After arriving in Tokyo to live with her uncle, Suzume collapses in a nearby park when she remembers once seeing a shooting star during the day. A handsome stranger brings her to her new home and tells her they'll meet again. Suzume starts her first day at her new high school sitting next to a boy who blushes furiously at her touch. And her homeroom teacher is none other than the handsome stranger!
HIRUNAKA NO RYUSEI © 2011 by Mika Yamamori/SHUEISHA Inc.
RATED T TEEN
VIZ

In this warmhearted romantic comedy, mistaken identity leads to a blossoming romance between two boys.

My Love Mix-Up!

Art by **Aruko**
Story by **Wataru Hinekure**

Aoki has a crush on Hashimoto, the girl in the seat next to him in class. But he despairs when he borrows her eraser and sees she's written the name of another boy—Ida—on it. To make matters more confusing, Ida sees him holding that very eraser and thinks Aoki has a crush on him!

RATED T TEEN · VIZ

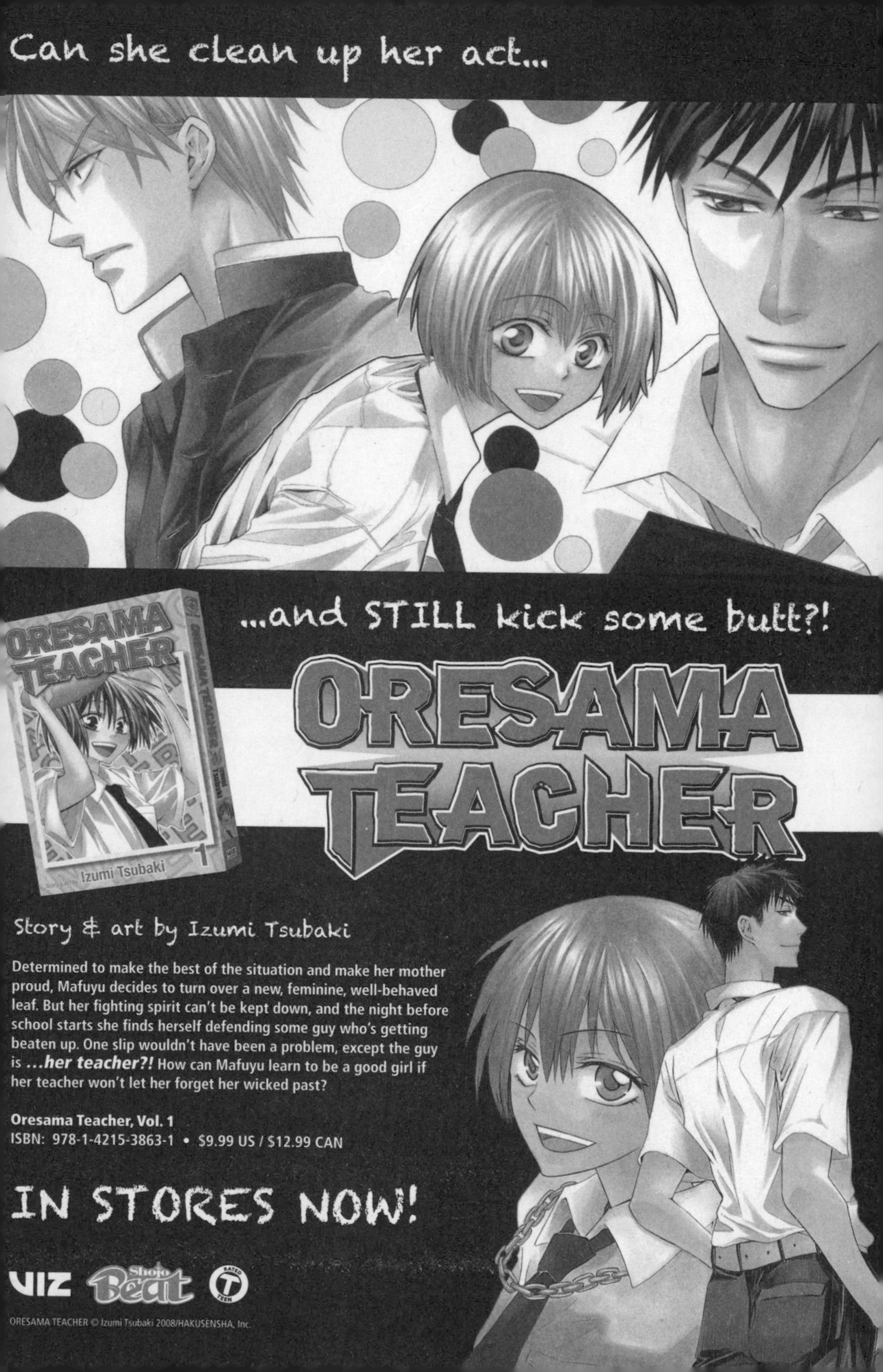
Can she clean up her act...
...and STILL kick some butt?!
ORESAMA TEACHER
ORESAMA TEACHER
Izumi Tsubaki
1
Story & art by Izumi Tsubaki
Determined to make the best of the situation and make her mother proud, Mafuyu decides to turn over a new, feminine, well-behaved leaf. But her fighting spirit can't be kept down, and the night before school starts she finds herself defending some guy who's getting beaten up. One slip wouldn't have been a problem, except the guy is ...her teacher?! How can Mafuyu learn to be a good girl if her teacher won't let her forget her wicked past?
Oresama Teacher, Vol. 1
ISBN: 978-1-4215-3863-1 • $9.99 US / $12.99 CAN
IN STORES NOW!
VIZ
Shojo Beat
ORESAMA TEACHER © Izumi Tsubaki 2008/HAKUSENSHA, Inc.

THE YOUNG MASTER'S REVENGE

When Leo was a young boy, he had his pride torn to shreds by Tenma, a girl from a wealthy background who was always getting him into trouble. Now, years after his father's successful clothing business has made him the heir to a fortune, he searches out Tenma to enact a dastardly plan—he'll get his revenge by making her fall in love with him!

RATED T TEEN

VIZ
viz.com

DROP IT! GOOD, GOOD!

YOU'RE READING THE WRONG WAY!

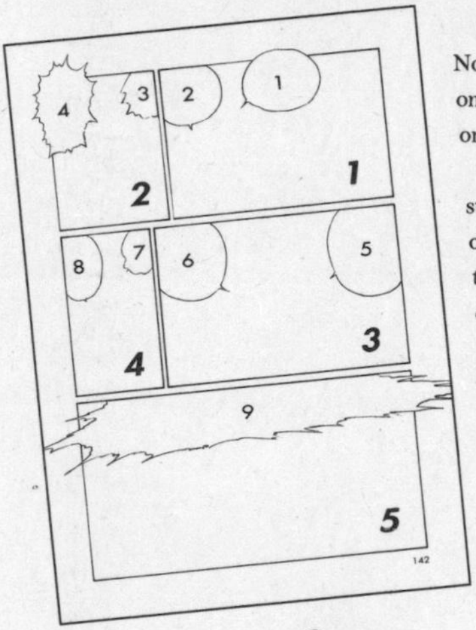
1
2
3
4
1
2
5
6
7
8
3
4
9
5
142

Now, watch me and listen up! I'm only explaining this once. To read *Wolf Girl and Black Prince* in its intended order, you need to flip it over and start again.

Wolf Girl and Black Prince reads from right to left, starting in the upper-right corner, to preserve the original Japanese orientation of the work. That means that the action, sound effects, and word-balloons are completely reversed from English order.

You got all that? That's a good pooch! Now, spin around three times, shake, and give me a "woof."

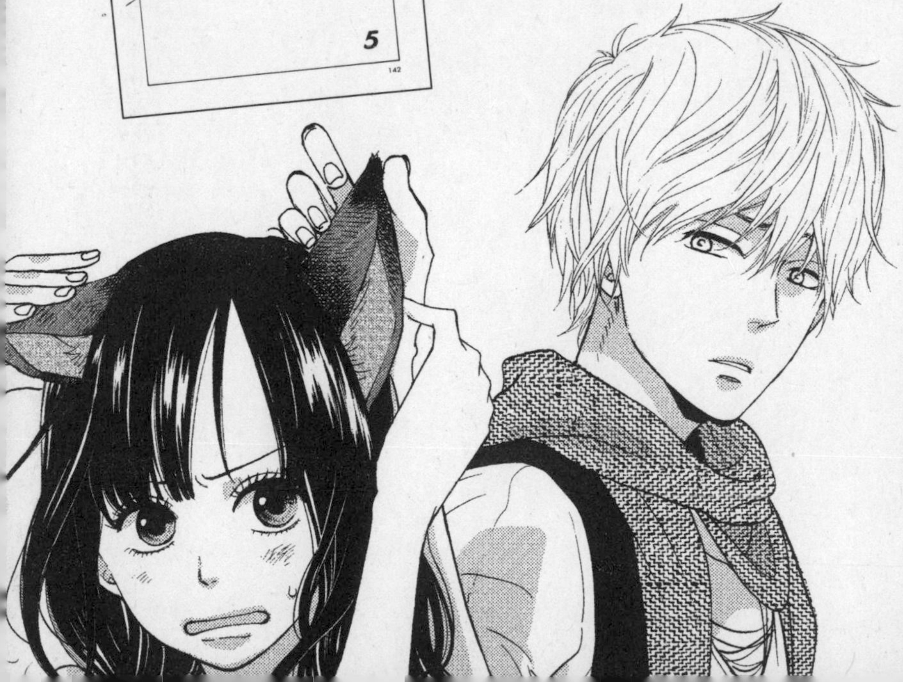